Radovich. 94.

MIGRATORY SHORE AND UPLAND GAME BIRD MANAGEMENT IN NORTH AMERICA

Edited By

THOMAS C. TACHA AND CLAIT E. BRAUN

Radovich-94.

MIGRATORY SHORE AND UPLAND

GAME BIRD MANAGEMENT

IN NORTH AMERICA

Edited by

THOMAS C. TACHA and CLAIT E. BRAUN

1994

Printed By
Allen Press
Lawrence, Kansas

Published By
The International Association of Fish
and Wildlife Agencies

In Cooperation with the Fish and Wildlife Service
U.S. Department of the Interior

The International Association of Fish
and Wildlife Agencies
Washington, D.C. 20036

Library of Congress Catalog Card Number 94-72747
Printed and bound in the United States of America

ISBN: 0-935868-75-5

This book is the second in a series on migratory shore and upland game birds in North America

Editor, Glen C. Sanderson
  Management of Migratory Shore and Upland Game Birds in North America

Editors, Thomas C. Tacha and Clait E. Braun
  Migratory Shore and Upland Game Bird Management in North America

CONTRIBUTORS

Biologists and researchers in member states of the International Association of Fish and Wildlife Agencies; the Fish and Wildlife Service and National Biological Survey, U.S. Department of the Interior; the Canadian Wildlife Service; Universities; and private conservation organizations have joined forces in a unique effort to provide this book. The work of more than 30 contributing authors from across North America has been augmented by advice and counsel from many others. The information in this book presents current research and management findings as well as references to previously published studies.

SUGGESTED CITATIONS

Tacha, T. C., and C. E. Braun, editors. 1994. Migratory Shore and Upland Game Bird Management in North America. International Association of Fish and Wildlife Agencies, Washington, D.C. 223 pp.

Braun, C. E. 1994. Band-tailed Pigeon. Pages 60–74 *in* T. C. Tacha and C. E. Braun, eds. Migratory Shore and Upland Game Bird Management in North America. International Association of Fish and Wildlife Agencies, Washington, D.C.

Printed by Allen Press, Lawrence, Kansas

About the Book

I am pleased to have the opportunity to recognize this important
publication. The U.S. Fish and Wildlife Service (Service) is proud to have
played a part in making this book possible. We provided a grant of
Wildlife Restoration funding because we and our State partners understood
the need for updating the information that has been gathered on these
species in recent years.

Upon reading this book, I am reminded of the importance of Conservation
Reserve Program lands, and our own acquisition efforts in the Lower Rio
Grande Valley. It also shows the past and future need for land management
on our National Wildlife Refuges such as Moosehorn in Maine. Our
regulation setting and harvest information activities with the States take
on more importance as we look to migratory shore and upland game bird
management in the 21st Century.

We in the Service are committed to the management needs identified in this
book. We are currently financing several States efforts to revamp their
licensing systems to identify migratory shore and upland game bird hunters.
This will allow for better definition of times, numbers, and places of
taking. We are working hard in the areas of pesticides where the
formulation and applications are changing rapidly.

Finally, we see through this book what needs to be done. More work with
Canada, Mexico, and States such as Nebraska is vital to the future of this
resource. By identifying these areas so clearly this book should help to
create the dialogues that will focus many different players on many
different fronts. This increase in partnerships will hopefully create the
real progress we all look for in this area.

Mollie Beattie
Director
U.S. Fish and Wildlife Service

Foreword

In his March, 1976 "Foreword" to the book "Management of Migratory Shore and Upland Game Birds in North America", then President of the International Association of Fish and Wildlife Agencies, O. Earle Frye, Jr., Tallahassee, Florida, wrote "It is difficult to predict the results of a particular action, how far the "ripples" will go, or in which direction. Some actions produce no results, others produce results well beyond anything anticipated. This publication is a case in point."

Earl Frye had no way of knowing how well the International's first book on migratory shore and upland game birds would be received by wildlife managers and that the ripples it generated would persist for nearly two decades and lead to the publication of this updated version 18 years later. The current interest in this group of species, which is spreading throughout North America, has surely surpassed anything anticipated by Earl Frye and the members of the National Program Planning Committee for Migratory Shore and Upland Game Birds who, back in 1967, had the wisdom and foresight to embark on a task of addressing the management and research needs of these important but poorly understood birds.

I, as President of the International, am especially proud of this publication. In my view it is another giant step forward in the management of a small, diverse, yet important group of species that historically received little emphasis as a result of being overshadowed by seemingly more important species and issues of the day. This book adds momentum to an already powerful movement, boosted by the growing interest in biodiversity and ecosystem management, aimed at meeting the contemporary needs of all wildlife and their habitats. I hope managers and researchers find this book useful as they face the complex challenges of the twenty-first century and work to preserve our quality of life, wildlife richness across North America, and ecosystem integrity while trying to meet the overwhelming human demands for natural resources.

I commend the International's Migratory Shore and Upland Game Bird Committee for recognizing the importance of these species and the need to update the original book. They have produced an excellent publication by selecting the dedicated and highly qualified wildlife professionals that served on the Ad Hoc Committee and Editorial Board for this book, and by selecting editors C. E. Braun and T. C. Tacha. I also commend the authors and editors for their skills, insight, expertise, and diligent work in bringing together, under one cover, our current knowledge of migratory shore and upland game bird management in North America.

Finally, on behalf of the International Association of Fish and Wildlife Agencies, I thank the U. S. Fish and Wildlife Service for helping to defray the costs of printing and distributing this book using Federal Aid administrative funds. Without the Service's assistance, the publication of this book would not have been possible.

As with the Association's first publication on migratory shore and upland game birds, there is no way to predict "how far the ripples will go" that result from this second publication, or in which direction they will travel. But, I am confident that wildlife managers and researchers from across North America, perhaps inspired by the following pages, will give the attention to these species they so rightly deserve.

Jerry M. Conley, President, 1993-1994
International Association of Fish and
Wildlife Agencies
Boise, Idaho
6 September 1994

PREFACE

Book History

The Migratory Shore and Upland Game Bird Committee (MSUGBC) of the International Association of Fish and Wildlife Agencies (IAFWA) determined in March 1990 that an ad hoc committee should be appointed to consider the need to update, revise, or prepare a followup to the book "Management of Migratory Shore and Upland Game Birds in North America" that was published in 1977. The rationale was that: 1) substantial changes had occurred in the status of several migratory shore and upland game bird (MSUGB) species, and 2) important new published information (including nearly 340 publications associated with the Accelerated Research Program) had become available since 1977. An ad hoc committee was appointed by MSUGBC chairman K. M. Babcock consisting of: T. C. Tacha (chairman), J. M. Anderson, R. R. George, and R. E. Tomlinson. The mandate of the ad hoc committee was (10 May 1990 letter from Babcock to Tacha) ". . . to communicate with appropriate biologists and administrators to determine: 1) use of the book, 2) interest in updating the publication, 3) potential authorship to the revision or rewrite, and 4) potential funding for such a venture."

A cover letter and preliminary questionnaire were developed and sent to solicit ideas from migratory bird biologists in 38 states. Biologists were identified by R. R. George from a list of people contacted earlier for another study regarding MSUGB species. The letter/questionnaire was sent on 2 August 1990 asking for responses by 1 September 1990. Of the 38 biologists contacted, 24 (63%) responded by returning the questionnaire.

A strong majority of state migratory bird biologists had read parts or all of the book, and thought it of average to outstanding importance to management of MSUGB species. Over 95% of the respondents indicated the book needed to be updated and that a revised updated edition of the same book was preferable.

These findings from the preliminary survey of state migratory bird biologists were reviewed by the MSUGBC at the IAFWA meetings in September 1990. A decision was subsequently reached to poll administrators, specifically Wildlife Division Chiefs or equivalents, of all 50 states and Puerto Rico. A cover letter and questionnaire were developed and sent by K. M. Babcock to solicit comments from the 51 wildlife administrators. The letter/questionnaires were sent in late October 1990 asking for responses by 1 December 1990.

Of the 51 administrators contacted, 48 (94%) responded by returning the questionnaire. A strong majority of state wildlife administrators had read parts or all of the book (88%), at least occasionally (75%), and thought it average to outstandingly important (83%) to management of MSUGB. Nearly 90% of the respondents indicated the book needed to be updated, and 78% suggested that a revised updated edition of the same book was preferable.

The MSUGBC concluded in March 1991 that: 1) the book was widely used for reference and/or as a guide in research/management of MSUGB, 2) there was wide interest among migratory bird biologists/administrators in updating the book, and 3) the book should be revised and updated in its current format using experts as authors as before. The MSUGBC then directed the ad hoc committee to investigate and identify possible costs and funding sources, potential editors, publishers, and authors, and a proposed schedule of events for revision of the book.

In September 1991, the MSUGBC and IAFWA approved C. E. Braun and T. C. Tacha as editors of the revised book. The MSUGBC and IAFWA also approved (Sep 1991) establishment of an Editorial Board for the book consisting of the editors and the ad hoc committee; this included T. C. Tacha (chairman), J. M. Anderson, C. E. Braun, R. R. George, and R. E. Tomlinson.

Changes From The 1977 Book

The Editorial Board developed a prospectus for this book that was approved by the MSUGBC and IAFWA in March 1992. Major changes from the 1977 book included deletion (in keeping with the book title) of chapters on unhunted species such as black and yellow rails and shorebirds, and addition of a chapter on white-tipped doves. Instead of forming committees to write each chapter as with the 1977 book, expert primary authors were selected for each chapter; primary authors were allowed to select their own coauthors. The resulting list of authors was representative of both the United States and

Canada, and a wide array of private, state, and federal agencies and academic institutions.

This book also used a formal manuscript review system, with at least 1 review required for each chapter by someone other than the chapter authors in addition to reviews by the editors. Some chapter authors reviewed other chapters. We thank the following for their assistance in reviewing chapters: J. C. Bartonek, T. S. Baskett, C. J. Conway, R. C. Drewien, W. E. Eddleman, L. H. Fredrickson, F. S. Guthery, W. B Krohn, S. M. Melvin, R. A. Ryder, D. E. Sharp, R. E. Tomlinson, and M. W. Weller.

New artwork for this book was prepared by Don Radovich, a long-time artist in Gunnison, Colorado. This book would not have been possible without the MSUGBC and the IAFWA. Funding to defray costs of printing and distributing 6,500 copies of this book was provided by U.S. Fish and Wildlife Service Cooperative Agreement 14-48-0009-93-1237 and the Sport Fish and Wildlife Restoration Program that uses excise taxes paid by hunters, anglers, and boaters. Copies of the book may be obtained free of charge from the Caesar Kleberg Wildlife Research Institute, Campus Box 218, Texas A&M University-Kingsville, Kingsville, Texas 78363.

Thomas C. Tacha and Clait E. Braun, Editors
August 1994

Your purchase
of hunting equipment
supports
Wildlife Restoration

Contents

Figs. 1, 2.   Examples of aquatic (Dead Creek Wildlife Management Area, Vermont, Photo by S. M. Melvin) and terrestrial (near LaVeta, Colorado, Photo by C. E. Braun) habitats used by migratory shore and upland game birds in North America.

Chapter 1

INTRODUCTION

KENNETH M. BABCOCK, Assistant Director, Missouri Department of Conservation, P.O. Box 180, Jefferson City, MO 65102

Hunting is an integral part of life for millions of North Americans. Each year a wide range of hunting activities rekindle traditional and cultural connections to our heritage and the natural world around us. Beyond the renewal of traditional and cultural values, hunting focuses attention on our responsibility to manage and care for the entire world in which we live.

The future of hunting depends upon answers to 2 broad questions. First, will the non-hunting citizenry recognize and appreciate the traditional and cultural values associated with hunting? Second, will the hunter and wildlife manager have the information and understanding necessary to ensure continued scientific justification for hunting? Answers to these questions depend upon our ability to educate and inform all people that professional wildlife managers have done a good job in the past, are doing a better job now, and will continue to improve in the future. Our credibility, both now and into the future, is linked to an improved understanding of wildlife population dynamics and the impacts of harvest on hunted species. Federal and state resource agencies throughout North America are challenged to generate and apply new information to guide decision making.

Migratory birds, especially those that are "webless," offer some of the most complex and greatest challenges of all. Complicating factors include the large number of species from several families and genera, the international significance of migratory behavior, diverse seasonal habitat requirements, and information gaps that exist among this group of birds.

Existing information deficiencies regarding migratory shore and upland game bird management is not a new revelation, nor have wildlife professionals been idly standing by. Thirty years ago, the International Association of Fish and Wildlife Agencies (IAFWA), The Wildlife Management Institute, the U.S. Fish and Wildlife Service (then the U.S. Bureau of Sport Fisheries and Wildlife), and other agencies and organizations led the charge to elevate attention on research and management needs of migratory shore and upland game birds. The Accelerated Research Program (1967-82), was the result of their cooperative efforts and resulted in numerous research projects addressing a wide range of "webless" migratory game bird issues. Research results appeared in 340 publications, greatly enhancing our ability to manage migratory birds. Much of this Accelerated Research Program (ARP) information was consolidated in the book *Management of Migratory Shore and Upland Game Birds in North America*, the forerunner to this publication.

Termination of ARP in 1982 left many questions about migratory shore and upland game birds unanswered. Since 1986, the IAFWA, through its Migratory Shore and Upland Game Bird Committee (MSUGB), has urged the U.S. Fish and Wildlife Service (USFWS) to reinstate ARP or develop a similar program. To date these efforts have been unsuccessful. However, a special task force of MSUGB committee members, including both state and federal representatives, has developed a proposal entitled "A Webless Migratory Game Bird Research Program" (WMGBR). The proposal requests a minimum annual appropriation of $750,000 in the USFWS budget to cost share research with state agencies, universities, and other groups with a stake in migratory bird management. This cooperative effort will address the information gaps among the webless species identified in this book and through management plans of the IAFWA, state agencies, and the USFWS. The WMGBR program, or a similar commitment, is vital if we are to manage webless migratory game birds responsibly in the future.

While hunting is an important and justifiable consideration in the management of "webless" migratory game birds, their significance transcends that relatively narrow focus. Today, as resource managers are shifting from a "game vs. non-game" mentality towards more holistic thinking, ecosystem approaches to wildlife conservation are emerging. Webless migratory game

1

birds use almost every conceivable habitat type, thus they can serve as barometers of ecosystem health throughout the continent. Additionally, they are appreciated and studied by scientists, bird watchers, and general nature enthusiasts. Migratory shore and upland game birds can be the common threads that link the different ecosystems and the many user groups.

The information provided in this book, and attention to the recommendations offered, will put us in good stead to manage migratory shore and upland game birds well into the next century. As a result, people will continue to enjoy many days afield in pursuit of doves, cranes, rails, snipe, woodcock, band-tailed pigeons, gallinules, moorhens, and coots with a shotgun, camera, or field guide. With public support based upon knowledge, these resources and the landscape upon which they depend will be sustained far into the future.

Chapter 2

MOURNING DOVE

ROY E. TOMLINSON, U.S. Fish and Wildlife Service, P.O. Box 1306, Albuquerque, NM 87103-1306
DAVID D. DOLTON, U.S. Fish and Wildlife Service, Henshaw Laboratory, 11500 American Holly Drive, Laurel, MD 20708-4016
RONNIE R. GEORGE, Texas Parks and Wildlife Department, 4200 Smith School Road, Austin, TX 78744
RALPH E. MIRARCHI, Department of Zoology and Wildlife Science, and Alabama Agricultural Experiment Station, Auburn University, Auburn, AL 36849-5414

Abstract: Mourning doves (*Zenaida macroura*) are the most abundant and widely-distributed game birds in North America. They breed in the southern portions of the Canadian provinces, all 48 conterminous states of the United States, Mexico, and the Greater Antilles. Most doves winter in the southern tier of states, Mexico, and Central America. In the United States, mourning doves are among the 10 most abundant bird species; the autumn dove population is estimated at about 475 million birds. Nevertheless, long-term population declines have occurred during 1966–93 in western and central sections of the country.

Since 1984, 36 of the 48 conterminous states permitted dove hunting seasons. On the average during 1983–87, 2.4 million hunters harvested about 45.6 million mourning doves/year. Mourning dove hunters annually spend an estimated $46 million on ammunition alone and contribute about $5 million in excise taxes to Federal Aid in Wildlife Restoration funds.

Major management needs include identification of the causes for population declines and institution of measures to reverse the trends, installation of a nationwide harvest information program, and establishment of an extension network to improve dove habitat on public and private lands. Primary research efforts should be directed toward evaluating land-use practices relative to dove populations, identifying the effects of biocides on dove populations, examining the relationship of hunting regulations on dove harvest and population trends, and measuring productivity and recruitment.

DESCRIPTION

The mourning dove is 1 of 12 native and introduced species of the Family Columbidae occurring north of Mexico (Am. Ornith. Union 1983). Five mourning dove subspecies are recognized; 2 are limited primarily to mainland North America, and the other 3 have relatively restricted insular distributions. The eastern subspecies (*Z. m. carolinensis*) breeds throughout the eastern third of temperate North America; the slightly smaller and paler western subspecies (*Z. m. marginella*) occupies much of the western two-thirds of the continent (Fig. 1). The line of demarcation in the United States between the 2 subspecies roughly coincides with the boundary between the eastern deciduous forests and the western grasslands. There is extensive mingling of these 2 races during migration in southern latitudes.

Small head, pointed tail, streamlined appearance, and rapid flight are prominent characteristics of mourning doves. Length and weight vary according to sex and subspecies (Mirarchi 1993c). Body length of *carolinensis* specimens average 32.1 cm (range 27.1–34.1 cm) for males and 27.3 cm (22.5–29.7 cm) for females; for

marginella, body length averages 29.8 cm (26.4–34.1 cm) for males and 28.1 (25.1–31.0) for females. Weight of *carolinensis* specimens averages 130 g (range 110–170 g) for males and 123 g (100–156 g) for females; for *marginella*, weight averages 116 g (96–143 g) for males and 108 g (86–142 g) for females. Coloration of both subspecies is slaty brown above and rufous tan below; *carolinensis*, however, gives a distinctly darker appearance, both in the hand and on the wing. Other distinguishing characteristics are a black spot behind and below the eye, a black bill, red or pink legs, and white-tipped tail feathers that flash during flight. Flight is direct and rapid, and the wing beat usually produces a prominent whistle, especially when the bird is flushed. The most obvious vocalization, the mournful 5–7-note perch coo, is given by the male mainly during spring and summer. A number of less prominent vocalizations are given by 1 or both sexes in different behavioral contexts (Sayre et al. 1993).

During the breeding season (Apr–Aug), males and females can be distinguished by external plumage characters. Adult males in breeding plumage typically have a light blue wash ex-

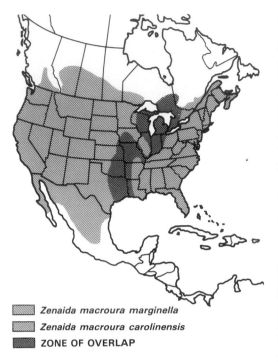

Zenaida macroura marginella

Zenaida macroura carolinensis

ZONE OF OVERLAP

Fig. 1.   Breeding ranges of the eastern and western mourning dove subspecies (from Baskett et al. 1993).

tending from the crown to nape and rosy breast feathers, whereas females have grayish brown crowns, brown napes, and tan breast feathers. Winter plumage patterns are similar, but more drab for both sexes. The gender of immature doves cannot be assigned accurately until they have molted at least through primary wing feathers V or VI. Occasionally, both males and females demonstrate plumage coloration similar to the opposite gender and can be misclassified by field technicians. In our judgement, the accuracy of field sex identification depends upon the experience of the handlers and time of year. If significant error is introduced, banded samples can demonstrate misleading estimates of sex ratio and annual survival by gender. The accuracy of age and gender determination was tested in a recent study in Missouri (Schulz et al. in prep.)

Newly-hatched doves possess whitish or buff-edged wing and back feathers and mottled breast, neck, and head feathers (Reeves and Amend 1970). The best characteristic used to distinguish between adult and immature doves is the presence of white or buff-colored edging on the wing coverts of juveniles (Mirarchi 1993a); these feathers are not lost until the primary molt

is nearly complete. Once the diagnostic covert feathers have been lost, the extent of wear on the distal edges of unmolted primaries VIII–X is useful; little wear is indicative of immatures, whereas heavy wear signifies adults (Wight et al. 1967). All birds that have completed the primary molt during August to December should be considered as "unknown age." Sadler et al. (1970) and Haas and Amend (1976, 1979) provide further discussion of age separation of mourning doves.

LIFE HISTORY
Spring Migration and Nesting Chronology

Spring migration of mourning doves to nesting areas begins in February or March, progresses slowly during April, and terminates in mid- to late May for most areas of the United States (Tomlinson 1993). Although few immature doves migrate and return to natal areas, a high percentage of adult males and females return to the previous year's nesting areas, and most select new sites within 60 m of the old locations (Tomlinson 1993). The extent of the nesting season and patterns of peak nesting vary considerably throughout the species' vast breeding range. In the United States, mourning doves in the North and West nest primarily between March and September, whereas doves in the South begin nesting in February and continue into October (Geissler et al. 1987, Sayre and Silvy 1993). In some southern states, doves have been reported nesting in all months of the year (Keeler 1977).

Nesting Biology

Mourning doves are monogamous and form pair bonds that persist through at least 1 nesting season (Sayre and Silvy 1993). Evidence suggests some doves may remain paired throughout the winter (Mackey 1965). Nevertheless, most doves probably are unpaired at onset of the breeding season. The overall sex ratios of adult doves banded during 1967–75 were 145:100 in the WMU and 187:100 in the CMU (Tomlinson et al. 1988). Although the ratios were probably inflated by capture methods that disproportionately targeted males, it is thought that some unmated males are present in the population throughout the season (Sayre et al. 1978, 1980; T. S. Baskett 1993; Sayre and Silvy 1993). This phenomenon suggests that an undetected differential mortality favoring males exists in all

Fig. 2. Male doves collect twigs and grass for delivery to their mates in construction of flat, and relatively flimsy, nests. Nests generally are located in trees at heights of 1–4.5 m, but extensive ground nesting also occurs in many areas, particularly in the prairie country of the central United States (Photo by R. E. Tomlinson).

Fig. 3. Two eggs are laid and both the male and female share in incubation of the eggs and in brooding and feeding of the squabs. The entire nesting cycle requires about 32 days and the young birds become independent of their parents sometime between 15 and 30 days after hatch (Photo by B. Reeves).

wild mourning dove populations (Martin and Sauer 1993, Tomlinson and Dunks 1993).

Mated males take the initiative in nest site selection and deliver twigs to the females for arrangement into flimsy nests (Fig. 2). Nests generally are placed in trees or shrubs at heights of 1–4.5 m, but in areas of the Great Plains and in the West, extensive ground nesting occurs. Nest construction takes 7–10 hours and may be spread over a period of 2–4 days (Blockstein 1986). Additional details of courtship and mating behavior are provided by Sayre et al. (1993) and Mirarchi (1993*b*).

Normal clutch size is 2 eggs, although 1, 3, and 4 are occasionally encountered. Three- and 4-egg clutches are thought to be the result of dump nesting by another female. Eggs are laid either on alternate days (24–48 hrs apart) or on consecutive days (12–24 hrs apart). Incubation probably begins immediately after the first egg is laid. Both the male and female share in incubation duties; the male typically is on the nest from mid-morning to late afternoon and the female during the night. Incubation normally requires 14–15 days. After hatching, squabs are brooded and fed by both parents (Fig. 3). A substance secreted from the crop, called "crop milk," is regurgitated and fed to the young (Mirarchi 1993*d*). As squabs grow older, the amount of crop milk produced by the parents decreases and is supplemented with seeds. At time of fledging, normally 14–15 days after hatching but sometimes as early as 10 days, the diet of squabs is nearly identical to that of adults.

Fledglings can survive independently of the parents 5–9 days after fledging (Mirarchi and Scanlon 1981), but normally are fed by the male until they are about 27 days old (Hitchcock and Mirarchi 1984). The entire nesting cycle requires about 32 days and the adult male continues to feed fledglings during the primary stages of the succeeding nesting attempt (Mirarchi 1993*b*, 1993*c*; Sayre and Silvy 1993). Adults may nest as often as 5–6 times a season in the South but only 2–3 times in northern areas. Sayre and Silvy (1993) estimated that each pair of mourning doves would have to average 3.7 and 4.7 annual nesting attempts (to fledge 2.2 and 2.8 young/pair) in the central and western United States, respectively, to maintain populations.

Food Habits

Mourning doves are primarily granivorous ground feeders, although they also pick up grit and insignificant amounts of animal matter and green forage (Lewis 1993). They avoid tall and rank vegetation and prefer relatively open areas for foraging. Small, even tiny, seeds are preferred and a large variety of species is consumed. Some preferred food plants are: pigweeds (*Amaranthus* spp.), spurges (*Euphorbia* spp.), crotons (*Croton* spp.), sunflower (*Helianthus* spp.), panic grasses (*Panicum* spp.), foxtails (*Hordeum* spp. and *Setaria* spp.), barnyard grass (*Echinochloa crusgalli*), and ragweed (*Ambrosia* spp.). Agricultural crops, particularly cereal grains, are important sources of food for doves in most areas; when agricultural foods are avail-

Fig. 4.   Doves generally drink water twice a day (late morning and late evening). Development of stock tanks during the late 19th and early 20th centuries increased the availability of water in the Southwest and West, and doves are known to visit them regularly (Photo by R. R. George).

able, they comprise >50% of the food volume (Lewis 1993). Individuals or flocks of doves may fly 30–50 km to feed in grain fields. Preferred grains are: wheat, sorghum, corn, rye, millets, and peanuts.

Survival and Mortality Factors

Mean annual survival rates of mourning doves vary widely among states. Generally, however, adults survive at rates between 42–52% and immatures at rates between 24–44% (Martin and Sauer 1993, Reeves et al. 1993, Tomlinson and Dunks 1993). Natural mortality factors include predation of adults and free-flying young by avian and mammalian predators (Sadler 1993a); destruction of eggs and nestlings by squirrels, snakes, grackles (*Quiscalus* spp.), blue jays (*Cyanocitta cristata*), and American crows (*Corvus brachyrhyncos*); and disease such as avian pox (*Poxvirus avium*) and trichomoniasis (*Trichomonas gallinae*). Man-caused mortality factors include destruction of habitat, pesticides, and hunting. The average life span of mourning doves is 1–1.5 years (Tomlinson and Dolton 1987).

Fall Migration

Southward migration begins in late August (Miles 1976, Tomlinson 1993) and ends at wintering areas in October and November. Immatures begin migration first and are followed by adult females and adult males in that order (Tomlinson 1993). Recent evidence suggests that some doves in middle to southern parts of the breeding range are completely nonmigratory (Channing 1979, Bivings 1980, Marion et al. 1981, Leopold and Dedon 1983).

HABITAT

Mourning doves are so adaptable in habitat selection that a complete description of breeding habitat is difficult at best (Eng 1986, Sayre and Silvy 1993). Although most doves nest in trees, ground nesting is known to be important, particularly in Great Plains and Great Basin states (Sayre and Silvy 1993). They generally shun deep woods or forest and select open woodlands and "edge" between forest and prairie communities for nesting. Humans have greatly modified the original vegetation of the United States, and these alterations generally have been beneficial to mourning doves. The clearing of forests in the East and parts of the West undoubtedly created favorable nesting conditions, but perhaps the most important change affecting mourning doves was plowing of the grasslands and introduction of irrigation in the Central and Western United States for cereal production (Tomlinson and Dunks 1993). Waste grains and weed seeds associated with these farming practices are important food sources. Planting of field and farmstead shelterbelts and development of stock ponds have provided substantially more nesting habitat and drinking water than originally available (Fig. 4). Additional nesting and roosting habitat was created when trees and shrubs were planted in cities and towns associated with farming communities.

Mourning dove nest site characteristics and preferences vary substantially. Doves nest in a variety of coniferous and deciduous tree species, shrubs, vines, building ledges, chimneys, and other less typical locations (Sayre and Silvy 1993). Most nests are constructed on horizontal limbs and are relatively free of any nearby concealing vegetation. Coniferous trees and ground sites are preferred early in the year before deciduous trees have developed leaves. Cemeteries, with their numerous tree and shrub species, provide especially good nesting habitat. In all situations, however, abundant food and water must be available within 20–30 km.

Sayre and Silvy (1993) listed primary and secondary mourning dove nest tree species by geographic area. Among those in the eastern United States were blue spruce (*Picea pungens*), Austrian pine (*Pinus nigra*), red pine (*P. resinosa*), shortleaf pine (*P. echinata*), red cedar (*Juniperus virginiana*), oak (*Quercus* spp.), and osage-orange (*Maclura pomifera*). In addition, orchard or ornamental species such as peach (*Prunus persica*), pecan (*Carya illinoensis*), grape (*Vitis* spp.), and rose (*Rosa* spp.) also were considered excellent nesting habitat. In the Midwest, elms (*Ulmus* spp.), blue spruce, white spruce (*Picea glauca*), honeylocust (*Gleditsia triacanthos*), osage-orange, hackberries (*Celtis* spp.), mesquite (*Prosopis* spp.), and live oak (*Q. virginiana*) are representative trees used by nesting doves. In the West, riparian trees and shrubs such as cottonwoods (*Populus* spp.), saltcedar (*Tamarix* spp.), willows (*Salix* spp.), and mesquite are particularly important for dove nesting. In addition, apple (*Malus* spp.), cherry (*Prunus* spp.), and citrus (*Citrus* spp.) orchards provide excellent nesting structures in many areas of the Far West and Southwest.

During autumn and winter, dove habitat preferences are determined primarily by food availability and roosting cover. Flocks of mourning doves move between roost sites and specific food sites (typically corn, millet, sorghum, or wheat fields) daily until the food is gone. The flocks then seek new feeding areas and considerable movement of dove flocks takes place during winter. Winter roost sites usually consist of small to medium-sized woodlots that provide protective cover.

DISTRIBUTION AND ABUNDANCE

The breeding distribution of mourning doves encompasses the southern portions of the Canadian provinces, the 48 conterminous United States, northcentral Mexico, and the Greater Antilles (Keeler 1977, Tomlinson et al. 1988, Aldrich 1993) (Fig. 5). The winter distribution generally extends south from the 40th Parallel (Interstate Highway 80) in the United States; most doves winter considerably farther south than that, but small groups of birds remain in areas as far north as southern Canada where food is available (Chambers et al. 1962, Keeler 1977, Dunks et al. 1982, Armstrong and Noakes 1983, Caron et al. 1986, Houston 1986, Tomlinson 1993) (Fig. 5). Doves are presumed to have less migratory inclination in the southern part of their breeding range, where it overlaps winter range.

Mourning doves are the most numerous and widely-distributed game birds in North America and rank among the 10 most abundant bird species in the United States (Robbins et al. 1986, Tomlinson and Dolton 1987). Recent estimates

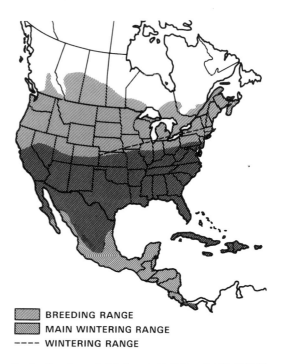

BREEDING RANGE
MAIN WINTERING RANGE
---- WINTERING RANGE

Fig. 5. Breeding and wintering ranges of mourning doves (from Baskett et al. 1993).

place the number of doves in the autumn population at about 475 million birds (Dunks et al. 1982, Tomlinson et al. 1988). The highest densities of breeding mourning doves are in the Great Plains states of North Dakota, South Dakota, Nebraska, and Kansas; in Arizona and southern California; and the Carolinas and Georgia (Fig. 6).

Kiel (1959) analyzed the existing banding and recovery records obtained during 1954–57 and concluded there were 3 clearly-defined areas within the United States that contained mourning dove populations that were largely independent of each other. As a result of this analysis, the Eastern (EMU), Central (CMU), and Western (WMU) Management Units (Fig. 7) were established as operational entities in 1960 (Kiel 1961). Two later banding analyses (Dunks et al. 1982, Tomlinson et al. 1988) suggested further division of the units into subunits that contained doves with similar migration patterns. Tomlinson (1993) divided the EMU into 6 regions, the CMU into 3 north-south tiers, and the WMU into 2 north-south tiers. Mexico and Central America were divided into 8 geographic regions with similar physiographic features and mourning dove band recovery patterns (Fig. 8). Al-

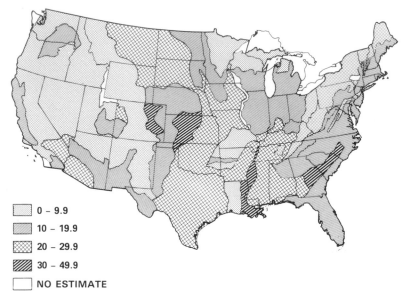

Fig. 6. Breeding densities (birds heard/route) of mourning doves in the United States, 1992–93 average.

though some overlap exists, dove migration and other habits generally are different enough among subpopulations that managers may wish to consider management options separately for each subunit at some point in the future.

Spring migration begins in February and March, progresses slowly through April, and terminates in mid- to late May for most areas of the United States. The breeding season begins in March, peaks in June and July, and essentially ends by the end of August. As the summer pro-

gresses, flocks grow larger and are composed of both young and adults that have finished nesting. Flocks locally move in response to food sources until mid-August when declines in numbers at breeding locations are noted. Immature doves tend to migrate before adults (Dunks et al. 1982, Tomlinson et al. 1988). Migrating doves move into southern states, Mexico, and Central America, as far south as northern Costa Rica (Dunks et al. 1982, Tomlinson et al. 1988). Of the doves banded in the United States and re-

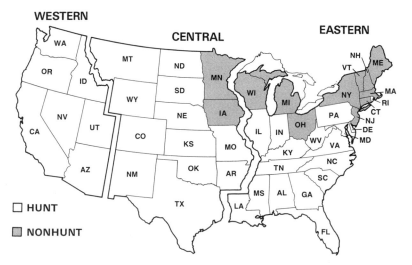

Fig. 7. Mourning dove management units with states permitting dove hunting, 1993.

WESTERN **CENTRAL** **EASTERN**

1 NORTHWEST COAST
2 NORTHERN HIGHLANDS
3 NORTHEAST COAST
4 WESTERN HIGHLANDS
5 CENTRAL HIGHLANDS
6 SOUTHERN
7 YUCATAN PENINSULA
8 CENTRAL AMERICA

Fig. 8.   Mourning dove management units, subunits, and Latin American harvest units (from Tomlinson 1993).

covered in Mexico, 78% were reported from the Western Highlands, a 5-state region of Jalisco, Michoacan, Guanajuato, Guerrero, and Colima on the west-central coast (Fig. 8) (Dunks et al. 1982). The rate of fall migration is leisurely, and doves average no more than 80–160 km/day. Doves from northern areas begin to arrive in southern states, such as Arizona and Texas, in September and increase through October. The peak recovery period in Mexico is mid-October, but this may reflect the later hunting season dates there rather than the actual arrival dates.

Populations Assessment

Development of a survey technique to detect and measure mourning dove population changes was a major objective of a cooperative dove investigation initiated in southeastern states in 1948 (Southeast. Assoc. Game and Fish Comm. 1957, Dolton 1993). The survey method, based on studies of McClure (1939) and refined by Foote and Peters (1952), consists of a series of

20-mile (32-km) routes on which cooperators stop every mile (1.6 km) and count the number of doves heard cooing during a 3-minute period (Fig. 9). The numbers of doves heard cooing/ route provide a mechanism to estimate population trends for states and management units over time. The numbers of doves seen on the same routes are used in a separate analysis to provide supplemental information.

Nationwide call-count survey routes are conducted by personnel of state and federal agencies during 20 May–5 June each year. The U.S. Fish and Wildlife Service (USFWS) coordinates the survey, analyzes the data, and prepares the annual summary of the results prior to the Public Hearing for Early Hunting Season Regulations in June. Data are grouped by physiographic region and weighted by the land area of each region within states, management units, and subunits. Analysis is accomplished using the route regression method, which incorporates linear regression on a logarithmic scale and takes into

Fig. 9.   Each year, over 1,000 mourning dove call-count routes are run throughout the United States. The average number of birds heard calling on the 20-stop routes provide annual indices to population size and trends over time in each of the 3 management units. Management decisions are guided by the long- and short-term trends from this survey (Photo by R. E. Tomlinson).

account differing abilities of individual observers to hear doves (Geissler and Sauer 1990). Variances of management unit, subunit, and state trends are estimated using trends and a statistical procedure known as bootstrapping.

The first call-count survey (in the 48 conterminous states) was conducted in 1953 on routes generally selected in high density areas (Dolton 1992). Between 1957 and 1966, the original routes, which did not provide a representative sample of the overall dove population, were replaced by randomly-selected routes, stratified by physiographic region (Foote et al. 1958). Randomized route selection was completed in 1966; since that time, surveys on between 1,000 and 1,100 routes have been conducted nationwide each year (Dolton 1993).

Status

Eastern Management Unit.—Most doves from the EMU *New England* region (geographic descriptions in Fig. 8) migrate through Mid-Atlantic states into the Carolinas and Georgia, with a few continuing to EMU South states (Tomlinson 1993). Although the long-term trend in New England is stable at 8–11 birds heard/route (Fig. 10), breeding dove populations appear to have increased during the past 20 years, and particularly the last 5 years (Table 1).

One segment of the *North-Central* population migrates into Alabama, Georgia, and Florida; the other moves into Louisiana and Texas. Breeding populations have fluctuated widely

from about 14 to 23 birds heard/route, but the long-term trend is stable (Fig. 10, Table 1).

Most doves from *Mid-Atlantic* states are recovered in the Carolinas and Georgia, presumably the wintering area. During the late 1960's, breeding population indices were at 16–18 doves heard/route, after which they declined to 11–13 doves in the mid–1970's (Fig. 10). Since then, the population has remained stable at 12–14 doves per route. No long-term trends have been detected.

Most doves originating from the *Mid-Central* states of Kentucky and Tennessee appear to remain there over winter, but the remainder fan into Louisiana, Mississippi, Alabama, Georgia, and Florida. Breeding populations, as measured by the call-count survey, appear to have declined from about 30–32 birds to 16–22 birds heard/route between 1966 and 1993 (Fig. 10, Table 1).

Dove populations in the *Carolinas* are sedentary and overwinter there, except for a few birds that move into Georgia and Florida. It appears that a steady decline from about 30 doves heard/route to 22 has occurred in the Carolinas during the past 15 years (Fig. 10, Table 1).

Doves from the EMU *South* show little tendency to migrate, although some birds from Louisiana and Mississippi move south and west into Texas and Mexico. Breeding doves in the South EMU appear to have been stable over the past 28 years (Fig. 10, Table 1).

Generally, doves from *EMU* states tend to move straight south or southeast and winter mainly in the Carolinas and the South EMU. Less than 2% of recoveries from doves banded in the EMU are in the CMU with less than 1% in Mexico and Central America. Thus, most doves that originate in the EMU migrate and winter within the unit, with only a few venturing outside. Breeding EMU dove populations have been relatively stable over the past 28 years (Fig. 10), but they declined between 1989 and 1993 (Table 1).

Central Management Unit.—Emigration from the *East CMU* is bifurcate; the main route is south and southwest into Louisiana, Texas, the Western Highlands of Mexico, and Central America, but significant numbers of doves move southeast into Alabama, Georgia, and Florida. A long-term decline was detected for breeding doves in the East CMU region, and populations are still at a level well below that of the late

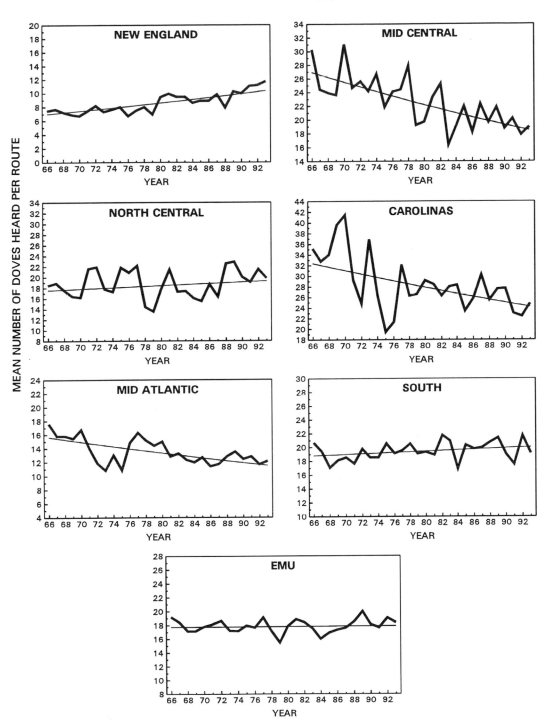

Fig. 10. Population indices and trends of breeding mourning doves in the Eastern Management Unit, 1966–93.

Table 1. Trends (% change[a] per year as determined by linear regression) in numbers of mourning doves heard along call-count survey routes, 1966–93.

Management unit/subunit	5-year (1989–93)			10-year (1984–93)			15-year (1979–93)			20-year (1974–93)			28-year (1966–93)		
	n	% change[b]	95% C.I.	n	% change[b]	95% C.I.	n	% change[b]	95% C.I.	n	% change[b]	95% C.I.	n	% change[b]	95% C.I.
Eastern Unit[c]															
New England	98	5.8***	2.0 9.3	111	2.3*	−0.3 4.8	120	1.3	−0.4 2.9	120	2.5***	1.1 4.0	134	1.5*	−0.2 3.0
North Central	94	−2.1	−4.8 0.6	99	3.7***	2.1 5.3	134	3.6***	2.0 5.2	134	0.8	−0.6 2.2	138	0.3	−1.1 1.7
Mid Atlantic	58	−5.1**	−10.1 −0.3	59	−1.1	−4.1 1.9	61	−0.4	−2.4 1.4	63	−1.1	−4.4 1.9	63	−1.1	−3.9 1.8
Mid Central	43	−3.1	−8.7 2.5	44	0.3	−2.4 3.0	46	−0.4	−2.7 1.8	50	−1.1	−3.3 0.8	56	−1.4	−3.4 0.5
Carolinas	41	−5.8***	−9.7 −1.9	46	−2.1**	−4.1 −0.3	49	−1.8**	−3.3 −0.2	49	−1.1	−2.8 0.7	49	−1.1	−2.8 0.6
South	120	−1.5	−4.4 1.5	127	0.6	−1.9 3.0	135	−1.1	−2.9 0.8	143	−0.2	−2.0 1.7	153	0.2	−1.5 2.0
Unit	454	−1.8**	−3.6 −0.1	486	1.3*	−0.1 2.7	545	0.4	−0.9 1.6	559	0.1	−1.0 1.3	593	0.0	−1.1 1.1
Central Unit[d]															
East	63	0.7	−2.7 4.0	64	0.7	−1.3 2.6	67	−1.1	−2.6 0.3	68	−1.3*	−2.7 0.0	73	−1.5***	−2.6 −0.4
Mid	253	1.5	−1.4 4.4	263	1.3	−0.5 3.2	276	−0.9	−2.1 0.3	285	−0.5	−1.6 0.7	329	−0.2	−1.2 0.8
West	82	−10.4***	−16.4 −4.1	86	−2.9**	−5.4 −0.5	88	−1.0	−3.3 1.2	91	0.2	−2.1 2.7	97	0.1	−2.1 2.2
Unit	398	0.7	−1.7 3.1	413	0.9	−0.7 2.5	431	−1.0*	−2.1 0.1	444	−0.6	−1.6 0.4	499	−0.4	−1.3 0.6
Western Unit[e]															
Interior	103	13.0***	5.1 21.1	111	−0.2	−2.6 2.3	116	−2.7***	−4.4 −1.1	122	−1.6*	−3.5 0.2	133	−1.6*	−3.2 0.1
Coastal	83	0.1	−5.2 5.5	97	−0.8	−3.0 1.5	101	−2.5***	−4.0 −1.0	107	−4.0***	−6.5 −1.7	118	−3.7***	−5.9 −1.6
Unit	186	8.4***	2.6 14.3	208	−0.5	−2.3 1.3	217	−2.7***	−4.0 −1.4	229	−2.6***	−4.3 −1.0	251	−2.4***	−4.0 −0.9

[a] Mean of route trends weighted by land area and population density. The estimated count in the next year is (%/100 + 1) times the count in the current year where % is the annual change. Note: extrapolating the estimated trend statistic (% change per year) over time (e.g., 28 years) may exaggerate the change over the period.

[b] *P < 0.10, **P < 0.05, ***P < 0.01.

[c] EMU subunits: New England (ME, NH, VT, NY, MA, RI, CT, PA, NJ); Mid Atlantic (DE, MD, WV, VA); North Central (WI, MI, IL, IN, OH); Mid Central (KY, TN); Carolinas (NC, SC); South (LA, MS, AL, GA, FL).

[d] CMU subunits: East (MN, IA, MO, AR); Mid (ND, SD, NE, KS, OK, TX); West (MT, WY, CO, NM).

[e] WMU subunits: Interior (ID, NV, UT, AZ); Coastal (WA, OR, CA).

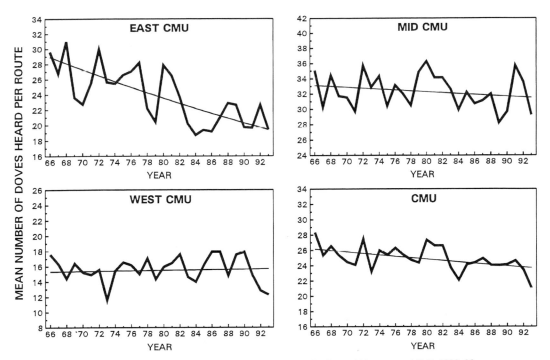

Fig. 11. Population indices and trends of breeding mourning doves in the Central Management Unit, 1966–93.

1960's (Fig. 11, Table 1). However, a gradual upturn during the past 10 years is cause for cautious optimism.

The migratory pattern of doves from the *Mid CMU* is straight south into Texas and Mexico, with some birds continuing into Central America. Few doves from this subunit are recovered in the EMU or WMU. Banding data suggest that Mid CMU states contribute more than half of the doves from the United States that winter in Mexico and Central America. Population indices indicate that breeding dove populations have remained stable at 30–36 doves/route (Fig. 11, Table 1).

Doves from the *West CMU* generally migrate straight south into Mexico, a few continuing into Central America. Banding data indicate that few birds from the West CMU remain within the subunit during winter, but move to Mexico's Central Highlands. Breeding doves in the West CMU have been relatively stable since 1966 with indices between 14 and 19 birds/route, but a decline during 1989–93 warrants close monitoring (Fig. 11, Table 1).

The general migratory pattern of *CMU* doves is fan-shaped; doves from the eastern part move into the EMU in substantial numbers, whereas doves from the rest of the unit migrate south

and southwest. The CMU contributes 75% of the doves originating in the United States and wintering in Mexico. A dove from the CMU is 13 times more likely to be recovered in Central America than a dove from the WMU. Except for doves in the East CMU, breeding populations as measured by the call-count survey generally appear to be stable (Fig. 11, Table 1).

Western Management Unit.—Migrating doves from the *Interior WMU* move straight south into Arizona, southern California, and the Western Highlands of Mexico. Banding data suggest that Interior WMU doves winter farther north than CMU doves (many in Arizona and California) and few continue to Central America. Annual indices for breeding doves in Interior states have declined from about 19 doves heard/route to 11 since 1966 and the decline has been particularly evident during the past 15 years (Fig. 12, Table 1). However, populations have shown a significant increase since 1989, coincident with restrictive regulations in Arizona, the major harvesting state of the subunit.

Most migrating doves from the *Coastal WMU* stay within the subunit but move east into Arizona and then into mainland Mexico. They winter from southern Arizona and southern California to the Western Highlands of Mexico. No

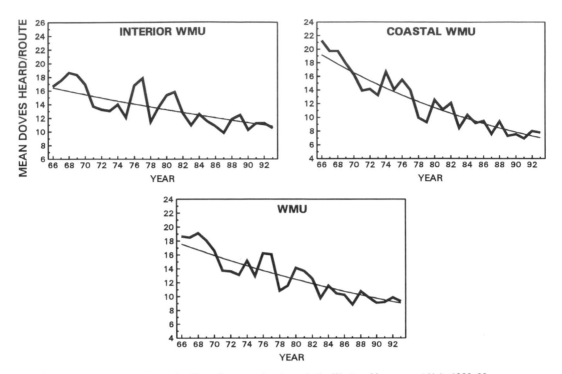

Fig. 12.   Population indices and trends of breeding mourning doves in the Western Management Unit, 1966–93.

doves from this tier of states continue into Central America. The breeding population in this subunit has registered the most precipitous decline in the United States, from approximately 25 doves heard/route in 1966 to <8 in 1991 (Fig. 12). The long-term downward trend is highly significant, but recent indices reflect a stabilization at low levels (Table 1).

Doves from the entire *WMU* migrate south and southeast. Wintering areas include the southern portions of California and Arizona to the Western Highlands of Mexico. Few doves migrate into southern Mexico or Central America. WMU doves in all areas are experiencing long-term declines (Fig. 12, Table 1).

HARVEST

Thirty-six of the 48 conterminous states have permitted dove hunting seasons since 1985 (Figs. 7, 13). In 1992, these states represented 87% of the breeding-dove population (call-count data, Dolton 1992), 86% of the land area, and 60% of the human population. In the EMU and CMU since 1982, federal hunting regulations frameworks have permitted annual dove hunting seasons with 2 geographic zones and 3 temporal splits in each state between 1 September and 15

January. Two options, either 70 days with bag/possession limits of 12/24 or 60 days with limits of 15/30, have been offered. During 1992 in the EMU, 11 states selected the former option and 6 the latter, whereas in the CMU, only 1 state selected the former and 11 the latter. Within the 2 units, only 1 state (South Dakota) elected to restrict further (season length). In the WMU, where populations have declined, Federal frameworks since 1987 have been restrictive. For the past 6 years, Arizona and California have been allowed a split season of 60 days (between 1–15 Sep and 1 Nov–15 Jan only) with bag/possession limits of 10/20. During the same time, the other WMU states were permitted a 30-consecutive-day season between 1 September and 15 January with limits of 10/20. In 1992, the Department of Wildlife elected to further restrict the season length to 15 days in Washington.

The annual harvest of mourning doves is estimated by many state wildlife agencies through mail or telephone questionnaire surveys. However, because each state's survey uses differing sampling frames and techniques, the precision of the estimates varies considerably among states. In addition, some states do not conduct harvest surveys at all and many states fail to conduct surveys in certain years, leaving gaps in the data. Therefore, long-term harvest trends for some states and all management units are difficult to obtain.

Harvest estimates for the entire United States have been made intermittently during the past 50 years (Table 2). During World War II (1942), the estimated dove harvest was >11 million birds. By 1982, the estimate had grown to 50 million. Since then, however, it appears that harvest has declined to about 41 million birds (1989, Table 2). According to Sadler (1993*b*), approximately 2.4 million United States hunters spent 10.4 million days dove hunting and harvested about 45.6 million doves on the average during 1983–87 (Table 3). Of the doves harvested, 28.5 million (62%) were in the EMU, 12.5 million (28%) in the CMU, and 4.6 million (10%) in the WMU. The average seasonal bag per hunter was 21.3 doves in the EMU, 16.1 in the CMU, and 15.0 in the WMU.

Baskett and Sayre (1993) estimated the number of dollars spent for shells (only) used in dove hunting ($70 million) and the amount from that source annually contributed to Federal Aid in Wildlife Restoration funds ($7.6 million). We conducted a similar exercise using more conservative base figures. We assumed a current harvest of 41 million doves (Table 2), 7 shells/bird bagged (less than the 8.7 of Haas [1977] in South Carolina), and an average cost of $4.00/box of shells; this resulted in an estimated annual expenditure for shells of $45.9 million and the amount contributed to Federal Aid funds at $5 million. Baskett and Sayre (1993:3) concluded that, "... as a direct result of dove hunting, millions of dollars are made available for state research and management programs for non-hunted wildlife as well as hunted species."

Martin and Sauer (1993) compared average dove harvests in the EMU during 2 periods (1966–71 and 1983–87) and concluded that harvest in that unit had remained relatively constant over time. This conclusion is consistent with the stable population trend observed in the EMU during the same period. In 9 states of the CMU with sufficient harvest data for varying time periods between 1966 and 1991, dove harvest exhibited upward trends in 2 states, downward in 2 states, and stable trends in 5 states (R. E. Tomlinson, unpubl. data from state surveys). Tomlinson and Dunks (1993) reported that seasonal harvest in the CMU essentially was stable

Fig. 13. Mourning doves are hunted in 36 of the 48 conterminous states. The estimated U.S. harvest is between 42 and 46 million doves per year (Sadler 1993). It is estimated that hunting doves annually generates over $5 million for Federal Aid projects (Photo by R. R. George).

between 1966 and 1987; however, data for Missouri, representing the East CMU, indicated decreasing harvest between 1977 and 1987, possibly the result of lower population numbers in that subunit. In the WMU, annual harvest has decreased from 7 million doves prior to 1976 to 3.5 million in the late 1980's (West. Migratory Upland Game Bird Tech. Comm. 1992, Reeves et al. 1993). These harvest declines are apparent in both the Interior and Coastal subunits. The number of WMU dove hunters remained at between 425,000 and 485,000 for many years despite lower annual bag sizes, but by 1987, the number of hunters had declined to about 275,000 (Reeves et al. 1993). The significant decline in hunter numbers and harvest in the WMU probably occurred because fewer doves were available, although factors such as increased costs of hunting and difficulty in gaining access to shooting areas may have contributed (West. Migratory Upland Game Bird Tech. Comm. 1992).

Table 2. Estimated harvest of mourning doves in the United States by selected year.

Year	Harvest (millions)	Reference
1942	11+	McClure 1944
1949	15	Dalrymple 1949
1955	19	Peters 1956
1965	41	Ruos and Tomlinson 1968
1972	49.4	Keeler 1977
1982	50.3	Sadler 1993
1983–87 ($\bar{x}$)	45.6	Sadler 1993
1988	41.8	Sadler 1993
1989	41.3	Sadler 1993

Table 3.   Average mourning dove harvest and hunting activity in the United States reported by state agencies, 1983–87 (modified from Sadler 1993).

Area	Hunters (n)	Days afield	Doves harvested	Average daily bag	Average seasonal bag
Eastern Management Unit					
New England					
Pennsylvania	161,200	642,585[a]	1,488,000	2.32	9.23
Rhode Island	No data	No data	10,000[b]		
Subtotals	161,200	642,585	1,498,000	2.33	9.29
North-Central					
Illinois	70,882	360,658	1,344,502	3.73	18.97
Indiana	15,735	100,316	162,230	1.62	10.31
Subtotals	86,617	460,974	1,506,732	3.27	17.40
Mid-Atlantic					
Delaware	6,515	33,483	102,755	3.07	15.77
Maryland	26,630	129,138	411,826	3.19	15.46
Virginia	62,558	271,467	931,776	3.43	14.89
West Virginia	11,455	44,184[b]	40,304[b]	0.91	3.52
Subtotals	107,158	478,272	1,486,661	3.11	13.87
Mid-Central					
Kentucky	85,994	438,569	1,930,005	4.40	22.44
Tennessee	139,514	527,907	3,183,702	6.03	22.82
Subtotals	225,508	966,476	5,113,707	5.29	22.68
Carolinas					
North Carolina	116,895	567,481	2,498,555	4.40	21.37
South Carolina	111,996	552,757	3,148,336	5.70	28.11
Subtotals	228,891	1,120,238	5,646,891	5.04	24.67
South					
Louisiana	110,600	462,777[a]	2,497,000	5.40	22.58
Mississippi	112,597	485,852	2,933,571	6.04	26.05
Alabama	98,264	552,992	3,029,572	5.48	30.83
Georgia	107,191	589,025	3,155,452	5.36	29.44
Florida	107,428	393,656	1,635,199	4.15	15.22
Subtotals	536,080	2,484,302	13,250,794	5.33	24.72
Unit totals	1,345,454	6,152,847	28,502,785	4.63	21.28
Central Management Unit					
East					
Missouri	60,901	290,184	999,369	3.44	16.41
Arkansas	42,918	201,715[a]	813,251	4.03	18.95
Subtotals	103,819	491,899	1,812,620	3.68	17.46
Mid					
North Dakota	15,951	52,136	83,418	1.60	5.23
South Dakota	16,454	73,344	264,240	3.60	16.06
Nebraska	34,510	177,759	588,912	3.31	17.06
Kansas	89,878	430,732	1,766,000	4.10	19.65
Oklahoma	75,002	431,172	1,854,041	4.30	24.72
Texas	393,259	1,370,392	5,207,490	3.80	13.24
Subtotals	625,054	2,535,535	9,764,101	3.85	15.62
West					
Montana	476	2,759	4,162	1.51	8.74
Wyoming	4,952	16,410	57,434	3.50	11.60
Colorado	29,945	122,658	414,376	3.38	13.84
New Mexico	17,517	115,221	495,452	4.30	28.28
Subtotals	52,890	257,048	971,424	3.78	18.37
Unit totals	781,763	3,284,482	12,548,145	3.82	16.05

Table 3. Continued.

Area	Hunters (n)	Days afield	Doves harvested	Average daily bag	Average seasonal bag
Western Management Unit					
Interior					
Idaho	7,950	29,850[c]	93,800	3.14	11.80
Nevada	7,100	18,189[c]	84,020	4.62	11.83
Utah	27,260	88,231[c]	248,460	2.82	9.11
Arizona	81,280	291,127[c]	1,534,980	5.27	18.89
Subtotals	123,590	427,397	1,961,260	4.59	15.87
Coastal					
Washington	8,600	20,770[c]	69,375	3.34	8.07
Oregon	14,550	44,319[c]	162,500	3.67	11.17
California	157,540	477,462[c]	2,376,980	4.98	15.09
Subtotals	180,690	542,551	2,608,855	4.81	14.44
Unit totals	304,280	969,948	4,570,115	4.71	15.02
United States totals	2,431,497	10,407,277	45,621,045	4.38	18.76

[a] Estimated from hunting/harvest data in nearby states.
[b] Estimated from information collected prior to 1983.
[c] Average for 1986 and 1987 only.

MANAGEMENT NEEDS

Habitat Management

Mourning dove habitat needs include trees in proper relation to open areas for nesting and roosting, a combination of wild and cultivated seeds for food, and water for drinking. Dove nesting and roosting habitats have been continuously destroyed during the past 50 years through urban development, agricultural practices, water reclamation projects, and other activities associated with human population growth (Braun et al. 1993, Reeves et al. 1993). Government and private landowners must be persuaded that indiscriminate bulldozing of phreatophytes in reclamation projects, and clearing of shelterbelts for efficient agricultural practices, often are unnecessary and harmful to wildlife. The same is true of the routine and heavy use of biocides to control pests during agricultural activities.

Fields used for feeding by mourning doves are characterized by abundance of small weed seeds and grain on relatively bare ground (R. K. Baskett 1993, Sayre and Silvy 1993). The presence of tall trees with bare limbs (snags) or utility lines where the birds congregate before alighting in fields also appears to be important. Manipulation of fields by mowing, light discing, grazing by livestock, and other agricultural practices can enhance dove feeding areas. Adjacent sources of drinking water are important, particularly if slopes of ponds and stock tanks are shallow and free of vegetation. There are few published sources for dove food and habitat management (reviewed by R. K. Baskett 1993), and a thorough treatise on the subject has not yet been developed, in some measure because complete knowledge of micro- and macrohabitat use is lacking.

Management manuals for different regions should be developed to educate landowners, land agencies, and conservation agencies in dove nesting and feeding habitat improvement methods. The manuals should be dynamic documents and easily updated when new management information is obtained. Additionally, some type of extension program is needed to gain the attention and cooperation of resource agencies and individuals. Initiatives should be established with landowners to improve habitat on private lands, and to demonstrate that the measures can be economically beneficial to individual farmers or ranchers. Opportunities exist for habitat improvement through 10-year contracts such as under the long-term Conservation Reserve Program (CRP), the annual Agricultural Conservation Program (ACP), and annual feed/grain set-aside programs of the Agricultural Stabilization and Conservation Service (ASCS). However, use of these programs would require an intensive monitoring system to ensure that farmers were indeed enhancing habitat for doves.

In the long run, additional funds will be needed to make such programs function. Wildlife agency adminstrators should be encouraged to use a larger proportion of their allocated Federal Aid reimbursement funds for mourning dove management. Braun et al. (1993) suggested that states establish annual mourning dove "stamps," required of dove hunters at a low cost, to finance management projects. Many states already have pheasant, waterfowl, and turkey stamps and the concept appears to be a reasonable method to accrue funding for dove management.

Mourning doves nest in urban and suburban areas, and these populations probably contribute substantially to the annual recruitment throughout their range. Many city people maintain bird feeders and water for bird watching and doves regularly use these facilities, sometimes to their detriment (through disease transmission). Dove managers typically have ignored this segment of the overall population. Studies should be initiated to assess the recruitment that urban doves contribute to total population numbers. Depending on the results, provision could be made for developing methods to enhance dove nesting and survival in urban and suburban environments.

Population Management

Subpopulations.—We have discussed mourning doves relative to breeding population subunits, as doves in each of these subunits exhibit distinctive migratory and survival characteristics. Tomlinson (1993) further discussed wintering areas of doves associated with breeding subpopulations. Management decisions should consider these relationships wherever practical. Any new banding programs, in addition to the primary objectives, should seek further definition of these subpopulations. This is not to say the 3 established management units are no longer germane to dove management, but to suggest that finer tuning may be desirable and even necessary in the future.

Surveys.—Although the higher cooing rates of unmated than mated males complicate use of call-count survey techniques in small areas where sex ratios may vary considerably (T. S. Baskett 1993), the mourning dove call-count survey has served well to detect long-term population declines in the WMU and East CMU and to indicate stable or increasing populations in other areas. Comparisons of trends from au-

dio counts with trends from independent visual counts have shown close correlation for dove populations in California, Missouri, and North Dakota (T. S. Baskett 1993). Nevertheless, recent examination of survey parameters (Sauer et al. 1994) indicates that certain physiographic regions and/or states are not being sampled at levels sufficient to provide precise trend estimates. The survey should be analyzed to identify where data are insufficient; sample sizes (number of routes) should be increased accordingly. Additionally, to better represent broad ecological types, a restratification may be necessary (Blankenship et al. 1971). Other sources of variability in survey results are diminished hearing ability of some observers (Ramsey and Scott 1981) and frequent changes of observers among years. An effort to improve observer participation is desirable. At present, the survey is restricted to the United States. Consideration should be given to expanding the survey into southern Canada and northern Mexico to sample populations in as much breeding habitat as possible.

A nationwide assessment of autumn and winter population distribution and abundance has been suggested to provide additional data for use in establishing hunting seasons. This might be a viable technique in the East where doves remain within EMU boundaries all year. However, in the CMU and WMU, where many doves annually migrate into Mexico and Central America, a fall and winter survey in the United States alone probably would be of limited value. We suggest that an autumn and/or winter survey be developed and tested in 2 or 3 southern EMU states to learn if wider application is warranted.

Banding.—The last nationwide, cooperative mourning dove banding program was conducted during 1967–75. Data from the program on survival rate, recovery rate, distribution, derivation, and other parameters were analyzed and published in the 1980's (Dunks et al. 1982, Tomlinson et al. 1988). Thus, the information now being used for many management decisions is over 15 years old. Although banding is often expensive and resulting data demonstrate high statistical variability without large sample sizes, this technique, in many cases, is the only tool available to obtain the needed information. Consideration should be given to inaugurating new, carefully designed and executed banding programs, at least in those areas that show decreasing population trends, for comparison with earlier data.

Harvest Management

Surveys.—The lack of a standardized survey to obtain reliable nationwide mourning dove harvest data has been a high priority issue for many years (Sadler 1993b). The most current estimates are composites from state surveys, each of which use different sampling techniques. In addition, some states either do not conduct harvest surveys or fail to maintain continuity from year to year. In 1990, an ad hoc committee of the International Association of Fish and Wildlife Agencies recommended a cooperative venture between the states and the USFWS to generate harvest information for all migratory game birds (Babcock et al. 1990). Subsequently, the National Migratory Bird Harvest Information Program (HIP) was established (U.S. Fish and Wildl. Serv. 1992). HIP is a cooperative permit system, in which individual states distribute Harvest Information Cards to hunters at the time annual hunting licenses are purchased, and obtain hunter names and addresses to enable the USFWS to conduct a mail questionnaire survey of migratory bird hunters throughout the United States. HIP is expected to provide more reliable mourning dove harvest estimates once it has been fully implemented in 1998. Until then, state wildlife agencies should be encouraged to stratify their license buyer files to enable more precise sampling and result in more accurate mourning dove harvest estimates.

Strategies.—Although the human population is growing, the number of hunters appears to be decreasing throughout the United States. It will be important to formulate sound mourning dove hunting and harvest strategies to accommodate changing hunting practices. We suggest these strategies can be developed in management plans for entire management units or geared to subunits and states, and include triggering mechanisms for restricting or liberalizing regulations. Whatever the strategy, it should include as much recreation as possible while protecting the resource. Education in the schools and public relations programs will be needed to explain the strategies and convince a highly urban society that hunting doves has a rightful place in the wise use of our renewable, natural resources.

In many parts of the country, farmers now grow fewer grain crops (e.g., sorghum and corn) than 25 years ago. These grain fields typically concentrated doves in quest of food during autumn and provided excellent hunting opportunity. In addition, farmers have become increasingly reluctant to allow hunting on the reduced numbers of grain fields. It will be necessary to develop incentives for landowners to grow crops that attract doves and to allow hunting on their lands. Development of state and federal hunting areas using improved field management techniques (R. K. Baskett 1993) will be increasingly important. Hunting regulations should ensure that measures governing baiting are just and that law enforcement is uniform geographically.

Management Plans

Braun et al. (1993) recommended that a comprehensive nationwide mourning dove management plan be developed to guide future management decisions. The Migratory Shore and Upland Game Bird Committee of the International Association of Fish and Wildlife Agencies (Spring 1991 Minutes) further recommended that management plans for each of the 3 management units be formulated first toward a national plan. We concur with development of the management unit plans and further suggest that each plan provide for subunit needs where applicable. Mourning Dove subcommittees should be appointed by each management unit technical committee to ensure that recommendations in the management plans are rigorously pursued, reviewed periodically, and updated often.

RESEARCH NEEDS

Mourning dove research needs are listed below in priority order.

1. With the aid of a Geographic Information System (GIS), evaluate the effects of land-use practices on mourning dove populations in areas where doves are declining. Considerations should include:
   a. changes in cropping practices (e.g., from grain crops to other crops and chronology of grain crop harvest);
   b. increases in farm size and removal of shelterbelts, hedgerows, etc.;
   c. conversion of rural habitat to urban areas;
   d. loss of nesting habitat through reclama-

tion, logging, agriculture, urban sprawl, etc.;

e. increased efficiency of grain harvest machinery (loss of food availability); and

f. changes in surface water availability.

2. Ascertain the effects of biocides on mourning dove survival and reproductive success.

3. In areas of dove declines, establish banding and radio-telemetry programs to estimate annual and periodic survival rates to compare with earlier estimates. Such studies should use reward bands and/or other methods to estimate band reporting rates.

4. Examine the relationship of hunting regulations (bag limits, season length, and timing) with dove harvest and breeding populations, including:

a. changes in harvest patterns;

b. compensatory vs. additive mortality;

c. all-day vs. half-day hunting; and

d. crippling rates.

5. Measure productivity of mourning doves through intensive nesting studies (geographically, by habitat type, by segment of breeding season, and in hunted vs. nonhunted areas).

6. In selected areas, establish wing-collection surveys to examine the utility of using age ratios to monitor annual changes in recruitment. Ideally, this should be conducted over a wide area to avoid differential age or gender migration biases and in conjunction with a banding program to derive correction factors for differential vulnerability.

7. Evaluate a winter survey to ascertain distribution and abundance of doves on wintering areas, including:

a. possible use of roadside counts during winter on already-established call-count survey routes; and

b. possible use of Christmas Bird Counts.

8. Reevaluate the nationwide call-count survey to improve efficiency and coverage by physiographic region, management unit, subunit, and state. Emphasis should be to:

a. decrease the incidence of observer change among years;

b. increase the numbers of routes in undersampled areas;

c. restratify survey units to reduce variability in index estimates; and

d. explore alternative techniques, e.g., routes with fewer stops and more repli-

cations, substituting with the Breeding Bird Survey, and others.

9. Document mortality factors other than hunting and examine their effects on mourning dove populations. Studies should include:

a. lead poisoning from spent shot;

b. disease (determine epidemiology);

c. avian, mammalian, and reptilian predation; and

d. toxicity of fungicides and insecticides used to protect commercial plant seed.

10. Develop improved methods for identifying external mourning dove age and sex characters by season.

11. Investigate the skewed sex ratio (disproportionate numbers of adult males to females) in the breeding population to:

a. learn if sex ratios derived from trapping operations are correct; and

b. identify the reasons for skewed sex ratios.

12. Refine the characteristics of subpopulations of breeding doves and relate them to wintering areas. Studies should:

a. examine survival differences among subunits and determine the reasons for them; and

b. learn if hunting regulations (e.g., zones and splits) can be used to target specific subpopulations to increase or decrease harvest.

13. Investigate the relationship between dove densities and habitat, including:

a. investigate the relationship of ground nesting to tree nesting by mourning doves and relate to production and densities in selected areas of their range;

b. investigate the recruitment that urban doves contribute to overall populations in selected areas;

c. ascertain which habitat practices can enhance dove breeding populations; and

d. evaluate impacts of U.S. Department of Agriculture programs (e.g., CRP and ACP) and land use on mourning dove population trends.

14. Examine the effects of intensively-managed shooting fields on local dove populations.

15. Investigate mortality factors in Mexico and Central America (e.g., habitat deterioration, hunting harvest, biocides).

16. Evaluate the geographic extent and size of non-migratory segments of populations and how they relate to hunting harvest.

17. Document the summer and winter range expansion and/or increased dove population size in northern parts of the range. Studies should include:
    a. basic breeding ecology;
    b. geographic extent of overwintering behavior and the influence of late-winter food plots in carrying doves through the winter; and
    c. food habits and energy needs early in the breeding season, before grain-producing crops and weeds have produced new seed.
18. Investigate illegal kill of mourning doves, including:
    a. double-bagging (whole-day vs. half-day hunting); and
    b. baiting laws.

RECOMMENDATIONS

The mourning dove chapter (Keeler 1977) in the first edition of this book (Sanderson 1977) listed a series of recommendations pertaining to mourning dove research and management. Because of a lack of funding and other factors, many of the recommendations have not been addressed. In addition, a considerable amount of new information on mourning doves has been gained and consolidated since 1977 (Baskett et al. 1993). Chief among these findings is the discovery that dove populations in the West and other locations have sustained long-term downward trends. The causes for these declines are unknown at present, but the situation is cause for concern. A concerted effort should be made to identify the responsible factors and initiate management practices to reverse the trends. We recommend the following procedures to address management of mourning doves throughout their range.

1. The USFWS and state agencies within the respective dove management units should develop a dedicated, long-term funding source (or sources) with which to conduct annual studies of identified mourning dove problems. Although research is critical, operational management also must be funded at adequate levels to address limiting factors.
2. Comprehensive mourning dove management plans with prioritized objectives should be developed for the 3 management units by the respective Migratory Shore and Upland Game Bird Technical committees in conjunction with the USFWS. These plans should be followed carefully and updated frequently.
3. Full implementation of the Migratory Bird Harvest Information Program also is critical to provide a standardized nationwide survey for obtaining more precise mourning dove harvest estimates in all states. The USFWS, the International Association of Fish and Wildlife Agencies, and individual states should ensure this program does not fail. This will require extraordinary cooperation among agencies because of the complexity of the techniques used to administer and conduct the program.
4. The USFWS and state agencies must cooperatively establish and fund research programs to identify causes for dove declines in specific areas, and develop management techniques to combat the problems.
5. State wildlife agencies in each management unit should work with the U.S. Soil Conservation Service, USFWS, the Agricultural Extension Service, and others to develop an extension program that would provide guidance to landowners in improving mourning dove habitats. Efforts should be made to exploit the Conservation Reserve Program (and successive programs) and the Agricultural Conservation Program to attain habitat improvement goals.

ACKNOWLEDGMENTS

We thank T. S. Baskett, K. Guyse, J. A. Roberson, J. H. Schulz, and P. M. Smith who reviewed drafts of this chapter and made suggestions that improved it. We also thank W. L. Kendall who provided statistical analysis for annual call-count data and P. D. Keywood who provided graphics assistance. Since 1940, a great number of researchers have contributed to the knowledge that has accumulated about mourning doves. We are indebted to all of these people for the background information presented in this chapter. Among those that made special contributions to the literature are: J. W. Aldrich for his early systematics and distribution work; T. S. Baskett and his Missouri graduate students, who contributed to several aspects of mourning dove biology; L. E. Foote and H. S. Peters, who were instrumental in initiation of the Southeastern dove study that provided much of the early life history information; H. C. Hanson and C. W. Kossack, whose book on Illinois doves is still a major reference; W. H. Kiel Jr., whose 1959 banding analysis led to the formation of the 3 management units; H. E. McClure whose original Iowa studies led to many other useful mourning dove techniques, such as the call-count survey; G. C. Moore and A. M. Pearson in Alabama and T. L. Quay in North Carolina, who contributed many of the earliest dove data, including techniques for distinguishing age and gender differences; and H. M. Wight, whose inquisitive mind led to most of the dove work that was done in Missouri and elsewhere during the 1950's and 1960's. We are particularly grateful to the editors and authors of "Ecology and Management of the Mourning Dove," the book that influenced many of the recommendations in this chapter.

LITERATURE CITED

ALDRICH, J. W. 1993. Classification and distribution. Pages 47–54 in T. S. Baskett, M. W. Sayre, R. E. Tomlinson, and R. E. Mirarchi, eds., Ecology and management of the mourning dove. Stackpole Books, Harrisburg, Pa.

AMERICAN ORNITHOLOGISTS' UNION. 1983. Checklist of North American birds, 6th ed. Allen Press, Lawrence, Kans. 877pp.

ARMSTRONG, E. R., AND D. L. G. NOAKES. 1983. Wintering biology of mourning doves, Zenaida macroura, in Ontario. Can. Field-Nat. 97:434–438.

BABCOCK, K. M., E. G. HUNT, AND P. S. DUNCAN. 1990. Waterfowl breeding ground surveys and migratory bird harvest surveys. Unpubl. Committee Rep., Int. Assoc. Fish and Wildl. Agencies. Washington, D.C. 28pp.

BASKETT, R. K. 1993. Shooting field management. Pages 495–506 in T. S. Baskett, M. W. Sayre, R. E. Tomlinson, and R. E. Mirarchi, eds., Ecology and management of the mourning dove. Stackpole Books, Harrisburg, Pa.

BASKETT, T. S. 1993. Biological evaluation of the call-count survey. Pages 253–268 in T. S. Baskett, M. W. Sayre, R. E. Tomlinson, and R. E. Mirarchi, eds., Ecology and management of the mourning dove. Stackpole Books, Harrisburg, Pa.

———, AND M. W. SAYRE. 1993. Characteristics and importance. Pages 1–6 in T. S. Baskett, M. W. Sayre, R. E. Tomlinson, and R. E. Mirarchi, eds., Ecology and management of the mourning dove. Stackpole Books, Harrisburg, Pa.

———, R. E. TOMLINSON, AND R. E. MIRARCHI, EDITORS. 1993. Ecology and management of the mourning dove. Stackpole Books, Harrisburg, Pa. 567 pp.

BIVINGS, A. E., IV. 1980. Breeding ecology of the mourning dove on the Texas A&M University campus. Ph.D. Thesis, Texas A&M Univ., College Station. 64pp.

BLANKENSHIP, L. H., A. B. HUMPHREY, AND D. MacDONALD. 1971. A new stratification for mourning dove call-count routes. J. Wildl. Manage. 35:319–326.

BLOCKSTEIN, D. E. 1986. Reproductive behavior and parental investment of mourning doves (Zenaida macroura). Ph.D. Thesis, Univ. Minnesota, Minneapolis. 222pp.

BRAUN, C. E., N. J. SILVY, T. S. BASKETT, AND R. E. TOMLINSON. 1993. Research and management needs. Pages 507–513 in T. S. Baskett, M. W. Sayre, R. E. Tomlinson, and R. E. Mirarchi, eds., Ecology and management of the mourning dove. Stackpole Books, Harrisburg, Pa.

CARON, M., R. OUELLET, AND M. LEPAGE. 1986. La situation de la tourterelle triste au Québec. Unpubl. Rep., Ministère du Loisir, de la Chasse et de la Pêche, Direction de la faune terrestre service de la petite faune, Québec City, Qué. 37pp.

CHAMBERS, G. D., H. M. WIGHT, AND T. S. BASKETT. 1962. Characteristics of wintering flocks of mourning doves in Missouri. J. Wildl. Manage. 26:155–159.

CHANNING, E. 1979. Movements of banded mourning doves near Turlock, California. Calif. Fish and Game 65:23–35.

DALRYMPLE, B. W. 1949. Doves and dove shooting. G. P. Putnam's Sons, New York, N.Y. 243pp.

DOLTON, D. D. 1992. Mourning dove breeding population status, 1992. Unpubl. Rep., U.S. Fish and Wildl. Serv., Laurel, Md. 15pp.

———. 1993. The call-count survey: historic development and current procedures. Pages 233–252 in T. S. Baskett, M. W. Sayre, R. E. Tomlinson, and R. E. Mirarchi, eds., Ecology and management of the mourning dove. Stackpole Books, Harrisburg, Pa.

DUNKS, J. H., R. E. TOMLINSON, H. M. REEVES, D. D. DOLTON, C. E. BRAUN, AND T. P. ZAPATKA. 1982. Migration, harvest, and population dynamics of mourning doves banded in the Central Management Unit, 1967–77. U.S. Fish and Wildl. Serv., Spec. Sci. Rep. Wildl. 249. 128pp.

ENG, R. L. 1986. Upland game birds. Pages 407–428 in A.Y. Cooperrider, R. J. Boyd, and H. R. Stuart, eds., Inventory and monitoring of wildlife habitat. U.S. Dep. Inter., Bur. Land Manage. Serv. Cent., Denver, Colo.

FOOTE, L. E., AND H. S. PETERS. 1952. Introduction. Pages 1–3 in Investigations of methods of appraising the abundance of mourning doves. U.S. Fish and Wildl. Serv., Spec. Sci. Rep. Wildl. 17.

———, ———, AND A. L. FINKNER. 1958. Design tests for mourning dove call-count sampling in seven southeastern states. J. Wildl. Manage. 22:402–408.

GEISSLER, P. H., AND J. R. SAUER. 1990. Topics in route regression analysis. Pages 54–57 in J. R. Sauer and S. Droege, eds. Survey designs and statistical methods for the estimation of avian population trends. U. S. Fish and Wildl. Serv., Biol. Rep. 90(1).

———, D. D. DOLTON, R. FIELD, R. A. COON, H. F. PERCIVAL, D. W. HAYNE, L. D. SOILEAU, R. R. GEORGE, J. H DUNKS, AND S. D. BUNNELL. 1987. Mourning dove nesting: seasonal patterns and effects of September hunting. U.S. Fish and Wildl. Serv., Resour. Publ. 168. 33pp.

HAAS, G. H. 1977. Unretrieved shooting loss of mourning doves in north-central South Carolina. Wildl. Soc. Bull. 5:123–125.

———, AND S. R. AMEND. 1976 Aging immature mourning doves by primary feather molt. J. Wildl. Manage. 40:575–578.

———, AND ———. 1979. Primary feather molt of adult mourning doves in South Carolina. J. Wildl. Manage. 43:202–207.

HITCHCOCK, R. R., AND R. E. MIRARCHI. 1984. Duration of dependence of wild fledgling mourning doves on parental care. J. Wildl. Manage. 48:99–108.

HOUSTON, C. S. 1986. Mourning dove numbers explode on the Canadian prairies. Am. Birds 40:52–54.

KEELER, J. E., CHAIRMAN. 1977. Mourning dove (*Zenaida macroura*). Pages 275–298 *in* G. C. Sanderson, ed., Management of migratory shore and upland game birds in North America. Int. Assoc. Fish and Wildl. Agencies, Washington, D.C.

KIEL, W. H., JR. 1959. Mourning dove management units—a progress report. U.S. Fish and Wildl. Serv., Spec. Sci. Rep. Wildl. 43. 24pp.

———. 1961. The mourning dove program for the future. Trans. North Am. Wildl. and Nat. Resour. Conf. 26:418–435.

LEOPOLD, A. S., AND M. F. DEDON. 1983. Resident mourning doves in Berkeley, California. J. Wildl. Manage. 47:780–789.

LEWIS, J. C. 1993. Foods and feeding ecology. Pages 181–204 *in* T. S. Baskett, M. W. Sayre, R. E. Tomlinson, and R. E. Mirarchi, eds., Ecology and management of the mourning dove. Stackpole Books, Harrisburg, Pa.

MACKEY, J. P. 1965. Cooing frequency and permanence of pairing of mourning doves. J. Wildl. Manage. 29:824–829.

MARION, W. R., T. E. O'MEARA, AND L. D. HARRIS. 1981. Characteristics of the mourning dove harvest in Florida. J. Wildl. Manage. 45:1062–1066.

MARTIN, F. W., AND J. R. SAUER. 1993. Population characteristics and trends in the Eastern Management Unit. Pages 281–304 *in* T. S. Baskett, M. W. Sayre, R. E. Tomlinson, and R. E. Mirarchi, eds., Ecology and management of the mourning dove. Stackpole Books, Harrisburg, Pa.

McCLURE, H. E. 1939. Cooing activity and censusing of the mourning dove. J. Wildl. Manage. 3:323–328.

———. 1944. Mourning dove management. J. Wildl. Manage. 8:129–134.

MILES, A. K. 1976. Fall migration of mourning doves in the Western Management Unit. M.S. Thesis, Oregon State Univ., Corvallis. 75pp.

MIRARCHI, R. E. 1993*a*. Aging, sexing, and miscellaneous research techniques. Pages 399–408 *in* T. S. Baskett, M. W. Sayre, R. E. Tomlinson, and R. E. Mirarchi, eds., Ecology and management of the mourning dove. Stackpole Books, Harrisburg, Pa.

———. 1993*b*. Energetics, metabolism, and reproductive physiology. Pages 143–160 *in* T.S. Baskett, M. W. Sayre, R. E. Tomlinson, and R. E. Mirarchi, eds., Ecology and management of the mourning dove. Stackpole Books, Harrisburg, Pa.

———. 1993*c*. Growth, maturation, and molt. Pages 129–142 *in* T. S. Baskett, M. W. Sayre, R. E. Tomlinson, and R. E. Mirarchi, eds., Ecology and management of the mourning dove. Stackpole Books, Harrisburg, Pa.

———. 1993*d*. The crop gland. Pages 117–128 *in* T. S. Baskett, M. W. Sayre, R. E. Tomlinson, and R. E. Mirarchi, eds., Ecology and management of the mourning dove. Stackpole Books, Harrisburg, Pa.

———, AND P. F. SCANLON. 1981. Effects of orphaning on captive fledgling mourning doves. J. Wildl. Manage. 45:218–222.

PETERS, H. S. 1956. 19 million doves. South. Outdoors 4(6):9.

RAMSEY, F. L., AND J. M. SCOTT. 1981. Tests of hearing ability. Avian Biol. 6:341–345.

REEVES, H. M., AND S. R. AMEND. 1970. External age and sex determination of mourning doves during the preseason banding season. Unpubl. Rep., U.S. Fish and Wildl. Serv., Laurel, Md. 5pp.

———, R. E. TOMLINSON, AND J. C. BARTONEK. 1993. Population characteristics and trends in the Western Management Unit. Pages 341–376 *in* T. S. Baskett, M. W. Sayre, R. E. Tomlinson, and R. E. Mirarchi, eds., Ecology and management of the mourning dove. Stackpole Books, Harrisburg, Pa.

ROBBINS, C. S., D. BYSTRAK, AND P. H. GEISSLER. 1986. The breeding bird survey; its first fifteen years; 1965–1979. U.S. Fish and Wildl. Serv., Resour. Publ. 157. 196pp.

RUOS, J. L., AND R. E. TOMLINSON. 1968. Mourning dove status report, 1966. U.S. Fish and Wildl. Serv., Spec. Sci. Rep. Wildl. 115. 49pp.

SADLER, K. C. 1993*a*. Other natural mortality. Pages 225–230 *in* T.S. Baskett, M. W. Sayre, R. E. Tomlinson, and R. E. Mirarchi, eds., Ecology and management of the mourning dove. Stackpole Books, Harrisburg, Pa.

———. 1993*b*. Mourning dove harvest. Pages 449–458 *in* T.S. Baskett, M. W. Sayre, R. E. Tomlinson, and R. E. Mirarchi, eds., Ecology and management of the mourning dove. Stackpole Books, Harrisburg, Pa.

———, R. E. TOMLINSON, AND H. M. WIGHT. 1970. Progress of primary feather molt of adult mourning doves in Missouri. J. Wildl. Manage. 34:783–788.

SANDERSON, G. C., EDITOR. 1977. Management of migratory shore and upland game birds in North America. Int. Assoc. Fish and Wildl. Agencies, Washington, D.C. 358pp.

SAUER, J. R., D. D. DOLTON, AND S. DROEGE. 1994. Mourning dove population trend estimates from call-count and North American breeding bird surveys. J. Wildl. Manage. 58:506–515.

SAYRE, M. W., AND N. J. SILVY. 1993. Nesting and production. Pages 81–104 *in* T. S. Baskett, M. W. Sayre, R. E. Tomlinson, and R. E. Mirarchi, eds., Ecology and management of the mourning dove. Stackpole Books, Harrisburg, Pa.

———, T. S. BASKETT, AND K. C. SADLER. 1980. Radiotelemetry studies of the mourning dove in

Missouri. Missouri Dep. Conserv. Terrestrial Ser. 9. 17pp.

———, ———, AND R. E. MIRARCHI. 1993. Behavior. Pages 161–180 *in* T. S. Baskett, M. W. Sayre, R. E. Tomlinson, and R. E. Mirarchi, eds., Ecology and management of the mourning dove. Stackpole Books, Harrisburg, Pa.

———, R. D. ATKINSON, T. S. BASKETT, AND G. H. HAAS. 1978. Reappraising factors affecting mourning dove perch cooing. J. Wildl. Manage. 42:884–889.

SCHULZ, J. H., S. L. SHERIFF, Z. HE, C. E. BRAUN, R. E. TOMLINSON, R. D. DROBNEY, D. D. DOLTON, AND R. A. MONTGOMERY. In prep. Accuracy of techniques used to assign mourning dove age and gender.

SOUTHEASTERN ASSOCIATION OF GAME AND FISH COMMISSIONERS. 1957. Mourning dove investigations, 1948–56. Southeast. Assoc. Game and Fish Comm. Tech. Bull. 1. 166pp.

TOMLINSON, R. E. 1993. Migration. Pages 57–80 *in* T. S. Baskett, M. W. Sayre, R. E. Tomlinson, and R. E. Mirarchi, eds., Ecology and management of the mourning dove. Stackpole Books, Harrisburg, Pa.

———, AND D. D. DOLTON. 1987. Current status of the mourning dove in the Western Management Unit. Proc. West. Assoc. Fish and Wildl. Agencies 67:119–133.

———, AND J. H. DUNKS. 1993. Population characteristics and trends in the Central Management Unit. Pages 305–340 *in* T. S. Baskett, M. W. Sayre, R. E. Tomlinson, and R. E. Mirarchi, eds., Ecology and management of the mourning dove. Stackpole Books, Harrisburg, Pa.

———, D. D. DOLTON, H. M. REEVES, J. D. NICHOLS, AND L. A. MCKIBBEN. 1988. Migration, harvest, and population characteristics of mourning doves in the Western Management Unit, 1964–1977. U.S. Fish and Wildl. Serv., Fish and Wildl. Tech. Rep. 13. 101pp.

U.S. FISH AND WILDLIFE SERVICE. 1992. Migratory bird harvest information program; proposed rule. Fed. Regist. 57:24736–24741. U.S. Gov. Printing Off., Washington, D.C.

WESTERN MIGRATORY UPLAND GAME BIRD TECHNICAL COMMITTEE. 1992. Pacific Flyway management plan for the Western Management Unit mourning dove. Unpub. Rep., U.S. Fish and Wildl. Serv., Off. Migratory Bird Manage., Portland, Oreg. 30pp.

WIGHT, H. M., L. H. BLANKENSHIP, AND R. E. TOMLINSON. 1967. Aging mourning doves by outer primary wear. J. Wildl. Manage. 31:832–835.

Chapter 3

WHITE-WINGED DOVE

RONNIE R. GEORGE, Texas Parks and Wildlife Department, 4200 Smith School Road, Austin, TX 78744
ROY E. TOMLINSON, U.S. Fish and Wildlife Service, P.O. Box 1306, Albuquerque, NM 87103
RONALD W. ENGEL-WILSON, Arizona Game and Fish Department, 2221 West Greenway, Phoenix, AZ 85023
GARY L. WAGGERMAN, Texas Parks and Wildlife Department, 410 North 13th Street, Edinburg, TX 78539
A. GORDON SPRATT, Florida Game and Freshwater Fish Commission, 1239 Southwest 10th Street, Ocala, FL 32674

Abstract: White-winged doves (*Zenaida asiatica*) are large semi-tropical columbids native to the south-western United States, Mexico, Central America, parts of South America, and some Caribbean islands. They also have been successfully introduced into Florida. White-winged doves are now expanding their breeding range northward into central Texas, and increasing numbers are wintering in central and southern Texas. There are 12 recognized subspecies, 4 of which breed in the United States. The Eastern and Western subspecies are the most widely distributed and most numerous, and the primary focus of this chapter. Total white-winged dove numbers are unknown, but the Eastern population may have numbered >16 million birds during the mid-1980's, making white-winged doves the second most numerous migratory game bird species in North America after mourning doves (*Zenaida macroura*). White-winged dove densities in major nesting colonies in Tamaulipas, Mexico, may reach >1,000 pairs/ha, but nesting habitat loss and overharvest appear to be continuing problems for this species. Increased funding for research and management should be high priority. Major management needs include improved population and harvest surveys. Priorities for habitat management include conservation and restoration of critical breeding and feeding habitats in Mexico and the United States as well as wintering habitats in Mexico and Central America.

DESCRIPTION

Bent (1932), Leopold (1959), Cottam and Trefethen (1968), Oberholser (1974), and Brown et al. (1977) provide extensive descriptions of white-winged doves. White-winged doves are large, semi-tropical, migratory columbids that are often conspicuous in appearance, voice, and abundance. A typical adult is 30 cm in length, has a wing span of 50 cm, and weighs 170 g (about ⅓ heavier than an adult mourning dove) Oberholser 1974). Adults are generally brown while juveniles are more grayish-brown in color. The most distinctive physical features of an individual are white wing bars. At rest, with the wings folded, the wing bar appears as a 1-cm wide white margin that follows the leading and lower edge of the wing. In flight, the wing bars are seen as brilliant white flashes on the upper surface of the wing that are clearly visible in good light for >200 m. Upon close examination, with the wing spread, the wing "bar" is revealed as 2 parallel white stripes that begin at mid-forewing and curve concentrically across the wing toward the body. These bars separate the brown or grayish-brown upper wing coverts from the black flight feathers. None of the other species of doves and pigeons native to the United States has these distinctive white wing bars.

White-winged doves are more robust and "pigeon-like" in general appearance than mourning doves. Compared to mourning doves, they have a larger head and bill, and the tail is square rather than tapered. Adult white-winged doves of both sexes have a ring of blue featherless skin around each eye, and the iris of the eye is red in color. In juveniles, there is no noticeable eye ring and the iris is black. Adults have red or pinkish-red legs and feet, whereas juveniles have pink or brownish-pink legs and feet. Adults also have solid black primary wing covert feathers whereas the black coverts of juveniles are edged with white or buff until these feathers are replaced by adult feathers in a molt pattern similar to that of mourning doves (Hanson and Kossack 1962, Mirarchi 1993). Accurate external sex classification of adult white-winged doves is difficult at best, although males are somewhat larger and more highly colored than females, with a brighter purple cast to the head and neck and a more conspicuous black "ear spot" (Cottam and Trefethen 1968).

Both males and females vocalize, but the call of the female (which is almost identical to the male) is much lower in volume and somewhat shorter and slurred (Cottam and Trefethen 1968). During the breeding season, males utter 2 common vocalizations: a burry "coo-uh-cuck-oo" and a "who cooks for you?" (Oberholser 1974:422). Calls are heard most frequently in early morning and late evening but also at mid-day during the breeding season. In the typical large and dense colonies of Mexico, the thousands or millions of calls merge into a continuous roar that can be heard under favorable weather conditions for >5 km.

White-winged doves are much more gregarious and inclined to fly in large flocks than mourning doves (Cunningham 1986). Even small flocks of white-winged doves are conspicuous, but late-summer and early autumn feeding flocks numbering in the thousands and sometimes millions are truly spectacular.

Saunders (1968) described 12 subspecies of white-winged doves in North, Central, and South America, 4 of which breed in the United States. These include Eastern (Z. a asiatica), Western (Z. a. mearnsi), Mexican Highland (Z. a. monticola), and Upper Big Bend (Z. a. grandis) subspecies. The Eastern and Western subspecies are by far the most widely-distributed and most numerous subspecies, and are emphasized in this chapter.

LIFE HISTORY

White-winged doves arrive during late April at breeding areas in the southwestern United States and northern Mexico from wintering areas in Mexico and Central America. In situations where thick native brush or citrus vegetation is extensive [e.g., the Lower Rio Grande Valley of Texas (LRGV) and northeastern Mexico], they may nest in large colonies with densities >500–1,000 nests/ha (Cottam and Trefethen 1968; Texas Parks and Wildl. Dep., unpubl. data). However, they also nest solitarily in areas of sparse vegetation in Arizona and Sonora, Mexico, deserts. Males establish and defend territories in suitable woody nesting habitat within reasonable flying distance of food and water. They use cooing and visual displays to attract a mate and discourage competing males. Males resort to physical combat (wing slaps) if necessary to drive off other males. Once a female has been attracted, precopulation behavior by the male includes extensive soft cooing, bowing, slow tail and wing-fanning, and mutual preening. Following copulation, the female selects a suitable nest site within the male's territory, and the female builds a nest with twigs, grasses, and other materials supplied by the male. The nest

is built over a period of 2–5 days and often is only slightly more substantial than that of a mourning dove.

A clutch of 2 eggs (occasionally 1, rarely 3) is laid by the female over a 2–3 day period. Incubation usually begins before the 2nd egg is laid, so the 1st chick usually hatches about a day before its sibling. Both adults assist with incubation; the male is usually on the nest from mid-morning until mid-afternoon, while the female usually incubates from mid-afternoon through mid-morning. The incubation period is about 14 days.

Adult white-winged doves of both sexes feed their young a secretion from their crops known as "crop milk" (Goodwin 1977:13). Although more curd-like in form, this substance is similar in chemical composition to milk produced by female mammals. This crop milk diet is gradually supplemented throughout the 1st week with regurgitated seeds. By the 2nd week, the young are being fed mostly seeds. Young white-winged doves grow rapidly and are able to leave the nest 13–16 days after hatching. The male parent usually continues to feed the young in the vicinity of the nest until they are about 4 weeks of age and able to fend for themselves. The female parent may begin laying another clutch in as little as 3 days after losing or completing an earlier clutch (Cottam and Trefethen 1968). Schacht et al. (1994) reported adult white-winged doves did not appear to be nutrient-limited during breeding seasons with average to above average rainfall, and actually increased body lipid mass by the end of the nesting season.

A pair of Eastern white-winged doves will successfully fledge an average of about 2.2 young per season (Texas Parks and Wildl. Dep., unpubl. data). Obviously, not all nesting attempts are successful. If white-winged doves arrive at traditional breeding sites to find nesting habitat altered or food or water no longer available, the entire colony may move elsewhere. Conversely, if they find previously acceptable woody nesting cover defoliated by drought or winter freezes, they may establish territories, form pair bonds, coo vigorously, and remain at the site for the entire breeding season without nesting unless timely rains restore the leafy cover.

White-winged dove nests are often destroyed by adverse weather, human disturbance, predators, and occasionally parasites (Cottam and Trefethen 1968). Heavy rains, hail, and high winds destroy nests and seriously affect nesting success in some years. Human disturbance may include agricultural activities (e.g., crop spraying, vegetation control), as well as urban and industrial development. In Latin America, there is some subsistence take of nesting white-winged doves and occasional intentional poisoning of large flocks in response to crop depredation. Tacha et al. (1994) documented widespread and chronic exposure of white-winged doves to anticholinesterase substances, probably organophosphorus insecticides, in the LRGV of Texas in 1991 and 1992.

A variety of predators including hawks, owls, jays, grackles, snakes, and mammals take eggs, young, and sometimes adults during the nesting season (Blankinship 1966, Dunks 1969, Evans 1972). The most significant predator on eggs and nestlings is probably the great-tailed grackle (*Quiscalus mexicanus*). Grackles cause the highest mortality early in the dove and grackle nesting season when the grackle's dietary demand for protein is highest. Later in the summer when grackles have completed their own nesting season, grackle predation on nests declines. White-winged doves receive some benefit from grackles because grackle nests tend to be sturdy, and white-winged doves will readily nest in an abandoned grackle nest (Cottam and Trefethen 1968). Blankinship (1970) believed Mexican crows (*Corvis imparatus*) were the most important predator on white-winged dove nests in northeastern Mexico.

Stabler (1961) documented the presence of *Trichomonas gallinae* in the saliva of all 51 white-winged doves he collected during the breeding season in the LRGV of Texas, but determined through laboratory analysis that it was an avirulent strain. Mortality due to virulent trichomoniasis is common in mourning doves (Haugen and Keeler 1952, George 1990), but unreported in whitewings. *Haemoproteus* spp., *Plasmodium* spp., *Trypanosoma* spp., and microfilaria have been detected in white-winged dove blood (Saunders 1959, Levine and Kantor 1959, Stabler 1961), but their effect on white-winged dove survival is unknown. Ectoparasites generally are not a serious problem for nesting white-winged doves, but occasionally bloodsucking louse flies (hippoboscids) and mosquitoes (*Culex* spp., *Aedes* spp., *Psorophora* spp., and *Anopheles* spp.) occur in such numbers that they cause adults to abandon their eggs and young (Cottam and Trefethen 1968, Scudday et al. 1980).

When white-winged dove nesting activity ceases in early August, the young of the year and the adults gradually form into larger and larger feeding flights prior to migration. Premigration feeding flights may be established in the vicinity of the original nesting colony, or further away, depending upon food availability. In late summer, white-winged doves may even wander northward in search for food. Birds banded as nestlings in Tamaulipas, Mexico, in June and July have been recovered >320 km north in Texas during September (Blankinship et al. 1972, George 1993b). Once a local feeding flight is established, however, morning and evening movements between the roost site and feeding site become predictable and usually continue until depletion of the food source, hunting pressure, changing photoperiod, or changing weather cause the birds to begin their southward migration in mid to late September.

HABITAT

Typical breeding habitat of white-winged doves in the southwestern United States and northern Mexico includes dense thorny native brush, cacti (*Cactacea*)–palo verde (*Cercidium* spp.) deserts, oak (*Quercus* spp.)–juniper (*Juniperus* spp.) forests, salt cedar or tamarisk (*Tamarix* spp.) and other riparian woodlands, citrus (*Citrus* spp.) orchards, and residential shade trees. White-winged doves are often colonial nesters in good habitat, but in more marginal habitat they nest only as scattered pairs.

Humid to semi-arid, tropical, thorny woodlands dominated by Texas ebony (*Pithecellobium ebano*), granjeno (*Celtis pallida*), anacua (*Ehretia anacua*), huisache (*Acacia smalli*), and brasil (*Condalia hookeri*) provide ideal white-winged dove nesting habitat for the Eastern population in the Mexican states of Tamaulipas, Coahuila, Nuevo Leon, and Veracruz, and the LRGV of Texas (Fig. 1). Mesquite (*Prosopis glandulosa*) is often an important component of this habitat, but these birds generally avoid nesting in mesquite trees, probably due to the open aspect of the limbs and foliage. Citrus orchards in Texas have been used extensively since the 1940's (in some years accounting for 50–90% of all nesting activity). However, severe freezes periodically kill or damage citrus orchards rendering them unsuitable as nesting habitat for 5–8 years. Eastern white-winged doves also adapted to nesting in citrus orchards in Mexico during the 1970's, where freezing

Fig. 1.   Adult white-winged dove on nest in anacua tree (Photo by M. T. Fulfer).

weather has done less damage to nesting habitat.

Residential shade and ornamental trees, bird feeders, and bird baths are important components of white-winged dove breeding habitat in Texas (Small et al. 1989, George 1991, West 1993, West et al. 1993). In 1993, the largest known nesting colony in the U.S. was within the city limits of San Antonio, Texas. These urban birds (Fig. 2) heavily use but are not totally dependent on residential food sources (e.g., bird feeders); white-winged doves in San Antonio make daily feeding flights to surrounding farmland 5–20 km from nesting areas (Texas Parks and Wildl. Dep., unpubl. data). White-winged doves preferentially selected liveoak (*Quercus virginiana*) and Arizona ash (*Fraxinus velutina*) trees for nesting in residential areas of San Antonio (West et al. 1993). Arizona cypress (*Cupressus arizonica*) was an important nesting tree for urban white-winged doves in western Texas (Small et al. 1989).

Sonoran and Mohave deserts and riparian woodlands (salt cedar and mesquite) along the Colorado River and its tributaries provide preferred nesting habitat for the Western population in southeastern Nevada, southeastern California, southern Arizona, western New Mexico, Baja California, and Sonora, Mexico. Unlike Eastern white-winged doves, which generally avoid nesting in mesquite trees, Western white-

winged doves will nest in mesquite, but not as readily as mourning doves (Cunningham 1986). Haughey (1986) reported saguaro cactus (*Carnegiea gigantea*) was extremely important for white-winged dove perching and food (nectar and fruit) in Arizona deserts. Unlike seeds produced by annuals or even perennial shrubs, saguaros and other cacti produce large quantities of fruit regardless of rainfall. Cottam and Trefethen (1968) and Haughey (1986) noted the original distribution of the Western population was closely linked to the distribution of saguaro and that such discrepancies (e.g., those in southwestern New Mexico, southern Nevada, southeastern Arizona, and southeastern California) may represent range extensions in response to agriculture. Citrus orchards in Arizona and elsewhere also provide important nesting habitat for the Western population.

White-winged doves feed primarily on seeds, mast, and fruit that vary in availability according to location, season, and precipitation. In Texas and northeastern Mexico brushlands, the fruit of granjeno, anacua, coma (*Bumelia angustifolia*), colima (*Zanthoxylum fagara*), brasil, privet (*Forestiera angustifolia*), and pigeon berry (*Rivina humilis*) are choice white-winged dove foods (Cottam and Trefethen 1968, Bautista J. and Brito C. 1992, Schacht et al. 1994). In open fields and pastures, the seed of native sunflower (*Helianthus annuus*), doveweed (*Croton* spp.), spurge (*Euphorbia* spp.), panic grass (*Panicum* spp.), foxtail (*Setaria* spp.), and other grasses and legumes are readily consumed by white-winged doves. In central Texas, the large white seed of introduced Chinese tallow trees (*Sapium sebiferum*) are consumed by wintering white-winged doves. In more arid areas of western Texas, seeds of leatherweed (*Jatropha dioica*) are an important food (Engel-Wilson and Ohmart 1978, Scudday et al. 1980).

Domestic grains including commercial sunflower, grain sorghum, corn, safflower, and wheat are important white-winged dove foods in farming areas throughout the species' range (Cottam and Trefethen 1968, Dolton 1975, Engel-Wilson and Ohmart 1978, Bautista J. and Brito C. 1992, Schacht et al. 1994). Rapid increases and declines in white-winged dove numbers often have been associated with abundance of food provided by agricultural grain crops as reported in Texas (Saunders 1940, Marsh and Saunders 1942), Arizona (Cottam and Trefethen 1968, Cunningham 1986), and Mexico (Ortega M. and

Fig. 2.   Part of an estimated 2,000–3,000 white-winged doves roosting in deciduous trees in the backyards of a residential area of Austin (central Texas) in mid-January 1993. Some white-winged doves (<5%) were cooing, indicating onset of courtship behavior. Prior to 1984, white-winged doves were unusual anywhere in Texas during the winter months, and white-winged doves were rare in central Texas at any season. White-winged doves are attracted to residential areas by bird feeders, water, and suitable roosting and nesting trees (Photo by G. L. Mills).

Zamora T. 1984; Purdy and Tomlinson 1982, 1991). Bucher (1986) reported white-winged doves in Mexico and eared doves (*Zenaida auriculata*) in South America showed similar population responses to agricultural grain. In Tamaulipas, Mexico, white-winged doves exhibited tremendous population growth during the 1970's and early 1980's coincident with agricultural development that greatly increased the availability of grain sorghum and irrigation water (Purdy and Tomlinson 1982, 1991; Bautista J. and Brito C. 1992). Conversely, white-winged dove populations declined dramatically in Arizona during the 1970's when economics forced a change from grain farming to cotton and alfalfa (Cunningham 1986). Thus, agricultural practices can greatly influence population size and distribution.

This preference for grain can cause problems for farmers (Cottam and Trefethen 1968, Purdy and Tomlinson 1982). Unlike mourning doves that feed exclusively on the ground, white-winged doves readily perch on sturdy sorghum or sunflower stalks and feed on the developing grain. When thousands of white-winged doves are attracted to a single field, serious crop depredations can occur, earning them the epithet "la plaga" (the plague) among many Mexican farmers.

In an Arizona study of colonial nesting birds adjacent to the lower Gila River (Cunningham 1986), white-winged doves relied almost exclusively on cultivated grains (particularly barley and sorghum), whereas mourning doves used a wide variety of weed seeds in addition to grains. Another study (Haughey 1986) investigated food habits of solitary-nesting white-winged doves in desert habitat of the Cabeza Prieta National Wildlife Refuge in southwestern Arizona. The 4 major food items (87% of the diet) were seeds of limberbush (*Jatropha cuneata*), saguaro cactus, Mexican jumping bean (*Sapium biloculare*), and ocotillo (*Fouquieria splendens*), with 20 other items comprising the remaining 13%. White-winged doves ate the seeds, fruit, and pollen of saguaro and were judged to be important pollinators for this cactus. In some areas of Arizona, acorns were an important food (Cottam and Trefethen 1968). In Sonora, Mexico, Western white-winged doves fed extensively on seeds of torchwood (*Bursera* spp.), organpipe cactus (*Lemaireocereus thruberi*), ocotillo, acanthus (Acanthacae), and a variety of legumes (Cottam and Trefethen 1968).

In all areas of their range, white-winged doves ingest small stones and the calcareous shells of snails and other gastropods (Cottam and Trefethen 1968, Haughey 1986, Bautista J. and Brito C. 1992 , Schacht et al. 1994). Haughey (1986) found 22% of the white-winged dove crops he examined in Arizona contained mammal or reptile bone fragments, apparently from mammal feces or raptor pellets. Stones aid in digestion by grinding food in the gizzard; shells and bones also provide calcium in the diet to enable adults to produce crop milk and eggshells.

Cottam and Trethethen (1968) noted that nesting colonies were near dependable water sources, and this appears to hold true today. Recently developed nesting colonies in Tamaulipas and Texas consistently have been close to major lakes, rivers, or irrigation systems (Ortega M. and Zamora T. 1984; Purdy and Tomlinson 1982, 1991; George 1991). Throughout the remainder of the year, wintering habitat for both Eastern and Western birds is remarkably similar to their breeding habitat (i.e., a mixture of brushlands, woodlands, or desert shrubs and cacti intermingled with agricultural grainfields). Waggerman and Sorola (1977) reported substantial grain sorghum, corn, sesame, and rice intermingled with native brush were important components of wintering habitat in Central America.

DISTRIBUTION AND ABUNDANCE

Although distributed mainly throughout Mexico and Central America, the breeding range of the 12 white-winged dove subspecies extends from the southwestern United States to northern Chile and includes several Caribbean islands (Cottam and Trefethen 1968, Saunders 1968, Goodwin 1977, Davis and Jenks 1983). The naturally occurring breeding ranges of the 4 subspecies of management interest to the United States encompass the southwestern United States and most of northern Mexico (Fig. 3). White-winged doves also have been successfully introduced into Florida.

Population Survey Methods

The Texas Parks and Wildlife Department (TPWD) and the Arizona Game and Fish Department conduct call-count surveys to derive annual indices to breeding population trends in their respective white-winged dove breeding areas during May. The Arizona survey is basically the same as the nationwide mourning dove call-count survey, in which the average numbers of birds heard calling on randomly-selected routes serve as the indices. This method probably samples solitary nesting areas in higher proportion than scattered high-density colonies. As a result, significant colonial population declines during the 1970's were largely undetected by the survey.

In Texas, the large numbers of birds encountered at each stop necessitated development of a more subjective technique. Call-count indices are expressed as breeding pairs/ha since TPWD studies conducted in the 1950's estimated that 1 calling white-winged dove = 5 pairs/ha, 3

BREEDING

WINTERING

RESIDENT

Fig. 3. Principal breeding and wintering areas of white-winged dove populations in North America.

calling birds = 15 pairs/ha, 6 birds = 30 pairs/ ha, almost steady cooing = 50 pairs/ha, and steady cooing with background monotone = 74 pairs/ha (Waggerman 1992). Because of the subjective judgment exercised by cooperators, and because the original assumption that number of calling males accurately reflected nesting density may be false (Rappole and Waggerman 1986, Baskett 1993), the Texas method probably yields questionable population estimates. However, because the survey is conducted in the same manner each year, it probably serves as a relatively-accurate indicator of long-term trends.

Production surveys are conducted annually in Texas and periodically in Tamaulipas, Mexico, to estimate nesting success and densities. In Texas, linear 0.1-ha (¼ ac) transects in native brush and 0.2-ha transects in citrus orchards are established in late April (Waggerman 1992). Nests found on transects are marked individually, mapped on a plat, and recorded on data sheets. All nests are checked weekly; total numbers of young fledged on each transect during

the breeding season (late Apr–late Aug) divided by total number of active nests counted at the peak of nesting activity gives a production index. A post-nesting population is estimated by multiplying the number of pairs in the estimated spring breeding population by the production index. Production surveys are sometimes disruptive to nesting birds and time-consuming to conduct since transects are often established in dense, thorny brush habitat and checked weekly throughout the nesting season. However, production surveys give information on reproductive activity that can be used in formulating and evaluating hunting regulations. At the present time, production surveys provide the most practical means of monitoring population status at major nesting colonies in Mexico.

Fall flight surveys also are conducted in Texas at 35 traditional roosting sites in the LRGV (Waggerman 1992). During August and early September, trained observers estimate the numbers of birds in each early morning feeding flight by making periodic counts over a specified pe-

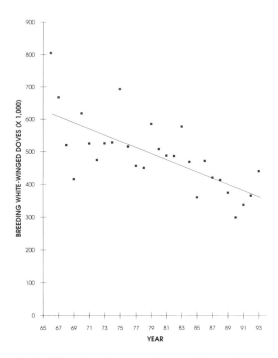

Fig. 4.   White-winged dove breeding population estimates in the Lower Rio Grande Valley of Texas, 1966–93, based on call-count surveys.

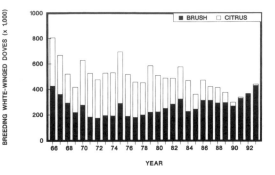

Fig. 5.   Relative use of native brush and citrus orchard nesting habitat by white-winged doves in the Lower Rio Grande Valley of Texas, 1966–93, based on call-count surveys.

riod of time. Since fall flights are poorly correlated with local production and conducted too late in the year to aid in establishing hunting regulations, the data are used mainly to monitor trends in local abundance, determine the origins and destinations of feeding flights (Texas or Mexico), and assist hunters in locating potential hunting areas.

These population survey methods, plus banding and recovery data, provide information on the distribution and abundance of each species of white-winged doves.

Zenaida asiatica asiatica.—Eastern white-winged doves breed in central and south Texas and northeastern Mexico and winter on the Pacific coasts of southern Mexico (mostly confined to the states of Oaxaca and Chiapas) and Central America to northern Costa Rica (Fig. 3). White-winged doves in the Caribbean Basin are thought to be part of the Eastern population.

The Eastern breeding population historically was primarily in the LRGV of Texas (Cameron, Hidalgo, Starr, and Willacy counties) and the adjoining Mexican state of Tamaulipas. White-winged dove populations increased in the LRGV following the introduction of irrigation and grain

farming in the early 1900's and reached a peak in 1923 estimated at 4–12 million birds (Saunders 1940, Marsh and Saunders 1942). Numbers then declined dramatically because of a combination of overharvest and continued agricultural and urban development that eliminated important native brush nesting habitat (Saunders 1940, Cottam and Trefethen 1968). White-winged doves in the LRGV adapted to nesting in citrus orchards during the 1940's, but suffered periodic population declines when citrus orchards were adversely affected by major freezes during 1951 and 1962. After an initial population recovery in the early 1960's, the breeding population in the LRGV has declined ($r = -0.71$, $P < 0.01$) about 9,600/year since 1966 (Fig. 4).

As recently as 1980, >80% of the white-winged doves in Texas nested in the LRGV. In a "normal" year, approximately 50% of these birds nested in citrus orchards, with the remainder in native brush (Fig. 5). However, freezing weather in December 1983 and 1989, combined with extended drought during 1987–90, decimated the citrus orchards and injured the hardy native brush. As a result, LRGV populations dependent upon this nesting habitat declined during the 1980's, but recovered to near prefreeze levels in 1993 despite the lack of mature citrus orchards (Table 1). Only 2% of the LRGV birds nested in citrus habitat in 1993; 98% nested in the more resilient native brush (Fig. 5).

White-winged dove populations increased substantially in south-central Texas, near San Antonio, at the same time populations were declining in the LRGV during the mid-1980's. The breeding population within the metropolitan area alone was estimated at >200,000 birds in

Table 1.   Western white-winged dove breeding population indices in Arizona expressed as the average number of calling males per 20-mile route (32-km), and Eastern white-winged dove breeding population estimates in Texas expressed as total birds, 1966–93. Date were derived from call-count surveys.

| Year | Arizona | Texas[a] | | | |
		Lower Rio Grande Valley	Lake Corpus Christi area[b]	San Antonio area[c]	Statewide
1966	48.4	805,000			805,000
1967	51.5	667,000			667,000
1968	52.3	520,000			520,000
1969	41.1	416,000			416,000
1970	33.9	618,000			618,000
1971	31.3	525,000			525,000
1972	35.4	475,000			475,000
1973	36.5	526,000			526,000
1974	31.1	529,000	63,280		592,280
1975	29.0	693,000	65,180		758,180
1976	30.9	516,000	46,641		562,641
1977	32.7	457,000	32,914		489,914
1978	35.6	451,000	43,403		494,403
1979	30.8	585,000	51,513		636,513
1980	34.9	508,000	57,853		565,853
1981	32.9	488,000	47,793		535,793
1982	29.3	487,000	55,316		542,316
1983	32.9	577,000	45,050		622,050
1984	31.1	469,000	53,198		522,198
1985	37.3	361,000	46,937		407,937
1986	34.1	472,000	47,850		519,850
1987	29.9	21,000	42,931		463,931
1988	26.7	414,000	50,601		464,601
1989	30.7	375,000	52,050	268,444	695,494
1990	28.0	299,000	69,350	318,363	686,713
1991	30.6	338,000	72,700	399,652	810,352
1992	30.8	366,000	69,150	340,966	766,116
1993	33.7	441,000	69,850	409,788	920,838

[a] Estimates do not include separate white-winged dove breeding populations in the Trans-Pecos region of western Texas.
[b] Surveys were expanded to include 4 counties in the Lake Corpus Christi area of southern Texas beginning in 1974.
[c] Surveys were expanded to include 13 counties in southcentral Texas including the San Antonio area beginning in 1989.

1990. Since 1990, the estimated numbers of white-winged doves elsewhere in Texas have exceeded those in the LRGV (George 1991, Table 1, Fig. 6). Whether this range expansion and increase in numbers outside the LRGV resulted from displacement of LRGV birds is unknown. The total Eastern white-winged dove breeding population in Texas was estimated at >920,000 in 1993 (Table 1).

Pioneering Eastern populations now appear to be firmly established as far north as Waco and Brownwood in central Texas (George 1991), and scattered nesting has been reported at Amarillo, Lubbock, and Fort Worth in northern Texas, as well as in Houston in southeastern Texas (Texas Parks and Wildl. Dep., unpubl. data). There also has been a substantial increase in the number of white-winged doves wintering in Texas (Fig. 2).

Modern agricultural development in Tamau-

lipas, Mexico, during the 1970's initially resulted in increased white-winged dove populations (Purdy and Tomlinson 1982, Ortega M. and Zamora T. 1984, George 1985, Purdy and Tomlinson 1991). Continuing destruction of nesting habitat in recent years, however, is adversely affecting the northeastern Mexico breeding population. Blankinship (1970) expressed concern about the increased clearing of nesting habitat in Tamaulipas during the 1960's. In 1966, he searched Tamaulipas, eastern Nuevo Leon, northern Vera Cruz, and northern San Luis Potosi and found 8 major nesting colonies (all in Tamaulipas). During 1966–68, these colonies contained an estimated 3.1–3.4 million breeding birds and produced an estimated fall flight of 5.3–6.2 million birds. With the continued clearing of land devoted mainly to irrigated cultivation of sorghum and other grains, the available food and drinking water increased

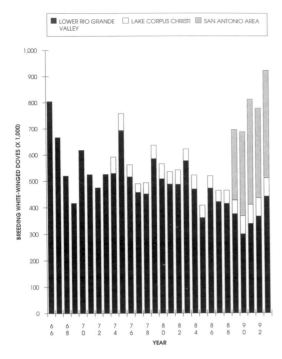

Fig. 6. Relative abundance of Eastern white-winged doves in the Lower Rio Grande Valley, Lake Corpus Christi, and San Antonio areas of Texas 1966–93, based on call-count surveys.

tremendously. White-winged dove populations responded accordingly, and fall flights were estimated to be 9 million in 1978, 12–16 million in 1982 (Purdy and Tomlinson 1991), and 16–19 million in 1984 (Ortega M. and Zamora T. 1984). There were 22 known colonies in Tamaulipas in 1978 (Ortega M. et al. 1979), but this number decreased to 16 by 1982 (Purdy and Tomlinson 1991). By 1991, the number of known colonies had shrunk to 10, and at least 3 of these were either small or degraded (Tomlinson 1991; U.S. Fish and Wildl. Serv., unpubl. data). The reasons for fewer colonies and decreasing populations since the mid-1980's were 3-fold: (1) continued destruction of native brush for agricultural development; (2) 2 severe freezes in 1983 and 1989 that killed or badly damaged nesting habitat; and (3) a prolonged drought from 1987 to 1990 that decimated the vegetation in all colonies and caused nearly complete nest failure in some areas each year. The initial increase in numbers in response to irrigated grain farming followed by the gradual decline of populations due to nesting habitat destruction in northeastern Mexico mirrored the situation that

occurred in the LRGV of Texas 40–50 years earlier.

Breeding white-winged doves were not endemic to Florida, but Cottam and Trefethen (1968) reported small numbers from Texas had been observed each year between Texas and Florida, suggesting eastward migration. One white-winged dove, banded near Tallahassee, Florida, later was found dead in western Cuba. Unknown to Cottam and Trefethen (1968), approximately 10 pairs of white-winged doves, obtained in Tampico, Mexico, and later identified as the Eastern subspecies, were released in Homestead, Dade County, Florida, in 1959 (Williams 1978, Saunders 1980). By the mid 1970's, this population had grown to an estimated 6,000–8,000 birds. Natural range expansion as well as a capture and release program begun in 1975 by the Florida Game and Fresh Water Fish Commission resulted in an established white-winged dove breeding population in the southeastern ⅓ of Florida with the greatest concentrations in the Homestead area south of Miami (J. R. Brady, pers. commun.; Fig. 3). Attempts to establish populations in central Florida citrus groves have been only partially successful (T. W. Regan, pers. commun.) White-winged doves have been a legal game species during the Florida dove hunting season since 1983. To date, a total of 12 Florida-banded white-winged doves have been recovered: 8 in Florida, 1 in Louisiana, 2 in Cuba, and 1 in Guatemala (U.S. Fish and Wildl. Serv., Bird Banding Lab., unpubl. data).

Zenaida asiatica mearnsi.—The Western white-winged dove population breeds in Arizona, California, Nevada, and New Mexico, as well as extensive areas of the adjacent states of Baja California and Sonora, Mexico (Fig. 3). Highest Western white-winged dove nesting densities north of the Mexican border have been mainly within the area bounded by Phoenix, Casa Grande, Gila Bend, and Buckeye, Arizona. Another colonial population has been centered along the Colorado River from about Needles, California, to the Mexican border. Unlike the Eastern population, little change in nesting distribution has been recorded during the past 15–30 years, but several factors have combined to adversely affect the population since about 1960: (1) suburban development and reclamation projects have eliminated a large part of the former nesting habitat; (2) agricultural development has cleared nesting areas, but the greatest change was a switch from grain crops (e.g., sorghum and wheat) to cotton and alfalfa, eliminating much of the food supply; and (3) as the metropolitan Phoenix area grew, increased hunting pressure caused overshooting in some areas, and there was a loss of nesting habitat as citrus orchards were converted into urban areas. Call-count surveys indicate white-winged dove populations in these affected areas are a small fraction of their former size, and the population index throughout Arizona has declined ($r = -0.65$, $P < 0.01$) at the rate of about 0.52 birds/route/year since 1966 (Table 1, Fig. 7). However, the solitary nesting populations throughout southern Arizona have remained relatively stable during this period.

The Western subspecies winters in Pacific coastal states of central Mexico, mainly from southern Sinaloa to northwestern Oaxaca (Fig. 3). Banding data suggest little overlap of wintering habitat occurs between the Eastern and Western populations. Thus, the 2 populations are mutually exclusive in both summer and winter distribution.

Zenaida asiatica grandis and *Z. a. monticola.*—The Upper Big Bend and Mexican Highland subspecies of white-winged doves breed in the Trans-Pecos region of western Texas, and the distribution of the latter extends sporadically from the adjacent states of Coahuila and Chihuahua through the highlands of central Mexico nearly to the Isthmus of Tehuantepec (Fig. 3). Since few samples of the Upper Big Bend subspecies have been banded, little is known about their winter distribution. However, they mostly winter in or near their breeding range (Saunders 1968).

The Mexican Highland subspecies has exhibited a northern breeding range expansion in recent years similar to the Eastern subspecies (Gallucci 1978, Scudday et al. 1980). Small et al. (1989) reported that white-winged doves in western Texas, previously confined to a narrow corridor paralleling the course of the Rio Grande, had moved northward into the central Trans-Pecos region. They suggested that range expansion and increased numbers of white-winged doves in the Trans-Pecos region were the result of increased nesting cover provided by the invasion of exotic salt cedar along the Rio Grande and its drainages, as well as increased nesting in native Arizona cypress trees planted as or-

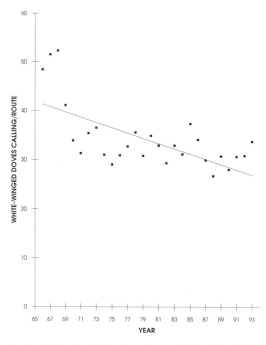

Fig. 7.   White-winged dove breeding population indices in Arizona, 1966–93, based on call-count surveys.

namentals in cities (e.g., Alpine, Texas). Increased grain farming in parts of the Trans-Pecos region also may have been a factor.

White-winged dove breeding populations in the Trans-Pecos region of Texas have not been surveyed completely due to the remoteness of the region, but >36,800 were counted in parts of 4 counties in this region in 1991 (Waggerman 1992).

Total Population Estimates

A complete census of white-winged doves cannot be undertaken with present technology, and the total number in the United States and Mexico is unknown. However, Ortega M. and Zamora T. (1984) using nest transects in the major nesting colonies in Tamaulipas, estimated a fall population fluctuating between 16 and 19 million in 1984. In that same year, Texas Parks and Wildlife Department personnel, using a modified call-count survey, estimated >522,000 adult white-winged doves within the breeding range of the Eastern population in Texas (Waggerman 1992). Although, assumptions and subjective decisions associated with these methods probably render the estimates suspect, they do

Fig. 8. White-winged dove hunter in domestic sunflower field in the Lower Rio Grande Valley of Texas (Photo by R. R. George).

suggest the Eastern population may have exceeded 16 million birds during the mid-1980's, making white-winged doves the second most numerous migratory game bird species in North America (after mourning doves). No effort currently is made to estimate total size of the Western population.

HARVEST

A comparison of average life spans of white-winged doves banded in Texas in the early 1960's with those banded at the same locations 10 years later indicated a decline from 2.90 to 1.67 years (George 1993*b*). Reasons for this decline are unknown and may include such factors as pesticides and diseases. Nevertheless, the number of

Fig. 9. Dove hunting operators in citrus orchards in the Lower Rio Grande Valley of Texas have found it pays to advertise with signs and posters along public roads. Day leases for white-winged dove hunting in Texas currently range from $25 to $75 per day (Photo by R. R. George).

hunters and harvest increased in both Texas and Mexico during that decade, and harvest cannot be ruled out as a factor. Unfortunately, there have been no recent banding programs in this area that could be used to estimate current survival rates for comparison (George 1993*b*).

White-winged doves seem more vulnerable to hunting pressure (Fig. 8) than mourning doves (George 1993*a*), and biologists from state and federal wildlife agencies in the United States have sought means of limiting the impact of hunting on white-winged doves. These restrictions have included shorter seasons, closed areas, and aggregate bag limits with other species, all of which limit harvest. These restrictions have resulted in varying success.

Regulations

White-winged dove hunting seasons have been allowed since 1912 and 1916 in Arizona and Texas, respectively (Cottam and Trefethen 1968). In both states, seasons and bag limits in the 1920's and 1930's were liberal and occurred during periods well within the breeding season (e.g., Jun–Aug), in contradiction to the Migratory Bird Treaty with Great Britain (for Canada). In Texas, it became obvious that liberal seasons could not be continued without adversely affecting populations (Saunders 1940, Marsh and Saunders 1942). In 1941, a Special White-winged Dove Hunting Season in an area paralleling the Rio Grande was established. The boundaries of the hunting area have varied over the intervening years, but the season dates, corresponding to the first 2 (occasionally 3) weekends of September (4–6 days of afternoon only shooting) have remained relatively constant (Table 2). Until 1984, separate daily bag limits of 10 or 12 white-winged *and* 10 or 12 mourning doves were permitted during the Texas white-winged dove season. In 1984, an aggregate bag limit of 10 doves was established from which only 2 could be mourning doves and 2 could be white-tipped doves (*Leptotila verreauxi*). Prior to 1983, white-winged dove hunting was not permitted anywhere in Texas except in the Special White-winged Dove Hunting Area (Fig. 9). However, in 1983, statewide aggregate daily bag limits were established during the regular mourning dove season that permitted 12 doves, no more than 2 of which could be white-winged doves and 2 of which could be white-tipped doves. In 1991, the statewide aggregate bag limit during the mourning dove season was further

Table 2. White-winged dove hunting regulations in Arizona, Texas, and Tamaulipas, Mexico, 1962–93.

	Arizona		Tamaulipas		Texas	
	Bag/possession	Date	Bag/possession[d]	Date	Bag/possession	Date
1962	25/25[a]	1–24 Sep, 8 Dec–2 Jan	10/20 M–F, 20/20 S–S	15 Sep–15 Jan	10/20[f]	7, 9 Sep
1963	25/25	1–25 Sep, 3–31 Dec			Closed	
1964	25/25	1–27 Sep, 12 Dec–3 Jan	12/12	15 Aug–14 Oct	10/20	5, 6, 12, 13 Sep
1965	25/25	1–26 Sep	10/10	1 Sep–31 Oct	10/20	4, 5, 11, 12 Sep
1966	25/25	1–25 Sep	10/10	15 Aug–15 Oct	12/24	3, 4, 5, 9, 10, 11 Sep
1967	25/25	1–24 Sep			12/24	2, 3, 9, 10 Sep
1968	25/25	1–24 Sep, 11 Dec–5 Jan			10/20	1, 2, 7, 8 Sep
1969	25/25	1–28 Sep, 21 Dec–11 Jan			10/20	6, 7 Sep
1970	10/10	1–20 Sep, 12 Dec–10 Jan			10/20	5, 6, 12, 13 Sep
1971	10/10	1–12 Sep			10/20	4, 5, 11, 12 Sep
1972	10/10	1–12 Sep			10/20	2, 3, 4 Sep
1973	10/10	1–23 Sep			10/20	1, 2, 8, 9 Sep
1974	10/10	1–22 Sep			10/20	1, 2, 7, 8 Sep
1975	10/10	1–21 Sep	10/60 M–T, 20/60 F–S	1 Aug–30 Sep	10/20	1, 2, 5, 7, 13, 14 Sep
1976	10/10	1–20 Sep			10/20	4, 6, 11, 12 Sep
1977	10/10	1–25 Sep			10/20	3, 4, 10, 11 Sep
1978	10/10	1–24 Sep	15/45 M–T, 25/75 F–S	1 Aug–15 Oct	10/20	2, 3, 9, 10 Sep
1979	10/10[a]	1–23 Sep	25/75	15 Aug–31 Oct	10/20	1, 2, 8, 9 Sep
1980	5/10 N, 6/12 S[b]	1–28 Sep	25/75	15 Aug–2 Nov	10/20	6, 7, 13, 14 Sep
1981	6/12	1–27 Sep	20/60	14 Aug–1 Nov	10/20	5, 6, 12, 13 Sep
1982	6/12	1–26 Sep	20/60	13 Aug–1 Nov	10/20[f]	4, 5, 11, 12 Sep
1983	6/12	1–25 Sep	20/60	13 Aug–29 Oct	10/20[g]	3, 4, 10, 11 Sep
1984	6/12	1–23 Sep	20/60	11 Aug–28 Oct	10/20[h]	1, 2, 8, 9 Sep
1985	6/12	1–22 Sep	20/60	15 Aug–25 Oct[e]	Closed	
1986	6/12	1–21 Sep	20/60	15 Aug–26 Oct	10/20	6, 7, 13, 14 Sep
1987	6/12	1–13 Sep	30/90	14 Aug–15 Nov	10/20	5, 6, 12, 13 Sep
1988	6/12	1–11 Sep	25/75	12 Aug–6 Nov	10/20	3, 4, 10, 11 Sep
1989	6/12	1–10 Sep[c]	25/75	11 Aug–12 Nov	10/20[i]	2, 3, 9, 10 Sep
1990	6/12	1–10 Sep	15/45	17 Aug–11 Nov	10/20[g]	1, 2 Sep
1991	6/12	1–10 Sep	20/60	21 Aug–17 Nov	10/20[j]	7, 8 Sep
1992	6/12	1–10 Sep	20/60	15 Aug–15 Nov	10/20	5, 6, 12, 13 Sep
1993	6/12	1–12 Sep	15/45	15 Aug–15 Nov[e]	10/20[j]	4, 5, 11, 12 Sep

[a] Mourning and white-winged doves had separate limits during 1962–79.
[b] Aggregate bag limits permitting either 10 or 12 doves, no more than 5 or 6 of which could be white-winged doves, have been in effect since 1980. N = northern areas and S = southern areas of Arizona.
[c] Shooting hours have been A.M. only since 1989.
[d] M–F = Monday–Friday, S–S = Saturday–Sunday, M–T = Monday–Thursday, F–S = Friday–Sunday.
[e] Approximate.
[f] White-winged dove hunting was confined to a 4–6 day period (weekends in Sep) in a special area paralleling the Rio Grande during 1962–82. The daily limits were 10 or 12 white-winged doves *and* 10 or 12 mourning doves. Shooting hours were P.M. only.
[g] During 1983–90, 2 white-winged doves also were permitted in an aggregate bag of 12 doves during the regular mourning dove season statewide.
[h] During the Special White-winged Dove Season starting in 1984, an aggregate bag limit of 10 doves was imposed, of which no more than 2 mourning doves and 2 white-tipped doves could be taken.
[i] The aggregate bag limit during the Special White-winged Dove Season in 1989–93 was 10 doves, no more than 5 of which could be mourning doves and 2 could be white-tipped doves.
[j] During 1991–93, 6 white-winged doves were permitted in an aggregate bag of 12 doves during the regular mourning dove season statewide (except in Cameron, Hidalgo, Starr, and Willacy counties, where the limit was 2 white-winged doves in the aggregate bag limit).

liberalized to permit 6 white-winged doves daily, except in the LRGV where the limit remained 2. These regulations were designed to allow additional hunting of the expanding populations in other areas of the state, and to divert hunting pressure from the LRGV.

In Arizona, the 1960's were characterized by liberal seasons of over 50 days and bag limits of 25 white-winged doves *and* 10 or 12 mourning doves (Table 2). Because white-winged dove populations declined as a result of changing agricultural practices, loss of nesting habitat, and overshooting, the season length was reduced in the 1970's to no more than 30 days, and the white-winged dove bag limit was lowered to 10. In the 1980's, poor response of these populations to management actions prompted the establishment of an aggregate bag limit of 10 or 12 mourning and white-winged doves of which no more than 6 could be white-winged doves.

Intensive investigations of hunting pressure on the Robbins Butte Wildlife Area in Arizona indicated local harvest rates could be excessive; up to 80% of the white-winged doves using the area immediately prior to the season were taken by hunters within the first few days. In addition, nesting studies on the same area indicated nesting attempts declined approximately 25% per year in 1983–85 (P. M. Smith, pers. commun.). Consequently, beginning in 1989, the Arizona Game and Fish Department restricted shooting hours to half-day (mornings only) in September to further reduce the white-winged dove harvest. Statewide, hunter success rates, numbers of hunters (except in 1992), total harvest, and call-count indices increased in 1990, 1991, and 1992. Nesting attempts on the Robbins Butte Area also increased 25% in 1990 and 1991, and 67% in 1992, in apparent response to the more restrictive regulations (P. M. Smith, pers. commun.).

White-winged dove call-count indices from areas in Arizona not associated with agriculture have not shown dramatic fluctuations over time. Solitary or dispersed-nesting white-winged doves (including urban birds) do not appear to be subjected to the same population pressures as colony-nesting birds.

In Mexico, white-winged dove seasons are permitted in several northeastern (Coahuila, Nuevo Leon, and Tamaulipas) and northwestern states (Chihuahua, Sonora, and Sinaloa), but the highest hunting pressure occurs in Tamaulipas. In that state, daily bag limits have varied during the past 20 years between 15 and 30 white-winged doves (possession limits, 30–90), and seasons generally have been 60–90 days long during mid-August to November (Table 2). In 1992, over 95% of the 5,528 estimated white-winged dove hunters in Tamaulipas were United States citizens (Torres 1992), and this high proportion of foreign hunters probably has been true for at least 10–25 years. Since 1988, an additional regulation has stipulated that all foreign hunters in Mexico must have a contract with a licensed Hunting Organizer and be accompanied by a guide on each hunt to and from a hunting area. This unpopular regulation was established by the Dirección General de Conservación Ecológica de los Recursos Naturales (DGCERN) to gain better control over United States hunters. However, it resulted in increasing the cost of hunting, barring most hunters that wished to hunt unguided, and giving control over dove and other hunting in Mexico to Hunting Organizers.

In Florida, increasing populations of white-winged doves and misidentification of this species resulted in an incidental but illegal harvest during the mourning dove season in the 1970's and early 1980's. After careful evaluation, hunting regulations were changed, and 4 white-winged doves have been permitted as part of a 12 dove aggregate daily bag since 1983 (T. W. Regan, pers. commun.).

Harvest Estimates

Texas.—Peak white-winged dove harvest in the LRGV of Texas probably occurred around 1923, but no harvest surveys were conducted at that time (Saunders 1940, Marsh and Saunders 1942). From about 1950 to 1976, the harvest of white-winged doves in Texas was estimated by a system where hunter vehicles were counted during aerial surveys, the number of hunters/vehicle and the average bag size were obtained from ground check stations, and the 2 data sets were integrated to produce a LRGV total. In 1976, a mandatory $3.00 (later $7.00) White-winged Dove Hunting Stamp was first used as a sampling frame to conduct a statewide mail questionnaire harvest survey (Waggerman 1977). Comparison of both methods in 1976 revealed that aerial counts underestimated the harvest by a factor of 2.4, probably because not all vehicles were counted (Table 3). The estimated number of white-winged doves/hunter-day in the LRGV was similar for both methods. The new method

Table 3. White-winged dove harvest statistics in the Lower Rio Grande Valley of Texas (LRGV), and in the entire Special White-winged Dove Hunting Area (SWWA) that includes the LRGV, during the special white-winged dove hunting season, 1962–92.

Date	Hunter days		Doves bagged		Doves/hunter day	
	LRGV	SWWA	LRGV	SWWA	LRGV	SWWA
1962[a]	16,281		114,789		7.1	
1963			Season closed			
1964	33,972		239,097		7.0	
1965	29,477		145,108		4.9	
1966	38,544		233,735		6.1	
1967	36,012		282,134		7.8	
1968	42,050		220,692		5.2	
1969	18,140		100,693		5.6	
1970	20,066		85,311		4.3	
1971	15,136		78,586		5.2	
1972	23,097		166,029		7.2	
1973	23,194		136,619		5.9	
1974	34,449		238,614		6.9	
1975	39,000		121,494		3.1	
1976[a]	36,612		162,914		4.4	
1976[b]	89,479	98,678	460,012	483,095	5.1	4.9
1977	66,864	78,093	403,513	438,195	6.0	5.6
1978	75,254	84,886	285,933	305,443	3.8	3.6
1979	80,654	91,216	461,842	497,816	5.7	5.5
1980	72,900	83,949	195,290	214,259	2.7	2.6
1981	71,979	86,179	222,088	262,265	3.1	3.0
1982	78,936	90,869	359,965	390,658	4.6	4.3
1983	67,942	90,980	230,816	273,434	3.4	3.0
1984	59,940	71,505	245,461	272,400	4.1	3.8
1985			Season closed			
1986	29,299	32,330	122,246	130,222	4.2	4.0
1987	33,242	38,519	123,643	140,880	3.7	3.7
1988	27,743	31,918	93,377	106,992	3.4	3.0
1989	25,167	32,906	75,430	98,861	3.0	3.0
1990	10,642	13,983	32,503	42,427	3.1	3.0
1991	11,882	14,433	22,392	35,589	1.9	2.3
1992	11,333	17,989	34,089	48,217	3.0	2.7

[a] During 1962–76, harvest in LRGV was determined by aerial survey of hunters' vehicles and ground check to determine number of hunters/vehicle, and the average number of white-winged doves/hunter.

[b] In 1976, Texas initiated a mail questionnaire survey of all white-winged dove stamp buyers statewide to determine harvest and compare old method (Footnote a) with new method.

for the first time provided harvest estimates for all areas of Texas where white-winged doves were legally hunted. The mail questionnaire was determined to be more accurate and less expensive (Waggerman 1977), and has been used since 1976. Harvest during the Texas Special White-winged Dove Season since 1976 has ranged from 22,000 in 1991 to 462,000 in 1979 in the LRGV (Table 3) and has declined ($r = -0.91$, $P < 0.01$) at the rate of 26,000 birds/year, 1976–92 due to declining populations and more restrictive regulations (Fig. 10).

Over 90% of the white-winged dove harvest in Texas occurred in the LRGV during 1976–82, (Table 3, Fig. 11). However, as white-winged doves continued to increase in other areas of the state, and regulations were changed in 1983 to

permit the taking of white-winged doves statewide as part of the aggregate bag during the regular mourning dove season, white-winged dove harvest throughout Texas increased substantially from 1983 through 1992. The LRGV accounted for only 13% of the statewide harvest by 1992 (Fig. 11).

Arizona.—Harvest statistics have been obtained annually since 1962 by the Arizona Game and Fish Department through a mail questionnaire survey of general hunting license holders. The white-winged dove harvest has varied from 75,000 in 1989 to 740,000 in 1968 (Table 4). In the 1960's with liberal bag limits, the annual harvest increased ($r = 0.90$, $P < 0.01$) from about 400,000 to 700,000 (Fig. 12). With declining populations and more restrictive hunting

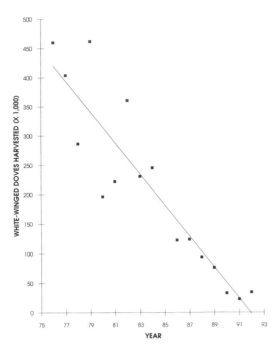

Fig. 10.   White-winged dove harvest trends during the special white-winged dove hunting season in the Lower Rio Grande of Texas, 1976–92, based on mail questionnaire surveys.

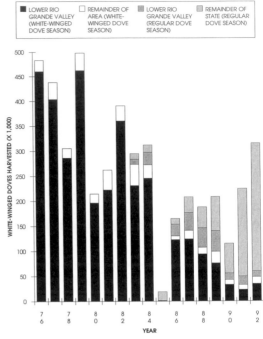

Fig. 11.   Relative harvest of white-winged doves in the Lower Rio Grande Valley and other legal harvest areas in Texas, during both the special white-winged dove season and the regular mourning dove season, 1976–92, based on mail questionnaire surveys.

regulations in the 1970's, the harvest of white-winged doves varied ($P > 0.10$) from about 450,000 to 300,000. Since 1980, under even more restrictive regulations, the harvest has remained relatively stable ($P > 0.10$) between 100,000 and 200,000. The average daily bag/hunter (Table 4) varied ($P > 0.05$) between 3 and 6 doves during the 1960's, declined ($r = -0.74$, $P < 0.05$) from about 2.5 in the early 1970's to 1.6 in the late 1970's, but increased ($r = 0.70$, $P < 0.01$) from about 0.7 to 1.5 during the 1980's. It appears that Arizona's white-winged dove population has stabilized at a lower level than in the 1960's, and that current hunting regulations are commensurate with that population.

Mexico.—White-winged dove hunting in Mexico has been popular with United States hunters since the mid-1970's. Individual and corporate groups generally have found more birds to hunt, more liberal regulations, and a different hunting experience than in the United States. Although United States hunters visit other areas of Mexico, Tamaulipas is the most popular white-winged dove hunting area in that country.

When United States citizens hunt in foreign countries, they are required by law to declare the number of birds or animals they killed and imported when returning to the United States. They are permitted to import 1 legal possession limit of each species hunted. In the case of white-winged doves, the possession limit has been 3 times the daily bag limit (Table 2). Since most guided hunts in Mexico are 3 days in length, a hunter is permitted to import his legal kill during his stay (usually 60 or 75 white-winged doves). The U.S. Fish and Wildlife Service game importation forms (Form 3-177) are retained by U.S. Customs and sent to the Service's Division of Law Enforcement at the end of the hunting season. Each year, the forms are reviewed by the Service's Office of Migratory Bird Management, and the dove and pigeon declarations are summarized for trend information (Table 5).

The number of white-winged doves declared at Texas/Mexico border ports increased ($r = 0.95$, $P < 0.01$) from about 17,000 birds in 1974 to over 1 million in 1987, the peak harvest year (Table 5). Routine examination of declarations forms indicated that most returning hunters had imported their legal possession limits. Reports from participants and eyewitness accounts, however, indicated that hunters actually bagged 3–4 times the number of declared white-winged doves (excess birds are eaten in camp or given to bird boys) (Tomlinson 1992). Thus, the actual harvest in 1987 was probably between 3 and 4 million birds, rather than the 1 million declared by hunters. In 1988, the harvest declined by nearly 50% from the previous year. This occurred as a result of: (1) a severe 4-year drought and a freeze during December 1989 that adversely affected breeding habitat and substantially reduced nesting success, and (2) the guide requirement that reduced the number of hunter declarations at Texas/Mexico border ports from 17,475 in 1987 to 11,222 in 1988 (−35%) (Tomlinson 1989). The downward trend ($r = -0.95$, $P < 0.01$) in harvest has continued to present. In retrospect, the guide requirement probably functioned as a management tool to reduce harvest to levels commensurate with population size. Torres (1992) interviewed hunters in hunting camps and estimated the white-winged dove harvest in Tamaulipas during 1992 at 1.3 million birds.

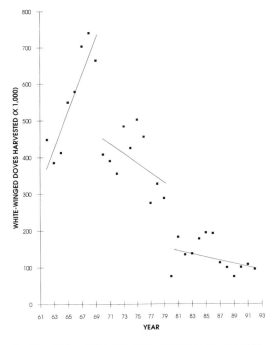

Fig. 12. White-winged dove harvest trends in Arizona, 1962–92, based on mail questionnaire surveys.

MANAGEMENT NEEDS

Habitat Management

Conservation and management of essential white-winged dove nesting and roosting habitat in the southwestern United States and northern Mexico continues to be the priority habitat management need. Woody habitat loss due to agricultural and urban development has resulted in total displacement of some breeding colonies, and dependence on freeze-prone citrus orchards by others. This massive loss of woody nesting cover primarily occurred in the LRGV of Texas before the 1930's (Saunders 1940), in Arizona in the 1960's (Rea 1983), and in northeastern Mexico in the 1970's (Purdy and Tomlinson 1982, 1991; Ortega M. and Zamora T. 1984).

In the LRGV of Texas, habitat acquisition programs by the U.S. Fish and Wildlife Service and the Texas Parks and Wildlife Department have resulted in public ownership of >18,000 ha (of a planned 40,000 ha) of actual or potential habitat for white-winged doves and other wildlife (D. R. Blankinship, pers. commun; Texas Parks and Wildl. Dep., unpubl. data). Much of this land had been previously cleared for agricultural production, and is currently being reforested with native brush to optimize its wild-

life habitat value (George 1985, Homerstad et al. 1988, Jahrsdoerfer and Leslie 1988).

Recognizing the economic value of white-winged dove hunting, the Mexican government has recently designated the brushy habitat used by the largest colony in Tamaulipas as a wildlife sanctuary. Other sanctuaries in Tamaulipas are needed, and similar habitat projects in western Mexico and Arizona are being considered.

Food availability is another important habitat management consideration for white-winged doves. Although many farmers in the LRGV of Texas readily plant domestic sunflowers or other grain as a white-winged dove attractant for the September hunting season, relatively few intentionally plant white-winged dove foods that mature earlier in the season. Schacht et al. (1994) recommended planting high-quality grain food plots that mature prior or during arrival of pre-nesting white-winged doves (mid–late Apr); this would enable doves to restore lipid losses incurred during migration and/or wintering and store energy for nesting, especially during drought when energy availability may be limited. Grain fields near traditional brushy nesting habitat are important throughout the nesting season. In areas where large populations occur,

Table 4. Arizona white-winged dove harvest statistics, 1962–92.

Year	Hunter (n)	Hunter days	Doves bagged	Doves/ season	Doves/ hunter day
1962	29,839	76,894	448,398	15.0	5.8
1963	29,322	96,837	385,249	13.1	4.0
1964	30,467	99,040	412,542	13.5	4.2
1965	31,058	99,916	549,045	17.7	6.0
1966	37,265	100,726	578,166	15.5	5.7
1967	36,975	179,085	703,157	19.0	3.9
1968	49,503	173,373	740,079	15.0	4.3
1969	54,547	197,347	664,053	12.2	3.4
1970	46,594	169,667	407,921	8.8	2.4
1971	46,090	167,288	390,016	8.5	2.3
1972	46,149	165,309	355,633	7.7	2.2
1973	54,982	211,166	484,095	8.8	2.3
1974	55,796	196,059	425,127	7.6	2.2
1975	58,129	196,645	502,225	8.6	2.6
1976	59,425	214,111	455,692	7.7	2.1
1977	45,136	161,739	274,998	6.1	1.7
1978	47,750	183,772	327,555	6.9	1.8
1979	43,573	176,899	288,516	6.6	1.6
1980	31,942	104,675	75,611	2.4	0.7
1981	38,122	209,671	182,535	4.8	0.9
1982	32,910	126,661	134,981	4.1	1.1
1983	26,404	118,320	137,284	5.2	1.2
1984	33,011	141,947	177,957	5.4	1.3
1985	37,985	135,320	194,508	5.1	1.4
1986	39,389	138,204	192,734	4.9	1.4
1987	29,648	108,287	112,838	3.8	1.0
1988	25,964	88,021	99,955	3.8	1.1
1989	21,115	62,514	74,944	3.5	1.2
1990	24,120	67,918	100,163	4.2	1.5
1991	25,556	71,368	107,455	4.2	1.5
1992	23,152	65,671	94,551	4.1	1.4

Table 5. Estimated annual harvest of white-winged doves in Texas and Arizona from state surveys and in Mexico from declarations by American hunters at border ports.

Year	Arizona	Mexico[a] Texas ports	Mexico[a] Ariz./N.M. ports	Texas
1962	448,398			
1963	385,249	17,004		
1964	412,542			
1965	549,045	24,922		
1966	578,166	54,256		
1967	703,157			
1968	740,079	139,956		
1969	664,053	183,379		
1970	407,921	178,591		
1971	390,016			
1972	355,633			
1973	484,095			
1974	425,127	168,112		
1975	502,225			
1976	455,692	165,036		483,095
1977	274,998	232,692		438,195
1978	327,555	260,977		305,443
1979	288,516	419,251	2,512	497,816
1980	75,611	636,478	2,623	214,259
1981	182,535	507,694	14,969	262,265
1982	134,981	548,273	4,170	390,658
1983	137,284	566,542	3,470	294,958
1984	177,957	777,815	19,585	312,792
1985	194,508	888,686	20,531	19,020
1986	192,734	796,844	13,587	169,517
1987	112,838	1,025,396	23,823	226,623
1988	99,955	592,803	23,168	201,000
1989	79,944	511,922	23,951	218,002
1990	100,163	346,602	26,432	124,255
1991	107,455	330,396	11,560	229,425
1992	94,551	137,982	16,590	325,890
Averages	325,096	396,317	14,784	277,248

[a] U.S. Fish and Wildlife Service, unpubl. data.

large-scale depredations of grain crops have been noted, particularly for the Eastern population (Cottam and Trefethen 1968). Care should be taken to minimize or disperse this problem when it occurs.

Large white-winged dove colonies are generally near reliable water sources, but dove numbers can be increased at many isolated, arid sites by providing reliable drinking water. Livestock watering troughs, wildlife guzzlers, residential lawn sprinklers, and bird baths are readily used by white-winged doves in arid and semi-arid areas.

We suggest that responsible wildlife agencies maintain active management programs to periodically assess habitat status and establish habitat renovation projects. We stress the programs be active and ongoing to avoid gradual, but highly-adverse, habitat loss. Extension programs in conjunction with other resource agencies (e.g., U.S. Soil Conservation Service, Agricultural Ex-

tension Service) should be established and actively maintained.

Population Management

Separate Populations.—Separate management of Eastern and Western populations of white-winged doves should continue. Furthermore, the geographic isolation of the Upper Big Bend and Mexican Highland subspecies in north-central Mexico and the Trans-Pecos region of western Texas (Saunders 1968) is sufficient to allow wildlife agencies to combine management of these 2 populations separately from either the Eastern or Western population if deemed necessary.

Standardized and statistically sound population surveys are needed throughout the breeding range to monitor the annual status of white-winged dove populations. At present, only the largest and/or most accessible white-winged dove populations are surveyed by the responsible agencies. In addition, a variety of survey techniques are used by the respective management agencies, and numbers reported by one agency may not be readily comparable with those of another. Because of extremely dense white-winged dove colonies in some Eastern areas, a traditional auditory survey may be impractical. Therefore, another method, such as the nest transect survey developed in Mexico (Nichols et al. 1986) or the electronic device developed in Texas (Waechtler and DeYoung 1990) might be adaptable to all areas regardless of nest densities. It would be desirable to develop a survey technique that could be conducted early enough in the breeding season to be useful in setting annual hunting regulations in June or July.

Monitoring status of wintering populations is important because white-winged doves from each of the 2 major breeding populations spend nearly 6 months in Mexico or Central America. For example, A. Alvarez G. (1992 letter to U.S. Fish and Wildl. Serv., Albuquerque, N.M.) stated that, in his opinion, 1987 was the last year white-winged doves migrated through El Salvador in great numbers, and that white-winged doves were almost nonexistent in that country in 1992. He added that since 1987, not only was the number of migrating birds greatly reduced, but that migration occurred later in the year (late Oct to mid-Nov rather than mid-Oct). We suggest that periodic and standardized surveys be developed and initiated in representative areas of the winter range.

Harvest surveys should be conducted annually to monitor trends. The Texas White-winged Dove Stamp, which is required of all white-winged dove hunters, and attendant mail questionnaire surveys, have allowed reasonably accurate estimates of Texas harvests since 1976. Similar small game harvest surveys in Arizona also have provided reasonably accurate estimates of Arizona white-winged dove harvests since 1962. In other white-winged dove harvest states of the United States (California, Nevada, New Mexico), no accurate harvest surveys have been conducted. The National Migratory Bird Harvest Information Program (U.S. Fish and Wildl. Serv. 1992) should be suitable to estimate white-winged dove harvest in all states beginning in 1998. Until that time, all white-winged

dove-hunting states are encouraged to continue the present surveys.

Hunter declarations of white-winged doves harvested by United States hunters at border ports (Tomlinson 1992) provide harvest trends, but the analysis does not accurately reflect actual harvest. A survey that sampled major hunting camps in Tamaulipas (e.g., Torres 1992) would be useful and should be continued on an annual basis.

Separate harvest estimates should be made for Eastern and Western populations, and for each state or country within the separate ranges. Formulae and rationale for deriving harvest objectives and allocations for each population jointly shared by the United States and Latin American countries should be formalized in management plans using the best available estimates of harvest and population size.

Banding Programs.—White-winged dove banding projects during the 1960's and 1970's were conducted in Arizona, the LRGV of Texas, and Tamaulipas, Mexico. Analyses of some of these data have been completed (e.g., Brown 1981, George 1993*b*). Data that have not been analyzed and/or published should be completed as soon as possible. In the past 20 years, substantial changes in habitats, ranges, and hunting practices have occurred. We suggest new banding programs be designed to provide information on the following objectives: (1) compare present white-winged dove survival and recovery rate estimates with those of the past; (2) compare migratory distribution, particularly of the Eastern population in Central America; (3) determine if distribution, survival, recovery, etc. are different between white-winged doves banded in southcentral Texas and the LRGV; (4) sample the Upper Big Bend and Mexican Highland subspecies to identify migration routes and wintering areas; and (5) determine if the introduced Florida population is migratory.

RESEARCH NEEDS

Funds for research on white-winged doves have been limited, but additional information is needed to provide optimum population, harvest, and habitat management. The research needs listed below are in descending priority order.

1. Accurately estimate harvest of white-winged doves in the United States using the National Migratory Bird Harvest Information

Program and encourage Latin America countries to develop similar harvest surveys.

2. Delineate numbers and trends of the Eastern and Western populations. Refine techniques for coordinated American/Mexican spring and summer breeding surveys, and compare with winter surveys to be developed in Mexico and Central America.
3. Inventory past and present status of nesting habitat and agricultural changes to make informed habitat management decisions.
4. Examine relationships of bag limits, aggregate bags, season lengths, season dates, shooting hours, and sanctuaries with magnitude of harvest in high harvest areas. Use banding studies to monitor changes in recovery and/or survival rates and use results to more carefully regulate harvest should it become necessary. Manipulate harvest regulations in experimental study areas in high-harvest regions to evaluate effectiveness of regulation alternatives.
5. Evaluate the importance of seasonal food availability on production and survival.
6. Develop more efficient methods of restoring nesting habitat.
7. Evaluate effects of agricultural chemicals, ingested lead shot, other toxins, and diseases on populations.
8. Define the taxonomic relationships of subspecies using DNA fingerprinting to allow a more precise biological definition of manageable units within populations.
9. Investigate the extent and causes of breeding range expansion (e.g., in Texas and Florida) and evaluate interaction of white-winged doves with other resident wildlife in these areas.
10. Evaluate the extent and causes of non-migratory behavior (i.e., wintering in the northern breeding range).
11. Determine productivity and recruitment to compare with survival estimates using nest studies, radiotelemetry, and wing collection programs.
12. Develop operational means of reducing nest mortality (by grackle predation), particularly for the Eastern population.

RECOMMENDATIONS

The following is a summary of specific recommendations presented in descending priority order.

1. The U.S. Fish and Wildlife Service (USFWS), the Central Flyway Council (CFC), the Pacific Flyway Council (PFC), and governments of Latin American countries should work jointly to develop and/or improve management plans for the Eastern and Western white-winged dove populations.
2. The USFWS, CFC, PFC, and governments of Latin American countries should conduct, assist, fund and/or promote funding of identified applied research.
3. The USFWS, Texas Parks and Wildlife Department, Arizona Game and Fish Department, and Dirección General de Conservación Ecológica de Recursos Naturales of Mexico should take the lead in forming a coalition of private, state, and federal agencies dedicated to prioritizing and funding protection and management of key breeding and wintering habitat areas in Arizona, Texas, Mexico, and Central America.
4. The Florida Game and Freshwater Fish Commission should evaluate the white-winged dove population in Florida and develop appropriate research, management, and funding strategies.

ACKNOWLEDGMENTS

Many past and present white-winged dove researchers, managers, educators, administrators, and enthusiasts made this chapter possible. In particular, we acknowledge the contributions of D. S. Blankenship, D. R. Blankinship, J. R. Brady, D. E. Brown, W. C. Brownlee, T. L. Clark, C. Cottam, L. R. Ditto, D. D. Dolton, J. H. Dunks, P. K. Evans, B. Hale, R. A. Haughey, J. M. Inglish, H. D. Irby, R. S. Jenks, W. H. Kiel, Jr., E. G. Marsh, R. D. Ohmart, P. C. Purdy, T. W. Regan, T. E. Retterer, J. A. Roberson, G. B. Saunders, J. F. Scuddy, P. D. Smith, T. C. Tacha, J. B. Trefethen, P. B. Uzzell, and C. K. Winkler. J. C. Barron, G. A. Boydston, K. D. Gruen, S. C. Marquardt, and D. M. McCarty analyzed data and prepared tables and figures. The assistance of J. W. Diden, R. L. Ledesma, K. B. Martin, and M. M. Mengers who typed and prepared numerous drafts of this chapter is greatly appreciated.

LITERATURE CITED

BASKETT, T. S. 1993. Biological evaluation of the call-count survey. Pages 253–268 in T. S. Baskett, M. W. Sayre, R. E. Tomlinson, and R. E. Mirarchi, eds. Ecology and management of the mourning dove. Stackpole Books, Harrisburg, Pa.

BAUTISTA J., M., AND A. BRITO C. 1992. Estudio sobre habitos alimenticios de la paloma de alas blancas (*Zenaida asiatica asiatica*) en el estado de Tamaulipas, Mexico. Unpubl. Rep., Dir. Gral. de Conser. Ecol. de los Recursos Naturales, Mexico City, D.F. 42pp.

BENT, A. C. 1932. Life histories of North America gallinaceous birds. U.S. Natl. Mus. Bull. 162. 490pp.

BLANKINSHIP, D. R. 1966. The relationships of white-winged dove production to control of great-tailed grackles in the Lower Rio Grande Valley of Texas. Trans. North Am. Wildl. and Nat. Resour. Conf. 31:45–58.

———. 1970. White-winged dove nesting colonies in northeastern Mexico. Trans. North Am. Wildl. and Nat. Resour. Conf. 35:171–182.

———, J. G. TEER, AND W. H. KIEL, JR. 1972. Movements and mortality of white-winged doves banded in Tamaulipas, Mexico. Trans. North Am. Wildl. and Nat. Resour. Conf. 37:312–325.

BROWN, D. E. 1981. Migratory game bird banding analysis. Performance Rep., Fed. Aid. Proj. W-53-R-31, W.P. 3, Job 2. Arizona Game and Fish Dep., Phoenix. 37pp.

———, D. R. BLANKINSHIP, P. K. EVANS, W. H. KIEL, JR., G. L. WAGGERMAN, AND C. K. WINKLER. 1977. White-winged dove. Pages 246–272 in G. C. Sanderson, ed. Management of migratory shore and upland game birds in North America. Int. Assoc. Fish and Wildl. Agencies. Washington, D.C.

BUCHER, E. H. 1986. The influence of changes in regional land-use patterns on *Zenaida* dove populations. Pages 291–303 in J. Pinowski and J. D. Summers-Smith, eds. Proc. Gen. Meeting Working Group on Granivorous Birds. INTECOL. Ottawa, Ont. and Syracuse, N.Y.

COTTAM, C., AND J. B. TREFETHEN, EDITORS. 1968. Whitewings: the life history, status, and management of the white-winged dove. D. Van Nostrand Co., Princeton, N.J. 348pp.

CUNNINGHAM, S. C. 1986. The comparative feeding and nesting ecology of mourning and white-winged doves in the Buckeye-Arlington Valley Area of Arizona. Unpubl. Rep., Arizona Game and Fish Dep., Phoenix. 121pp.

DAVIS, C. A., AND R. S. JENKS. 1983. Distribution, abundance, and habitat of white-winged doves in New Mexico. Final Rep., U.S. Fish and Wildl. Serv. Contract 14-16-0009-81-006. New Mexico State Univ., Las Cruces. 148pp.

DOLTON, D. D. 1975. Patterns and influencing factors of white-winged dove feeding activity in the Lower Rio Grande Valley of Texas and Mexico. M.S. Thesis, Texas A&M Univ., College Station. 145pp.

DUNKS, J. 1969. Whitewings vs. grackles. Texas Parks and Wildl. 27(7):2–5.

ENGEL-WILSON, R. W., AND R. D. OHMART. 1978. Assessment of vegetation and terrestrial vertebrates along the Rio Grande between Fort Quitman, Texas and Haciendita, Texas. U.S. Sect.,

Int. Boundary and Water Comm. Contract IBM 77–17. Arizona State Univ., Tempe. 88pp.

EVANS, P. K. 1972. Grackle control as an aid to white-winged dove management. Proc. Southeast. Assoc. Game and Fish Comm. 26:296–298.

GALLUCCI, T. 1978. The biological and taxonomic status of the white-winged doves of the Big Bend of Texas. M.S. Thesis, Sul Ross State Univ., Alpine, Tex. 208pp.

GEORGE, R. R. 1985. White-winged dove management in Texas with implications for northeastern Mexico. Unpubl. Rep., First Reg. Conf. on Parks and Wildl. of the Rio Grande Border States, Laredo, Tex. 9pp.

———. 1990. Investigation of migratory shore and upland game bird losses in Texas. Final Rep., Fed. Aid. Proj. W-125-R, Job 3. Texas Parks and Wildl. Dep., Austin. 4pp.

———. 1991. The adaptable whitewing. Texas Parks and Wildl. 49(9):10–15.

———. 1993a. Hunting in the Southwest. Pages 459–474 in T. S. Baskett, M. W. Sayre, R. E. Tomlinson, and R. E. Mirarchi, eds. Ecology and management of the mourning dove. Stackpole Books, Harrisburg, Pa.

———. 1993b. White-winged dove banding analysis. Final Rep., Fed. Aid Proj. W-128-R, Job 6. Texas Parks and Wildl. Dep., Austin. 85pp.

GOODWIN, D. 1977. Pigeons and doves of the world. Cornell Univ. Press. Ithaca, N.Y. 446pp.

HANSON, H. C., AND C. W. KOSSACK. 1962. The mourning dove in Illinois. Illinois Dep. Conserv. Tech. Bull. 2. 133pp.

HAUGEN, A. O., AND J. KEELER. 1952. Mortality of mourning doves from trichomoniasis in Alabama during 1951. Trans. North Am. Wildl. Conf. 17: 141–151.

HAUGHEY, R. A. 1986. Diet of desert nesting western white-winged doves. M.S. Thesis, Arizona State Univ., Tempe. 80pp.

HOMERSTAD, G. E., G. L. WAGGERMAN, AND R. R. GEORGE. 1988. The reforestation of cropland in the Lower Rio Grande Valley of Texas with emphasis on white-winged dove nesting habitat. Second Reg. Conf., Rio Grande Border States on Parks and Wildl. Saltillo, Coahuila, Mexico. 13pp.

JAHRSDOERFER, S. E., AND D. M. LESLIE, JR. 1988. Tamaulipan brushland of the Lower Rio Grande Valley of south Texas: description, human impacts, and management options. U. S. Fish and Wildl. Serv., Biol. Rep. 88(36):63pp.

LEOPOLD, A. S. 1959. Wildlife in Mexico, the game birds and mammals. Univ. California Press, Berkeley. 568pp.

LEVINE, N. D., AND S. KANTOR. 1959. Check-list of blood parasites of birds of the order Columbiformes. Wildl. Dis. 1:1.

MARSH, E. G., AND G. B. SAUNDERS. 1942. The status of white-winged dove in Texas. Wilson Bull. 54:145–146.

MIRARCHI, R. E. 1993. Aging, sexing, and miscellaneous research techniques. Pages 399–408 in T. S. Baskett, M. W. Sayre, R. E. Tomlinson, and R. E. Mirarchi, eds. Ecology and management of the mourning dove. Stackpole Books. Harrisburg, Pa.

NICHOLS, J. D., R. E. TOMLINSON, AND G. L. WAGGERMAN. 1986. Estimating nest detection probabilities for white-winged dove nest transects in Tamaulipas, Mexico. Auk 103:826–828.

OBERHOLSER, H. C. 1974. The bird life of Texas. Univ. Texas Press, Austin. 1,069pp.

ORTEGA M., H., AND H. V. ZAMORA T. 1984. Estudio de la paloma de alas blancas en Tamaulipas, 1984. Unpubl. Rep., Fifth Latin American Workshop on Function and Manage. of Natl. Wildl. Refuges. Santa Ana Natl. Wildl. Refuge. Alamo, Tex. 10pp.

———, F. TREVIÑO L., A. ARAGON T., AND J. CRUCES D. 1979. Estudio de la paloma de alas blancas (Zenaida asiatica asiatica) durante su época de reproducción en el estado de Tamaulipas–Temporada 1978. Unpubl. Rep., SARH, Dir. Gral. de Fauna Silvestre, Cd. Victoria, Tamps., México. 25pp.

PURDY, P. C., AND R. E. TOMLINSON. 1982. Agricultural development in relation to the eastern white-winged dove. Unpubl. Rep., Tamaulipan Biotic Province Symp. Corpus Christi, Tex. 20pp.

———, AND ———. 1991. The eastern white-winged dove: factors influencing use and continuity of the resource. Pages 255–265 in J.G. Robinson and K.H. Redford, eds. Neotropical wildlife use and conservation. Univ. Chicago Press. Chicago, Ill.

RAPPOLE, J. H., AND G. L. WAGGERMAN. 1986. Calling males as an index of density for breeding white-winged doves. Wildl. Soc. Bull. 14:151–155.

REA, A. M. 1983. Once a river. Univ. Arizona Press, Tucson. 285pp.

SAUNDERS, G. B. 1940. Eastern white-winged dove (Melopelia asiatica asiatica) in southeastern Texas. Unpubl. Rep., U.S. Biol. Surv., Washington, D.C. 132pp.

———. 1959. Microfilarial and other blood parasites in Mexican wild doves and pigeons. J. Parasitol. 45:69–75.

———. 1968. Seven new subspecies of white-winged doves from Mexico, Central America and Southwestern United States. North Am. Fauna 65. 30pp.

———. 1980. The origin of white-winged doves breeding in South Florida. Florida Field Nat. 8(2):50–51.

SCHACHT, S. J., T. C. TACHA, AND G. L. WAGGERMAN. 1994. Bioenergetics of white-winged dove reproduction in the Lower Rio Grande Valley of Texas. Wildl. Monogr. In review.

SCUDDAY, J. F., T. L. GALLUCCI, AND P. S. WEST. 1980. The status and ecology of the white-winged dove of Trans-Pecos Texas. Final Rep., U.S. Fish and Wildl. Serv. Contract 14–16-00-2096. Sul Ross State Univ., Alpine, Tex. 157pp.

SMALL, M. F., R. A. HILSENBECK, AND J. F. SCUDDY. 1989. Resource utilization and nesting ecology of the white-winged dove (Zenaida asiatica) in central Trans-Pecos, Texas. Texas. J. Agric. and Nat. Resour. 3:37–38.

STABLER, R. M. 1961. A parasitological survey of fifty-one eastern white-winged doves. J. Parasitol 47:309–311.

TACHA, T. C., S. J. SCHACHT, R. R. GEORGE, AND E. F. HILL. 1994. Anticholinesterase exposure of white-winged doves breeding in the Lower Rio Grande Valley, Texas. J. Wildl. Manage. 58:213–217.

TOMLINSON, R. E. 1989. Hunter declarations at border ports of doves and pigeons bagged in Mexico. Unpubl. Rep., U.S. Fish and Wildl. Serv., Albuquerque, N.M. 12pp.

———. 1991. Report on white-winged dove status surveys in northeastern Mexico, June 1–July 31, 1991. Unpubl. Trip Rep., U.S. Fish and Wildl. Serv., Albuquerque, N.M. 13pp.

———. 1992. Hunter declarations at border ports of doves and pigeons bagged in Mexico. Unpubl. Rep., U.S. Fish and Wildl. Serv., Albuquerque, N.M. 15pp.

TORRES, C., F. 1992. Aprovechamiento cinegético de la paloma de alas blancas (Zenaida asiatica) en el estado de Tamaulipas, México. Unpubl. Rep., Facul. Med. Vet. y Zootec., Univ. Autónoma de Tamulipas, México. 17pp.

U.S. FISH AND WILDLIFE SERVICE. 1992. Migratory bird harvest information program; proposed rule. Fed. Regist. 57:24736–24741.

WAECHTLER, D. G., AND C. A. DE YOUNG. 1990. Evaluation of an electronic device for counting the calls of white-winged doves. Texas J. Agric. and Nat. Resour. 4:55–58.

WAGGERMAN, G. 1977. White-winged dove harvest regulations. Performance Rep., Fed. Aid Proj. W-30-R, Job 1, Texas Parks and Wildl. Dep., Austin. 21 pp. plus Appendix by J. H. Dunks. The white-winged dove harvest in Texas. 20pp.

———. 1992. White-winged dove density, distribution, movement, and harvest. Performance Rep., Fed. Aid Proj. W–128-R, Job 2, Texas Parks and Wildl. Dep., Austin. 18pp.

———, AND S. SOROLA. 1977. Whitewings in winter. Texas Parks and Wildl. 35(10):6–9.

WILLIAMS, L. E. 1978. Environmental assessment report, white-winged dove relocation experiment. Fed. Aid Proj. W–41. Florida Game and Freshwater Fish Comm., Tallahasse. 14pp.

WEST, L. M. 1993. Ecology of breeding white-winged doves in the San Antonio metropolitan area. M.S. Thesis, Texas Tech Univ., Lubbock. 64pp.

———, L. M. SMITH, R. S. LUTZ, AND R. R. GEORGE. 1993. Ecology of urban white-winged doves. Trans. North Am. Wildl. and Nat. Resour. Conf. 58:70–77.

Chapter 4

WHITE-TIPPED DOVE

GARY L. WAGGERMAN, Texas Parks and Wildlife Department, 410 North 13th Street, Edinburg, TX 78539
GARY E. HOMERSTAD, Texas Parks and Wildlife Department, 2601 North Azalea Street, Victoria, TX 77902
RONNIE R. GEORGE, Texas Parks and Wildlife Department, 4200 Smith School Road, Austin, TX 78744
WAYNE A. SHIFFLETT, Buenos Aires National Wildlife Refuge, P.O. Box 109, Sasabe, AZ 85633

Abstract: White-tipped doves (*Leptotila verreauxi*) are large tropical columbids native to southern Texas, Mexico, Central America, and portions of South America. They have been a legally hunted game species in the United States since 1984. Their range in the United States is a 14-county area of southern Texas. White-tipped doves are sedentary and do not migrate. In southern Texas they nest in native brush and citrus orchards. The annual breeding population has been stable in Texas for the past 10 years, except for declines during years following major freezes that adversely affect citrus and native brush nesting habitat. A limited harvest of 2 white-tipped doves per day is allowed during the special white-winged (*Zenaida asiatica*) and mourning (*Z. macroura*) dove hunting seasons. Improvements in harvest surveys are needed. Other management and research needs include more detailed breeding population surveys in the northern part of their range, and additional life history data.

DESCRIPTION

White-tipped doves are the only species of the genus *Leptotila* that occurs in the United States (Leopold 1959). White-tipped doves are large, mostly terrestrial doves that seem more inclined to walk than fly (Fig. 1). They are dark olive brown above and light gray below with a light-colored forehead. The most distinct features are the chestnut or rusty-red underwing linings. They have an iridescent nape and hindneck; whitish below, washed with purplish or purplish buff anteriorly and pale buff posteriorly. The bill is black, the iris yellow or orange, and the bare skin around the eye is red or blue. The feet and legs are carmine. First-year males and females attain adult plumage by the post-juvenal molt (Oberholser 1974). Leopold (1959) noted the similarity of *Leptotila* wings to those of American woodcock (*Scolopax minor*). Both of these species spend most of their time in brush and have evolved wings shaped for flying around obstacles. Leopold (1959) described a special attenuated outer primary in *Leptotila*, and surmised this adaption allows the birds to quickly change direction and speed. The common name of white-tipped dove is derived from the rounded, white-tipped tail; however, this seems a poor choice of names since both white-winged and mourning doves have white on the tail. Another common name for this species, white-fronted dove, apparently referred to the light-colored forehead on some individuals (Fig. 2). Males and females are generally similar in appearance, but females are more dull in color and smaller in size.

Oberholser (1974) gave the following measurements (mm) for white-tipped doves: adult male wings 140.0–158.0 ($x = 146.3$), tail 96.0–117.6 (106.7), bill (exposed culmen) 14.0–17.0 (15.7), tarsus 27.4–33.0 (29.7), and middle toe without claw 22.1–25.4 (24.1). Adult females have wings 129.5–152.4 (142.7), tail 94.5–114.6 (103.4), bill 14.5–17.0 (16.3), tarsus 26.9–31.0 (29.2), and middle toe 22.1–24.9 (23.9). Measurements given by other authors were usually within these limits (Bent 1932, Leopold 1959, Boydstun 1982). The average weight for adult white-tipped doves is 186.6 g (Oberholser 1974), although Leopold (1959) gave a range of weights of 145–205 grams. Neither report separated weights by gender. Boydstun (1982) weighed 24 adult white-tipped doves and found weights ranging from 150.4 to 229.7 g, with an average of 187.5.

LIFE HISTORY

White-tipped doves are year-round residents that rarely travel more than 1.6 km in their lifetime from the place they hatch (Boydstun 1982). However, from a legal standpoint, white-tipped doves (Family Columbidae) are classified as a migratory species under the Migratory Bird Treaty Act. The breeding season extends from February into September, but most nesting oc-

Fig. 1.   White-tipped dove feeding on the ground in South Texas. This species is mostly terrestrial (Photo by L. R. Ditto).

Fig. 2.   White-tipped dove in South Texas (Photo by L. R. Ditto).

curs between April and August. The courtship call is a low and soft 3-note coo (Leopold 1959). Unless quite close to the calling bird, one will only hear the last note, which is drawn out for 3–4 seconds. The tone is similar to the sound made when a person blows softly across the mouth of a large empty bottle, hence their common name, "jug blower."

The typical nest of white-tipped doves is more substantial than that of other doves and pigeons. It is constructed of heavier twigs and is usually bowl shaped (Fig. 3). Nests are placed in trees or shrubs at heights from 1 to 8 m. The usual clutch size is 2 eggs, but occasionally 1 and rarely 3 eggs are laid. Eggs are elliptical to oval in shape, cream buff to white in color, and measurements range from 21.6 to 23.0 mm in circumference and 29.6 to 31.0 mm in length (Bent 1932, Skutch 1964, Leopold 1959). Both sexes share incubation duties and eggs hatch in about 14 days. Young grow rapidly and are capable of short flights by 10–12 days of age (Fig. 4). A complete nesting cycle takes 30–35 days. Even though white-tipped doves have a long nesting season and a relatively short nesting cycle, only one documented instance of double brooding has been reported. Boydstun and DeYoung (1987) recorded a radio-marked bird that successfully fledged 2 broods of 2 young each. They reported 80% of the nests studied ($n = 41$) in 1980 fledged at least 1 young. Nest success has not been studied extensively for white-tipped doves. However, since they nest in habitats similar to white-winged doves, they encounter similar nest predators. The primary avian predator is the great-tailed grackle (*Quiscalus mexicanus*). Snakes, rodents, and other small mammals

also take a significant proportion of eggs and young. White-tipped doves have higher nest success than white-winged and mourning doves, probably due to their more substantial nest (Boydstun and DeYoung 1985).

The 41 nests studied by Boydstun (1982) were in 11 plant species: honey mesquite (*Prosopis glandulosa*), spiny hackberry (*Celtis pallida*), sugar hackberry (*C. laevigata*), palm (*Washingtonia* spp.), baccharis (*Baccharis* spp.), huisache (*Acacia smallii*), cedar elm (*Ulmus crassifolia*), Lindheimer pricklypear (*Opuntia lindheimeri*), citrus (*Citrus* spp.), snake-eyes (*Phaulothamnus spinescens*), and brazil (*Condalia hookeri*). Eight of the nests were constructed in vegetation draped with old-man's beard (*Clematis drummondii*). One nest was in Spanish moss (*Tillandsia usneoides*).

White-tipped doves feed on seeds of forbs such as pigeon berry (*Rivina humilis*), grasses, and fruit of trees such as sugar hackberry, anaqua (*Ehretia anacua*) spiny hackberry, brazil,

Fig. 3.   White-tipped dove nest inside of a freeze-killed citrus tree trellised with annual sunflowers and the vine old-man's beard (*Clematis drummondii*) in the early summer in the Lower Rio Grande Valley of South Texas. This nesting habitat was destroyed before the next nesting season when the citrus orchard was bulldozed and replanted (Photo by R. R. George).

Fig. 4.   Adult white-tipped dove on nest in prickly-pear cactus feeding two young in South Texas (Photo by L. E. Krueger).

and citrus (W. A. Shifflett, unpubl. data). They also consume seeds of cultivated crops such as sorghum, corn, and sunflower, although they rarely venture far from the edge of wooded areas.

HABITAT

In the Lower Rio Grande Valley of Texas, as throughout its range, the primary habitat of white-tipped doves is thickets of native brush. White-tipped doves are usually found in the tallest trees and densest brush (Oberholser 1974). Historically, these doves used native brush as roosting, feeding, and nesting areas. Boydstun and DeYoung (1988) found that most individuals in woodland or citrus habitats spent at least 9 months of the year within a range of generally less than 10 ha. Between the late 1970's and 1983 (when the first of 2 killing freezes occurred), there was increased use of citrus for nesting by white-tipped doves in the Lower Rio Grande Valley. However, the number of birds nesting in native brush remained fairly stable during these years, giving rise to speculation that white-tipped doves either exceeded the carrying capacity of surrounding brush tracts or moved when brush was destroyed. Leopold (1959) reported that in Mexico, white-tipped doves thrived in cutover forests broken with trails and openings. This description is similar to habitats used by doves in southern Texas.

Native brush composition in southern Texas varies with soil type and available moisture, but contains combinations of the following impor-

tant woody species: Texas ebony (*Pithecellobium ebano*), anaqua, brazil, lime pricklyash (*Zanthoxylum fagara*), spiny hackberry, sugar hackberry, cedar elm, coma (*Bumelia celastrina*), lotebush (*Zizyphus obtusifolia*), Texas persimmon (*Diospyros texana*), and mesquite. Native brush typically forms a dense, tangled thicket that provides the cover preferred by white-tipped doves. The understory component of these thickets is often sparse, except in openings and along edges, and this allows the doves to walk about freely on the ground.

Fields and other disturbed areas such as roadsides are used as feeding areas by white-tipped doves nesting in nearby brush habitat. These areas may be cultivated grain fields with an active crop, stubble with waste grain, or they may be old fields with primarily herbaceous cover.

Mature citrus trees are densely foliated and are composed of a tangle of intertwined limbs that include horizontal limbs used by nesting doves. All but the best cared-for orchards contain a certain amount of herbaceous, weedy growth that provides fruits and seeds consumed

Fig. 5.   Distribution of white-tipped doves in North America.

by doves. White-tipped doves will probably reoccupy citrus orchards when the orchards have fully recovered from the 1989 freeze damage, possibly as soon as 1995.

DISTRIBUTION AND ABUNDANCE

White-tipped doves occur from southern Texas to southern Brazil, Uruguay, and eastern Argentina (Goodwin 1967, Am. Ornithol. Union 1983) (Fig. 5). In the United States, white-tipped doves were first reported in the Lower Rio Grande Valley of Texas in 1878 (G. B. Sennett in Bent 1932). By 1923, Bent (1932) reported they were "quite common" locally around Resaca de la Palma near Brownsville, Texas, where they were generally restricted to dense native brush thickets near the Rio Grande. In the late 1960's and early 1970's, white-tipped doves were still found only in the dense riparian brush along the Rio Grande in the Lower Rio Grande Valley (W. A. Shifflett, pers. observ.). During the 1970's there was a gradual movement of white-tipped doves into native brushlands north of the river and nearby citrus orchards. White-tipped doves

have not become as abundant as mourning and white-winged doves. However, in recent years, they have increased in number and distribution in South Texas.

In the United States, white-tipped doves now occur in the southernmost counties in Texas. Boydstun and DeYoung (1985) surveyed all counties south of a line from Corpus Christi to Laredo and found white-tipped doves in Cameron, Willacy, Hidalgo, Starr, Zapata, Webb, Brooks, and Kenedy counties. Oberholser (1974) gave the same distribution as Boydstun and DeYoung (1985), except for observation records from the Big Bend area of western Texas prior to 1970. Personnel on the Chaparral Wildlife Management Area, in LaSalle County, reported white-tipped doves during Christmas Bird Counts in 1991 and 1992; and 2 white-tipped doves were taken by hunters on this area in 1988 (D. R. Synatzske, Tex. Parks and Wildl. Dep., pers. commun.). This represents a slight range expansion (80 km) north of previous descriptions. A 6-year breeding bird atlas for Texas has just been completed, with results for white-

Table 1. White-tipped dove breeding surveys in the Lower Rio Grande Valley, Texas, 1983–92.

Year	Stops (*n*)	White-tipped doves/stop
1983	401	0.97
1984	359	0.89
1985	395	0.93
1986	400	1.36
1987	400	1.02
1988	436	0.97
1989	477	0.91
1990	452	0.74
1991	318	0.77
1992	365	1.11

Table 2. White-tipped dove harvest estimates for the Special White-winged Dove Season in the Lower Rio Grande Valley, Texas, 1984–92.

Year	Hunters (*n*)	Harvested (*n*)
1984	59,940	11,917
1985	Season closed	
1986	29,299	2,127
1987	31,919	3,863
1988	27,743	2,054
1989	22,564	2,677
1990[a]	25,167	1,237
1991[a]	10,642	1,406
1992	11,333	1,440

[a] Two-day hunting season.

tipped doves similar to those in previous investigations (K. A. Arnold, Texas A&M Univ., pers. commun.).

White-tipped doves have become more important to hunters since the 1970's. In 1979, illegal possession of white-tipped doves in hunter bags constituted 31% of the total violations in southern Texas. As a result, the Texas Parks and Wildlife Department developed a call-count survey that could be used to estimate trends in the annual breeding population. The resulting white-tipped dove call-count survey is currently being conducted each year simultaneously with the white-winged dove survey. Results of these annual surveys suggest that calls/stop have remained relatively stable during the past 10 years (Table 1).

HARVEST

White-tipped doves became legal game beginning with the 1984 hunting season (Homerstad 1984). During the 1984 special white-winged dove hunting season along the Rio Grande, 2 white-tipped doves per day were allowed in the aggregate bag limit of 10 doves. Two white-tipped doves also were allowed daily during the regular mourning dove season statewide that same year. The special white-winged dove season (and concurrent white-tipped dove hunting) was closed the next year (1985) due to loss of nesting habitat associated with a severe freeze in December 1983. The special white-winged dove hunting season reopened in 1986, and usually consists of 4 one-half days during the first 2 weekends in September. During the regular Texas mourning dove season (70 days), 2 white-tipped doves are allowed in the daily bag throughout the state, even though white-

tipped doves currently occur only in southern Texas.

Estimates of hunting pressure and harvest during the special white-winged dove season and the regular mourning dove season are obtained through hunter questionnaires mailed to a random sample of hunters purchasing a White-winged Dove Stamp (required to take white-winged doves). Trends in hunter numbers over the 8 years of white-tipped dove hunting indicate an overall decline in the Lower Rio Grande Valley where most white-tipped doves are harvested (Table 2). This dramatic decline in hunter numbers during the white-winged dove hunt is most likely due to decreases in white-winged dove populations resulting from 2 freezes and a drought that adversely affected breeding habitat, and to restrictive hunting regulations. The total number of white-tipped doves harvested per year (1,200–3,900) has been more stable (except 1984) than number of hunters.

MANAGEMENT NEEDS
Habitat Management

The greatest threat to maintaining a white-tipped dove breeding population in southern Texas is the continual loss of native brush habitat to agricultural and urban development. Most native brush is restricted to near the river in the Lower Rio Grande Valley, adjacent to irrigation canals and drainage ditches, around resacas (oxbow lakes), or in areas that are not suitable for agriculture or other development. Only 4–6% of the original riparian and delta brush remains in the Valley (U.S. Fish and Wildl. Serv. 1983). Over 50% of the native brush that still exists has been acquired by either the state of Texas for white-winged dove management, or by the U.S. Fish and Wildlife Service as part of a wildlife corridor acquisition project. The 2 freezes in 1983 and 1989 reduced the citrus habitat by 80–90% (from 28,000 to 6,000 ha).

Population Management

Even though trends in the white-tipped dove breeding population appear to be stable, populations should be closely monitored using standardized call-count or other procedures along randomly selected routes. White-tipped doves may occur over a greater area than is presently known, and be more adaptable than believed; the white-tipped dove distribution needs to be better defined. Since they are so restrictive in their daily and seasonal movements, white-tipped doves may be candidates for translocation into suitable habitats in unoccupied areas.

The current harvest surveys may be providing misleading information on location and size of the white-tipped dove harvest as the result of inadequate sampling. The sampling method should be examined and redesigned, if necessary, to provide more precise estimates of harvest and distribution.

RESEARCH NEEDS

1. More research is needed to answer basic life history questions such as annual productivity, food habits, and water requirements. The answers to these questions may allow current efforts to better manage for other wildlife species (e.g., white-winged doves).
2. Banding is needed to provide data on survival and harvest rates, as well as documenting that populations do not migrate.
3. Improved population surveys should be developed. The call-count survey for white-tipped doves, currently conducted only in the Lower Rio Grande Valley, should be expanded to the rest of southern Texas. This could be accomplished with a slight modification of mourning dove call counts on routes in southern Texas or other parts of the state.
4. Improved harvest surveys should be developed. Current mail questionnaire surveys are adequate to estimate harvest. However, due to the large number of hunters that hunt in parts of the state that do not have any white-tipped doves, there needs to be either more information on identification of doves on the questionnaire, or a separate telephone fol-

lowup survey to identify true harvest locations.

RECOMMENDATIONS

1. Management is a local responsibility that should be shared by the Texas Parks and Wildlife Department and the U.S. Fish and Wildlife Service within the national refuges, state parks, and wildlife management areas in southern Texas.
2. Information on basic life history (e.g., the number of nests per year, nest success, preferred nest trees, etc.) is a priority.
3. Current management and habitat acquisition efforts by both state and federal agencies need to continue because management programs that benefit white-winged doves or endangered felines also benefit white-tipped doves and many other species.

ACKNOWLEDGMENTS

White-tipped dove researchers are few and most have provided information for this chapter. In particular we acknowledge the contributions of S. J. Benn, C. P. Boydstun, V. F. Cogar, C. A. DeYoung, L. R. Ditto, J. R. Fugate, M. W. Graham, P. I. James, L. E. Krueger, and J. A. Roberson. S. C. Marquardt prepared the distribution figure. The assistance of K. L. Meinen who typed and prepared numerous drafts of this chapter is greatly appreciated.

LITERATURE CITED

AMERICAN ORNITHOLOGISTS' UNION. 1983. Checklist of North American birds. 6th Ed. Allen Press, Lawrence, Kans. 877pp.

BENT, A. C. 1932. Life histories of North American gallinaceous birds. U.S. Natl. Mus. Bull. 162. 490pp.

BOYDSTUN, C. P. 1982. Evaluations of the current status of white-fronted doves in South Texas. M.S. Thesis, Texas A&I Univ., Kingsville. 57pp.

———, AND C. A. DEYOUNG. 1985. Distribution and relative abundance of white-tipped doves in South Texas. Southwest. Nat. 30:567–571.

———, AND ———. 1987. Nesting success of white-tipped doves in South Texas. J. Wildl. Manage. 51:791–793.

———, AND ———. 1988. Movements of white-tipped doves in southern Texas. Southwest. Nat. 33:365–367.

GOODWIN, D. 1967. Pigeons and doves of the world. Brit. Mus. Nat. Hist. Cornell Univ. Press. Ithaca, N.Y. 446pp.

HOMERSTAD, G. E. 1984. Texas' newest game bird. Texas Parks and Wildl. 42(9):8–11.

LEOPOLD, A. S. 1959. Wildlife of Mexico. Univ. California Press, Berkeley. 568pp.

OBERHOLSER, H. C. 1974. The bird life of Texas. Univ. Texas Press, Austin. 1,069pp.

SKUTCH, A. F. 1964. Life histories of Central American pigeons. Wilson Bull. 76:211–247.

U.S. FISH AND WILDLIFE SERVICE. 1983. Land protection plan for Lower Rio Grande Valley National Wildlife Refuge. Unpubl. Final Rep., Region II, Albuquerque, N.M. 64pp.

Chapter 5

BAND-TAILED PIGEON

CLAIT E. BRAUN, Colorado Division of Wildlife, Wildlife Research Center, 317 West Prospect Road, Fort Collins, CO 80526

Abstract: Two populations (Coastal and Interior) of band-tailed pigeons (*Columba fasciata*) exist north of Mexico. Breeding occurs in mixed conifer woodlands from British Columbia south into California in Coastal areas and northern Colorado and central Utah south into Mexico in the Interior. Winter-use areas are primarily in southern California and Mexico. Band-tailed pigeons have low productivity but high survival. Population size is highest in Coastal areas and lowest in the Interior. Habitat problems appear to be most severe and increasing in Coastal areas. Management efforts in the immediate past have been hindered by a lack of funding and uniformly approved and implemented management plans. Major challenges include development and initiation of surveys (e.g., population, harvest, wing collection), identifying habitat requirements, and establishing consistent sources of funding for management and research. Although band-tailed pigeon research and management efforts generally have declined since 1977, major needs identified in 1977 are still germane today. However, there is a greater urgency to accomplish them because of demonstrated population declines in the Coastal population. Fortunately, there appears to be renewed interest in pigeon management and research in both geographic areas north of Mexico. The most important management and research needs are identified and prioritized.

DESCRIPTION

Two subspecies of band-tailed pigeons are recognized north of Mexico with the Interior race (*C. f. fasciata*) (referred to as the Four Corners population) breeding primarily in the Rocky Mountains south of Wyoming. The Coastal race (*C. f. monilis*) (referred to as the Pacific Coast population) occurs primarily west of the crest of the Cascade–Sierra Nevada ranges from British Columbia and southeast Alaska south into Baja California (Am. Ornithol. Union 1957). Seasonally, some band-tailed pigeons occur in scattered localities along the eastern flank of the Cascade–Sierra Nevada ranges (Jeffrey 1977). Although the races are geographically separated, some interchange occurs between the 2 populations (Schroeder and Braun 1993).

Both races of band-tailed pigeons are robust and are similar in appearance. Adults are blue-gray overall with a white crescent on the iridescent nape of the neck, have yellow legs and feet, a yellow bill tipped with black, dark wings, and a long tail with a prominent black zone tipped with a wide, pale gray band from which the species draws its name (Ridgway 1916) (Fig. 1). The Interior race is somewhat smaller and has lower adult body mass (rarely >400 g) (C. E. Braun, unpubl. data) than the Coastal race (adults usually >400 g) (Drewien et al. 1966; F. J. Ward, unpubl. data). The Coastal race of band-tailed pigeons is generally darker than the Interior race but sufficient overlap occurs to make plumage coloration a poor criterion for subspecific separation. Males and females differ in both races; males are larger and have more purple or pinkish coloration than the brownish-colored females (Braun et al. 1975, Braun 1976, Passmore and Jarvis 1979). Immatures are gray with pale gray feet and bills, no neck crescent, and have buffy-edged wing coverts and primaries (Silovsky et al. 1968, White and Braun 1978).

LIFE HISTORY

Northward migration of band-tailed pigeons from winter-use areas begins in March–early April with first arrivals observed primarily where artificial food sources are abundant (e.g., livestock feeding areas, old grain fields, suburban bird feeders) (Neff 1947, Smith 1968, Fitzhugh 1970, Braun 1976). The number of birds observed in breeding areas increases during April and May with spring migration assumed to be terminated by early June.

Depending upon location of breeding and natal areas, and possibly food availability (Neff 1947, Gutierrez et al. 1975), fall migration is initiated in September and continues through October (Neff 1947, Smith 1968, Jarvis and Passmore 1992, Schroeder and Braun 1993). Little is known about sequence and speed of migration, although adults that complete nesting early

Fig. 1.   Adult band-tailed pigeon (Photo by R. B. Gill).

are believed to be the first to migrate. Migration can either be slow with pigeons lingering in summer-use areas (probably related to food availability) or relatively swift (Schroeder and Braun 1993). Not all pigeon populations are migratory in the Coastal area (Smith 1968) and records of pigeons remaining in northern California (Neff 1947, Fitzhugh 1970) and as far north as the Fraser Lowlands and Vancouver Island (Campbell et al. 1990) during late fall and winter are not uncommon.

Adult band-tailed pigeons have high fidelity (>90% of all recaptures in subsequent years are within 50 km of banding locale) to areas where initially captured (presumed nesting areas) (Braun 1972, Kautz 1977, Curtis 1981, Jarvis and Passmore 1992, Schroeder and Braun 1993). Studies of radio-marked band-tailed pigeons (Curtis and Braun 1983a) indicated that most marked adults feed (and are captured) within 15 km of nesting sites. Schroeder and Braun (1993) reported that 299 females banded as immatures were recaptured in later years an average of 36.7 km from initial banding location, while 298 immature males were recaptured an average of 26.0 km from initial banding locations. These average distances are slightly longer than those of adult males (16.0 km) and females (20.8 km). Thus, most immature band-tailed pigeons that are recaptured return as breeding adults to the general area where they were reared.

Band-tailed pigeons are monogamous but length of pair bond is unknown. Pairing is probably initiated in winter flocks as courtship behavior has been observed in winter-use areas (C.

E. Braun, pers. observ.) and during migration (Peeters 1962). Courtship activities of males (calling, bowing, chases, and circular glide flights) (Peeters 1962) are most frequently observed at foraging sites from May into early August (Glover 1953, Curtis 1981). While most pigeons are apparently paired during spring and summer, unmated males occur in feeding aggregations throughout the breeding period (Glover 1953, Peeters 1962, Curtis 1981). Cooing vocalizations by band-tailed pigeons may occur at any time of the day and probably throughout the year (C. E. Braun, pers. observ.), depending on location (Gutierrez et al. 1975). However, cooing tends to increase in March and reaches highest frequencies in May–July (Keppie et al. 1970). Initiation of calling is closely associated with time of sunrise and is thought to be related to light intensity (Sisson 1968, Keppie 1973).

Nesting band-tailed pigeons may be territorial (Glover 1953, Peeters 1962) although Neff (1947), based on reports of others, suggested that communal nesting may occur. Studies of radio-marked band-tailed pigeons in Colorado indicate the Interior race, at least, is a solitary nester (Curtis and Braun 1983a). Nests of band-tailed pigeons are loosely constructed and are often little more than twig platforms (Glover 1953, MacGregor and Smith 1955, Peeters 1962, Curtis and Braun 1983a). Nest height, location in tree, shrub or tree type, age of tree or shrub, elevation, and aspect vary greatly throughout the species' range (Neff 1947, Glover 1953, MacGregor and Smith 1955, Peeters 1962, Curtis and Braun 1983a). Conifers are used most frequently for nesting, with nests 4–10 m above ground near the bole in dense foliage. Trees used for nesting tend to be on edges of openings or on steep slopes (Neff and Niedrach 1946, Peeters 1962). Both sexes cooperate in nest construction (Peeters 1962), although the female does most of the twig placement (Willard 1916, Peeters 1962). Trees used for nesting may be used repeatedly (Bent 1932, MacGregor and Smith 1955, Peeters 1962); this may give an appearance of communal nesting in areas where nests may persist for several years.

Active nests of band-tailed pigeons have been reported in some portion of the species' range in every month of the year (Swarth 1900, Thayer 1909, Stephens 1913, Lamb 1926, Abbott 1927, Vorhies 1928, Allen 1941, Neff 1947, MacGregor and Smith 1955). However, north of

Mexico most nests are initiated from early May through August (Grinnell 1913, Michael 1928, Neff 1947, Glover 1953, MacGregor and Smith 1955, Peeters 1962).

Crop gland activity and gonadal development have been used to examine the breeding cycle of band-tailed pigeons (Houston 1963, March and Sadleir 1970, Ziegler 1971, Gutierrez et al. 1975). Pigeons in northern California and British Columbia arrive and remain in breeding condition until late summer (Houston 1963, March and Sadleir 1970), with crop gland activity being highest in August (March and Sadleir 1970, Ziegler 1971, March and McKeown 1973). In the Interior population, band-tailed pigeons breed from May through August with gonadal regression beginning in September (Gutierrez et al. 1975). Studies of gonadal material (March and Sadleir 1970, Gutierrez et al. 1975) indicate that 2 nestings may be attempted per season. Most nests contain only 1 egg, but clutches of 2 have been reported in the wild (Neff 1947, MacGregor and Smith 1955, Fitzhugh 1970). Guitierrez et al. (1975) found that 8% of females may lay 2 eggs/clutch.

Timing of nesting is variable and depends on food availability (Gutierrez et al. 1975). Band-tailed pigeons are capable of breeding when light periods are as short as 10 hours/day. Thus, in years with good food supplies, pigeons may breed and nest early with several nesting attempts throughout the favorable period. If early food supplies are poor, they may delay breeding to take advantage of late food abundance (Gutierrez et al. 1975).

The incubation period is 19–20 days (Neff 1947, MacGregor and Smith 1955); both members of the pair incubate the egg(s) (Neff 1947, MacGregor and Smith 1955, Peeters 1962). Based on capture records away from the nest during the nesting season, females predominated in trap samples after 1000 MDT and before 1600 MDT, with males dominating captures before 1000 MDT. Sexes were equally represented in samples captured after 1600 MDT (Braun et al. 1975). Jarvis and Passmore (1992) reported similar schedules for band-tailed pigeons observed/captured at mineral sites in Oregon. Both sexes feed the nestling(s) for 20–28 days until the young fledge (Neff and Niedrach 1946; MacGregor and Smith 1955; Peeters 1962; J. A. White, unpubl. data; C. E. Braun, pers. observ.). Males may continue feeding fledglings after they leave the nest (J. A. White and C. E. Braun,

unpubl. data). Captive females are able to initiate a second clutch before the initial young has fledged. These observations suggest the assumed length of nesting cycle (40–49 days) can be truncated under ideal conditions (ad libitum food) (J. A. White and C. E. Braun, unpubl. data).

Young band-tailed pigeons are fed crop milk that is regurgitated by adults (Neff 1947, Peeters 1962, Ziegler 1971). Examination of crops with active (Ziegler 1971) glands indicates that different stages occur that are related to amount of crop milk produced (March and Sadleir 1970). By late stages of nestling development, young may be obtaining mostly regurgitated seeds and fruits. Calcium intake by adults is extremely important during the nesting cycle, especially during rearing of young prior to fledging (March and Sadleir 1972, 1975; March and McKeown 1973). Numerous studies have demonstrated the importance of mineral springs or mineral graveling sites as sources of calcium (Neff 1947, Morse 1950, Einarsen 1953, Fitzhugh 1970, Jarvis and Passmore 1992). Use of mineral sites is most notable in the Coastal population (particularly in Oregon and Washington) and, to a much lesser extent, in the Interior population (Packard 1946, Fitzhugh 1970). These differences may be moisture related, as pigeons in both populations should have similar mineral needs. Most mineral needs in the Interior population are probably met by abrasion of grit that, at least in Colorado, is highly basic (C. E. Braun, unpubl. data).

Diets of band-tailed pigeons vary seasonally and with location. New buds and flowers of a variety of deciduous trees and shrubs, especially oak (*Quercus*), madrone (*Arbutus*), elder (*Sambucus*), cherry (*Prunus*), cascara (*Rhamnus*), huckleberry (*Vaccinium*), and *Rubus* are important in spring and fruits of these species become important as they develop and mature (Gilman 1903, Neff 1947, Glover 1953, Peeters 1962, Smith 1968, March and Sadleir 1972, Fry and Vaughn 1977, Jarvis and Passmore 1992). This list is not all inclusive, as most flowering and fruiting shrubs and trees within the range of band-tailed pigeons are used as a food source at some time (Neff 1947). Pigeons also use a variety of cultivated crops including fruits of olives, grapes, and cherries, and seeds of wheat, peas, barley, corn, and oats. Use of cultivated crops is especially prevalent in early spring and winter for the Coastal population, and throughout April–October for the Interior race.

Fig. 2. Band-tailed pigeons commonly forage on waste grain (Photo by C. E. Braun).

Braun (1973) speculated that abundance of pigeons in Colorado was dependent upon distribution of grain fields in mountainous areas. Food availability strongly influences timing and duration of band-tailed pigeon nesting (Gutierrez et al. 1975). Natural foods are preferred, but band-tailed pigeons readily exploit waste or stored grains and even bird feeders. Corn seems to be the most preferred grain, possibly because of the size of kernels, but field peas and wheat also are readily consumed. Barley and oats are used, but not as extensively. Once band-tailed pigeons start feeding on a specific food, they tend to specialize on that food until it is no longer available. Band-tailed pigeons do not alight on standing grain, and field feeding is on waste or shattered grains (Fig. 2). However, they feed on cut barley before harvest (C. E. Braun and J. E. Kautz, pers. observ.), shocked wheat (Neff 1947), and have been suspected of feeding on sprouting grain (Neff 1947, Smith 1968). Observations and collections in Colorado (C. E. Braun, unpubl. data) and California (Smith 1968) demonstrated that pigeons only took unsprouted grain from the soil surface.

Use of free water by band-tailed pigeons has been reported (Neff 1947, Einarsen 1953, Smith 1968), especially related to obtaining minerals (Jarvis and Passmore 1992). While need for water would appear to be greatest when pigeons are foraging on grains and acorns, immediate water availability should not be a problem because of the pigeon's great mobility (Schroeder and Braun 1993).

Numerous efforts have been made to estimate annual survival rates of band-tailed pigeons (Mace and Batterson 1961, Wight et al. 1967,

Smith 1968, Silovsky 1969, Braun 1972, Braun et al. 1975, Pederson and Nish 1975, Kautz and Braun 1981, Jarvis and Passmore 1992, Schroeder and Braun 1993). Some of these efforts were based on inadequate sample sizes and inappropriate analyses. Annual survival rates of adults estimated from early banding samples varied from 57% (Smith 1968) for pigeons banded in California, to 71% (Wight et al. 1967) for pigeons banded in Oregon. These studies used composite-dynamic life tables that may have introduced error (Burnham and Anderson 1979).

Annual survival estimates using Brownie-Robson models (Brownie et al. 1978) were 73% for adults and 66% for immature pigeons banded in Colorado (Kautz and Braun 1981). Schroeder and Braun (1993) reanalyzed the Colorado data set with Program JOLLYAGE using recaptures and recoveries (Pollock et al. 1990), and derived annual survival estimates of 60% (±3%, 95% CI) for adults and 53% (±7%, 95% CI) for immatures. Estimated annual survival rates for Coastal adult band-tailed pigeons varied from 60 to 77% and averaged about 67% in Washington, Oregon, and California (unpubl. data, R. E. Tomlinson, pers. commun. 1993). The estimated recovery rates for Coastal adults varied from 1.3 to 5.1% and averaged 2.8%. Recovery rates from the Interior population are lower (1.0–2.5%) than those for Coastal pigeons. However, depending on actual reporting rates, hunting mortality appears to be low in both regions.

Natural predators of band-tailed pigeons appear confined mainly to raptors (Willard 1916, McLean 1925, Bond 1946, Neff 1947, Marshall 1957, Beebe 1960, Smith 1968). Egg and squab loss may be one of the most important mortality factors (Peeters 1962). The presence of *Trichomonas gallinae* that causes trichomoniasis in band-tailed pigeons has been documented in studies in Colorado (Stabler and Matteson 1950, Stabler 1951, Stabler and Braun 1975), California (Stabler and Herman 1951, Stabler and Braun 1979), and Arizona (Sileo and Fitzhugh 1969). A California strain of *T. gallinae* has been demonstrated to be particularly lethal (Stabler and Braun 1979) and 15–16,000 pigions were estimated to have died in 1988 (D. P. Connelly, pers. commun.). A variety of other parasites has been reported from band-tailed pigeons, none of which pose a major threat to pigeon populations (Wood and Herman 1943, Stabler and Holt 1963, Olsen and Braun 1976, Pence and

Fig. 3. Foraging and nesting areas of band-tailed pigeons in south-central Colorado (Photo by C. E. Braun).

Canaris 1976, Stabler et al. 1977, Olsen and Braun 1980, Stabler and Stromberg 1981). Pesticide poisoning of pigeons may occur but is undocumented. High residues of mercury were not found to be affecting band-tailed pigeons in Colorado (Braun et al. 1977). While use of persistent pesticides has decreased in the United States, organochlorine pesticides are still commonly used in Mexico (Mora and Anderson 1991).

HABITAT

Band-tailed pigeons inhabit coniferous forests, especially pine-oak (*Pinus-Quercus*) woodlands (Neff 1947, Marshall 1957, Braun 1973, Braun et al. 1975, Pederson and Nish 1975). Interior pigeons nest in mountainous terrain with highest densities occurring at elevations of 1,600 to 2,700 m that are dominated by ponderosa pine (*P. ponderosa*) and varieties of oak, but pigeons also occur into lodgepole pine (*P. contorta*) and spruce-fir (*Picea-Pseudotsuga-Abies*) forests at higher elevations (Fig. 3). Nesting occurs in all habitat types, and foraging frequently extends to cultivated fields, along stream courses, and in livestock feeding areas (Braun et al.

1975, Braun 1976, Kautz 1977). During migration stopovers, habitats similar to those used for foraging in summer and fall (especially areas where acorns are abundant) are commonly used. Pigeons of the Interior race winter in Mexico primarily in oak-pine woodlands and montane conifer forests along the Sierra Madre Occidental (Fig. 4), but descend at times into the subtropical Sinaloan deciduous forest (Braun et al. 1975).

Band-tailed pigeons of the Coastal population use a variety of forest types, principally below 1,000 m. Some areas are dominated by species of pine and oak while others are dominated by spruce, fir (especially Douglas-fir, *Pseudotsuga menziesii*), redwood (*Sequoia sempervirens*), cedar (*Thuja*), hemlock (*Tsuga*), and alder (*Alnus*) (Neff 1947, Glover 1953, Jeffrey 1989, Jarvis and Passmore 1992). Coastal areas are floristically and structurally variable depending on logging and fire history, cultivation, and urbanization. Typical habitats used by band-tailed pigeons vary markedly from south to north: southern California (pine-oak); northern California (spruce-fir-alder); and northern Oregon through Washington (fir-hemlock-cedar-spruce) (Neff

Fig. 4.   Interior band-tailed pigeons winter in the Sierra Madre Occidental of Mexico (Photo by C. E. Braun).

1947, Glover 1953, Jeffrey 1989, Jarvis and Passmore 1992). Published reports on migration stopovers are general (Einarsen 1953, Morse 1957) and of limited value. Coastal band-tailed pigeons winter in California and Baja California primarily in pine-oak woodlands and coastal chaparral (*Adenostoma, Arctostaphylos, Ceanothus, Quercus*) (Jeffrey 1977) and adjacent agricultural areas at elevations of 10 to 500 m.

DISTRIBUTION AND ABUNDANCE

Coastal band-tailed pigeons occur (and probably breed) from extreme southeastern Alaska and western British Columbia south into Washington, Oregon, California, and extreme western Nevada, primarily west of the Cascade and Sierra Nevada ranges, into Baja California (Fig. 5). The Interior race breeds from northern Colorado and east-central Utah south through Arizona, New Mexico, extreme west Texas into the Sierra Madre Occidental of Mexico (Braun et al. 1975, Am. Ornithol. Union 1983). Coastal band-tailed pigeons winter from central California into northern Baja California. Some pi-

geons remain north of southern California along the coast in winter and may represent non-migratory populations. Interior pigeons winter from northern Mexico south to at least Michoacan (Braun et al. 1975, Am. Ornithol. Union 1983). Band-tailed pigeons in Mexico and southern California may represent both migratory and non-migratory populations.

Band-tailed pigeons breed in Mexico and South America, with similar forms breeding in Jamaica (*C. caribaea*) and Chile (*C. araucana*) (Goodwin 1970). Little is known about band-tailed pigeons south of the United States, and further study may describe additional races or conclude that *C. fasciata* is a superspecies (Goodwin 1970, Am. Ornithol. Union 1983).

Estimates of abundance are lacking because of the difficulty in locating and observing individual band-tailed pigeons. However, indices of breeding population abundance are obtained from 3 separate surveys. Band-tailed pigeons are encountered on some Breeding Bird Surveys (BBS) in British Columbia and all of the states of both the Coastal and Interior populations (Pe-

C.f. monilis

C.f. fasciata

☐ BREEDING

▨ WINTER

Fig. 5.   Distribution of band-tailed pigeons in North America (after Braun et al. 1975).

Table 1.   Trends in band-tailed pigeon breeding populations as reflected by the Breeding Bird Survey, 1968–93 (analysis provided by C. T. Moore, Natl. Biol. Surv.).

Population/state	Routes (*n*)	Annual change (%)	SE
Coastal			
British Columbia	24	−4.1**	1.9
California	98	−3.2**	1.5
Oregon	23	−2.7*	1.4
Washington	23	−4.2***	1.4
All areas	168	−3.5***	0.9
Interior			
Arizona	8	−0.6	3.7
Colorado	11	2.9	3.0
New Mexico	8	11.9	18.7
Utah	4	3.1	5.8
All areas	31	0.5	5.7

* $P < 0.10$, ** $P < 0.05$, *** $P < 0.01$.

terjohn and Sauer 1993, 1994). Audio counts of band-tailed pigeons are conducted during June in Washington (McCaughran and Jeffrey 1980, Jeffrey 1989), and visual counts are conducted during August at mineral sites in Oregon (Jarvis and Passmore 1992). The BBS surveys in the Coastal area indicate a long-term (1966–93) downward trend in British Columbia, Washington, Oregon, and California (Table 1). The BBS information fails to demonstrate trends in either direction for the Interior states, but sample sizes are low and variances are high. The annual call-count survey in Washington gives a long term (1975–93) downward population trend ($P < 0.05$) of 6% per year, and mineral spring counts in Oregon indicate a similar (1968–93) downward trend ($P < 0.01$) of 67 birds/year (West. Migratory Upland Game Bird Tech Comm. 1994). Thus, the 3 surveys all suggest that Coastal band-tailed pigeon populations have declined substantially during the past 15–30 years. Insufficient information exists to evaluate population trends in the Interior states.

Braun (unpubl. data) estimated fall population size in Colorado to be about 70,000 birds

in 1972 based on recapture rates of banded pigeons, and speculated the total size of the Interior population north of Mexico was <250,000 birds. About 4,000 pigeons were harvested each fall during the early 1970's (Braun et al. 1975). If the recovery rates during this period of 1–2% (Kautz and Braun 1981) reliably reflected the harvest, the fall population estimate of <250,000 birds in the Interior population during the early 1970's was probably reasonable. Reported harvests of band-tailed pigeons in the Coastal population between 1957 and 1987 varied from 217,000 (1976) to 724,000 (1972) and averaged 414,000 (Jarvis and Passmore 1992). Direct recovery rates for pigeons banded in the 1960's in California and Oregon were 2.3 to 5.5% (Wight et al. 1967, Smith 1968, Silovsky 1969). If a reporting rate of 32% and a crippling rate of 30% are assumed, the kill rate was between 10.3 and 24.6. Using these rates to extrapolate population size in 1972, when 724,000 birds were reported harvested, the Coastal population is estimated to have been between 2.9 and 7.1 million birds. This extrapolation is speculative, but indicates the probable disparity in size between the Coastal and Interior populations. While few data are available for speculative estimates of the size of either population, the available trend data indicate the Coastal population is markedly lower in recent years than prior to 1975. This agrees with Jarvis and Passmore's (1992) estimate that population size in the late 1980's was only 30–50% of that in the 1960's.

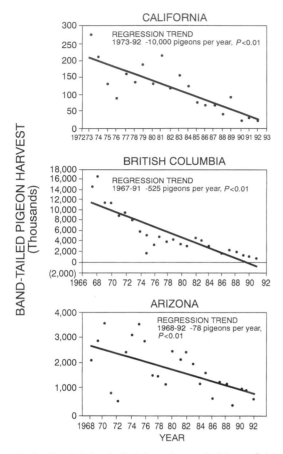

Fig. 6. Trends in band-tailed pigeon harvest in Arizona, California, and British Columbia (data provided by R. E. Tomlinson, pers. commun.).

al states during later years (the season was closed in Washington during 1991–93 by the Washington Division of Wildlife) reflected concern of managers that population levels were declining. In contrast, bag/possession limits for the Interior states have remained constant at 5/10 since the season was opened in 1968 (R. E. Tomlinson, pers. commun.).

Harvest of band-tailed pigeons in the 3 Coastal states decreased from about 550,000 birds in 1968 to 70,000 in 1988, a decline ($P < 0.01$) of 20,000 pigeons per year (Fig. 6) (West. Migratory Upland Game Bird Tech. Comm. 1994). Pigeon harvest in British Columbia also declined 525 birds/year ($P < 0.01$) from 14,000 in 1967 to under 500 in 1991 (Fig. 6) (Legris and Levesque 1991, West. Migratory Upland Game Bird Tech. Comm. 1994). Although some of the decrease in Coastal band-tailed pigeon harvest resulted from hunting season restrictions between 1976 and 1993 (including lower bag limits, shorter seasons, and delayed season opening dates), smaller population size undoubtedly also contributed to lower harvests. For the Interior population, harvests prior to 1973 generally ranged from 1,800 to 3,400 birds (Braun et al. 1975). Current data (1973–92) are not available for the Interior states, as only Arizona has maintained an adequate harvest survey. However, the Arizona harvest during 1968–91 ranged from about 3,500 birds in 1970 to 250 in 1989 (Fig. 6), and the trend ($P < 0.01$) is downward at 78 pigeons/year (R. E. Tomlinson, pers. commun.).

HARVEST

Hunting of band-tailed pigeons is administered jointly by federal (U.S. and Canada) and state/provincial wildlife agencies. Federal governments generally work in conjunction with appropriate state/provincial wildlife agencies to establish frameworks under which state/provincial agencies select season dates and bag limits. United States frameworks permitted bag/possession limits as follows for the Coastal population: 1932–75, 6/6 to 10/10; 1976–86, 5/5 (6/6 in California during 1976–78); 1987–88, 4/4; 1989–93, 2/2 (West. Migratory Upland Game Bird Tech. Comm. 1994). Band-tailed pigeons were also hunted in Nevada in 1981–91, but harvests were so small the hunt was discontinued (J. C. Bartonek, pers. commun.). Limits in British Columbia were 10/20 from 1976 to 1990 and 5/10 in 1991–92. Restrictive limits in Coast-

MANAGEMENT NEEDS
Habitat Management

Detailed knowledge of habitats essential for maintenance of stable breeding populations of band-tailed pigeons is limited. The major components of pigeon habitat appear to be suitable and secure forested nesting areas, foraging sites (including mineral sources), and escape/roosting habitats. Widespread alteration of nesting and foraging habitats may be partly responsible for long-term declines in Coastal populations and should be evaluated. Investigations should concentrate on areas where forestry practices have reduced old-growth forests to remnants and replaced them with even-age monocultures of fast-growing conifers. Modern silvicultural practices, including use of herbicides to control deciduous shrubs/trees, have the potential to greatly reduce berry-producing plants throughout the range of band-tailed pigeons, especially in Coastal areas from northern California into British Columbia. These foraging areas (including mineral sources) are important for band-tailed pigeons, as food availability appears to affect timing and duration of nesting (Gutierrez et al. 1975) and probably nesting success and fledging rates. Controlled manipulation of foraging areas appears possible, and could stabilize and improve reproductive success.

Pigeons are easily attracted to grain at livestock feeding sites, storage areas, harvested crop fields, bird feeders, etc. This is especially true for the Interior population during all seasons, and for the Coastal population during spring migration, early summer before mast becomes available, and during fall migration. Data from Colorado (Braun 1976, Kautz 1977, Curtis 1981, Curtis and Braun 1983*b*) and California (F. J. Ward, unpubl. data) indicate that band-tailed pigeons can be easily attracted to artificial bait sites maintained specifically for them. Furthermore, pigeons use these sites throughout the breeding season in Colorado (Kautz 1977, Curtis 1981). Thus, management of foraging areas specifically for band-tailed pigeons should be possible to stabilize and increase production.

Research is needed to provide detailed information on preferred habitats used throughout all life processes of band-tailed pigeons for both populations. For example, do breeding pigeons prefer continuously forested tracts, or areas with numerous open areas created by fire or other factors? Experimental manipulation of habitat types is needed to learn how pigeons respond to logging and associated forestry practices (e.g., controlled fires, herbicidal control of deciduous trees and shrubs, even-age tree management, and clear vs. selective cutting practices). It is important to understand how size of areas logged and managed for regeneration of forests affects pigeon nesting and movements.

Efforts also are needed at migration stopover and winter-use sites to identify habitat components attractive to and essential for band-tailed pigeons. Suburban areas should be included in consideration of pigeon habitat, as they appear to attract substantial numbers of pigeons for breeding/nesting and foraging. Suburban areas also may contribute to transmission of trichomoniasis through interactions with other native and non-native columbids at feeding and watering areas. Management to improve habitats and alleviate conditions in chronic problem areas could have important benefits to band-tailed pigeons over a larger area. Thus, funding for sustained management and research is needed and has the highest priority.

Population Management

Although a small amount of interchange of individuals occurs between the 2 identifiable band-tailed pigeon populations (Schroder and Braun 1993), management has been and should be continued separately. Furthermore, consideration should be given to regulating subpopulations (Braun 1972, Jarvis and Passmore 1992), as there are sufficient data to indicate that band-tailed pigeons have fidelity to breeding areas (Kautz 1977, Jarvis and Passmore 1992, Schroeder and Braun 1993). Thus, separate hunting regulations could be established for different regions within a state (Braun 1972). This measure could provide special protection of local breeding populations when and where needed (Jarvis and Passmore 1992). Regulation of pigeon harvest in areas away from breeding habitats needs further research.

At present there is no standardized population survey technique for band-tailed pigeons throughout their range, despite substantial efforts to develop a call-count survey (Sisson 1968, Keppie et al. 1970, Fitzhugh 1974, Keppie 1977, McCaughran and Jeffrey 1980). This technique is being used in Washington (Jeffrey 1989), but it appears to have limited utility throughout the breeding range of both populations because of low pigeon densities and poor access (few roads) in suitable breeding habitats (Jeffrey 1989).

Pigeons are systematically counted at approximately 25 mineral sites during August in Oregon (Jarvis and Passmore 1992), and 9 consistently-run counts are used as annual indices to population trends (West. Migratory Upland Game Bird Tech. Comm. 1994). This technique may have limitations, as locations of all mineral sites used by pigeons are not known (thus, a random sample cannot be drawn for surveys), pigeons in some areas (especially in the Interior) use mineral sites sparingly or not at all, and timing of use may depend upon the types of food available. Furthermore, pigeons do not use mineral sites equally in all areas of their range. Further evaluation of mineral site counts as a monitoring technique for band-tailed pigeons is needed.

Breeding Bird Surveys coordinated by the U.S. Fish and Wildlife Service and Canadian Wildlife Service presently appear to have limited use for detecting trends in band-tailed pigeon populations within their range because of sparse placement of routes, low densities of pigeons, and inadequate sampling of appropriate habitats. Braun (1976) and Kautz (1977) suggested monitoring pigeon populations by flocks based on capture-recapture. However, this method is costly and not feasible for many flocks, and may result in reduction of band reporting rates. Curtis and Braun (1983b) recommended establishing permanent feeding stations in selected breeding areas and using periodic counts of pigeons at these sites to estimate trends in populations. This technique may be possible in some areas when food is limiting (Kautz 1977, Curtis 1981), but has not been tested over large areas. Other census methods have been attempted (Jeffrey 1977) and discontinued because of apparent low densities, irregular distribution, poor access, etc. Thus, despite considerable effort and expense, there is still a need to develop survey methods to reliably estimate population trends of band-tailed pigeons throughout their range.

Considerable numbers of band-tailed pigeons were banded during the mid 1960's to mid 1970's; the information on survival rates, recovery rates, and distribution of recoveries provided a better understanding of population dynamics. Since these data are now 20–30 years old, consideration should be given to initiate new banding programs to obtain up-to-date information for comparison. Experience in Colorado (Braun 1976, Kautz 1977, Curtis 1981, Curtis and Braun 1983b) and California (F. J. Ward, unpub. data) indicate that band-tailed pigeons are easy to attract to bait sites for capture. Thus, efficient banding programs can apparently be established and maintained for as many years as needed.

Knowledge of harvest age ratios can provide estimates of annual productivity and recruitment. Wing surveys were extensively used in the early 1970's in the range of the Interior population, and were beneficial in understanding timing of nesting, productivity, and migration (Braun et al. 1975). Wing surveys have been conducted sporadically in Oregon and (more recently) throughout California and Oregon. Sample sizes and distribution of wing surveys should be improved to better understand population dynamics of band-tailed pigeons. However, caution should be used in interpreting wing survey data because of differential vulnerability of juveniles and adults to harvest (Kautz 1977, Kautz and Braun 1981, Jarvis and Passmore 1992). Also, early age ratios may have been biased downward because of poorly developed external wing age classification techniques.

Harvest Management

States in the Coastal area conduct mail-questionnaire harvest surveys of general license holders to estimate trends in band-tailed pigeon harvest, but procedures and sampling rates vary by state. In some years, surveys were not conducted, leaving gaps in the data base. Thus, the quality of data used to construct the band-tailed pigeon harvest trend in Coastal states (Fig. 6) may be compromised to an unknown extent. Band-tailed pigeon hunters in British Columbia are required to have a federal migratory bird hunting permit. The permittees have been sampled through annual harvest surveys conducted by the Canadian Wildlife Service since 1964 (Benson 1968, 1971; Cooch et al. 1973). However, the sampling error has been great and harvest estimates were accompanied by high variances. Nevertheless, all 3-state and the province estimates probably reflect long-term trends in harvests (West. Migratory Upland Game Bird Tech. Comm. 1994). Since 1992, harvest estimates have improved as the result of mandatory state-issued permits which provide a sampling frame for questionnaire surveys.

The Four Corners states implemented hunting of band-tailed pigeons of the Interior population under state permit requirements in the late 1960's and early 1970's (Braun et al. 1975). All pigeon hunters were required to have a permit; names and addresses from these permits were the basis for sampling hunters (usually 100% surveys) about their hunting activities. These permits were subsequently discontinued (except in Arizona and Utah) because band-tailed pigeon hunter activity and harvest were low, and administrators did not perceive the value of long-term data collection. In recent years, some states of the Interior area have obtained pigeon harvest data from questionnaires mailed to samples of general license buyers. However, the few pigeon hunters in each state are rarely contacted because of low sampling intensity. Thus, projections for statewide harvest levels have little validity because of high variances around the estimates.

A uniform means of deriving harvest data for each population (Interior and Coastal) is needed. A National Migratory Bird Harvest Information Program was proposed and implemented (U.S. Fish and Wildl. Serv. 1992, 1993) that will provide a suitable sampling frame for band-tailed pigeons. However, implementation will not be complete for all states until 1998. Permits to hunt pigeons are now required in all states and harvest surveys are conducted by the individual states using lists of permittees. Efforts must be made to ensure that these 2 methods are smoothly integrated so that annual harvest estimates can be compared over time to provide long-term trends.

RESEARCH NEEDS

Funding for research on band-tailed pigeons has been limited since cessation in 1982 of the Accelerated Research Program for Migratory Shore and Upland Game Birds that was initiated in 1968 (Sandfort 1977). Reasons for inadequate funding for band-tailed pigeon research and management are attributed to lack of support by federal, state, and private agencies and individuals because: population size has been relatively low, population declines were not recognized until recently, and pigeon hunting was not as popular as hunting other migratory birds such as waterfowl. Because of the uncertain status of both populations, funding for sustained management and research is urgently needed and has the highest priority. Research needs in descending order of priority follow.

1. Develop separate integrated, cooperative management/research plans for both populations of pigeons north of Mexico. This has recently (1994) been accomplished for the Pacific Coast population.
2. Develop reliable population monitoring techniques for use throughout the range of band-tailed pigeons. Past experience suggests that techniques associated with pigeon foraging have the best chances of success.
3. Examine the effects of forestry management practices (e.g., clear-cutting and herbicide use) on nest densities, nest success, annual production, and recruitment to breeding populations especially as related to food abundance and availability.
4. Investigate the relationship of food (including minerals) to timing and duration of breeding/nesting. If a clear relationship is demonstrated, nest success and production of pigeons may be enhanced by food/mineral provisioning.
5. Test field procedures to control outbreaks of trichomoniasis in migration stopover and winter-use sites, especially in suburban areas.
6. Describe the seasonal habitats essential for maintaining pigeon populations. The lack of information on how Coastal pigeons use habitats is especially acute.
7. Derive estimates of hunting crippling loss by habitat types. Unretrieved kill is believed to be one-half to equal the retrieved harvest although data to support this contention are lacking.
8. Examine the incidence of early season harvest (<20 Sep) and its effects on annual production and survival of breeding adults.
9. Investigate the ecology of pigeons in winter-use areas, especially in relation to agricultural and forest management practices and daily movements. This need may be urgent for pigeons from the Interior population that winter in Mexico.
10. Experiment with hunting regulations in areas used primarily for breeding, migration, and winter-use to learn at what harvest levels subpopulations or flocks are negatively affected. This will require intensive banding efforts in breeding and winter-use areas.
11. Examine use of harvest age ratios as a measure of annual productivity. Are early migration of progeny of first nests and interrupted molting of primaries/secondaries important problems confusing identification of immature pigeons and use of harvest age ratios?
12. Evaluate the reproductive performance and survival patterns of resident vs. migratory populations, especially those associated with suburban areas.
13. Examine the relationships of resident and migratory populations of band-tailed pigeons in northern and central Mexico. Do populations use habitats differentially, temporally and spatially?
14. Examine the genetic differences, using mtDNA, between band-tailed pigeons of the Coastal and Interior populations, and those seasonally resident throughout Mexico and Central America.

RECOMMENDATIONS

1. Develop a consistent source of funding for management and research.
2. Implement integrated, cooperative management/research plans for both populations of pigeons north of Mexico. Periodically examine and revise the plans as necessary.
3. Implement a range-wide, uniform harvest monitoring program.
4. Implement population monitoring surveys that have reasonable chances for success.
5. Initiate research on effects of forest management practices on pigeon nesting and production.
6. Manage selected areas specifically for band-tailed pigeons. This could involve both breeding and winter-use areas.
7. Implement regulations to reduce harvest of pigeons in breeding and nesting/squab rearing areas.
8. Implement annual or periodic wing collections in major harvest areas to derive long-term estimates of changes in productivity.
9. Initiate intensive banding efforts in localized breeding areas to estimate annual recovery and survival rates.
10. Initiate research on the relationship of food and mineral abundance on timing and duration of nesting.

ACKNOWLEDGMENTS

Preparation of this chapter was facilitated by the Colorado Division of Wildlife's tolerance of my interest in band-tailed pigeons and by their initial assignment of my position to conduct research on this species starting in 1969. I thank W. W. Sandfort (now retired) for his enlightened leadership during that period. Many people shared ideas and field work with me on pigeons. I especially thank F. J. Ward and H. M. Wight (both deceased) for stimulating me to think about Coastal band-tailed pigeons, R. M. Stabler and O. W. Olsen (both deceased) for encouraging me to examine the effects of parasites on pigeon ecology, H. M. Reeves and R. E. Tomlinson for forcing me to be critical and providing encouragement, R. F. McDonald and K. P. Baer (both deceased) for field support in Colorado (RFM) and Mexico (KPB), and the dedicated pigeon trappers that worked within Colorado. These included J. E. Kautz, J. A. White, M. R. Stromberg, and P. D. Curtis. I especially thank my family (particularly JAB and NJKB) for allowing pigeons into their life. This manuscript was improved by the reviews of J. C. Bartonek, R. L. Jarvis, J. E. Kautz, L. A. Robb, M. A. Schroeder, T. C. Tacha, and R. E. Tomlinson. However, I take full responsibility for all speculation and interpretation of the data available. This is a joint contribution from the Accelerated Research Program for Migratory Shore and Upland Game Birds (1969–82) and the Colorado Division of Wildlife, Federal Aid in Wildlife Restoration Projects W-88-R and W-167-R.

LITERATURE CITED

ABBOTT, C. G. 1927. Notes on the nesting of the band-tailed pigeon. Condor 29:121–123.

ALLEN, W. I. 1941. Nesting of band-tailed pigeons of Altadena, California. Condor 43:156–157.

AMERICAN ORNITHOLOGISTS' UNION. 1957. Check-list of North American birds. 5th ed. Lord Baltimore Press, Baltimore, Md. 691pp.

———. 1983. Check-list of North American birds. 6th ed. Allen Press, Lawrence, Kans. 877pp.

BEEBE, F. L. 1960. The marine peregrines of the northwest Pacific coast. Condor 62:145–189.

BENT, A. C. 1932. Life histories of North American gallinaceous birds: Orders Galliformes and Columbiformes. U.S. Natl. Mus. Bull. 162. 490pp.

BENSON, D. A. 1968. Waterfowl harvest and hunter activity in Canada during the 1967–68 hunting season. Can. Wildl. Serv. Prog. Notes 5. 6pp.

———. 1971. Report on sales of the Canada migratory game bird hunting permit and waterfowl harvest and hunter activity, 1970. Can. Wildl. Serv. Prog. Notes 22. 29pp.

BOND, R. M. 1946. The peregrine population of western North America. Condor 48:101–116.

BRAUN, C. E. 1972. Movements and hunting mortality of Colorado band-tailed pigeons. Trans. North Am. Wildl. and Nat. Resour. Conf. 37: 326–334.

———. 1973. Distribution and habitats of band-tailed pigeons in Colorado. Proc. West. Assoc. State Game and Fish Comm. 53:336–344.

———. 1976. Methods for locating, trapping and banding band-tailed pigeons in Colorado. Colorado Div. Wildl. Spec. Rep. 39. 20pp.

———, W. J. ADRIAN, AND R. E. KEISS. 1977. Mercury residues in Colorado band-tailed pigeons. J. Wildl. Manage. 41:131–134.

———, D. E. BROWN, J. C. PEDERSON, AND T. P. ZAPATKA. 1975. Results of the Four Corners cooperative band-tailed pigeon investigation. U.S. Fish and Wildl. Serv., Resour. Publ. 126. 20pp.

BROWNIE, C., D. R. ANDERSON, K. P. BURNHAM, AND D. S. ROBSON. 1978. Statistical inference from band recovery data—A handbook. U.S. Fish and Wildl. Serv., Resour. Publ. 131. 212pp.

BURNHAM, K. P., AND D. R. ANDERSON. 1979. The composite dynamic method as evidence for age-specific waterfowl mortality. J. Wildl. Manage. 43:356–366.

CAMPBELL, R. W., N. K. DAWE, I. McTAGGART-

COWAN, J. M. COOPER, G. W. KAISER, AND M. C. E. McNALL. 1990. The birds of British Columbia. Vol. II. Royal British Columbia Mus., Victoria. 636 pp.

COOCH, F. G., G. W. KAISER, AND L. WICHT. 1973. Report on 1972 sales of the Canada migratory game bird hunting permit, migratory game bird harvest and hunter activity. Can. Wildl. Serv. Prog. Notes 34. 10pp.

CURTIS, P. D. 1981. Evaluation of daily counts of band-tailed pigeons as a census method. M.S. Thesis, Colorado State Univ., Fort Collins. 113pp.

———, AND C. E. BRAUN. 1983*a*. Radiotelemetry location of nesting band-tailed pigeons in Colorado. Wilson Bull. 95:464–466.

———, AND ———. 1983*b*. Recommendations for establishment and placement of bait sites for counting band-tailed pigeons. Wildl. Soc. Bull. 11:364–366.

DREWIEN, R. C., R. J. VERNIMEN, S. W. HARRIS, AND C. F. YOCOM. 1966. Spring weights of band-tailed pigeons. J. Wildl. Manage. 30:190–192.

EINARSEN, A. S. 1953. Problems of the band-tailed pigeon. Proc. West. Assoc. State Game and Fish Comm. 33:140–146.

FITZHUGH, E. L. 1970. Literature review and bibliography of the band-tailed pigeon of Arizona, Colorado, New Mexico, and Utah. Arizona Game and Fish Comm. Spec. Rep. 53pp.

———. 1974. Chronology of calling, egg laying, crop gland activity, and breeding among wild band-tailed pigeons in Arizona. Ph.D. Thesis, Univ. Arizona, Tucson. 74pp.

FRY, M. E., AND C. E. VAUGHN. 1977. Acorn selection by band-tailed pigeons. Calif. Fish and Game 63:59–60.

GILMAN, M. F. 1903. More about the band-tailed pigeon (*Columba fasciata*). Condor 5:134–135.

GLOVER, F. A. 1953. A nesting study of the band-tailed pigeon (*Columba f. fasciata*) in northwestern California. Calif. Fish and Game 39: 397–407.

GOODWIN, D. 1970. Pigeons and doves of the world. 2nd ed. Brit. Mus. Nat. Hist., London, U.K. 446pp.

GRINNELL, J. 1913. The outlook for conserving the band-tailed pigeon as a game bird of California. Condor 15:25–40.

GUTIERREZ, R. J., C. E. BRAUN, AND T. P. ZAPATKA. 1975. Reproductive biology of the band-tailed pigeon in Colorado and New Mexico. Auk 92: 665–677.

HOUSTON, D. B. 1963. A contribution to the ecology of the band-tailed pigeon, *Columba fasciata*, Say. M.S. Thesis, Univ. Wyoming, Laramie. 74pp.

JARVIS, R. L., AND M. F. PASSMORE. 1992. Ecology of band-tailed pigeons in Oregon. U.S. Fish and Wildl. Serv., Biol. Rep. 6. 38pp.

JEFFREY, R. G., CHAIRMAN. 1977. Band-tailed pigeon (*Columba fasciata*). Pages 208–245 *in* G. C. Sanderson, ed. Management of migratory shore and upland game birds in North America. Int. Assoc. Fish and Wildl. Agencies, Washington, D.C.

———. 1989. The band-tailed pigeon: distribution, effects of harvest, regulations, mortality rates, and habits, 1968–79. Final Rep., Washington Dep. Wildl., Olympia. 98pp.

KAUTZ, J. E. 1977. Effects of band-tailed pigeon behavior on estimates of population parameters. M.S. Thesis, Univ. British Columbia, Vancouver. 70pp.

———, AND C. E. BRAUN. 1981. Survival and recovery rates of band-tailed pigeons in Colorado. J. Wildl. Manage. 45:214–218.

KEPPIE, D. M. 1973. Morning commencement of calling of band-tailed pigeons in Oregon. Murrelet 54:28–30.

———. 1977. Morning versus afternoon calling of band-tailed pigeons. J. Wildl. Manage. 41:320–322.

———, H. M. WIGHT, AND W. S. OVERTON. 1970. A proposed band-tailed pigeon census—a management need. Trans. North Am. Wildl. and Nat. Resour. Conf. 35:157–171.

LAMB, C. C. 1926. The Viosca pigeon. Condor 28: 262–263.

LEGRIS, A. M., AND H. LEVESQUE. 1991. Migratory game birds harvested in Canada during the 1990 hunting season. Can. Wildl. Serv. Prog. Notes 197. 40pp.

MACE, R. U., AND W. M. BATTERSON. 1961. Results of a band-tailed pigeon banding study at Nehalem, Oregon. Proc. West. Assoc. State Game and Fish Comm. 41:151–153.

MACGREGOR, W. F., AND W. M. SMITH. 1955. Nesting and reproduction of the band-tailed pigeon in California. Calif. Fish and Game 41:315–326.

MARCH, G. L., AND B. A. McKEOWN. 1973. Serum and pituitary prolactin changes in the band-tailed pigeon (*Columba fasciata*) in relation to the reproductive cycle. Can. J. Physiol. and Pharmacol. 51:583–589.

———, AND R. M. F. S. SADLEIR. 1970. Studies on the band-tailed pigeon (*Columba fasciata*) in British Columbia. I. Seasonal changes in gonadal development and crop gland activity. Can. J. Zool. 48:1353–1357.

———, AND ———. 1972. Studies on the band-tailed pigeon (*Columba fasciata*) in British Columbia. II. Food resource and mineral-graveling activity. Syesis 5:279–284.

———, AND ———. 1975. Studies on the band-tailed pigeon (*Columba fasciata*) in British Columbia. III. Seasonal changes in body weight and calcium distribution. Physiol. Zool. 48:49–56.

MARSHALL, J. T., JR. 1957. Birds of the pine-oak woodland in southern Arizona and adjacent Mexico. Pacific Coast Avifauna 32. 125pp.

McCAUGHRAN, D. A., AND R. JEFFREY. 1980. Estimation of the audio index of relative abundance of band-tailed pigeons. J. Wildl. Manage. 44:204–209.

McLEAN, D. D. 1925. A western goshawk scatters Yosemite's band-tailed pigeon colony. Yosemite Nature Notes 4:103.

MICHAEL, C. W. 1928. Nesting time of band-tailed pigeons in Yosemite Valley. Condor 30:127.

MORA, M. A., AND D. W. ANDERSON. 1991. Seasonal and geographical variation of organochlorine residues in birds from northwest Mexico. Arch. Environ. Contam. Toxicol. 21:541–548.

MORSE, W. B. 1950. Observations on the band-tailed pigeon in Oregon. Proc. West. Assoc. State Game and Fish Comm. 30:102–104.

————. 1957. The bandtail—another forest crop. Am. Forests 63(9):24–25, 32, 34.

NEFF, J. A. 1947. Habits, food, and economic status of the band-tailed pigeon. U.S. Fish and Wildl. Serv., North Am. Fauna 58. 76pp.

————, AND R. J. NIEDRACH. 1946. Nesting of the band-tailed pigeon in Colorado. Condor 48:72–74.

OLSEN, O. W., AND C. E. BRAUN. 1976. New species of *Splendidofilaria* and *Chandlerella* (Filarioidea: Nematoda), with keys to the species from the band-tailed pigeon (*Columba fasciata*) in the Rocky Mountain region. Great Basin Nat. 36: 445–457.

————, AND ————. 1980. Helminth parasites of band-tailed pigeons in Colorado. J. Wildl. Dis. 16:65–66.

PACKARD, F. M. 1946. Some observations of birds eating salt. Auk 63:89.

PASSMORE, M. F., AND R. L. JARVIS. 1979. Reliability of determining sex of band-tailed pigeons by plumage characters. Wildl. Soc. Bull. 7:124–125.

PEDERSON, J. C., AND D. H. NISH. 1975. The band-tailed pigeon in Utah. Utah Div. Wildl. Resour. Publ. 75-1. 75pp.

PEETERS, H. J. 1962. Nuptial behavior of the band-tailed pigeon in the San Francisco Bay area. Condor 64:445–470.

PENCE, D. B., AND A. G. CANARIS. 1976. *Tinaminyssus juxtamelloi* sp. n. (Acari: Dermanyssidae; Rhinonyssinae) from the nasal passages of the band-tailed pigeon, *Columba fasciata*, in New Mexico. J. Parasitol. 62:116–118.

PETERJOHN, B. G., AND J. R. SAUER. 1993. North American breeding bird survey annual summary 1990–1991. Bird Populations 1:1–15.

————, AND ————. 1994. Population trends of woodland birds from the North American Breeding Bird Survey. Wildl. Soc. Bull. 22:155–164.

POLLOCK, K. H., J. D. NICHOLS, C. BROWNIE, AND J. E. HINES. 1990. Statistical inference for capture-recapture experiments. Wildl. Monogr. 107. 97pp.

RIDGWAY, R. 1916. The birds of North and Middle America. U.S. Natl. Mus. Bull. 50:288–292.

SANDFORT, W. W. 1977. Introduction. Pages 1–3 *in* G. C. Sanderson, ed. Management of migratory shore and upland game birds in North America. Int. Assoc. Fish and Wildl. Agencies, Washington, D.C.

SCHROEDER, M. A., AND C. E. BRAUN. 1993. Movement and philopatry of band-tailed pigeons captured in Colorado. J. Wildl. Manage. 57:103–112.

SILEO, L., JR., AND E. L. FITZHUGH. 1969. Incidence of trichomoniasis in the band-tailed pigeons of southern Arizona. Bull. Wildl. Dis. Assoc. 5:146.

SILOVSKY, G. D. 1969. Distribution and mortality of the Pacific Coast band-tailed pigeon. M.S. Thesis, Oregon State Univ., Corvallis. 70pp.

————, H. M. WIGHT, L. H. SISSON, T. L. FOX, AND S. W. HARRIS. 1968. Methods for determining age of band-tailed pigeons. J. Wildl. Manage. 32: 421–424.

SISSON, L. H. 1968. Calling behavior of band-tailed pigeons in reference to a census technique. M.S. Thesis, Oregon State Univ., Corvallis. 57pp.

SMITH, W. A. 1968. The band-tailed pigeon in California. Calif. Fish and Game 54:4–16.

STABLER, R. M. 1951. A survey of Colorado band-tailed pigeons, mourning doves, and wild common pigeons for *Trichomonas gallinae*. J. Parasitol. 37:471–472.

————, AND C. E. BRAUN. 1975. Effect of virulent *Trichomonas gallinae* on the band-tailed pigeon. J. Wildl. Dis. 11:482–483.

————, AND ————. 1979. Effects of a California-derived strain of *Trichomonas gallinae* on Colorado band-tailed pigeons. Calif. Fish and Game 65:56–58.

————, AND C. M. HERMAN. 1951. Upper digestive tract trichomoniasis in mourning doves and other birds. Trans. North Am. Wildl. Conf. 16:146–163.

————, AND P. A. HOLT. 1963. Hematozoa from Colorado birds. I. Pigeons and doves. J. Parasitol. 49:320–322.

————, AND C. P. MATTESON. 1950. Incidence of *Trichomonas gallinae* in Colorado mourning doves and band-tailed pigeons. J. Parasitol. 36: 25–26.

————, AND M. R. STROMBERG. 1981. Hematozoa from band-tailed pigeons (*Columba fasciata*) from New Mexico. J. Ariz.-Nev. Acad. Sci. 16: 60–61.

————, N. J. KITZMILLER, AND C. E. BRAUN. 1977. Blood parasites from band-tailed pigeons. J. Wildl. Manage. 41:128–130.

STEPHENS, F. 1913. Early nesting of the band-tailed pigeon. Condor 15:129.

SWARTH, H. S. 1900. Avifauna of a 100-acre ranch. Condor 2:14–16.

THAYER, J. E. 1909. Letter to the editor. Condor 11:142–143.

U.S. FISH AND WILDLIFE SERVICE. 1992. Migratory bird harvest information program; proposed rule. Fed. Regist. 57:24736–24741.

————. 1993. Migratory bird harvest information program; final rule. Fed. Regist. 58:15093–15098.

VORHIES, C. T. 1928. Band-tailed pigeon nesting in Arizona in September. Condor 30:253.

WESTERN MIGRATORY UPLAND GAME BIRD TECHNICAL COMMITTEE. 1994. Pacific Flyway management plan for the Pacific Coast population of band-tailed pigeons. Pacific Flyway Counc., Portland, Oreg. 39pp.

WHITE, J. A., AND C. E. BRAUN. 1978. Age and sex determination of juvenile band-tailed pigeons. J. Wildl. Manage. 42:564–569.

WIGHT, H. M., R. U. MACE, AND W. M. BATTERSON. 1967. Mortality estimates of an adult band-tailed pigeon population in Oregon. J. Wildl. Manage. 31:519–525.

WILLARD, F. C. 1916. Nesting of the band-tailed pigeon in southern Arizona. Condor 18:110–112.

WOOD, S. F., AND C. M. HERMAN. 1943. The occurrence of blood parasites in birds from southwestern United States. J. Parasitol. 29:187–196.

ZIEGLER, D. L. 1971. Crop-milk cycles in band-tailed pigeons and losses of squabs due to hunting pigeons in September. M.S. Thesis, Oregon State Univ., Corvallis. 48pp.

Chapter 6

SANDHILL CRANE

THOMAS C. TACHA, Caesar Kleberg Wildlife Research Institute, Campus Box 218, Texas A&M University–Kingsville, Kingsville, TX 78363

STEPHEN A. NESBITT, Florida Game and Fresh Water Fish Commission, 4005 South Main Street, Gainesville, FL 32601

PAUL A. VOHS,[1] National Biological Survey, Iowa Cooperative Fish and Wildlife Research Unit, Department of Animal Ecology, Science Hall II, Iowa State University, Ames, IA 50011

Abstract: Sandhill cranes (*Grus canadensis*) are classified into 3–6 subspecies in 9 populations. Populations in Cuba, Florida, and Mississippi are nonmigratory; Cuban and Mississippi cranes are endangered. The Lower Colorado River Valley population is unhunted and is presumed stable. Three populations are hunted. Greater than 90% of the harvest is from the Mid-continent population. Pacific Coast (Pacific Flyway) and Rocky Mountain populations are hunted and stable. The Mid-continent population occurs as 2 distinct subpopulations totalling about 560,000 birds. Numbers of both subpopulations are currently considered stable. The Western subpopulation has 530,000 birds, 11% juveniles in winter, and an annual harvest rate of about 4%. The Gulf Coast subpopulation numbers ≥30,000 cranes, has 18% juveniles in winter, and a harvest rate of ≤13%. Major Mid-continent population management needs include improved population surveys and separate assessment and management of subpopulations. A management plan is needed for the Eastern greater sandhill crane population, and management plans for the Central Valley and Pacific Coast populations need to be updated. Data related to harvest should include improved estimates of subsistence harvests in Alaska and Canada, estimates of recreational and subsistence harvests in Mexico and Siberia, and estimates of unretrieved harvest throughout North America. Priorities for habitat management include conservation and management of essential habitat complexes (especially native grassland habitats) in the North Platte and Platte River valleys, Nebraska, <20 saline pluvial lakes in western Texas, and numerous acquisition and enhancement projects in the western United States. Research is needed to better delineate western populations, develop accurate population and harvest surveys by population and subpopulation, and to evaluate influence of regulations on harvest.

All populations of sandhill cranes are included in this chapter, but we emphasize those with active management plans and those subject to recreational harvest in our Management Needs and Recommendations sections. We focus on the Mid-continent population because it provides >90% of the North American recreational harvest of cranes.

DESCRIPTION

Sandhill cranes have heavy bodies and long necks and legs (Walkinshaw 1949, Tacha et al. 1992). Height extends to 1.2 m, wing span to 2 m, and weight may reach 5.5 kg. Feet are ansiodactic with a functionally vestigial elevated hallux. The bill is elongate and strong. Sexes are monochromatic gray and generally indistinguishable even with cloacal examination (Tacha and Lewis 1979). Juveniles have a feathered crown and brown nape feathers (Tacha and Vohs 1984). Adults have red, pappilos skin on the crown and gray nape feathers. Walkinshaw (1949, 1973) and Tacha et al. (1992) provide detailed descriptions of sandhill cranes.

Six subspecies and 9 populations of sandhill cranes have been identified (Tacha et al. 1992). The American Ornithologists' Union (1957) recognizes *G. c. canadensis* (lesser), *G. c. pratensis* (Florida), and *G. c. tabida* (greater) as subspecies. Lewis (1977) and others have also recognized *G. c. nesiotes* (Cuban), *G. c. pulla* (Mississippi), and *G. c. rowani* (Canadian) subspecies. Four of the 9 populations are composed of greater sandhill cranes: Eastern, Rocky Mountain, Lower Colorado River Valley, and Central Valley (Tacha et al. 1992). Populations in Cuba (Cuban subspecies), Florida (Florida subspecies), and Mississippi (Mississippi subspecies) are nonmigratory. The Pacific Coast Population (also known as the Pacific Flyway Population) includes primarily the lesser subspecies. The Mid-continent population, including both Western and Gulf Coast subpopulations, has been de-

---

[1] Present address: National Biological Survey, Information Transfer Center, 1201 Oak Ridge Drive, Suite 200, Fort Collins, CO 80525.

scribed as a mixture of lesser, Canadian, and greater subspecies (Lewis 1977). However, Tacha et al. (1985*b*) studied the Mid-continent population and suggested the medium-size Canadian subspecies could not and should not be separated from the smaller lesser subspecies and the larger greater subspecies because there was: 1) a continuum in size that had been arbitrarily divided into subspecies, 2) random pairing among birds classified as being different subspecies, and 3) substantial overlap in breeding ranges.

LIFE HISTORY

Sandhill cranes are among the oldest existing species of birds (2.5 million years) (Tacha et al. 1992). They are well known for their bugling calls, especially a duet by mated pairs referred to as the Unison Call. While their appearance is rather drab, their behavior is complex. Social behaviors (agonistic, courtship, preflight, and alert) that communicate information account for only 5% of diurnal time allocations but are critical to establishing and maintaining social relationships that facilitate survival and reproduction.

Social Organization

Mated adult pairs and families are the primary social units of sandhill cranes (Tacha 1988). These primary units combine with unpaired adults and subadults in migratory populations into large, socially unstable aggregations during migration and wintering.

Sandhill cranes are perennially monogamous and delay breeding (Walkinshaw 1949, 1973; Tacha 1988; Nesbitt 1992). In Mid-continent cranes, pairs are formed as early as age 3; 20% form pairs by age 4, and 90–100% by age 7 (Tacha et al. 1989). In contrast, Florida cranes pair as early as 14 months of age, and the average pair forms at age 21 months (Nesbitt and Wenner 1987). Pair bonds may form and dissolve before successful reproduction occurs (Nesbitt and Wenner 1987), but following reproduction, mate changes are rare unless a mate dies (Littlefield 1981*a*, Bishop 1988, Tacha 1988, Nesbitt 1989).

Mid-continent cranes apparently form pairs during spring migration, and dancing may play an important role in mate selection (Tacha 1988). Pairing activities occur in native grassland (wet meadow) habitats in the North Platte and Platte River valleys. Pair bonds are maintained outside the breeding season by the pair staying in close proximity and by using the Unison Call.

Mid-continent cranes may reproduce successfully as early as age 5, but >75% are not successful until ≥8 years of age (Tacha et al. 1989). Eastern greater and Florida cranes have reproduced as early as age 3 (Nesbitt and Wenner 1987). However, the average age of first reproduction is 4 years in Eastern greater and 5 years in Florida cranes (Nesbitt 1992).

Reproduction and Recruitment

Mean date of nest initiation ranges from 22–24 February in Florida to 16 June on Banks Island, N.W.T. (Walkinshaw 1949, Tacha et al. 1992). Average clutch size is 1.9 (mode 2 and range 1–3) for several populations and is smaller in more northern-breeding birds. The interval between egg laying is typically 1–2 days; incubation begins with laying of the first egg and lasts for 30 days. Both sexes incubate; males and females share daylight incubation duties about equally, but the female is the primary nest attendant at night (Nesbitt 1989). Nest success varies among years and locations but averages about 50% (Tacha et al. 1992). Sandhill cranes raise a single brood per year but will renest following loss of eggs in northern nesting populations or loss of eggs or young in southern populations.

Precocial young leave the nest <24 hours after hatch (Tacha et al. 1992). Both parents feed the young, but females do most post-hatch brooding. Young Rocky Mountain cranes fledge at 67–75 days (Drewien 1973), but in captivity the mean is 53.4 ± 2.4 (SD) days (Baldwin 1977). Post-fledging brood size averages 1.31 and ranges from 1.21 to 1.35 (Tacha et al. 1992). Percentage of post-fledged juveniles in several populations averaged 11.0 (range 6.6–18.3). Young are usually separated from the parental pair at about 10 months of age (Tacha 1988, Nesbitt 1992).

Survival and Non-hunting Mortality

The survival rate of Florida sandhill cranes from hatching to fledging was 0.65 and 0.82 from fledging to independence (Nesbitt 1992). Average annual survival rate for Florida and Eastern greater sandhill cranes, all age groups combined, was 0.88 (Tacha et al. 1992). Maximum known age of a wild bird was 19.4 years from the Mid-continent Population (Klimkiewicz and Futcher 1989) and 21.6 years for a bird from Florida (Tacha et al. 1992).

Annual non-hunting mortality probably approximates 5% among fledged sandhill cranes (Tacha et al. 1992). Avian botulism (*Clostridium botulinum*), avian cholera (*Pasteurella* spp.), and mycotoxins cause noteworthy mortality (Windingstad 1988). Avian tuberculosis (*Mycobacterium avium*), aspergillosis (*Aspergillus* spp.), lead poisoning, and power line collisions are other causes of mortality (Tacha et al. 1992). Predation of cranes, once fledged, is relatively rare.

Diet and Nutrition

Omnivorous sandhill cranes exploit foods by probing subsurfaces with bills and by gleaning seeds and other foods on the land surface or in shallow marshes (Walkinshaw 1949, Tacha et al. 1992). Mid-continent cranes spend 1.4–6.4% of their diurnal time searching for food, up to 17.1% gleaning surface foods, and 17.9–60.4% probing for subsurface foods (Tacha et al. 1987).

Cranes eat a variety of foods, and the specific diet depends on food availability in different seasons and/or locations (Tacha et al. 1992). Diets during migration and winter seem not to vary among age, sex, or social classes. Cultivated grains are major food items whenever and wherever they are available.

Animal matter is important to sandhill cranes, yet rarely exceeds 5–10% of the diet by volume or weight (Tacha et al. 1992). Invertebrate and vertebrate prey are important sources of exogenous protein and provide essential amino acids and calcium rarely available in grain diets (Reineke and Krapu 1986). Indogenous (carcass) protein of adult Mid-continent cranes varies little throughout the annual cycle (Iverson 1981, Krapu et al. 1985), suggesting cranes can meet most of their protein demands via food intake.

Lipid (fat) reserves of Mid-continent cranes vary widely (Tacha et al. 1992). The lowest postreproductive lipid levels occurred in mid-August when cranes arrived in Saskatchewan (Tacha et al. 1985a), but cranes gained an average of 9 g lipid/day eating high-energy grains in Saskatchewan. Lipid levels remained constant through departure from Saskatchewan, staging in Oklahoma, wintering in western Texas, and spring arrival in Nebraska (Iverson 1981; Tacha et al. 1985a, 1987). Cranes deposited an average of 12.8 g lipid/day in Nebraska during spring migration and maintained the accumu-

lated lipid levels through Saskatchewan and central Alaska to nesting areas in western Alaska. The birds lost 4 g/day during prenesting (Iverson 1981, Krapu et al. 1985, Tacha et al. 1987).

Fat stores probably accumulated during fall in Saskatchewan and spring in Nebraska because food resources (grains) with high metabolizable energy were available in concentrated form and accessible with minimum energy expenditures (Tacha et al. 1987). Lipids were replenished during later stages of spring migration by stops to exploit grain fields, and by increases in foraging time compared to Nebraska. Lipid losses during prenesting were due to low food availability for lipid replenishment and to energy expenditures for territorial defense and egg production. Krapu et al. (1985) speculated that presence of waste grain has allowed Mid-continent cranes to obtain and transport maximum lipids to nesting areas where these lipids facilitate relatively early reproduction, and that early reproduction has allowed increased recruitment when compared to the period prior to agricultural development in the Great Plains and Alaska.

HABITAT

Mid-continent Population

Typical breeding territories in the Yukon-Kuskokwim Delta, Alaska were in wet marsh or sedge meadow areas (Boise 1976). Broods spent the most time in taller *Elymus* vegetation along slough banks, heath tundra, and short-grass meadows. Walkinshaw (1973) reported use of similar habitats in tundra areas of northern Canada. Carlisle (1982) found cranes nesting in open, wet, sedge marsh adjacent to wooded areas in central Alberta (Fig. 1).

Sandhill cranes staging in southeastern Saskatchewan in fall roost in shallow, open wetlands and feed in small grain fields (Stephen 1967). In eastern North Dakota, cranes roost in shallow lakes and marshes, feed in harvested grain fields, and loaf in hayfields and pastures (Melvin and Temple 1983). Cranes in western North Dakota preferred to roost within large expanses of shallow saline water with a soft substrate, and far from bare shoreline (Soine 1982).

Optimum habitat complexes for spring migrants staging in the North Platte River Valley included a river or shallow wetland roost site, an interspersion of 30–70% corn stubble, 5–40%

Fig. 1.   Sandhill crane nest in sedge marsh with 2 eggs (Photo by M. C. Tacha).

pasture, ≥13% alfalfa, and ≥1 wetland within 4 km of the roost site (Iverson et al. 1987) (Figs. 2, 3). Krapu et al. (1984) found similar habitats important in the Platte River Valley during spring.

Folk and Tacha (1991) documented substantial reductions in sandhill crane use of the North Platte River Valley between 1980 and 1989, and suggested that reductions in availability of off-river wetlands and corn stubble may have been responsible. Folk and Tacha (1990) characterized spring roosting habitat in the North Platte River Valley and demonstrated that roost space was not limiting abundance of sandhill cranes in central Nebraska. Iverson et al. (1987) and Folk and Tacha (1990) recommended preservation and/or management of essential habitat complexes along the river. The wet-meadow component was the most limiting feature in habitat complexes in the North Platte and Platte River valleys.

Cranes stopping in southeastern Saskatchewan and central Alaska during spring roost in shallow wetlands (Iverson et al. 1987). Cranes use wheat stubble in Saskatchewan and barley fields in Alaska as food sources.

Cranes roost on <20 saline pluvial lakes in western Texas and concentrate on those with at least 1 freshwater spring (Iverson et al. 1985a). Numbers of freshwater springs on the lake and the percentage of the surrounding area in sorghum stubble explained 95% of the variation in roost site selection (Iverson et al. 1985b). Cranes

Fig. 2.   Sandhill cranes (note neck-banded pair) in a hay field in the North Platte River Valley (Photo by T. C. Tacha).

Fig. 3. Aerial view of typical roost sites (note visible sandbars) in the North Platte River near Hershey, Nebraska (Photo by T. C. Tacha).

avoided cotton stubble, plowed fields, and brushlands.

Cranes wintering along the Gulf Coast of Texas roosted on shallow, open-water marshes and spent the day in coastal prairie, scrub oak brushland, freshwater marshes, and sorghum stubble fields (Guthery 1975). Cranes wintering in New Mexico roosted in shallow river or lake areas and spent most of the day in irrigated croplands and pastures (Walker and Schemnitz 1987). In southeastern Arizona, cranes roosted in shallow water in playa lakes and spent the day loafing in grasslands or wetlands and feeding in grain (especially corn) stubble fields (Perkins and Brown 1981).

Other Populations

Sandhill cranes from the Rocky Mountain and Lower Colorado River Valley populations nest in isolated, well-watered river valleys, marshes, and meadows at elevations above 1,500 m (Drewien 1973, Drewien and Bizeau 1974). Most nest in wet meadow-shallow marsh zones along the marsh edge. The largest concentrations in fall in Idaho occur at Gray's Lake and Teton Basin (Drewien and Bizeau 1974) where cranes feed in grainfields, primarily barley. In New Mexico during winter, livestock farms with irrigated pasture, cotton farms, and truck gardening areas are available (Lewis 1977). In the Rio Grande Valley, cranes concentrate on refuges and on dairy farms where grains were raised.

Eastern greater sandhill cranes nest in isolated, open marshes or bogs surrounded by shrubs and forests (Walkinshaw 1973). They concentrate in fall in Michigan in large marshes with little human intrusion (Walkinshaw 1973). The birds roost in shallow water at night and feed in alfalfa, pasture, or hay fields until wheat fields are harvested. Later on the birds use newly planted fall wheat. Later in the fall, waste corn becomes available and the birds prefer corn stubble. Pastures are little used during fall. In Indiana, cranes use isolated roost sites with water less than 20 cm deep over a firm bottom (Lovvorn and Kirkpatrick 1981). Migrants preferred corn stubble and avoided soybeans, winter wheat, and fallow-pasture areas in fall (Lovvorn and Kirkpatrick 1982). Spring migrants preferred unplowed corn stubble and showed a preference for fallow-pasture areas. Cranes use prairie wetlands and pasture areas of central Florida during winter (Wenner and Nesbitt 1987).

Birds of the Central Valley population nest in flooded meadows and marshes in the Great Basin and in the southern Cascade Mountains of Oregon and California (Littlefield and Ryder 1968). Nesting habitat for the birds includes open meadows with scattered stands of bulrush (*Scirpus* spp.), cattails (*Typha* spp.), and bur-reed (*Sparganium* spp.) (Littlefield 1981*b*). Much of the nesting is in the Great Basin where surrounding vegetation consists of sagebrush (*Artemisia* spp.) and scattered junipers (*Juniperus* spp.). Nesting habitat outside the basin is surrounded by sagebrush, willow (*Salix* spp.), pine (*Pinus* spp.), and Douglas-fir (*Pseudotsuga menziesii*). The birds feed in irrigated pastures, milo, wheat, barley, rice, and corn fields as well as saltgrass (*Distichlis* spp.) flats during winter.

Cranes in western Cuba and on the Isle of Pines inhabit dry, isolated regions and may not visit marshes (Walkinshaw 1949). Drinking water comes from small streams, springs, and rainpools. Most territories are sparingly grown to shrubs and trees, often sometimes park-like, often rather flat, but birds may be found in rocky and mountainous terrain. Pine- or palm-dotted areas and large savannas are used for feeding, roosting, nesting, and rearing of young.

The Florida population is associated with freshwater marshes in Florida and Georgia (often surrounded with grassy uplands). In Okefenokee Swamp, cranes use the open, less wooded herbaceous marsh ares, making little or no use of drier upland habitats (Bennett 1989). In Florida, cranes use prairies, pastures, other open (low growth) uplands, and herbaceous wetlands. Transition areas between wetlands and upland habitats receive high use (Nesbitt and Williams 1990). Peanut and corn fields, and other agricultural areas (feed lots, dairy farms, etc.), are heavily used during winter and early spring. Cranes also use the forested edges surrounding these habitats. Forest edges are used for midday loafing in summer and provide mast in the fall.

In fall and winter, the Mississippi population of cranes mainly roost in Pascagoula Marsh and fly to small cornfields or pastures to feed (Val-entine 1981). Some of the birds fly to crop fields to feed and some spend the day feeding in swamps and savannas within the breeding range. In spring, summer, and fall, the birds feed on the breeding grounds in savannas, swamps, and open pine fields (Valentine and Noble 1970). From the 1950's to present, savannas declined from 74 to 14% of the habitat in the area, woodland increased from 18 to 70%, agricultural land from 8 to 9%, and urban lands from a trace to 6% (Smith and Valentine 1987).

Little is known about nesting habitat of the Pacific Coast population but it is probably similar to the Mid-continent population. Pacific Coast sandhill cranes staging in the eastern Copper River Delta in Alaska roost primarily in wetlands associated with medium shrub and intertidal mudflat habitats and feed primarily in wet meadow habitats (Herter 1982). Little is known about their wintering habitat, but it is probably similar to the Central Valley population because they commingle.

DISTRIBUTION AND ABUNDANCE
Non-hunted Populations

Ranges of the 3 non-migratory populations are discrete and non-overlapping (Fig. 4). The Cuban population inhabits western Cuba and the Isle of Pines. The Florida population occurs throughout peninsular Florida into Georgia (Okefenokee Swamp). The Mississippi population occurs only in Jackson County, Mississippi. Populations in Cuba and Mississippi contain <200 cranes and are endangered (Table 1). The Cuban population seems to be slowly declining (Tacha et al. 1992); the Mississippi population is stable due to release of young produced in captivity (Ellis et al. 1992). The Florida population seems stable (Table 1).

The Central Valley population nests in northeastern California, west of the Cascade Range in Oregon and Washington and into British Columbia, and winters in the Central Valley of California (Fig. 4). The Eastern population, associated with the Great Lakes Region, nests from eastern Minnesota, Wisconsin, and Michigan to southern Ontario and winters in the southeastern United States, primarily Florida and southern Georgia. These populations of greater sandhill cranes seem to be increasing (Table 1).

The Lower Colorado River Valley population nests in northeastern Nevada and adjacent parts of Idaho and Utah and winters in the Colorado

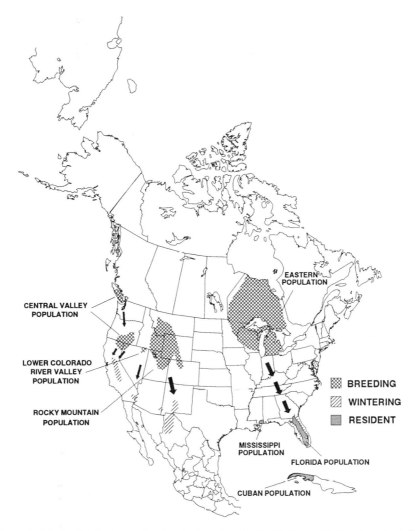

Fig. 4. Breeding and wintering distributions and major migration routes of the Central Valley, Cuban, Eastern, Florida, Lower Colorado River Valley, Mississippi, and Rocky Mountain populations of sandhill cranes.

River Valley of Arizona and California, and the Imperial Valley (Fig. 4). This population is probably stable, but there have been no recent (last 15+ years) surveys.

Hunted Populations

The Rocky Mountain population nests in northwestern Colorado, western Wyoming and Montana, southeastern Idaho, and northern Utah. It winters primarily in the middle and lower Rio Grande Valley of New Mexico, but also westward into southeastern Arizona and southward to Chihuahua, Mexico. The San Luis Valley in Colorado serves as the major migration stopover in both fall and spring. The Rocky Mountain population is hunted and stable (Table 1).

The Pacific Coast population nests in southwestern Alaska and winters in the Central Valley of California (Fig. 5). The population numbers about 25,000, is hunted in Alaska primarily for recreation, and seems to be stable (Table 1).

The Mid-continent population nests in eastern Siberia, western and interior Alaska, and Canada west of Hudson and James bays, and winters in southern and western Texas, central and eastern New Mexico, and central and northern Mexico (Fig. 5). The birds congregate briefly at many stopover areas during spring and fall migration, but 80–90% concentrate for up to 6 weeks in

Table 1. Current population estimates, status, and long-term (10–20 year) trends in populations of sandhill cranes (modified from Tacha et al. 1992).

Population/subpopulation	Status[a]	Current size	Long-term trend
Cuba	Endangered	<200	Declining
Florida	Unhunted	4,000–6,000	Stable
Mississippi	Endangered	120–130	Increasing
Eastern	Unhunted	24,000–26,000	Increasing
Rocky Mountain	Hunted	18,000–20,000	Stable
Central Valley	Unhunted	6,000–7,000	Increasing
Lower Colorado River Valley	Unhunted	1,400–2,100	Stable
Pacific Coast (Pacific Flyway)	Hunted	≤25,000	Stable
Mid-continent	Hunted	≥560,000	Increasing
Western	Hunted	≥530,000	Increasing
Gulf Coast	Hunted	≥30,000	Stable

[a] Endangered = protected under the federal Endangered Species Act, Unhunted = not subject to recreational hunting, Hunted = subject to recreational hunting.

spring in the North Platte and Platte River valleys, Nebraska (Tacha et al. 1992).

The Western subpopulation of the Mid-continent population nests in western Canada, western and interior Alaska, and eastern Siberia and migrates through central Alberta, southern Saskatchewan, western portions of North and South Dakota, Nebraska, Oklahoma, and eastern portions of Montana, Wyoming, and Colorado to wintering areas in western Texas, eastern and southern New Mexico, southeastern Arizona, and central and northern Mexico (Fig. 5) (Tacha et al. 1984, 1992). The birds stop in southern Saskatchewan and western North Dakota during fall. In spring, they stop in Nebraska along the more western portions of the Platte River and the North Platte River Valley.

The Gulf Coast subpopulation of the Mid-continent population nests in northwestern Minnesota, southwestern Ontario, eastern and northern Manitoba, and north-central Canada and migrates through eastern North and South Dakota and central Nebraska, Kansas, and Oklahoma to wintering areas along the Texas Gulf

Table 2. Estimated hunting mortality of Mid-continent sandhill cranes in North America, 1975–92 (from Sharp and Vogel 1992; D. E. Sharp, 1993 unpubl. rep.).

Year	Retrieved harvest				Unretrieved harvest[c]	Totals
	Cent. Flyway	Canada	Alaska[a]	Mexico[b]		
1975	9,497	6,165	1,642	1,730	3,807	22,841
1976	7,393	1,636	873	990	2,178	13,071
1977	12,151	367	620	1,314	2,890	17,342
1978	10,146	876	310	1,133	2,493	14,958
1979	10,379	3,798	675	1,485	3,267	19,605
1980	10,152	5,582	1,050	1,678	3,692	22,155
1981	10,134	2,961	553	1,365	3,003	18,015
1982	7,916	2,837	1,746	1,250	2,750	16,499
1983	12,959	3,098	1,805	1,786	3,930	23,578
1984	11,271	3,717	2,376	1,786	3,820	22,920
1985	12,776	5,159	1,270	1,921	4,225	25,351
1986	12,487	6,106	731	1,932	4,251	25,508
1987	12,770	5,268	1,014	1,905	4,191	25,149
1988	12,772	6,946	1,443	2,116	4,655	27,933
1989	13,639	4,985	625	1,921	4,225	25,352
1990	18,041	4,840	1,116	2,400	5,279	31,676
1991	13,074	5,394	1,116	1,958	4,308	25,851
1992	12,391	5,394[d]	1,116	1,890	4,158	24,949

[a] No survey data were available for 1990–92; the long-term average of 1,116 was used.
[b] Harvests in Mexico were estimated to be 10% of known harvests in Canada and the United States.
[c] Unretrieved harvest was estimated to be 20% of retrieved harvest.
[d] No survey data were available for 1992; 1991 data were used.

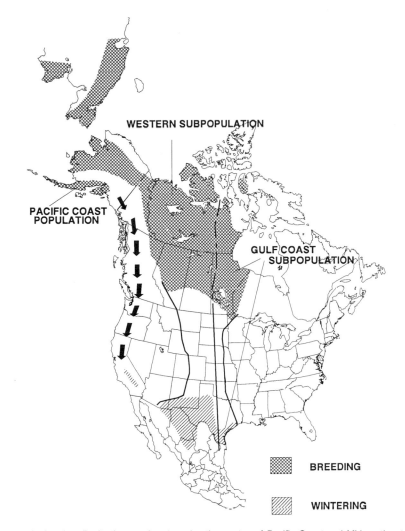

WESTERN SUBPOPULATION

PACIFIC COAST
POPULATION

GULF COAST
SUBPOPULATION

BREEDING

WINTERING

Fig. 5. Breeding and wintering distributions and major migration routes of Pacific Coast and Mid-continent populations of sandhill cranes. Western and Gulf Coast subpopulations of the Mid-continent population have geographic separation during migration and wintering (solid line), but the subpopulation boundary (dashed line) during the breeding season is less well known.

Coast (Fig. 5) (Tacha et al. 1984, 1986, 1992). The birds may stop in eastern North Dakota and central Kansas during fall and in central and more eastern parts of the Platte River Valley during spring (Melvin and Temple 1980, 1983; Tacha et al. 1984).

The Mid-continent population numbers about 560,000 birds (Table 1). Population trends have been upward over the last 20 years, but the population may have stabilized in the last 5–10 years (Sharp and Vogel 1992, unpubl. Alaska sandhill crane breeding population index). The Gulf Coast subpopulation of about 30,000 birds appears stable. The Western subpopulation approximates 530,000, and is probably responsible

for the changes in population trends observed for the collective Mid-continent population (Table 1).

HARVEST

Mid-continent Population

The history of Mid-continent crane harvests was detailed by Lewis (1977), Miller (1987), and Sharp and Vogel (1992). Recent hunting seasons began in 1961. Harvest has increased since 1975 (Table 2), primarily in the 8 Central Flyway states where sandhill cranes are currently hunted (Sharp and Vogel 1992).

Detailed harvest surveys became possible be-

Table 3. Estimated hunting mortality of Rocky Mountain and Pacific Coast populations of sandhill cranes 1981–92.

Year	Rocky Mountain harvests			Pacific Coast harvests		
	Retrieved[a]	Unretrieved[b]	Totals	Retrieved[c]	Unretrieved[b]	Totals
1981	20	4	24	166	33	199
1982	152	30	182	524	105	629
1983	189	38	227	542	108	650
1984	134	27	161	713	143	856
1985	178	36	214	381	76	457
1986	603	121	724	219	44	263
1987	915	183	1,098	304	61	365
1988	476	35	511	433	87	520
1989	713	143	856	188	38	226
1990	181	36	217	335	67	402
1991	240	48	288	335	67	402
1992	386	77	463	335	67	402

[a] Data from Sharp (1993, unpubl. rep.).
[b] Unretrieved harvest was estimated to be 20% of retrieved harvest.
[c] Harvest of the Pacific Coast population is assumed to be 30% of Alaska harvest (Pacific Flyway Council 1983b). Alaska harvest data are from Table 2.

cause hunters in the U.S. (except Alaska) were required to obtain a free federal Sandhill Crane Hunting Permit starting in 1975 (Sharp and Vogel 1992). Hunters had to provide their name and address to obtain the permit. Questionnaires were sent to hunters shortly after the seasons, and follow-up questionnaires were sent to non-respondents (Miller 1987). Crane harvests in Alaska and Canada were estimated from surveys associated with respective U.S. duck stamps and Canadian Migratory Bird Hunting Permits.

Numbers of active crane hunters in the United States have remained at about 8,000 since 1975, but average days spent hunting per season declined from about 4 in 1975 to 2.7 in 1991 (Sharp and Vogel 1992). Hunter bag increased from 1.3 to 2.4, explaining increases in harvest.

Similar hunting frameworks have been in effect for the past 10 years (Sharp and Vogel 1992). A 3-bird daily bag, 6 in possession; season dates during September–February; and season lengths up to 93 days in all or parts of New Mexico, Oklahoma, and Texas, was the general framework. Other states could have a season up to 58 days in length. In Mexico, sandhill cranes are currently (1993) hunted in 9 northern and central states with season lengths of 101–122 days and daily bag limits of 1–3 birds.

Rocky Mountain and Pacific Coast Populations

Recreational hunting of the Rocky Mountain population of greater sandhill cranes has been allowed in 1 or more states of the U.S. since 1981 (Pacific and Central Flyway Councils 1991). The population is currently regularly hunted in Mexico, Arizona, Wyoming, and New Mexico, and experimentally in Utah and southwestern New Mexico. Annual retrieved harvest peaked near 1,000 on 1987, but has not exceeded 400 since 1989 (Table 3). Harvests by permit only are determined annually based on population size and recruitment with the objective of maintaining the population at 18,000–22,000 birds. Rigorous protocols control the overall annual harvest objective, allocations of harvest to interested states, and development of new or expanded hunting opportunities in any U.S. states where Rocky Mountain cranes occur.

Recreational hunting of the Pacific Coast population of lesser sandhill cranes is limited to southern Alaska (Pacific Flyway Council 1983b). Retrieved harvest is assumed to be 30% of the total sandhill crane harvest in Alaska, and estimates have varied from 166 to 713 during 1981–92 (Table 3).

MANAGEMENT NEEDS
Habitat Management

The single most-important factor regulating sandhill crane populations is habitat availability (Tacha et al. 1992). Thus, maintenance of essential habitats is the primary need for all populations of sandhill cranes. Wetland conservation is particularly important throughout the ranges of non-migratory populations and in migration staging and wintering areas of migratory populations.

Mid-continent Population.—Conservation

and management of essential habitat complexes in the North Platte and Platte River valleys, Nebraska are priority habitat management needs. Existing optimum complexes in central Nebraska require aggressive protection via acquisition or perpetual easements obtained by appropriate private, state, or federal agencies. Adequate North Platte and Platte River instream flows must be maintained for cranes because river flows affect distribution and abundance of roost sites, and (probably) availability and quality of adjacent wet meadow habitats. However, conservation and management of habitat complexes should be the priority focus of crane habitat management activities in central Nebraska.

Wet meadow habitat is the most common element missing from potentially optimum crane habitat complexes in central Nebraska. Wet meadows are important for pair formation activities and foraging. Temporary or semipermanent palustrine wetlands in shallow depressions and/or old oxbows within pastures adjacent (and probably hydrologically linked) to active river channels provide the best wet meadows. Reversing drainage, rewatering with increased in-stream flows or other means during the critical spring period, and/or reversion from row crops will restore wet meadows. Restoration of selected wet meadows to add the single missing component of otherwise optimum habitat complexes would be cost-effective.

Conservation of the <20 saline pluvial lakes and associated freshwater springs in western Texas that provide roosting and drinking sites is essential. Concentrations of 300,000 cranes have been observed on one of these lakes, and >100,000 birds commonly roost on several others. The number of active fresh-water springs related to a lake strongly influence sandhill crane use. Management opportunities include acquisition and/or easements protecting existing basins and springs, and using windmills or other cost-effective means of supplying freshwater where limiting. Wide dispersal of wintering cranes among the limited number of preferred roost lakes to protect the birds from disease and drought should be a priority management objective in western Texas.

Other Populations.—The management plan for the Rocky Mountain population indicates there is a need to identify, classify, rank, and catalog habitats used by Rocky Mountain cranes throughout their range to facilitate protection of important habitats (Pacific and Central Flyway Councils 1991). Specific habitat preservation priorities include protection of 600 ha of farmland adjacent to Willcox Wildlife Management Area in Arizona and provision of 200 ha of wet hay meadow and grain fields along the Yampa and Elk rivers in Routt County, Colorado. In Idaho, habitat priorities include protection of roost sites, loafing sites, and feeding areas along the Teton River in Teton County; providing 50–200 ha of cropland adjacent to Blackfoot Reservoir in Caribou County; and providing 25–200 ha of cropland in Bear Lake County near Bear Lake National Wildlife Refuge. New Mexico habitat priorities include protection of river sand bars, riparian wooded areas, and well-drained irrigable cropland in the Middle Rio Grande Valley; retention of water in the Rio Grande; and maximizing production of wildlife crops on state and federal agricultural lands. Habitat priorities in Utah include protection of 200 ha of farmland along the Bear River in Rich County and 200 ha of farmland in the Cache Valley, and developing and improving farming programs at Ouray National Wildlife Refuge. Priorities in Wyoming include protection of roost sites, loafing sites, and feeding areas to support 4,000–6,000 cranes in premigration staging areas such as the Salt River, lower Bear River, Eden-Farson Agricultural Project, and the Wind River Irrigation Project; providing adequate grain croplands on Ocean Lake Wildlife Habitat Management Unit for 600–1,000 cranes during premigration staging; developing a long-term strategy to protect and enhance wetlands on the lower Bear River; and to develop Cokeville Meadows National Wildlife Refuge. Many of the cropland priorities in different states are proposed to alleviate crop depredation problems.

Habitat needs for the Pacific Coast population include priorities to identify and catalog habitats used by Pacific Coast cranes, and to protect roost sites and other key wintering habitats in California (Pacific Flyway Council 1983b). Habitat priorities for the Central Valley population include the need to inventory and preserve key habitats throughout the range, but especially in the Silvies and Warner valleys of Oregon and Surprise and Big valleys of California (Pacific Flyway Council 1983a). An additional refuge, managed primarily for wintering sandhill cranes, is needed in the San Joaquin portion of the Central Valley. The Pacific Fly-

Table 4.   Demographic variables associated with the Western and Gulf Coast subpopulations of the Mid-continent population of sandhill cranes (data are from Iverson et al. 1985a, Tacha 1981, Tacha and Vohs 1984, and Tacha et al. 1984, 1985b, 1986, 1992 except as noted).

Variable	Subpopulation	
	Western	Gulf Coast
Number of birds	530,000+	30,000+
Subspecies		
% G. c. canadensis	80	33
% G. c. tabida	<1	9
Adult sex ratio, % males	40	46
Avg. annual recruitment rate, % young in winter	11	18
Avg. annual harvest rate, % of population[a]	4	13

[a] Includes estimates of retrieved and unretrieved harvest in the U.S. and Canada from Novara and Handy (1991) and the preceding 10 years of similar reports, and from Sharp and Vogel (1992), allocated to subpopulations based on geographic separation identified in Tacha et al. (1984, 1986).

way Council (1983a) also provided a series of habitat enhancement recommendations for private and public lands in the Central Valley population range, especially for Malheur National Wildlife Refuge. Habitat needs for the Lower Colorado River Valley population include identification and protection of key habitats throughout the range, but especially in nesting areas (Pacific Flyway Council 1989). Specific recommendations included protection of wetlands associated with nesting and delaying mowing of hay until 1 August and limiting cattle grazing and fencing in nesting areas; development of migration stopover habitat at Kirch Wildlife Management Area in Nevada; and protection of winter roost sites southeast of Brawley, California, and at all lower Colorado River national wildlife refuges (especially Cibola).

Population Management

Mid-continent Population.—Western and Gulf Coast subpopulations should be managed as separate entities. The initial "Management Guidelines for Mid-continent Sandhill Cranes" was adopted by the Central Flyway Council in July 1981, and was revised in 1993 (Central and Pacific Flyway Councils 1993). Both versions were based on management of the Mid-continent population as one unit.

Evidence for subpopulations as distinct entities began with sightings of neck-banded birds showing separate fall migration routes and wintering areas (Tacha et al. 1984). In addition to geographic separation during fall and winter (when hunting occurs), Iverson et al. (1983) found differences in internal parasites that suggested separation during nesting. Important de-

mographic differences were evident between subpopulations (Table 4). Tacha et al. (1986) refined the geographic separation of subpopulations during winter, and Tacha et al. (1985b, 1986, 1992) reiterated the need for independent management of subpopulations.

Improved surveys are needed to accurately monitor Mid-continent population and subpopulation trends. Tacha et al. (1984, 1986) estimated 530,000 cranes in the Western subpopulation, and Tacha et al. (1986) estimated at least 30,000 cranes in the Gulf Coast subpopulation, leading to the estimate of 560,000 in the Mid-continent population. Miller (1987) estimated 540,000 Mid-continent birds. A vertical photographic transect survey was used to estimate about 510,000 Mid-continent cranes staging in the North Platte and Platte River valleys, Nebraska during March 1982 (Benning and Johnson 1987). There are no recent estimates of Mid-continent population size. However, Muehl (1994) used a stratified random sample of ¼-sections in the wintering area of the Gulf Coast subpopulation and estimated 166,000 (SE = 81,000) cranes in that subpopulation in late November 1992. This estimate is preliminary, but the random ¼-section ground counts hold promise as an inventory technique for the Gulf Coast subpopulation.

Winter surveys in western Texas are only effective during dry years when the Western subpopulation of Mid-continent cranes is concentrated. Mid-continent cranes concentrate in the North Platte and Platte River valleys during spring migration, and aerial surveys to estimate their numbers have been conducted since 1975 (Benning and Johnson 1987). The current annual photo-corrected-ocular-transect survey has been conducted since 1981. Numbers of additional cranes observed outside the transect survey area are added to produce an annual, but highly variable, index of Mid-continent population size (Table 5). A 3-year average (Table 5) is used to smooth index trends (Sharp and Vogel 1992). The 3-year averages vary widely, lower the utility of the index, and extend the number of years of surveys needed to detect statistically significant changes. The current (1993) management plan calls for maintaining the Mid-continent population (as measured by the spring index) at 404,000 ± 15%.

The spring survey, as currently conducted, is not recording a consistent proportion of Mid-continent cranes. The variability of the index, minimal contribution (<2%) of external surveys, and major discrepancy between the 510,000–560,000 population size and the index average of 360,000, suggests that current procedures are inadequate.

Two major variables control numbers of cranes estimated in the transect survey area. Peak crane numbers in Nebraska may occur before or after the transect survey. Numbers of cranes in the transect survey area can change dramatically from 1 day to the next. Also, an increasing proportion of the Mid-continent population may not stage in Nebraska. Folk and Tacha (1991) documented substantial reductions in crane use of the North Platte River Valley (part of the transect survey area) between 1980 and 1989 that were highly associated with declining habitat quality. Improved procedures are needed to more accurately estimate numbers and trends of each subpopulation (Research Needs).

We suggest winter survey methods be developed to accurately estimate numbers of the Gulf Coast subpopulation (Research Needs), and the Western subpopulation be surveyed during winter when drought occurs (Iverson et al. 1985*a*, Tacha et al. 1986). Spring vertical-photographic-transect surveys (Benning and Johnson 1987) should be conducted at regular intervals (e.g., every 5 years), with new procedures developed (Research Needs) to locate and estimate numbers of cranes outside the transect survey area. Results of winter and spring surveys should be compared when appropriate.

Other Populations.—The Pacific and Central Flyway Councils (1991) have set a population objective of 18,000–22,000 for the Rocky Mountain population of sandhill cranes. These pop-

Table 5. Population index of Mid-continent sandhill cranes estimates during coordinated spring surveys in the Central Flyway during 1982–93 (from Sharp and Vogel 1992 and J. W. Solberg, unpubl. reps.).

Year	Annual index	3-year average
1982	437,100	
1983	354,900	
1984	282,700	358,233
1985	530,463	389,354
1986	356,340	389,834
1987	416,408	434,404
1988	471,187	414,645
1989	393,895	427,163
1990	438,694	434,592
1991	341,785	391,458
1992	420,100	400,167
1993	446,800	402,867

ulation levels provide for consumptive and nonconsumptive use while limiting crop depredations, and are consistent with current habitat availability. Population status is monitored annually, primarily by spring aerial surveys in the San Luis Valley of Colorado where nearly all the Rocky Mountain population concentrates during northward migration. Aerial survey data are adjusted for both visibility bias (photo-correction) and to remove *G. c. canadensis* (correction factor from concurrent ground surveys to determining proportion of lesser sandhill cranes present). The resulting index is considered sufficiently accurate to monitor the Rocky Mountain population relative to the population objective and to influence subsequent harvest objectives. The index was within the population objective range during 4 of the 7 years 1987–93 (Table 6). Survey conditions can range from poor to ideal in spring, and emphasis is placed on those surveys with ideal conditions when making management decisions based on the spring index.

The management plan for the Pacific Coast population suggests maintaining the wintering population of lesser sandhill cranes in California at the current level of 20,000–25,000 (Pacific Flyway Council 1983*b*). The primary means of monitoring trends in this population are by evaluating changes in portions of the annual Alaska breeding crane survey conducted in the Bristal Bay and Upper Cook Inlet lowlands, and counts conducted on wintering areas. Winter counts are difficult because the lesser subspecies from the Pacific Coast population mix with the greater subspecies from the Central Valley popula-

Table 6.   Population index of Rocky Mountain sandhill cranes estimated during spring surveys in the San Luis Valley, Colorado 1984–93 (from D. E. Sharp, 1993 unpubl. rep.).

Year	Survey estimate	Adjusted for visibility bias[a]	Adjusted to remove G. c. candensis[b]	Survey conditions
1984	10,952	14,263		Poor
1985	18,393	21,448		Ideal
1986	14,031	15,958		Poor
1987	12,754	14,074	13,175	Poor
1988	17,765	19,951	18,665	Poor
1989	17,706	18,816	17,399	Ideal
1990	21,301	24,676	21,292	Ideal
1991	20,356	18,502	16,130	Ideal
1992	23,516	23,516	20,014	Poor
1993	17,582	17,582	16,457	Poor

[a] The survey estimate was adjusted for visibility bias using aerial photography.
[b] The photo-corrected estimate was adjusted to remove G. c. canadensis using proportions of G. c. canadensis observed in ground counts conducted concurrent with air surveys.

tion. Both breeding and winter surveys would be aided by better delineation of populations in Alaska and California, respectively.

The Pacific Flyway Council (1983a) has indicated the need to increase fall numbers of the Central Valley population of sandhill cranes to 4,000. However, Pogson and Lindstedt (1991) estimated 5,000–7,000 in the population, primarily due to increased numbers from British Columbia detected during improved winter surveys and increased concentration of sandhill cranes during their study. Winter surveys may hold the best potential for monitoring this population, but problems with unknown subspecific composition and mixing with other populations need additional investigation.

The Lower Colorado River Valley population objective is 2,400–2,600 during winter (Pacific Flyway Council 1989). The current population size is stable at 1,400–2,100 (Table 1) based on winter surveys. These winter counts are questionable due to unknown levels of mixing with other populations.

Adequate monitoring of population trends seems to be in progress for the Rocky Mountain population. However, adequate techniques are needed to identify subspecies and populations in wintering areas of the Pacific Coast, Central Valley, and Lower Colorado River Valley populations before winter surveys can be used reliably for monitoring. Breeding surveys may be adequate for monitoring the Pacific Coast population, but the breeding range of this population needs better delineation. Surveys during

migration seem unreliable except for the Rocky Mountain population.

Harvest Management

Mid-continent Population.—The Federal Sandhill Crane Hunting Permit and attendant surveys have allowed reasonably accurate estimates of crane harvest in the Central Flyway since 1975. This procedure should be continued until sampling of hunters is assumed by the National Migratory Bird Harvest Information Program. Continuing both surveys for 2–3 years would provide continuity and useful comparisons.

Recreational harvest estimates from Canada are probably adequate. However, estimates of recreational harvest in Mexico and Siberia and subsistence harvest in Mexico, Canada, Siberia, and Alaska are needed. Although some data are currently being collected on sport harvest in Mexico and subsistence harvest in Canada and Alaska, reliable surveys and publication of results are needed for all of the above areas. Valid estimates are needed of unretrieved harvest (currently assumed to be 20% of retrieved harvest based on hunter estimates). No viable data are available, but about 30% of the total harvest of Mid-continent cranes is assumed to come from Mexico (10%) and from unretrieved harvest (20%). Subsistence harvest is not currently considered in calculations of total harvest.

Separate harvest estimates should be made for the Western and Gulf Coast subpopulations. Formulae and rationale for deriving harvest objectives and allocations for each subpopulation in the U.S. and Canada should be formalized (in the "Management Plan") using the best estimates of all subsistence harvests, recreational harvests in Mexico and Siberia, and trends in subpopulation size.

Rocky Mountain and Pacific Coast Populations.—Recreational harvest of the Rocky Mountain population is monitored adequately through the hunting permit system. Recreational harvest of the Pacific Coast population in Alaska is monitored via surveys of duck stamp purchasers hunting in southern coastal Alaska. Estimates from this source are probably inaccurate, but implementation of the National Migratory Bird Harvest Information Program should allow better estimates. Improved estimates are needed of subsistence harvests in Mexico and Alaska, recreational harvests in Mexico, and unretrieved harvest in all areas where these populations are hunted.

Harvest Rates and Harvest Objectives.— Sandhill cranes have relatively low recruitment rates that limit the ability of populations to recover from declines. Thus, careful and reasonably precise harvest management is required for populations subject to recreational harvest.

Crude estimates of current harvest rates (total retrieved and unretrieved harvest/population size) are 4% for the Western subpopulation and 13% for the Gulf Coast subpopulation of Mid-continent cranes, <2% for the Pacific Coast population, and about 2–3% for the Rocky Mountain population. Assuming 4–6% additive natural mortality for each population (Tacha et al. 1992), average annual mortality of hunted populations and subpopulations varies from 7 to 19%.

The Western subpopulation of Mid-continent cranes and the Pacific Coast population both probably average about 11 and 8.4% young, respectively, in winter populations (Table 3, Herter 1982), and combined harvest and natural mortality do not seem to exceed recruitment. Recruitment in the Rocky Mountain population averaged about 5.6% during 1985–92, with a crude annual mortality rate apparently near 6–9% (R. C. Drewien, unpubl. data). This suggests that harvest of the Rocky Mountain population should not be increased from current levels unless recruitment increases, and underscores the need for continuing relatively precise management of harvests and monitoring of recruitment and population size on an annual basis. The 13% harvest rate of the Gulf Coast subpopulation (circa 3,900 retrieved and unretrieved harvest/ 30,000) seems high, even though adding 4–5% natural mortality does not exceed the estimated 18% recruitment. This high harvest rate may be due to a poor estimate of population size (30,000); using the preliminary estimate of 166,000 from Muehl (1994) would reduce the harvest rate to 2.3%, the overall mortality rate to 6–8%, and suggest substantial growth in the subpopulation.

The analysis of current harvest rates is crude, and is intended only to provide a general sense of the propriety of current harvest management for sandhill cranes in North America. Most important, this analysis demonstrates the need to clearly understand how appropriate harvest depends on population size and objectives, annual recruitment, and natural and total mortality. Proper management of hunted crane popula-

tions requires valid estimates of all forms of harvest (recreational, subsistence, unretrieved), annual recruitment, and population size. Understanding variation in population size will depend upon precise estimates of survival.

RESEARCH NEEDS

Funds for research to improve management of sandhill cranes have been limited, yet substantial additional information is required to facilitate population, harvest, and/or habitat management. The research needs listed are in priority order.

1. Delineate numbers and trends of the Western and Gulf Coast subpopulations of Mid-continent sandhill cranes. Random ¼-section ground surveys (Muehl 1994) hold promise for inventory of the Gulf Coast subpopulation. Compare results of spring transect surveys with winter surveys. Place radio transmitters on a relatively large sample of birds in representative wintering areas and track through spring migration; use results from 2–3 years to estimate the average percentage of birds in the spring transect survey area, annual variation, and location of birds outside the survey area.

2. Estimate subsistence harvests in Alaska and Canada and subsistence and recreational harvests in Mexico and Siberia. Develop reliable surveys and obtain international cooperation to acquire data.

3. Estimate unretrieved harvest in major harvest areas. Compare estimates from hunter reports to data obtained from direct observation of hunters.

4. Improve population delineation and range boundaries, and numbers of cranes in the Pacific Flyway. Collar and/or radiomarking and adequate tracking efforts on breeding, migration staging, and wintering areas will be required. Cost-effective annual inventory methods need to be developed.

5. Examine relationships of bag limits, season lengths, and season dates with magnitude of harvest in high-harvest areas of Mid-continent cranes. Use findings to more carefully regulate harvest should it become necessary. Manipulate harvest regulations in experimental study areas in high-harvest regions to evaluate effectiveness of regulation alternatives.

6. Identify annual variation in recruitment of

young into the fall flight for each population and subpopulation. Methods have been developed (Tacha and Vohs 1984), but data from at least 5 consecutive years are needed to identify stability and predictability of recruitment.

7. Define the taxonomic relationships of subspecies to subpopulations and populations. Systematic sampling of cranes from throughout the breeding range of the Mid-continent population and analyses of morphometrics and mtDNA are needed to allow more precise biological definition of manageable units.

8. Develop, test, and recommend techniques that effectively reduce or eliminate crop depredations by sandhill cranes.

9. Document pre-fledging survival and energetics of reproduction.

10. Develop and test population models applicable to subpopulations of Mid-continent sandhill cranes.

RECOMMENDATIONS

Specific recommendations are presented in descending order of priority.

1. The U.S. Fish and Wildlife Service (USFWS) and the Central Flyway Council (CFC) should implement independent population assessment and harvest management for each subpopulation of Mid-continent sandhill cranes.

2. The USFWS, CFC, and Canadian Wildlife Service should conduct, assist, fund, and/or promote funding of the applied research identified while maintaining ongoing surveys and other management efforts.

3. The USFWS and Mississippi Flyway Council should develop and implement a management plan for the Eastern population of greater sandhill cranes. The USFWS and Pacific Flyway Council should immediately update management plans for the Pacific Coast (Pacific Flyway) and Central Valley populations, and update all others at 5–10 year intervals.

4. The USFWS and the Nebraska Game and Parks Commission should take the lead in forming a coalition of private, state, and federal agencies dedicated to delineating specific priorities for, and funding acquisition/protection and management of, crane habitat complexes in central Nebraska.

5. The USFWS and the Texas Parks and Wildlife Department should prioritize and fund protection and management of key saline pluvial lakes used in winter by cranes in western Texas.

6. The USFWS, Pacific Flyway Council, and relevant state agencies should review and fund habitat needs identified in management plans for populations of sandhill cranes in the western U.S.

ACKNOWLEDGMENTS

We thank S. L. Beasom and F. S. Guthery for reviewing an early draft of this manuscript. The manuscript benefitted greatly from critical reviews by J. C. Bartonek, R. C. Drewien, and D. E. Sharp. J. Herbert and C. D. Littlefield also provided valuable comments.

LITERATURE CITED

AMERICAN ORNITHOLOGISTS' UNION. 1957. A.O.U. checklist of North American birds. Lord Baltimore Press. Baltimore, Md. 691pp.

BALDWIN, J. H. 1977. A comparative study of sandhill crane subspecies. Ph.D. Thesis, Univ. Wisconsin, Madison. 150pp.

BENNETT, A. J. 1989. Movements and home range of Florida sandhill cranes. J. Wildl. Manage. 53: 830–836.

BENNING, D. S., AND D. H. JOHNSON. 1987. Recent improvements to sandhill crane surveys in Nebraska's central Platte Valley. Pages 10–16 in J. C. Lewis, ed. Proc. 1985 Int. Crane Workshop. U.S. Fish and Wildl. Serv., Grand Island, Nebr.

BISHOP, M. A. 1988. Factors affecting productivity and habitat use of Florida sandhill cranes: an evaluation of three areas in central Florida for a nonmigratory population of whooping cranes. Ph.D. Thesis, Univ. Florida, Gainesville. 190pp.

BOISE, C. M. 1976. Breeding biology of the lesser sandhill crane Grus canadensis canadensis (L.) on the Yukon-Kuskokwim Delta, Alaska. M.S. Thesis, Univ. Alaska, Fairbanks. 79pp.

CARLISLE, M. J. 1982. Nesting habitat of sandhill cranes in central Alberta. Pages 44–55 in J. C. Lewis, ed. Proc. 1981 Int. Crane Workshop. Natl. Audubon Soc., Tavernier, Fla.

CENTRAL AND PACIFIC FLYWAY COUNCILS. 1993. Management plan for the Mid-continent population of sandhill cranes. U. S. Fish and Wildl. Serv., Migratory Bird Manage., Off., Golden, Colo. 44pp.

DREWIEN, R. C. 1973. Ecology of Rocky Mountain greater sandhill cranes. Ph.D. Thesis, Univ. Idaho, Moscow. 153pp.

———, AND E. G. BIZEAU. 1974. Status and distribution of greater sandhill cranes in the Rocky Mountains. J. Wildl. Manage. 38:720–742.

ELLIS, D. H., G. H. OLSEN, G. F. GEE, J. M. NICOLICH, K. E. O'MALLEY, M. NAGENDRAN, S. G. HEREFORD, P. RANGE, W. T. HARPER, R. P.

INGRAM, AND D. G. SMITH. 1992. Techniques for rearing and releasing non-migratory cranes: lessons from Mississippi sandhill crane program. Pages 135–141 *in* D. W. Stahlecker, ed. Proc. 1991 North Am. Crane Workshop. Platte River Trust, Grand Island, Nebr.

FOLK, M. J., AND T. C. TACHA. 1990. Sandhill crane roost site characteristics in the North Platte River Valley. J. Wildl. Manage. 54:480–486.

———, AND ———. 1991. Distribution of sandhill cranes in the North Platte River Valley 1980 and 1989. Prairie Nat. 23:11–16.

GUTHERY, F. S. 1975. Food habits of sandhill cranes in southern Texas. J. Wildl. Manage. 39:221–223.

HERTER, D. R. 1982. Staging of sandhill cranes on the Copper River Delta, Alaska. Pages 273–280 *in* J. C. Lewis, ed. Proc. 1981 Int. Crane Workshop. Natl. Audubon Soc., Tavernier, Fla.

IVERSON, G. C. 1981. Seasonal variation in lipid content and condition indices of sandhill cranes from mid-continental North America. M.S. Thesis, Oklahoma State Univ., Stillwater. 38pp.

———, P. A. VOHS, AND T. C. TACHA. 1985a. Distribution and abundance of sandhill cranes wintering in western Texas. J. Wildl. Manage. 49:250–255.

———, ———, AND ———. 1985b. Habitat use by sandhill cranes wintering in western Texas. J. Wildl. Manage. 49:1074–1083.

———, ———, AND ———. 1987. Habitat use by mid-continent sandhill cranes during spring migration. J. Wildl. Manage. 51:448–458.

———, ———, A. A. KOCAN, AND K. A. WALDRUP. 1983. Some helminth parasites of sandhill cranes from mid-continental North America. J. Wildl. Dis. 19:56–59.

KLIMKIEWICZ, K. M., AND A. G. FUTCHER. 1989. Longevity records of North American birds. J. Field Ornithol. 60:469–494.

KRAPU, G. L., D. E. FACEY, E. K. FRITZELL, AND D. H. JOHNSON. 1984. Habitat use by migrant sandhill cranes in Nebraska. J. Wildl. Manage. 48:407–417.

———, G. C. IVERSON, K. J. REINEKE, AND C. M. BOISE. 1985. Fat deposition and usage by arctic nesting sandhill cranes during spring. Auk 102:362–368.

LEWIS, J. C., CHAIRMAN. 1977. Sandhill crane. Pages 4–53 *in* G. C. Sanderson, ed. Management of migratory shore and upland game birds in North America. Int. Assoc. Fish and Wildl. Agencies, Washington, D.C.

LITTLEFIELD, C. D. 1981a. Mate swapping of sandhill cranes. J. Field Ornithol. 52:244–245.

———. 1981b. The greater sandhill crane. Pages 163–166 *in* J. C. Lewis and H. Masatomi, eds. Crane research around the world. Int. Crane Found., Baraboo, Wis.

———, AND R. A. RYDER. 1968. Breeding biology of the greater sandhill crane on Malheur National Wildlife Refuge, Oregon. Trans. North Am. Wildl. and Nat. Resour. Conf. 33:444–454.

LOVVORN, J. R., AND C. M. KIRKPATRICK. 1981. Roosting behavior and habitat of migrant greater sandhill cranes. J. Wildl. Manage. 45:842–857.

———, AND ———. 1982. Field use by staging

eastern greater sandhill cranes. J. Wildl. Manage. 46:99–108.

MELVIN, S. M., AND S. A. TEMPLE. 1983. Fall migration and mortality of Interlake, Manitoba sandhill cranes in North Dakota. J. Wildl. Manage. 47:805–817.

MILLER, H. W. 1987. Hunting in the management of mid-continent sandhill cranes. Pages 30–46 *in* J. C. Lewis, ed. Proc. 1985 Int. Crane Workshop. U. S. Fish and Wildl. Serv., Grand Island, Nebr.

MUEHL, G. T. 1994. Distribution and abundance of water birds and wetlands in coastal Texas. M.S. Thesis, Texas A&M Univ.–Kingsville, Kingsville. 130pp.

NESBITT, S. A. 1989. The significance of mate loss in Florida sandhill cranes. Wilson Bull. 101:648–651.

———. 1992. First reproductive success and individual productivity in sandhill cranes. J. Wildl. Manage. 56:573–577.

———, AND A. S. WENNER. 1987. Pair formation and mate fidelity in sandhill cranes. Pages 117–122 *in* J. C. Lewis, ed. Proc. 1985 Int. Crane Workshop. U.S. Fish and Wildl. Serv., Grand Island, Nebr.

———, AND K. S. WILLIAMS. 1990. Home range and habitat use of Florida sandhill cranes. J. Wildl. Manage. 54:92–96.

NOVARA, A. N., AND M. HANDY. 1991. Sandhill crane harvest and hunter activity in the Central Flyway during the 1990–91 hunting season. U.S. Fish and Wildl. Serv., Off. Migratory Bird Manage. Adm. Rep. 14pp.

PACIFIC FLYWAY COUNCIL. 1983a. Management plan for the Central Valley population of greater sandhill cranes. U.S. and Wildl. Serv., Migratory Bird Manage. Off., Portland, Oreg. 28pp.

———. 1983b. Management plan for the Pacific Flyway population of lesser sandhill cranes. U.S. Fish and Wildl. Serv., Migratory Bird Manage. Off., Portland, Oreg. 19pp.

———. 1989. Management plan for the Lower Colorado River Valley population of greater sandhill cranes. U.S. Fish and Wildl. Serv., Migratory Bird Manage. Off., Portland, Oreg. 32pp.

PACIFIC AND CENTRAL FLYWAY COUNCILS. 1991. Management plan for the Rocky Mountain population of greater sandhill cranes. U.S. Fish and Wildl. Serv., Migratory Bird Manage. Off., Portland, Oreg. 55pp.

PERKINS, D. L., AND D. E. BROWN. 1981. The sandhill crane in Arizona. Ariz. Game and Fish Dep. Spec. Publ. 11. 47pp.

POGSON, T. H., AND S. M. LINDSTEDT. 1991. Distribution and abundance of large sandhill cranes, *Grus canadensis*, wintering in California's Central Valley. Condor 93:266–278.

REINEKE, K. J., AND G. L. KRAPU. 1986. Feeding ecology of sandhill cranes during spring migration in Nebraska. J. Wildl. Manage. 50:71–79.

SHARP, D. E., AND W. O. VOGEL. 1992. Population status, hunting regulations, hunting activity, and harvest of mid-continent sandhill cranes. Pages 24–32 *in* D. W. Stahlecker, ed. Proc. 1991 North Am. Crane Workshop. Platte River Trust, Grand Island, Nebr.

SMITH, E. B., AND J. M. VALENTINE, JR. 1987. Habitat changes within the Mississippi sandhill crane range in Jackson County, Mississippi (1942–1984). Pages 342–354 in J. C. Lewis, ed. Proc. 1985 Int. Crane Workshop. U.S. Fish and Wildl. Serv., Grand Island, Nebr.

SOINE, P. J. 1982. Roost habitat selection by sandhill cranes in central North Dakota. Pages 88–94 in J. C. Lewis, ed. Proc. 1981 Int. Crane Workshop. Natl. Audubon Soc., Tavernier, Fla.

STEPHEN, W. J. D. 1967. Bionomics of the sandhill crane. Can. Wildl. Serv. Rep. Ser. 2. 48pp.

TACHA, T. C. 1981. Behavior and taxonomy of sandhill cranes from mid-continental North America. Ph.D. Thesis, Oklahoma State Univ., Stillwater. 110pp.

———. 1988. Social organization of sandhill cranes from mid-continental North America Wildl. Monogr. 99. 37pp.

———, AND J. C. LEWIS. 1979. Sex determination of sandhill cranes by cloacal examination. Pages 81–83 in J. C. Lewis, ed. Proc. 1978 Int. Crane Workshop. Natl. Audubon Soc., New York, N.Y.

———, AND P. A. VOHS. 1984. Some population parameters of sandhill cranes from mid-continental North America. J. Wildl. Manage. 48:89–98.

———, ———, AND G. C. IVERSON. 1984. Migration routes of sandhill cranes from mid-continental North America. J. Wildl. Manage. 48:1028–1033.

———, C. JORGENSON, AND P. S. TAYLOR. 1985a. Harvest, migration, and condition of sandhill cranes in Saskatchewan. J. Wildl. Manage. 49: 476–480.

———, P. A. VOHS, AND W. D. WARDE. 1985b. Morphometric variation of sandhill cranes from mid-continental North America. J. Wildl. Manage. 49:246–250.

———, D. E. HALEY, AND R. R. GEORGE. 1986. Population and harvest characteristics of sandhill cranes in southern Texas. J. Wildl. Manage. 50: 80–83.

———, P. A. VOHS, AND G. C. IVERSON. 1987. Time and energy budgets of sandhill cranes from mid-continental North America. J. Wildl. Manage. 51: 440–448.

———, AND P. A. VOHS. 1989. Age of sexual maturity in sandhill cranes from mid-continental North America. J. Wildl. Manage. 53:43–46.

———, S. A. NESBITT, AND P. A. VOHS. 1992. Sandhill crane. in A. Poole, P. Stettenheim, and F. Gill, eds. The birds of North America, No. 31. Acad. Nat. Sci., Philadelphia and Am. Ornithol. Union, Washington, D.C. 24pp.

VALENTINE, J. M., JR. 1981. The Mississippi sandhill crane, 1980. Pages 167–174 in J. C. Lewis and H. Masatomi, eds. Crane research around the world. Int. Crane Found., Baraboo, Wis.

———, AND R. E. NOBLE. 1970. A colony of sandhill cranes in Mississippi. J. Wildl. Manage. 34: 761–768.

WALKER, D. L., AND S. D. SCHEMNITZ. 1987. Food habits of sandhill cranes in relation to agriculture in central and southwestern New Mexico. Pages 201–212 in J. C. Lewis, ed. Proc. 1985 Int. Crane Workshop. U.S. Fish and Wildl. Serv., Grand Island, Nebr.

WALKINSHAW, L. H. 1949. The sandhill cranes. Cranbrook Inst. Sci. Bull. 29. Bloomfield Hills, Mich. 202pp.

———. 1973. Cranes of the world. Winchester Press, New York, N.Y. 370pp.

WENNER, A. S., AND S. A. NESBITT. 1987. Wintering of greater sandhill cranes in Florida. Pages 196–200 in J. C. Lewis, ed. Proc. 1985 Int. Crane Workshop. U.S. Fish and Wildl. Serv., Grand Island, Nebr.

WINDINGSTAD, R. M. 1988. Nonhunting mortality in sandhill cranes. J. Wildl. Manage. 52:260–263.

Chapter 7

AMERICAN WOODCOCK

J. ASHLEY STRAW, JR.,[1] Migratory Bird Management Office, U.S. Fish and Wildlife Service, Laurel, MD 20708-4016
DAVID G. KREMENTZ, Southeast Research Group, National Biological Survey, Warnell School of Forest Resources, The University of Georgia, Athens, GA 30602-2152
MICHAEL W. OLINDE, Louisiana Department of Wildlife and Fisheries, P.O. Box 98000, Baton Rouge, LA 70898
GREG F. SEPIK, U.S. Fish and Wildlife Service, Moosehorn National Wildlife Refuge, P.O. Box X, Calais, ME 04619

Abstract: American woodcock (*Scolopax minor*) are managed as 2 populations, roughly separated by the Appalachian Mountains. Both the Eastern and Central populations have declined since 1968. The total United States harvest was >1.1 million in 1990 and the average composition was 26% juvenile males, 25% juvenile females, 21% adult males, and 28% adult females. Band recovery rates range from 2.5 to 4.7%. Major management needs include harvest estimates for the United States, a habitat management manual for wintering areas, techniques for monitoring habitat changes on a continental scale, and increased emphasis on management of early-successional forest habitat on private lands. Major research needs include identifying habitat requirements of woodcock in winter and improving understanding of woodcock population dynamics.

DESCRIPTION

Woodcock (*Scolopax* spp.) belong to Order Charadriiformes, Family Scolopacidae and Subfamily Scolopacinae, with 6 species recognized by Howard and Moore (1991). American woodcock (*S. minor*) are native to only the eastern portion of the Nearctic and have no recognized subspecies. European woodcock (*S. rusticola*) occur throughout much of the Palearctic region.

A variety of local names have been applied to American woodcock and contribute to confusion regarding distribution and abundance of this bird during the colonial period. Some local names include: timberdoodle, snipe, brush/cane/wood snipe, hill partridge, bec noir, bog borer, and bog sucker. Pettingill (1936:187) presents a more exhaustive list.

Woodcock weights vary with sex, age, feeding conditions, and time of year, but are generally highest immediately before fall migration when juveniles weigh as much as adults. Females collected in Maine during late October averaged 215 g while males averaged 174 g (Mendall and Aldous 1943, Owen and Krohn 1973). Woodcock plumage has a pattern of mottled browns, blacks, and buff that provides effective camouflage against a backdrop of fallen leaves. Short, powerful wings permit excellent maneuverability and facilitate flight through thickets and tangled brush as woodcock travel between feeding areas, singing-grounds, and roosting areas. The 3 outermost primaries are narrow and cause the distinctive "twittering" sound characteristic of the male's courtship display and flushed woodcock. The short legs are composed of "white" muscle tissue and are poorly positioned for long periods of walking; woodcock usually fly between singing grounds, nocturnal roosting sites, and feeding areas.

The most distinctive features of woodcock are the large bill and the position of the eyes. The bill is 60–75 mm in length (Mendall and Aldous 1943) and has a prehensile tip that can be opened to capture food even while thrust in soil. The underside of the mandible and tongue are roughened and enhance the woodcock's grasp on earthworms and other invertebrates. The eyes are large and set far back in the head, providing a field of view behind, above, and to the front. This adaptation enables woodcock to detect approaching predators while feeding.

Female woodcock are larger than males when fully grown, permitting gender identification on the basis of body measurements. Bill length is considered the most reliable criteria for distinguishing gender (Mendall and Aldous 1943), as woodcock with bills <68 mm are usually males ($\bar{x}$ = 64.7, SD = 2.8) and woodcock with bills >68 mm are usually females ($\bar{x}$ = 71.0, SD = 2.6). Other reliable criteria include length of the wing (Artmann and Schroeder 1976), and width of primaries VIII–X (Greeley 1953).

Age of woodcock chicks to 15 days can be

---

[1] Deceased.

estimated from bill length based on the formula:

$$AGE = \frac{BILL\ LENGTH\ -\ 14}{2}$$

where age is in days and bill length is in millimeters (Ammann 1982). Approximate ages of older chicks can be estimated from a growth curve (Ammann 1982:fig. 1).

During early summer, 3 age classes can be identified: young of the year (identified by juvenal plumage until Jul–Aug [Duvall 1955]), second-year birds (identified by the presence of juvenal secondaries [Martin 1964]), and after-second-year birds. After molt in late summer, presence of juvenal secondaries is used to distinguish between hatching-year and after-hatching-year birds, and is the basis for age classification of wings collected during the U.S. Fish and Wildlife Service's (USFWS) "Wing Collection Survey." Primary wear is also used to differentiate between hatching-year and after-hatching-year birds during fall (Sheldon et al. 1958).

LIFE HISTORY

Spring Migration

Gonadal recrudescence begins in late January or February (Stamps and Doerr 1977, Roberts and Dimmick 1978, Walker and Causey 1982, Whiting and Boggus 1982, Olinde and Prickett 1991), coinciding closely with departure from wintering areas. However, during warm winters, some woodcock remain in the southern United States and begin nesting during February (Causey et al. 1974, 1987). Woodcock that breed in southern states may subsequently migrate northward. Causey et al. (1987) documented 2 examples, 1 involving a brood hen and the other, an unrelated chick, that were banded in spring in Alabama and shot that fall in Michigan. Woodcock are among the earliest spring migrants, arriving in northern breeding areas while snow and freezing temperatures are still common (late Mar–early Apr). Woodcock have moderate natal site fidelity. In a review of recoveries of chicks banded in Michigan, indirect (after year of banding) recoveries of woodcock shot in September were seldom (<5%) >48 km from site of banding (J. A. Straw, unpubl. data), suggesting that woodcock return to breed within several kilometers of where they hatched.

Courtship

Courtship continues after arrival in breeding areas. As long as temperatures are above freezing, males move at dusk and dawn to singing grounds in forest openings or fields and perform their courtship display. During the seasonal peak of courtship activities, the normal display period lasts approximately 40–50 minutes, consisting of 9–13 courtship flights (Mendall and Aldous 1943). Courtship begins with a ground display where the male utters a nasal "peent" every 2–4 seconds for about 1 minute. The ground display is followed by 45–60 seconds of aerial display (flight song) where the male flies in spirals above the singing ground and utters a melodic, warbling call while creating a distinctive whistling sound with the outer primaries of his wings. After alighting at the departure point, the male repeats the sequence of ground and aerial displays. On moonlit nights during the peak season of courtship activity, some males continue to perform sporadically throughout the night (Sheldon 1971).

Although males usually use >1 singing ground during a breeding season, 1 singing ground serves as a focal point of activity (McAuley et al. 1993). Furthermore, males have high affinity for the preferred singing ground in subsequent years, with about 30% of recaptures occurring on the same singing grounds, and 95% within 1.5 km of a singing ground used in a previous year (Sheldon 1971, Godfrey 1974, Dwyer et al. 1988). Although capable of breeding in their first year, many males present at singing grounds do not participate in courtship activities (Sheldon 1971, Godfrey 1974). These non-displaying (sub-dominant) males serve a vital function. Dominant males have high mortality rates on singing grounds (J. R. Longcore, unpubl. data) and are quickly replaced by sub-dominant males when killed (Modafferi 1967, Sheldon 1971, Godfrey 1974, Ellingwood 1983). The presence of non-displaying males results in a variable number of males per active singing ground. Over a 5-year period, Dwyer et al. (1988) observed a range of 1.2–2.4 males per active singing ground in Maine.

Females arrive in breeding areas at approximately the same time as males, and mating may occur several times during the following 2–3 weeks. A female may visit as many as 3 males per evening and >1 female may visit a male during 1 crepuscular period (McAuley et al. 1993). Visitation of singing grounds by females is most common prior to nesting; however, visitation is sporadic and a given female may visit singing grounds during only 14% of available crepuscular periods (McAuley et al. 1993). During most crepuscular periods, the hen remains in diurnal cover or moves to another forested cover.

Nesting

Females have high nest site fidelity. Dwyer et al. (1982) recaptured 6 hens with broods near ($\bar{x}$ = 303.5 m) previous (≥ 1 year) capture sites, and 5 brood-hens (initially banded as chicks) were recaptured 5 to 1,380 m from their initial capture sites. Woodcock construct a simple nest consisting of a shallow depression lined with leaves, usually in early growth hardwoods (Mendall and Aldous 1943, Maxfield 1961, Sheldon 1971, Kinsley et al. 1982, Gregg 1984) (Fig. 1). Mean clutch size is about 4 eggs (3.9, Mendall and Aldous 1943; 3.8, McAuley et al. 1990). Nest success is high; estimates range from 43 to 67% (Mendall and Aldous 1943, Gregg 1984, McAuley et al. 1990) and woodcock readily renest after losing a clutch or brood. Thus, woodcock have a fairly high reproductive potential despite their small clutch size.

In contrast to the strong nest site fidelity associated with successful nesting attempts, renesting attempts are several kilometers ($\bar{x}$ = 6.7 km) distant from the destroyed nest. Also, average clutch size of the second nest ($\bar{x}$ = 3.0) is smaller than the first (McAuley et al. 1990). The incidence of nest loss is variable from year to year, but tends to be highest when weather is cold and wet during incubation (Gregg 1984). There is no evidence of hens laying a second clutch after a brood has been raised successfully (McAuley et al. 1990).

Incubation lasts 21 days and is performed solely by the female (Mendall and Aldous 1943). Peak hatch ranges from approximately 1 March in Alabama (Causey 1981) to mid-May in northern breeding areas (Sheldon 1971, Dwyer et al. 1982, Gregg 1984). Females continue to visit singing grounds during incubation, but at reduced rates (McAuley et al. 1993). Dwyer et al. (1988) and McAuley et al. (1993) speculate this continued contact encourages the male to continue courtship displays, ensuring the female can be inseminated if the first clutch is lost.

Woodcock young are precocial, but require maternal feeding the first 7 days (Gregg 1984)

Fig. 1. The nest of an American woodcock (Photo by U.S. Fish and Wildlife Service).

and periodic brooding the first 15–20 days (Vander Haegen 1992). Within a few hours of hatching, young are led 100–200 m from the nest (Ammann 1982). Woodcock chicks feed almost exclusively on invertebrates and grow rapidly. Young are capable of short flights after 18 days, while sustained flight and brood dispersal occurs after 4–5 weeks. By 5 weeks, young are almost fully grown and difficult to distinguish from adults. Survival of young from hatching to fledging is variable and dependent primarily upon weather (D. G. McAuley, unpubl. data).

Survival of adults during courtship and nesting also varies with weather (J. R. Longcore, unpubl. data). Persistent snow in spring can prevent feeding and lead to high mortality (Dwyer et al. 1988). Similarly, a lack of snow cover and cold temperatures during winter can result in deep frost depths that reduce availability of earthworms (Vander Haegen et al. 1993) and lead to decreased survival of woodcock (J. R. Longcore, unpubl. data).

Summer

Adults undergo a complete feather molt during summer, finally replacing primaries VIII–X in September or early October. Juveniles undergo a partial molt during July–October. Owen and Krohn (1973) provide a detailed report of woodcock molt patterns and associated changes in body weights.

Most woodcock move to a nocturnal roost at dusk and return to their diurnal covert at dawn. The nocturnal roost is most often a field or a forest opening, but sometimes is a forested area similar to the diurnal covert. Use of fields versus forested areas as roost sites varies by age and gender, with males of all ages and juvenile females being most likely to use fields. Percentage of individuals using fields varies by age and gender but peaks in July (range 61–87%) and declines through late summer and early fall (range 28–53%) (Sepik and Derleth 1993b).

Average monthly diurnal home range in Maine was <20 ha with few differences between age and gender classes. Sizes of diurnal home ranges and movement patterns were smaller for woodcock using sapling stage stands ($\bar{x}$ = 14.6 ha) than for woodcock using older stands ($\bar{x}$ = 29.6 ha) (Sepik and Derleth 1993b). Average monthly nocturnal home ranges of woodcock were variable (range 17–34 ha). Average monthly movement between nocturnal and diurnal sites was also variable (range 137–1,020 m).

Summer (15 Jun–20 Oct) survival rates of adult woodcock ($\bar{x}$ = 0.914) are significantly higher than juvenile survival rates ($\bar{x}$ = 0.675) (Derleth and Sepik 1990). The primary source of mortality during summer is predation (Derleth and Sepik 1990), but starvation also can be important. Sepik et al. (1983) and Dwyer et al. (1988) observed decreased survival rates of juveniles during a drought.

Fall Migration and Winter

Departure from breeding areas begins in October with southward movements continuing into late December. Woodcock in Maine achieved maximum weight by 20 October and were believed physiologically prepared to migrate at that time (Owen and Krohn 1973). However, peak departure from Moosehorn National Wildlife Refuge in eastern Maine occurs during the first week of November (Sepik and Derleth 1993a). Migration in Pennsylvania occurs between 18 November and 8 December (Coon et al. 1976). Migration chronology is affected by wintering latitude and weather, especially strong cold fronts. Evidence of differential migration chronology by age and gender has been supported (Williams 1969, Gregg 1984) and not supported (Sepik and Derleth 1993a).

Weather factors such as temperature and moisture influence food availability and, thus, selection of wintering areas by woodcock. Root (1988) believed the northern wintering distribution of woodcock was related to the January 0 C isotherm. The abundance and distribution of woodcock in Louisiana also varies with winter severity (Williams 1969). Furthermore, during wet winters, woodcock winter more extensively in Texas than during normal or dry winters (R. M. Whiting, pers. commun.). Period survival rates (15 Dec–15 Feb) of woodcock are about 0.8 (Krementz et al. 1994). Most mortality during winter is attributed to predation, although prolonged cold temperatures may result in localized mortality due to starvation (Sheldon 1971).

Woodcock are susceptible to contaminants under certain circumstances. There was a complete closure of woodcock hunting in New Brunswick in 1970 and a partial closure in 1971 in response to concerns over DDT concentrations that resulted from spruce budworm control efforts (Pearce 1971). Woodcock may be exposed to pesticides being used to control either forest or agricultural pests, but the hazard from agricultural pesticides is highest in wintering areas when woodcock are feeding in agricultural fields. Earthworms are fairly resistant to many chemicals and, therefore, may carry toxicants (Davey 1963). Also, since woodcock are first-order predators, there is opportunity for biological magnification of persistent chemicals. Woodcock continue to use nocturnal roost sites during winter. Roosting behavior is variable with birds sometimes roosting in fields or remaining in their diurnal covert. In contrast to summer roosting behavior (Krohn 1970), feeding occurs in nocturnal roosting fields, possibly because of increased energy requirements that cannot be met during diurnal and crepuscular feeding periods (Glasgow 1958, Sheldon 1971, Stribling and Doerr 1985). Courtship flights may occur at any time on the wintering grounds, but are most common during warm spells shortly before spring migration.

Dwyer and Nichols (1982) estimated annual survival rates from band recoveries (Table 1). Survival rate estimates of adults were higher than for juveniles and estimates of female survival rates were greater than males. Overall survival rates for the Central population were greater than overall survival rates for the Eastern population.

HABITAT

Breeding

Singing Grounds.—Male woodcock use a variety of openings as courtship sites including clearcuts, natural openings, roads, pastures, cultivated fields, lawns, and reverting agricultural fields (Mendall and Aldous 1943, Liscinsky 1972). Openings <10 m across may be used by a single male, while larger areas may contain several courting birds (Liscinsky 1972, Rabe and Prince 1982).

The vegetative structure of singing grounds is variable both locally and throughout the breeding range. Openings with surrounding tall vegetation may inhibit use (Gutzwiller and Wakeley 1982), while openings with scattered shrubs were preferred in Pennsylvania (Gutzwiller and Wakeley 1982) and Michigan (Rabe and Prince 1982). Kinsley et al. (1982) found that use of an opening was influenced by amount of litter cover, density of small and large woody shrubs, distance to water, and age of the stand. Sheldon (1971) and Gutzwiller et al. (1983) found vegetative structure of an opening more important than species composition in affecting use by woodcock.

Dwyer et al. (1988) suggested that quality of nesting and brood rearing habitat surrounding an opening determined whether the site was used as a singing ground. Other researchers have also noted that most singing grounds were <100 m from diurnal cover (Mendall and Aldous 1943, Maxfield 1961, Sheldon 1971, Kinsley et al. 1982).

Nesting and Brood Rearing.—Woodcock nest in a variety of habitat types, but most nests are in young, second-growth hardwood stands (Mendall and Aldous 1943, Sheldon 1971, Bourgeois 1977). Nests are often at the base of a tree or shrub (Coon et al. 1982, Gregg 1984), near feeding areas (Mendall and Aldous 1943, Gregg 1984), and <150 m from a singing ground (Mendall and Aldous 1943, Blankenship 1957, Sheldon 1971, Gregg 1984).

Vegetative structure at nest sites is highly variable. In Pennsylvania, density of woody shrubs was about 49,000 stems/ha (Coon et al. 1982, Kinsley and Storm 1989) compared to 20,630 stems/ha in Alabama (Roboski and Causey 1981), and 14,600 stems/ha in New York (Parris 1986). This variability may reflect limited availability of nest sites influenced by weather conditions at time of nest site selection (Sepik et al. 1989). Coon et al. (1982) found low

Table 1. Mean annual survival rates of preseason-banded American woodcock, 1967–75 (after Dwyer and Nichols 1982).

Age/sex	Eastern population		Central population	
	Survival rate	SE	Survival rate	SE
Adult male	0.354	0.052	0.400	0.150
Adult female	0.491	0.073	0.525	0.096
Juvenile male	0.202	0.048	0.356	0.124
Juvenile female	0.358	0.077	0.313	0.094

selectivity in choice of nest sites on the basis of habitat characteristics.

Ideal brood habitat is characterized by dense, hardwood cover on good soils that support an abundance of earthworms. A dense canopy serves to protect broods from avian predators and shades out herbaceous plants allowing broods ready access to earthworms. Brood use of a site is correlated with earthworm abundance (Rabe and Prince 1982, Parris 1986).

Diurnal Habitat.—There is wide variation in plant species composition at diurnal habitat sites, but several plant species-groups are important indicators of potential woodcock habitat because they are early-successional or have growth forms that provide proper habitat structure. Stands of hawthorn (*Crataegus* spp.), alder (*Alnus* spp.), aspen (*Populus* spp.), and dogwood (*Cornus* spp.) are frequently indicators of good woodcock habitat.

A critical determinant of woodcock use of a site is abundance of earthworms. Earthworm biomass at sites used by woodcock in Maine (Nicholson et al. 1977, Sepik and Derleth 1993*b*) and New York (Parris 1986) averaged about 8 g/m² (dry weight). When biomass was below this level, woodcock use declined (Parris 1986). Vegetative composition of a site can influence earthworm abundance (Reynolds et al. 1977, Parris 1986), but soil characteristics, hydrology, and land-use history are of equal or greater importance. In glaciated areas of the breeding range, previously-farmed land with moderately-drained, fine-textured soils hold more earthworms (Owen and Galbraith 1989).

Dense stands of young hardwoods characterize optimal diurnal habitat structure on breeding areas (Morgenweck 1977, Rabe 1977, Hudgins et al. 1985, Parris 1986, Phelps 1986). Woodcock are sometimes found in stands of mature forest, but only if there is a dense understory (Sheldon 1971, Rabe 1977). Straw et al.

Fig. 2.   A mosaic of clearcuts at Moosehorn National Wildlife Refuge, Maine, used to create habitat for American woodcock (Photo by U.S. Fish and Wildlife Service).

(1986) found that optimal diurnal habitat in Pennsylvania occurred in stands with 4,900 saplings/ha, maximum canopy cover of large shrubs (≥32%), and an open overstory (14.3 m²/ha basal area). Sites with <2% exposed mineral soil, <12% cover of small or large shrubs, <1,500 saplings/ha and ≥20 m²/ha basal area were avoided by woodcock. Woodcock use of coniferous stands is minimal in northern breeding areas, except during periods of drought (Sepik et al. 1983).

Nocturnal Habitat.—Many woodcock leave diurnal areas at dusk and fly to openings such as clearcuts, abandoned agricultural fields, pastures, and soybean fields throughout most of the year (Dunford and Owen 1973, Owen and Morgan 1975, Connors and Doerr 1982, Sepik et al. 1986). Woodcock in breeding areas are not selective with regard to these nocturnal roost sites, except they avoid openings with vegetation that is either sparse or dense. Some birds (predominantly females) do not use openings, but instead remain in diurnal covers or move to an alternate forest cover at night (Glasgow 1958, Horton and Causey 1979, Sepik and Derleth 1993*b*).

Creation and Maintenance of Habitat.— Quality woodcock habitat can be created on most sites with suitable soils (Fig. 2). When viewed in a successional context, a clearcut may serve as a nocturnal roost site and singing ground, then nesting, brood-rearing, and diurnal habitat, and ultimately become unsuitable for woodcock as succession proceeds. Optimizing timber operations for woodcock involves entering a forest every 5–10 years to cut small areas adjacent to previous cuts to juxtapose habitat elements critical for woodcock. Shelterwood cuts, clearcuts, heavy thinnings, and group-selection cuts can all be used to create good woodcock habitat in breeding areas. Unmerchantable sites can be treated with forestry site-preparation equipment, herbicides, or burned to set back succession. Sepik et al. (1981) detailed habitat requirements and management options for creating woodcock habitat as did Roberts (1989).

Wintering

Diurnal Habitat.—Typical diurnal woodcock habitat in the lower Mississippi River bottomland hardwoods was described by Glasgow (1958) as consisting of woodlands with scattered thickets of cane (*Arundinaria gigantea*) and blackberry (*Rubus* spp.). Britt (1971) and Dyer and Hamilton (1977) compared habitat conditions at woodcock flushing sites (Fig. 3) to random plots in the same region that Glasgow (1958) worked. Britt (1971) found that blackberry/ dewberry, greenbriars (*Smilax* spp.), supplejack (*Berchemia scandens*), and water oak (*Quercus nigra*) were more common understory plants at flushing sites. Switch-cane, when present on an area, was also associated with flush sites. Britt (1971) stressed the importance of dense stands of other mid-story and shrub species such as devil's-walking-stick (*Aralia spinosa*), swamp dogwood (*Cornus drummondii*), hawthorn, and tree saplings with high vertical-stem densities. He determined that canopy closure (structure) was more important than overstory species composition. Dyer and Hamilton (1977) found similar understory plant species associated with flushing sites.

Although bottomland hardwood sites are traditionally considered the best woodcock habitat, pinelands and their associated drainages in the southeast are extensive and also offer woodcock wintering habitat (Reid and Goodrum 1953; Glasgow 1953, 1958; Pursglove 1975; Kroll and Whiting 1977; Pace and Wood 1979; Johnson and Causey 1982). Understory species composition on pineland sites is different from that of bottomland sites. Glasgow (1953) listed yellow jasmine (*Gelsemium sempervirens*), Japanese honeysuckle (*Lonicera japonica*), grape (*Vitis* spp.), poison ivy (*Toxicodendron radicans*), blackberry, yaupon (*Ilex vomitoria*), French mulberry (*Callicarpa americana*), waxmyrtle (*Myrica cerifera*), rose (*Rosa* spp.), blueberry (*Vaccinium* spp.), and southern crabapple (*Malus angustifolia*) as common understory plants within pineland woodcock habitat. Understory structure is of greater importance than plant species composition, except that species composition influences structure and earthworm populations.

Selection of diurnal habitat (pineland or bottomland) by woodcock is variable with regard to site and weather. Pineland sites provide suitable habitat for woodcock only when adequate moisture is present (Boggus and Whiting 1982). When moisture levels are reduced, woodcock tend to concentrate in mixed pine-hardwoods, and hardwood drainages and seeps. Within these areas, many bottomland understory species associated with woodcock flushing sites such as switch-cane, blackberry/dewberry, greenbriars, and supplejack are more prevalent. Pursglove (1975), and Pace and Wood (1979) also noted that highest woodcock concentrations were associated with mixed pine-hardwood stands and adjacent stream bottoms rather than predominantly pine areas. Excessive moisture can be a limiting factor when bottomland sites are flooded.

Fig. 3.   Two English setters point an American woodcock (Photo by T. J. Dwyer).

A factor that sometimes limits use of pineland sites by woodcock is excessive ground cover. In such situations, prescribed burning may increase use, but only when adequate vegetative structure and earthworms are already present. Johnson and Causey (1982) reported that a fall or early winter burn removes sufficient ground cover to facilitate foraging, while retaining adequate structural cover for protection.

Nocturnal Habitat.—Nocturnal roosting fields are a critical habitat element in wintering areas because these sites are used for feeding (Glasgow 1958, Horton and Causey 1979, Connors and Doerr 1982). D. G. Krementz (unpubl. data) found that woodcock travel short distances (≤2 km) from diurnal areas to nocturnal roosting fields, indicating the importance of juxtaposition of suitable roosting cover and diurnal cover for optimum use of both.

A variety of sites is used for nocturnal roosting. Glasgow (1958) indicated that most sites offered a herbaceous or brushy canopy at least 0.5–1 m high, interspersed with sparse ground cover on soils with sufficient moisture to maintain earthworms near the surface. In pineland areas, woodcock often used former homesites for nocturnal feeding, showing particular preference for those that had been grazed. Overhead cover on these sites was provided by plants such as bitterweed (*Helenium tenuifolium*), goatweed (*Croton capitatus*), coneflower (*Rudbeckia* spp.), St. Andrew's cross (*Hypericum* spp.), winged sumac (*Rhus copallina*), huckleberry, and blackberry. Bluestems (*Andropogon* spp.), panic grasses (*Panicum* spp.), bullgrasses (*Paspalum* spp.), carpet grass (*Axonopus affinis*) and sedges (*Carex* spp.) dominated the understory vegetation.

Agricultural fields are also used as nocturnal roosting sites. Crop fields used include corn, cotton, sugar cane, and soybeans (Glasgow 1958, Connors and Doerr 1982, Stribling and Doerr 1985). Fields that received the highest use were not fall-plowed and had persistent stalks that provided cover. Stribling and Doerr (1985) found that woodcock used fall-plowed soybean fields but not fall-plowed corn fields, even though earthworms were equally abundant in the latter. They also found that earthworms collected in soybean fields had higher protein content than those collected in corn fields and hypothesized this factor might account for greater use of soybean fields. Recent banding efforts in Louisiana suggest a preference for soybean fields that were row-planted rather than flat-planted (no-till) (M. Olinde, pers. commun.). Areas planted in rows may provide cover in the form of topographic relief. Further, Stribling and Doerr (1985) speculated that fields planted in rows with accumulated crop residues in the troughs prevented the soil from freezing and provided important shelter from wind during cold weather.

Pastures within alluvial floodplains are also frequently used as nocturnal feeding sites by woodcock (Glasgow 1958). Recently abandoned and active pastures contained a variety of grasses and broadleaf weeds, while older pastures contained blackberry, rose, and small early successional trees. Burning improved the quality of fields dominated by dense vegetative cover by removing ground cover while preserving a light canopy of woody stems.

Habitat management in wintering areas should include management of nocturnal roosting fields. We suggest that a good roosting field should provide adequate earthworms with low pesticide loads, ease of movement, and protection from predators (especially owls). Ground cover should be minimal with an abundance of exposed soil to facilitate walking and probing. A light, broken canopy of overhead vegetation 0.5–1 m high should be present to make it difficult for predators to locate foraging woodcock.

Losses

Since the turn of the century, bottomland hardwoods have been drained and cleared for flood control and agricultural purposes. Although early diversions of land use were not thought to limit woodcock populations, concern was later expressed by Glasgow (1958), Sheldon (1971:139), and Owen et al. (1977:168–169) because of the large area involved. During rapid farm mechanization from the mid-1950's to mid-1970's, 2.7 million ha of forested wetlands were cleared nationally (Haynes et al. 1988) with about 80% of that loss in the southeastern United States. The largest losses of bottomland hardwoods occurred in important woodcock wintering areas along the Lower Mississippi River and Atchafalaya River basins. Haynes et al. (1988) estimated that 25% of the remaining forested wetlands would be lost by 1995.

Habitat loss throughout the breeding range has been as extensive as loss of habitat on the wintering range, but more insidious. Natural forest succession has consumed thousands of hectares of woodcock breeding habitat. Rates of forest regeneration through timber harvesting have not kept pace with habitat losses due to succession. Over the past 20 years, this imbalance caused net decreases in the area of seedling-sapling forest in several northern states.

DISTRIBUTION AND ABUNDANCE
Breeding Range

American woodcock occur throughout eastern North America (Figs. 4, 5). Although woodcock are found well within the "Eastern Boreal Forest Region" (Soc. Am. For. 1975:fig. 1), the northern limit of breeding is indistinct. Sheldon (1971) suggests the northern extreme of woodcock range may be James Bay or southern Hudson Bay. J. C. Davies (pers. commun.) confirms courtship activity as far north as Moosonee, Ontario (51°N) while Nero (1977) documents breeding in Manitoba as far north as 50°N and courtship activity as far north as Gillam, Manitoba (56°N). Additional research is needed to confirm breeding at latitudes north of 50°N. Newfoundland is the northeast limit of breeding (Mendall and Aldous 1943; R. I. Goudie, pers. commun.). The probable northwestern extent of breeding is the Manitoba-Saskatchewan border (Mendall and Aldous 1943; Nero 1977; J. Christie, pers. commun.; W. H. Koonz, pers. commun.). The western limit of breeding (Fig. 4) follows Robbins et al. (1966).

Management Units

Woodcock are managed on the basis of Eastern and Central regions or populations (Owen et al. 1977) (Fig. 4). Coon et al. (1977) reviewed development of the concept of harvest units for woodcock and recommended the current regions over several alternative configurations. The selected configuration was justified because there was little interchange between regions based on band recoveries (Krohn 1972, Krohn and Clark 1977), and because regional boundaries conformed to the boundary between the Atlantic and Mississippi waterfowl flyways.

Breeding Densities

The North American Woodcock Singing-ground Survey (SGS) provides estimates of relative abundance of breeding woodcock throughout much of the primary breeding range (Sauer and Bortner 1991) (Fig. 4). This survey is based on a network of about 1,500 5.4-km routes on randomly selected secondary roads and has been conducted annually since 1968. Observers count the number of woodcock heard at 10 stops. The number of woodcock heard per route is an index of the relative density of woodcock in a geographic area. Changes in number of woodcock heard over time reflect population trends.

Because of the dynamic nature of woodcock habitat, counts along individual routes will rise and fall over time. However, because routes were randomly established (along secondary roads), the resulting trends should be representative of regional changes in habitat quality and woodcock populations (Sauer and Bortner 1991). Therefore, just as observed changes in the number of woodcock heard along an individual route probably reflect the effect of habitat changes on local populations, the observed SGS trends for states and provinces reflect the changing status of woodcock habitat (and hence, woodcock populations) in those areas.

Because breeding densities in southern states are low, the SGS is not conducted there (Fig. 4). Much of the northernmost breeding range is inaccessible; therefore, the SGS samples few areas north of 50°N.

Based on the SGS, highest densities of breeding woodcock occur in southern Ontario and Quebec, coinciding approximately with the Northern Forest Region (Soc. Am. For. 1975: fig. 1). While this forest region traverses both the Eastern and Central woodcock management

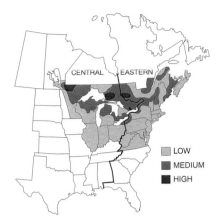

Fig. 4. Density and extent of breeding of American woodcock. Density is average number of woodcock heard per Singing-ground Survey route 1970–88 (from Sauer and Bortner 1991) except for Manitoba which is from 1989–92.

regions, woodcock are more abundant in the Central Region.

Woodcock increased in abundance and expanded their range in Manitoba during the 1970's (Nero 1977). Surveys conducted since 1988 showed high densities of breeding woodcock in central and southeastern Manitoba. This increased abundance of woodcock in Manitoba since the early 1970's is probably due to fires, recent timber operations in boreal forest and parkland areas, and an abundance of abandoned fields and pastures as a result of land use and ownership changes over the past 20 years.

Wintering Range

We used data from the National Audubon Society's Christmas Bird Counts to supplement wintering range information provided by Owen et al. (1977). The Christmas Bird Count (CBC) is the only systematic and widespread survey conducted across the wintering range of woodcock. These counts are conducted within a 2-week period of Christmas in a specified 24-km circle. An analysis of 5 years of these data (1985–89) was conducted on all routes. Data were adjusted for effort (party hours) and examined using program SURFER (Golden Software Inc., Golden, Colo.) to estimate wintering distribution and densities. Data from SURFER, abundance data from Glasgow (1958), and recommendations of R. R. George (pers. commun.) and R. M. Whiting (pers. commun.) were used to identify wintering areas (Fig. 5). The range of wintering woodcock suggested by this analysis is broader than indicated by Owen et al.

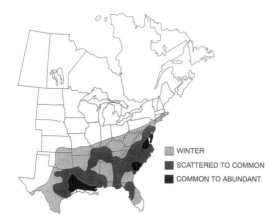

Fig. 5.   Density and extent of wintering by American wood-cock.

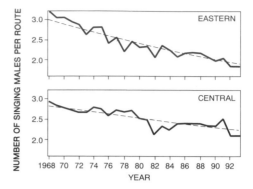

Fig. 6.   Long-term trends and annual indices of number of woodcock heard on woodcock Singing-ground Survey, 1968–93.

(1977). Data from program SURFER showed woodcock wintering further north and in a larger portion of Texas. Some of the discrepancy in the northern limits of the wintering range may be due to timing of CBC's. Counts conducted to 1 week before Christmas (still within the CBC time frame) may census migrating woodcock.

Three areas had high numbers of woodcock in the CBC: eastern Texas to central Louisiana, the coastal plain of South Carolina, and the lower Delmarva Peninsula to eastern Virginia. Recent increases in logging activity may be partly responsible for increasing attractiveness of the pineywoods of eastern Texas to wintering woodcock (R. R. George, pers. commun.). The lower Delmarva Peninsula is a combination migration corridor and wintering area. In particular, Cape Charles, Virginia has been regarded as a migration stopover where the highest counts in the nation are regularly recorded.

Population Trends

Population trends of woodcock are primarily monitored through the North American Woodcock Singing-ground Survey. Trend analyses of the Singing-ground Survey (Straw 1993) indicated that the Eastern population index declined at an average rate of 1.8%/year during 1968–93 (Fig. 6). There was a significant ($P <$ 0.05) decline during 1985–93. The Central population also had a significant long-term (1968–93) decline of -0.9/yr ($P < 0.01$) as well as a significant short-term (1985–93) decline of -1.7%/yr ($P < 0.01$). Individual states/provinces that showed significant long-term declines

were Connecticut, Ohio, Maine, Maryland, Massachusetts, New Brunswick, New Jersey, Nova Scotia, Pennsylvania, Rhode Island, Vermont, Virginia, and Wisconsin (Fig. 7).

HARVEST

United States Regulations

Hunting seasons for migratory birds in the United States are modified at the federal level through changes in frameworks within which states select seasons. During 1970–present, changes have been made in framework dates, bag limits, and number of days for hunting woodcock.

The opening framework date for the Eastern Region was 1 September from 1965 to 1981, 3 October in 1982, and 1 October 1983–present. The 1 September opening date for the Central Region has remained unchanged since 1961.

Management concerns regarding the opening framework date include balancing physiological condition of woodcock at the time of the opening against lost hunting opportunity if woodcock migrate prior to the opening date. Some biologists have questioned the wisdom of allowing woodcock hunting as early as 1 September. While woodcock chicks are fully mature by 1 September, molt of adult females appears to be delayed during drought years and some biologists have speculated these females may be more vulnerable to harvest. Another concern of mid-latitude states regarding their own choice of opening date is that opening the season too early may place excessive harvest pressure on local populations prior to arrival of migrants.

The closing framework date for hunting has

been altered more often in the past than the opening date. From 1965 to 1969, the closing date was 31 January in both regions. From 1970 to 1971 it was 15 February, and from 1972 to 1984 it was 28 February. The closing date was 31 January during 1985–present in the Eastern Region. In 1991, the closing date was changed to 31 January in the Central Region in response to concerns about the potential impact of February hunting on annual survival and early nesting attempts.

Issues that administrators should consider when selecting closing dates include nature of late-season mortality (compensatory vs. additive), impact and ethics of hunting while nesting is ongoing, and impact and ethics of hunting during spring migration. These issues must be balanced against potential loss of recreational opportunities. Many landowners in Louisiana do not make their land available to woodcock hunters until February due to deer-hunting leases. Also, woodcock are taken opportunistically in southern states by quail hunters (M. W. Olinde, pers. observ.). As many states have quail seasons open during February, a closed woodcock season at this time decreases opportunity.

The season length framework was 65 days during 1967–85 in both management regions. Season length was reduced to 45 days in the Eastern Region (21 Aug 1985 Fed. Regist. 50 FR33737) in 1985 due to concern over the continued decline of the Eastern population. Season length has varying effects on woodcock harvest in different states. Northern states are potentially limited by the number of days woodcock are present. Seasons in mid-latitude states may miss major migrations if season length is too restrictive. Woodcock are present in many southern states during all of December and January, and hunting opportunity in these states would probably be reduced if season length were restricted.

The daily bag limit permitted by federal harvest frameworks was 5 in both management regions during 1963–85. The bag limit in the Eastern Region was changed to 3 in 1985, concurrent with the reduction in season length. Increases in bag limits tend to rapidly reach a point of diminishing returns, as few hunters are actually limited by the bag limit. However, woodcock are often found in high concentrations, and the potential for excessive harvests exists if the bag limit is too large.

The most significant harvest management ac-

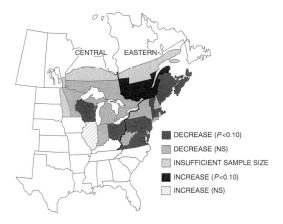

Fig. 7. Long-term (1968–92) trends in number of American woodcock heard on the Singing-ground Survey by state and province.

tion was taken in the Eastern Region in 1985 when the bag limit was reduced from 5 to 3, the season length reduced from 65 to 45 days, and the closing date changed to 31 January. Based on a comparison of 1982–84 vs. 1985–87 (J. A. Straw, unpubl. data), the daily and seasonal bags of cooperators in the Wing-collection Survey were reduced by 6 and 7%, respectively. Average harvest estimates from the Annual Questionnaire Survey of U.S. Waterfowl Hunters decreased 17%. However, much of this decrease is attributable to a decrease in the estimated number of hunters (16%).

United States Harvest

The woodcock harvest in the United States is currently monitored by the USFWS by 2 methods. The Waterfowl Harvest Surveys section of the Migratory Bird Management Office (MBMO) conducts the Annual Questionnaire Survey (AQS) of U.S. Waterfowl Hunters to estimate harvest of all migratory game birds by waterfowl hunters. The Population Assessment Section of MBMO conducts the Woodcock Wing-collection Survey (WCS). Data from the WCS include hours hunted and number of woodcock killed. From this information, changes in the daily and seasonal bag are estimated by the base-year method (Clark 1970, Straw 1993). In addition to federal surveys, many states conduct annual or periodic surveys (mostly mail surveys) of resident hunters that provide estimates of woodcock hunter numbers and harvest.

The contact procedures used by both federal

Table 2. Woodcock harvest and hunters (thousands) estimated by state surveys and the U.S. Fish and Wildlife Service's Annual Questionnaire Survey of U.S. Waterfowl Hunters in 1990.

State	State surveys		Annual questionnaire survey		Year[a]
	Harvest	Hunters	Harvest	Hunters	
Alabama	3.7	1.3	0.8	0.3	
Arkansas			1.5	0.6	
Connecticut	20.4	75.5	6.9	3.3	
Delaware	1.7	0.8	1.4	0.5	
Florida	3.4	0.9	1.9	0.6	
Georgia	9.1	3.2	2.8	1.1	1982
Illinois	11.3	6.1	8.1	3.0	
Indiana	5.1	3.9	2.9	1.0	
Iowa	2.3	2.7	2.5	1.3	
Kansas			0.4	0.2	
Kentucky	16.8	5.5	2.5	0.9	1989
Louisiana	143.0	21.0	39.7	6.2	
Massachusetts	33.0	13.9	11.1	4.7	1985
Maryland	6.6	2.4	1.9	1.3	
Maine	107.6	24.2	13.5	3.1	1983
Michigan	241.0	75.0	61.9	16.0	
Minnesota	114.0	27.0	36.1	12.0	
Missouri	19.0	5.7	3.5	1.3	
Mississippi	18.0	24.0	3.4	0.5	
North Carolina	17.7	4.3	3.9	1.6	1989
Nebraska			1.1	0.3	
New Hampshire			5.1	2.4	
New Jersey	28.0	2.7	7.7	2.6	
New York	44.9	17.4	15.5	6.7	
Ohio	10.5	5.9	8.5	3.1	1988
Oklahoma	7.2	2.1	1.1	0.5	
Pennsylvania	50.9	30.0	18.1	8.0	
Rhode Island			1.3	0.4	
South Carolina	8.2	3.8	2.3	1.1	1984
Tennessee	13.1	4.1	4.9	1.3	1986
Texas	7.7	2.4	4.0	1.3	
Virginia	10.0	3.5	5.2	1.8	1989
Vermont			6.0	1.4	
Wisconsin	139.8	37.2	44.0	13.9	
West Virginia			0.4	0.2	
Totals	1,094.0	406.5	331.9	104.5	

[a] Data for state surveys are from 1990 unless otherwise noted.

surveys have shortcomings. The AQS relies on randomly selected participants; however, it addresses only the harvest of woodcock by purchasers of Migratory Bird Hunting and Conservation (Duck) Stamps. This is a serious omission because the relative number of non-waterfowl hunters who hunt woodcock may vary by state and year in response to differing hunting opportunities, including the abundance of grouse, quail, and waterfowl. Participants in the WCS are not randomly selected. The WCS solicits past participants, their friends, hunters who requested to participate, and waterfowl hunters who indicated on the AQS that they also hunt woodcock. The upcoming National Migratory Bird Harvest Information Program is designed to

provide a suitable sampling framework from which accurate harvest estimates of woodcock can be made.

Recent United States harvest estimates based on the AQS are approximately 325,000 per year, although this does not include harvest by non-waterfowl hunters. Owen et al. (1977) estimated a national harvest of 1.5 million woodcock and over 0.5 million hunters by totaling estimates from all state hunter surveys. We surveyed state agencies to obtain similar values for 1970–90. We estimated a national harvest in 1991 of at least 1.1 million woodcock taken by 400,000 woodcock hunters (Table 2). Most of this harvest occurred in the Great Lakes states, Louisiana, and the Northeast.

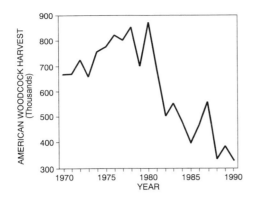

Fig. 8. Total United States harvest of American woodcock, 1970–90.

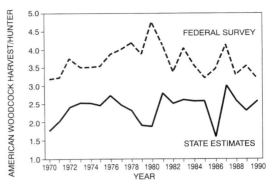

Fig. 9. Mean seasonal bag of all woodcock hunters as estimated by state surveys and the Annual Questionnaire Survey, 1970–90. Estimates from state surveys are based only on states which had estimates of harvest and number of hunters available. Annual Questionnaire Survey estimates are for all states which hunted woodcock.

Total United States harvest based on the AQS declined during 1970–91, especially during the 1980's (Fig. 8). This decline was primarily due to declining hunter numbers; average seasonal bag as estimated by both the AQS and state surveys was stable over this period (Fig. 9). Some of the decline in harvest may also be due to fewer woodcock. The WCS furnishes estimates of cumulative changes in the daily and seasonal bag of comparable hunters, thus reflecting changes in opportunity or days afield independent of changes in the hunter population. The daily bag in the Eastern Region and the seasonal bag in both regions have declined since 1970 (Straw 1993). This suggests that woodcock in the Eastern Region have declined, and that cooperators in the Central Region are spending less days afield than previously.

Canadian Regulations and Harvest

Hunting regulations in Canada are set by the Canadian Wildlife Service in cooperation with provincial wildlife agencies. Ontario has 4 zones and Quebec has 5 zones with seasons that open at progressively later dates by latitude. Woodcock hunting seasons in some areas of Canada open as early as 1 September, and usually close long after all woodcock have migrated south. The bag limit throughout Canada has remained at 8 since 1970.

Harvests in Canada approximate 100,000 woodcock, with Ontario and Quebec accounting for more than 75% of the total annual harvest. The remainder of the harvest occurs in the maritime provinces of New Brunswick, Nova Scotia, and Prince Edward Island (Hounsell 1991). Although daily and seasonal bags per successful hunter have increased over the past 10 years, the number of woodcock hunters in Canada has declined.

Harvest Rates

Band recovery rates for woodcock vary from 2.5 to 4.7% (Table 3). Recovery rates for females were higher than for males, but did not differ between young and adults. Recovery rates were also higher for the Eastern Region than the Central Region.

Dwyer and Nichols (1982) discussed the relationship between recovery rates, hunting mortality, and annual mortality. Low recovery rates may suggest that hunting mortality accounts for only a small percentage of the total annual mortality of woodcock. However, they cautioned that reporting rates are unknown and crippling loss must be considered. Pursglove (1975) estimated crippling loss for woodcock may be as high as 17%. Dwyer and Nichols (1982) concluded that even if it could be estimated, knowledge of the harvest rate does not in and of itself permit inferences to be drawn regarding the effect of hunting on woodcock populations.

Sex and age composition of the harvest is measured by the WCS and an equivalent Canadian survey. Composition of the United States harvest is approximately 51% juveniles and 49% adults. Within the juvenile harvest, males and females are equally represented (51 vs. 49%), but this is not true in the adult harvest where females are more common than males (57 vs. 43%). Adult

Table 3. Mean annual recovery rates of preseason-banded American woodcock, 1967–75 (after Dwyer and Nichols 1982).

Age/sex	Eastern population		Central population	
	Recovery rate	SE	Recovery rate	SE
Adult male	0.036	0.005	0.031	0.007
Adult female	0.036	0.005	0.047	0.008
Juvenile male	0.029	0.003	0.025	0.004
Juvenile female	0.046	0.007	0.032	0.006

males are less abundant in the population than adult females due to differential survival rates, although there also may be a slight harvest bias towards adult females (Dwyer and Nichols 1982).

MANAGEMENT NEEDS

Habitat

Continued habitat loss throughout breeding and wintering range will reduce woodcock populations and associated recreational opportunities. Historic causes of habitat loss have been drainage and land-use conversion in wintering areas and forest succession in northern breeding areas. Rates of habitat loss must be monitored so that appropriate agency goals for information and education can be set and habitat work on public and private lands can be planned. The best sources of information on recent habitat trends will probably be the U.S. Forest Service Forest Inventory and Analysis data and the Canadian Forest Service Forest Inventory. Incorporation of aerial photography (Dwyer et al. 1983) and satellite imagery into a Geographic Information System also has great potential for delineating patterns of woodcock habitat loss.

Protection and management of key sites used during the winter and migration should be a priority. Areas of extraordinary value to woodcock that are in danger of being degraded should be identified, and preservation and maintenance of these lands as quality woodcock habitat should be assured through acquisition or other methods (U.S. Fish and Wildl. Serv. 1990). Additional areas should be protected through market-based incentive programs, zoning, and wetland regulations.

Research on habitat requirements of wintering woodcock should be quickly followed by habitat manipulation experiments and ultimately, the development of a habitat management manual for wintering woodcock. The Migratory Bird Management Office of the USFWS

receives many requests regarding habitat management for woodcock in wintering areas. These requests are increasing as the public expresses more interest in managing land to benefit woodcock, and wildlife in general.

State, federal, and provincial agencies need to create habitat on public and private lands. This will benefit local woodcock populations and focus public attention on needs of woodcock and other early-successional species. Public agencies that own land suitable for woodcock should be encouraged to incorporate woodcock habitat management into their land management practices wherever possible. However, the public attitude towards management of public lands for early-successional wildlife has not been favorable. To gain public support for this type of habitat management, wildlife biologists need to be proficient in salesmanship and create an interest in woodcock and other early-successional species. When communicating with private landowners, biologists should transfer information on woodcock habitat management techniques in a manner that results in the greatest number of hectares managed. Existing government programs (e.g., Conservation Reserve Program, Agricultural Conservation Reserve, Stewardship Incentive Program) should be exploited to provide economic incentives to landowners who manage for multiple benefits, including woodcock.

Population Status

The status of woodcock populations is assessed annually for the purpose of recommending annual hunting regulations. The Singing-ground Survey (SGS) provides part of the basis for that assessment. Where possible, operational and analytical procedures should be improved to make the SGS a better tool for managing woodcock populations. For example, original route randomization maps should be reviewed to identify how many 10° blocks originally selected for establishing SGS routes were roadless in 1968 but are now accessible. It may be desirable to establish survey routes in these areas.

The Wing-collection Survey provides annual estimates of production and hunter success. However, a major criticism of the survey is that cooperators are not a random sample of woodcock hunters. Analytical techniques are used to correct for biases resulting from this shortcoming. Improvements to this survey should include a review of analytical techniques to see if biases can be further reduced. Improvements to the sampling procedure should begin after implementation of the National Migratory Bird Harvest Information Program.

Production estimates for the current year are desirable (Dwyer et al. 1988), but such information is difficult and expensive to obtain. Furthermore, such information is necessary only if hunting regulations strongly influence population dynamics. Decisions regarding initiation of expensive new surveys should wait until additional studies of the influence of hunting on woodcock population dynamics are completed.

Harvest

It is necessary to understand the relationship between harvest regulations and actual harvest to make appropriate harvest regulation recommendations. Knowledge of the magnitude (including error) and geographic distribution of harvest is needed annually. Implementation of the National Migratory Bird Harvest Information Program will provide a suitable sampling universe of woodcock hunters to accurately estimate national woodcock harvests. This information will be used in the annual regulations process.

RESEARCH NEEDS

Continued investigations of the relationship of woodcock survival and reproductive rates to density-independent and density-dependent factors are needed. In particular, the effects of hunting on local and regional populations are unknown. To learn if hunting is compensatory or additive, research needs to identify density-dependent mortality factors, estimate their magnitude, and identify their role in population dynamics. The role of immigration and emigration in sustaining local populations that are subject to high hunting mortality should also be evaluated.

Estimates of harvest rates are needed to evaluate harvest regulations and to understand the role of harvest in the population dynamics of woodcock. Telemetry can be used to estimate harvest rates for that part of a season that woodcock remain on a study area. However, banding must be used to estimate harvest rates over the course of fall and winter. Crippling loss and band reporting rates must be examined so that harvest rates can be estimated from banding data. A feasibility study is needed to identify

the cost of a reward band study to estimate the reporting rate for woodcock bands.

During the past 15 years, little research has been conducted on the effects of contaminants on woodcock. Over this same time period, pesticide formulations and methods of application have changed considerably. The potential impact of modern pesticides on woodcock, habitat, and earthworm abundance needs to be evaluated.

Knowledge regarding habitat management in wintering areas is inadequate and has changed little since Owen et al. (1977) identified this research need. Progress towards this objective will require identification of wintering habitat requirements followed by experimental habitat manipulations. To be useful, such experiments should test habitat models over a wide geographic range and several years.

To recoup recent habitat losses, agencies should re-evaluate methods of stimulating habitat creation on private lands. Most new initiatives that aspire to encourage habitat creation on private lands use the same methods of contacting the public, contact the same persons as previous initiatives, and attempt to motivate those persons with the same techniques that were used (with mixed success) 20 years ago. Modern marketing techniques should be applied to future efforts. Research needs to identify individuals who have control of forested lands and are likely to implement woodcock habitat practices. After target groups have been identified, research should focus on discovering impediments to progress (e.g., why aren't these individuals creating habitat now? Is it lack of information, negative attitudes towards timber harvesting, a lack of cash incentives or something else?). Finally, research should focus on how to best contact and motivate target groups.

RECOMMENDATIONS

1. The U.S. Fish and Wildlife Service (USFWS) regions 3, 4, and 5 should implement the American Woodcock Management Plan (U.S. Fish and Wildl. Serv. 1990).
2. The USFWS, in cooperation with states, provinces, and flyways, should pursue the identified research needs.
3. The USFWS should continue development and implementation of the National Migratory Bird Harvest Information Program.
4. The USFWS, in cooperation with states, provinces, and flyways, should identify crit-

ical areas for protection, management or acquisition. Also, regional habitat demonstration areas should be created.

ACKNOWLEDGMENTS

We thank W. B. Krohn for reviewing this manuscript. D. G. McAuley and C. C. Allin also provided helpful comments. We thank J. Christie, J. C. Davies, R. R. George, R. I. Goudie, W. H. Koonz, and R. M. Whiting for helpful comments on distribution of woodcock.

LITERATURE CITED

AMMANN, G. A. 1982. Age determination of American woodcock chicks by bill length. Pages 22–25 in T. J. Dwyer and G. L. Storm, tech. coords. Woodcock ecology and management. U.S. Fish and Wildl. Serv., Wildl. Res. Rep. 14.

ARTMANN, J. W., AND L. D. SCHROEDER. 1976. A technique for sexing woodcock by wing measurement. J. Wildl. Manage. 49:572–574.

BLANKENSHIP, L. H. 1957. Investigations of the American woodcock on Michigan. Ph.D. Thesis, Michigan State Univ., Lansing. 217pp.

BOGGUS, T. G., AND R. M. WHITING, JR. 1982. Effects of habitat variables on foraging of American woodcock wintering in east Texas. Pages 148–153 in T. J. Dwyer and G. L. Storm, tech. coords. Woodcock ecology and management. U.S. Fish and Wildl. Serv., Wildl. Res. Rep. 14.

BOURGEOIS, A. 1977. Quantitative analysis of American woodcock nest and brood habitat. Proc. Woodcock Symp. 6:108–118.

BRITT, T. L. 1971. Studies of woodcock on the Louisiana wintering ground. M.S. Thesis, Louisiana State Univ., Baton Rouge. 105pp.

CAUSEY, M. K. 1981. Alabama woodcock investigations. Final Rep., P-R Proj. W-44-5, Alabama Dep. Conserv. and Nat. Resour., Montgomery. 22pp.

———, M. K. HUDSON, AND T. P. MACK. 1987. Breeding activity of American woodcock in Alabama as related to temperature. Proc. Southeast. Assoc. Fish and Wildl. Agencies 41:373–377.

———, J. ROBOSKI, AND G. HORTON. 1974. Nesting activities of the American Woodcock (*Philohela minor* Gmelin) in Alabama. in J. H. Jenkins, chairman. Proc. 5th Am. Woodcock Workshop. Athens, Ga.

CLARK, E. R. 1970. Woodcock status report, 1969. U.S. Fish and Wildl. Serv., Spec. Sci. Rep. Wildl. 133. 35pp.

CONNORS, J. I., AND P. D. DOERR. 1982. Woodcock use of agricultural fields in coastal North Carolina. Pages 139–147 in T. J. Dwyer and G. L. Storm, tech. coords. Woodcock ecology and management. U.S. Fish and Wildl. Serv., Wildl. Res. Rep. 14.

COON, R. A., P. D. CALDWELL, AND G. L. STORM. 1976. Some characteristics of a fall migration of female woodcock. J. Wildl. Manage. 40:91–95.

———, T. J. DWYER, AND J. W. ARTMANN. 1977. Identification of harvest units for the American woodcock. Proc. Woodcock Symp. 6:147–153.

———, B. K. WILLIAMS, J. S. LINDZEY, AND J. L. GEORGE. 1982. Examination of woodcock nest sites in central Pennsylvania. Pages 55–62 in T. J. Dwyer and G. L. Storm, tech. coords. Woodcock ecology and management. U.S. Fish and Wildl. Serv., Wildl. Res. Rep. 14.

DAVEY, S. P. 1963. Effects of chemicals on earthworms: a review of the literature. U.S. Fish and Wildl. Serv., Spec. Sci. Rep. Wildl. 74. 20pp.

DERLETH, E. L., AND G. F. SEPIK. 1990. Summerfall survival of American woodcock in Maine. J. Wildl. Manage. 54:97–106.

DUNFORD, R. D., AND R. B. OWEN, JR. 1973. Summer behavior of immature radio-equipped woodcock in central Maine. J. Wildl. Manage. 37:462–468.

DUVALL, A. J. 1955. The juvenal plumage of the American woodcock. U.S. Fish and Wildl. Serv., Spec. Sci. Rep. Wildl. 31. 54pp.

DWYER, T. J., AND J. D. NICHOLS. 1982. Regional population inferences for the American woodcock. Pages 12–21 in T. J. Dwyer and G. L. Storm, tech. coords. Woodcock ecology and management. U.S. Fish Wildl. Serv., Wildl. Res. Rep. 14.

———, E. L. DERLETH, AND D. G. MCAULEY. 1982. Woodcock brood ecology in Maine. Pages 63–70 in T. J. Dwyer and G. L. Storm, tech. coords. Woodcock ecology and management. U.S. Fish and Wildl. Serv., Wildl. Res. Rep. 14.

———, D. G. MCAULEY, AND E. L. DERLETH. 1983. Woodcock singing-ground counts and habitat changes in the northeastern United States. J. Wildl. Manage. 47:772–779.

———, G. F. SEPIK, E. L. DERLETH, AND D. G. MCAULEY. 1988. Demographic characteristics of a Maine woodcock population and effects of habitat management. U.S. Fish and Wildl. Serv., Fish and Wildl. Res. Rep. 4. 29pp.

DYER, J. M., AND R. B. HAMILTON. 1977. Analysis of several site components of diurnal woodcock habitat in southern Louisiana. Proc. Woodcock Symp. 6:51–62.

ELLINGWOOD, M. R. 1983. American woodcock singing grounds, summer fields, and night surveys in West Virginia. M.S. Thesis, West Virginia Univ., Morgantown. 147pp.

GLASGOW, L. L. 1953. The American woodcock (*Philohela minor*) in Louisiana. Proc. Southeast. Assoc. Game and Fish Comm. 7:20–28.

———. 1958. Contributions to the knowledge of the ecology of the American woodcock, (*Philohela minor* Gmelin), on the wintering range in Louisiana. Ph.D. Thesis, Texas A&M Univ., College Station. 158pp.

GODFREY, G. A. 1974. Behavior and ecology of American woodcock on the breeding range in Minnesota. Ph.D. Thesis, Univ. Minnesota, Minneapolis. 333pp.

GREELEY, F. 1953. Sex and age studies in fall-shot woodcock (*Philohela minor*) from southern Wisconsin. J. Wildl. Manage. 17:29–32.

GREGG, L. 1984. Population ecology of woodcock

in Wisconsin. Wisconsin Dep. Nat. Resour., Tech. Bull 144. 51pp.

GUTZWILLER, K. J., AND J. S. WAKELEY. 1982. Differential use of woodcock singing grounds in relation to habitat characteristics. Pages 51–54 *in* T. J. Dwyer and G. L. Storm, tech. coords. Woodcock ecology and management. U.S. Fish and Wildl. Serv., Wildl. Res. Rep. 14.

———, K. R. KINSLEY, G. L. STORM, W. M. TZILKOWSKI, AND J. S. WAKELEY. 1983. Relative value of vegetation structure and species composition for identifying American woodcock breeding habitat. J. Wildl. Manage. 47:535–540.

HAYNES, R. J., J. A. ALLEN, AND E. C. PENDLETON. 1988. Reestablishment of bottomland hardwood forests on disturbed sites: an annotated bibliography. U.S. Fish and Wildl. Serv., Biol. Rep. 88. 104pp.

HORTON, G. I., AND M. K. CAUSEY. 1979. Woodcock movements and habitat utilization in central Alabama. J. Wildl. Manage. 43:414–420.

HOUNSELL, R. G. 1991. Status of the woodcock in Canada 1990. Can. Wildl. Serv., Sackville, N.B.

HOWARD, R., AND A. MOORE. 1991. A complete checklist of the birds of the world. 2nd ed. Harcourt Brace Jovanovich, Publ., New York, N.Y. 598pp.

HUDGINS, J. E., G. L. STORM, AND J. S. WAKELEY. 1985. Local movements and diurnal-habitat selection by male American woodcock in Pennsylvania. J. Wildl. Manage. 49:614–619.

JOHNSON, R. C., AND M. K. CAUSEY. 1982. Use of longleaf pine stands by woodcock in southern Alabama following prescribed burning. Pages 120–125 *in* T. J. Dwyer and G. L. Storm, tech. coords. Woodcock ecology and management. U.S. Fish and Wildl. Serv., Wildl. Res. Rep. 14.

KINSLEY, K. R., AND G. L. STORM. 1989. Structural characteristics of woodcock nesting habitat. J. Penn. Acad. Sci. 62:142–146.

———, S. A. LISCINSKY, AND G. L. STORM. 1982. Changes in habitat structure on woodcock singing grounds in central Pennsylvania. Pages 40–50 *in* T. J. Dwyer and G. L. Storm, tech. coords. Woodcock ecology and management. U.S. Fish and Wildl. Serv., Wildl. Res. Rep. 14.

KREMENTZ, D. G., J. T. SEGINAK, D. R. SMITH, AND G. W. PENDLETON. 1994. Survival rates of American woodcock wintering along the Atlantic coast. J. Wildl. Manage. 58:147–155.

KROHN, W. B. 1970. Woodcock feeding habits as related to summer field usage in central Maine. J. Wildl. Manage. 34:769–775.

———. 1972. American woodcock banding and recovery data, 1950–1970. U.S. Fish and Wildl. Serv., Adm. Rep. 213. 11pp.

———, AND E. R. CLARK. 1977. Band-recovery distribution of eastern Maine woodcock. Wildl. Soc. Bull. 5:118–122.

KROLL, J. C., AND R. M. WHITING. 1977. Discriminate function analysis of woodcock winter habitat in east Texas. Proc. Woodcock Symp. 6:63–71.

LISCINSKY, S. A. 1972. The Pennsylvania woodcock management study. Pennsylvania Game Comm., Res. Bull. 171. 95pp.

MARTIN, F. W. 1964. Woodcock age and sex determination from wings. J. Wildl. Manage. 28:287–293.

MAXFIELD, H. K. 1961. A vegetational analysis of fifty woodcock singing grounds in central Massachusetts. M.S. Thesis, Univ. Massachusetts, Amherst. 31pp.

MCAULEY, D. G., J. R. LONGCORE, AND G. F. SEPIK. 1990. Renesting by American woodcock (*Scolopax minor*) in Maine. Auk 107:407–410.

———, ———, AND ———. 1993. Behavior of radio-marked breeding American woodcock. *In* J. R. Longcore and G. F. Sepik, eds. Eighth woodcock symp. U.S. Fish and Wildl. Serv., Biol. Rep. 16:116–125.

MENDALL, H. L., AND C. M. ALDOUS. 1943. The ecology and management of the American woodcock. Maine Coop. Wildl. Res. Unit., Univ. Maine, Orono. 201pp.

MODAFFERI, R. D. 1967. A population behavior study of male American woodcock on central Massachusetts singing grounds. M.S. Thesis, Univ. Massachusetts, Amherst. 57pp.

MORGENWECK, R. O. 1977. Diurnal high use areas of hatching-year female American woodcock. Proc. Woodcock Symp. 6:155–160.

NERO, R. W. 1977. The American woodcock in Manitoba. Blue Jay 35:240–256.

NICHOLSON, C. P., S. HOMER, R. B. OWEN, JR., AND T. G. DILWORTH. 1977. Woodcock utilization of commercial timberlands in the Northeast. Proc. Woodcock Symp. 6:101–108.

OLINDE, M. W., AND T. E. PRICKETT. 1991. Gonadal characteristics of February-harvested woodcock in Louisiana. Wildl. Soc. Bull. 19:465–468.

OWEN, R. B., JR., AND W. J. GALBRAITH. 1989. Earthworm biomass in relation to forest types, soil, and land use: implications for woodcock management. J. Wildl. Manage. 17:130–136.

———, AND W. B. KROHN. 1973. Molt patterns and weight changes of the American woodcock. Wilson Bull. 85:31–41.

———, AND J. W. MORGAN. 1975. Summer behavior of adult radio-equipped woodcock in central Maine. J. Wildl. Manage. 39:179–182.

———, J. M. ANDERSON, J. W. ARTMANN, E. R. CLARK, T. G. DILWORTH, L. E. GREGG, F. W. MARTIN, J. D. NEWSOM, AND S. R. PURSGLOVE, JR. 1977. American woodcock (*Philohela minor = Scolopax minor* of Edwards 1974). Pages 149–186 *in* G.C. Sanderson, ed. Management of migratory shore and upland game birds in North America. Int. Assoc. Fish and Wildl. Agencies, Washington, D.C.

PACE, R. M., III, AND G. W. WOOD. 1979. Observations of woodcock wintering in coastal South Carolina. Proc. Southeast. Assoc. Game and Fish Comm. 33:72–80.

PARRIS, R. W. 1986. Forest vegetation, earthworm, and woodcock relationships. Ph.D. Thesis, State Univ. New York, Syracuse. 240pp.

PEARCE, P. A. 1971. Woodcock pesticide problems in Canada. *In* G. A. Ammann, chairman. Fourth American woodcock workshop proc. Higgins Lake, Mich.

PETTINGILL, O. S. 1936. The American woodcock, *Philohela minor* (Gmelin). Memoirs Boston Soc. Nat. Hist. 9(2). 391pp.

PHELPS, N. E. 1986. The influence of earthworm abundance on woodcock diurnal habitat use in Maine. M.S. Thesis, Pennsylvania State Univ., State College. 76pp.

PURSGLOVE, S. R. 1975. Observations on wintering woodcock in northeast Georgia. Proc. Southeast. Assoc. Game and Fish Comm. 29:630–639.

RABE, D. L. 1977. Structural analysis of woodcock diurnal habitat in northern Michigan. Proc. Woodcock Symp. 6:125–134.

———, AND H. H. PRINCE. 1982. Breeding woodcock use of manipulated forest-field complexes in the aspen community type. Pages 114–119 *in* T. J. Dwyer and G. L. Storm, tech. coords. Woodcock ecology and management. U.S. Fish and Wildl. Serv., Wildl. Res. Rep. 14.

REID, V., AND P. GOODRUM. 1953. Wintering woodcock populations in west-central Louisiana, 1952–53. U.S. Fish and Wildl. Serv., Spec. Sci. Rep. Wildl. 24. 68pp.

REYNOLDS, J. W., W. B. KROHN, AND G. A. JORDAN. 1977. Earthworm populations as related to woodcock habitat usage in central Maine. Proc. Woodcock Symp. 6:135–146.

ROBBINS, C. S., B. BRUUN, AND H. S. ZIM. 1966. Birds of North America. Golden Press. New York, N.Y. 340pp.

ROBERTS, T. H. 1989. American woodcock (*Scolopax minor*): Sect. 4.1.2, U.S. Army Corps Engineers wildlife resources management manual. Tech. Rep. EL–89–5, U.S. Army Engineers Waterways Exp. Stn., Vicksburg, Miss.

———, AND R. W. DIMMICK. 1978. Distribution and breeding chronology of woodcock in Tennessee. Proc. Southeast. Assoc. Fish and Wildl. Agencies 32:8–16.

ROBOSKI, J. C., AND M. K. CAUSEY. 1981. Incidence, habitat use, and chronology of woodcock nesting in Alabama. J. Wildl. Manage. 45:793–797.

ROOT, T. 1988. Atlas of wintering North American birds. Univ. Chicago press, Chicago, Ill. 312pp.

SAUER, J. R., AND J. B. BORTNER. 1991. Population trends from the American woodcock singing-ground survey, 1970–88. J. Wildl. Manage. 55: 300–312.

SEPIK, G. F., AND E. L. DERLETH. 1993a. Premigratory dispersal and fall migration of American woodcock in Maine. *In* J. R. Longcore and G. F. Sepik, eds. Eighth woodcock symp. U.S. Fish and Wildl. Serv., Biol. Rep. 16:36–40.

———, AND ———. 1993b. Habitat use, home range size and patterns of moves of the American woodcock in Maine. *In* J. R. Longcore and G. F. Sepik, eds. Eighth woodcock symp. U.S. Fish and Wildl. Serv., Biol. Rep. 16:41–49.

———, R. B. OWEN, JR., AND M. W. COULTER. 1981. A landowner's guide to woodcock management in the northeast. Maine Agric. Exp. Stn., Misc. Rep. 253. 23pp.

———, ———, AND T. J. DWYER. 1983. The effect of drought on a local woodcock population. Trans. Northeast Fish and Wildl. Conf. 40:1–8.

———, ———, ———, AND E. L. DERLETH. 1989. Habitat requirements and management of woodcock in the Northeast: assessment of knowledge and needs. Pages 97–109 *in* J. C. Finley and M. C. Brittingham, eds. Timber management and its effects on wildlife. Proc. Penn. State For. Resour. Issues Conf. Pennsylvania State Univ., University Park.

———, D. M. MULLEN, T. J. DWYER, E. L. DERLETH, AND D. G. MCAULEY. 1986. Forest-wildlife management techniques on the Moosehorn National Wildlife Refuge. Pages 333–340 *in* J. A. Bissonette, ed. Is good forestry good wildlife management? Maine Agric. Exp. Stn., Misc. Publ. 689.

SHELDON, W. G. 1971. The book of the American woodcock. Univ. Massachusetts Press, Amherst. 277pp.

———, F. GREELEY, AND J. KUPA. 1958. Aging fall-shot American woodcocks by primary wear. J. Wildl. Manage. 22:310–312.

SOCIETY OF AMERICAN FORESTERS. 1975. Forest cover types of North America, report of the committee on forest types. F. H. Eyre, chairman. Soc. Am. For., Bethesda, Md. 67pp.

STAMPS, R. T., AND P. D. DOERR. 1977. Reproductive maturation and breeding of woodcock in North Carolina. Proc. Woodcock Symp. 6:185–190.

STRAW, J. A., JR. 1993. American woodcock harvest and breeding status, 1992. U.S. Fish and Wildl. Serv., Adm. Rep., 15pp.

———, J. S. WAKELEY, AND J. E. HUDGINS. 1986. A model for management of diurnal habitat for American woodcock in Pennsylvania. J. Wildl. Manage. 50:378–383.

STRIBLING, H. L., AND P. D. DOERR. 1985. Nocturnal use of fields by American woodcock. J. Wildl. Manage. 49:485–491.

U.S. FISH AND WILDLIFE SERVICE. 1990. American woodcock management plan. U.S. Fish and Wildl. Serv., Washington, D.C. 11pp.

VANDER HAEGEN, W. M. 1992. Energetic aspects of woodcock habitat use during the breeding season at Moosehorn National Wildlife Refuge. Ph.D. Thesis, Univ. Maine, Orono. 103pp.

———, R. B. OWEN, JR., AND W. B. KROHN. 1993. Effects of weather on earthworm abundance and foods of the American woodcock in spring. *In* J. R. Longcore and G. F. Sepik, eds. Eighth woodcock symp. U.S. Fish and Wildl. Serv., Biol. Rep. 16:26–31.

WALKER, W. A., AND M. K. CAUSEY. 1982. Breeding activity of American woodcock in Alabama. J. Wildl. Manage. 46:1054–1057.

WILLIAMS, S. O., III. 1969. Population dynamics of woodcock wintering in Louisiana. M.S. Thesis, Louisiana State Univ., Baton Rouge. 68pp.

WHITING, R. M., AND T. G. BOGGUS. 1982. Breeding biology of American woodcock in east Texas. Pages 132–138 *in* T. J. Dwyer and G. L. Storm, tech. coords. Woodcock ecology and management. U.S. Fish and Wildl. Serv., Wildl. Res. Rep. 14.

Chapter 8

COMMON SNIPE

KEITH A. ARNOLD, Department of Wildlife and Fisheries Sciences, Texas A&M University, College Station, TX 77843-2258

Abstract: Two subspecies of common snipe (*Gallinago gallinago*) occur in North America; *G. g. gallinago* occurs only in the Aleutian Islands while *G. g. delicata* breeds widely throughout North America and is subject to hunting. Most harvest is incidental to waterfowl hunting and few data are available on size of annual harvest. No population estimates are available. Breeding occurs across the northern forest region, primarily in wetlands with high organic soils. Winter habitat includes a variety of wetlands, primarily in the coastal marshlands of the Gulf of Mexico. Little management currently exists for this species. Habitat loss likely will have the greatest impact on distribution and abundance of common snipe.

Common snipe remain one of the least studied of North American game birds. During 1971–93, only 4 papers of significance were published on the North American subspecies. The vast majority of published reports dealt with the Eurasian *G. g. gallinago*; where applicable, these reports were used to supplement information on the North American subspecies.

DESCRIPTION

Common snipe are small-bodied shorebirds, measuring from 265 to 295 mm including the bill. The long, straight bill averages about 64 mm. Wingspan may reach 450 mm, while weight is around 100 g (range 70–155 g). Their anisodactyl feet have a vestigial, elevated hallux. Common snipe are sexually monochromatic, generally dark, variegated birds with a white abdomen and brown under-tail coverts. (Tuck 1972, Fogarty et al. 1977).

The bill is flesh-colored, darkening distally to a dull, dark brown. The irides are deep brown. Legs and feet vary from greenish gray to yellowish green. Two dark stripes cross the crown, and a dark eye-stripe and a dusky spot on the cheek give the head a distinctive pattern. Light feather edgings on the dark brown dorsal feathers form lines or strips along sides of the back. The rump is a distinctive buffy rufous, highly visible in flight. The buffy breast has dark markings that give a streaky appearance. The lower breast and abdomen are white, with dark barring on the upper sides; the lower tail coverts are brownish. The middle rectrices are black; the outer feathers become progressively less black and more brown, with increasing amount of white at the tips. The outer pair of rectrices has much white with dark bars that become less evident towards the base of the feather. The dark wings have a broken pattern on the secondaries and coverts similar to the back (Tuck 1972, Fogarty et al. 1977).

Sloan (1967) described a technique for classifying gender of common snipe on the basis of the rectices, but Booth (1968) and Hoffpauir (1969) considered this technique unreliable. Females generally weigh more and have longer bills and males generally have longer outer rectrices, but sufficient overlap exists in all of these characters to preclude use in external identification of gender (Tuck 1972). Green (1991) reported that in *G. g. gallinago*, a discriminant function incorporating bill length and length of the outer rectrix correctly classified gender of 82–85% of the birds examined. Working with wintering birds in Louisiana, Booth (1968) reported that a discriminant function analysis of 6 feather variables separated sexes with <3% overlap. Applicability of this method across the species remains untested.

Tuck (1972) recognized 8 subspecies of common snipe worldwide. However, 2 of those subspecies are considered full species by some (Am. Ornithol. Union 1983). *Gallinago g. gallinago* and *G. g. delicata* occur in North America, the former only in the Aleutian Islands.

LIFE HISTORY

Tuck's (1972) monograph remains the major source of life history information about common snipe. Much of the following information is from that source, along with more recent accounts, including some from the Eurasian *G. g. gallinago*.

Spring Migration and Nesting

Migration from the wintering grounds in the southern United States begins in late February or early March. Fogarty (1970) described behavior that precedes migration as the flushing and wheeling of flocks that drop abruptly to the ground. Migration begins during this period on the first moonlit night, even though some birds remain in Florida into early April. In Texas, snipe frequently remain on the wintering grounds until late March, with stragglers sometimes found into early May (Arnold and Jirovec 1978). White and Harris (1966) reported similar ranges of dates for departure of wintering snipe from the Humboldt Bay region of California. Large flocks arrive in lower Canada concurrent with departures from wintering areas. Males arrive 10–15 days before females and quickly establish territories, even though breeding numbers may not peak until late May. McKibben and Hofmann (1985) reported that snipe arrive on California breeding grounds in the last half of March, with breeding activity well underway by early April. Arrival dates in Colorado breeding areas approximate those reported for California (Johnson and Ryder 1977).

Arrival on the breeding grounds prompts courtship flights by males. These flights are accompanied by bleating or whinnying sounds, and flights intensify with arrival of females. Although these flights may occur at any time of the day, they usually take place at dusk and on moonlit nights. Flight sounds have been attributed to the shape of the outer rectrices, but Sutton (1981) suggested these sounds probably result from movement of the entire tail, rather than the outer rectrices. Males may rise to over 90 m in these flights, before plummeting downward at a 45-degree angle; the tail is spread horizontally and the wings held at 45-degree angles. This flight display may be repeated up to 8 times a minute.

Sutton (1923) described the pair formation display as the male holding his wings over his back as he approaches the female as he drops to the ground in a graceful downward-curving path, with dangling or trailing feet. The precopulatory display terminates with the male approaching the female; he drops his wings and struts before the female with his tail fanned, often with the tail turned upward to display the upper surface to his mate. The female may join in this display.

Females select nest sites. The nest begins as a simple scrape, but layers are added as egg-laying progresses, and a canopy may result. Johnson and Ryder (1977) reported that snipe in Colorado typically place the nest in grasses or sedges on moist but unflooded ground near water. The clutch consists of 4 heavily blotched, buffy eggs, but 3-egg clutches are not uncommon (Tuck 1972). Eggs are deposited from mid-April to early June, but fresh clutches sometimes are found in August. In Colorado, Johnson and Ryder (1977) reported the onset of incubation as ranging from 2 May through 4 July with the majority beginning in May. Other late dates include 24 July in Utah (Bent 1927) and 1 September in California (Bryant 1915). Females incubate for about 19 days, but males remain in close attendance to the nest. In Europe, the female leaves the nest for short periods during daylight to feed, with time away increasing with increasing ambient temperatures (Green et al. 1990).

Common snipe chicks vocalize up to 24 hours before hatching. Hatching may take 1–6 hours and the precocial chick dries within an hour of completion of hatching. Only 10% of the adult mass at hatching, chicks have feet nearly as large as adults. Mass at hatching correlates with the estimated fresh mass of the egg in European snipe (Green 1985b). The male often leads 1st- and 2nd-hatched chicks away from the nest, while the female remains for any additional eggs to hatch. Adults apparently divide parental duties between them. Adults have no defense from predators other than flight, but have evolved effective distraction displays. The display becomes quite intense in late incubation or with young chicks.

Young common snipe develop and grow rapidly. Tuck (1972) found that in Newfoundland, chicks double their mass in the 1st week and double it again in the 2nd week. At 3 weeks the chicks were as heavy as molting adults. The bill and flight feathers also grow rapidly, especially in the first 4 weeks; adult lengths are reached at 7–8 weeks of age. On seasonally flooded pasture lands in Great Britain, Green (1984) found that biomass density of soil invertebrates and penetrability of the soil influenced the growth rate of snipe chicks. Chicks will drink as early as day 1 and even peck at the ground. Although parents present food to chicks for the first several days, chicks begin to probe as early as day 6 and are probably self-sustaining at 10 days. First

Fig. 1. Common snipe foraging habitat in central Texas (Photo by A. L. Barr).

sustained flight takes place at about 3 weeks. At about this same time, adults begin their prebasic molt and chicks start to associate with others of their own age class.

Fall Migration and Wintering

Young-of-the-year begin gathering in flocks in late July, with flocks building to large numbers by mid-August. Tuck (1972) believed young snipe migrate together, probably prior to adults. Snipe arrive at wintering areas in northwestern California in the first week of October (White and Harris 1966); populations build to a peak in mid-November, then decease as heavy rains increase causing the snipe to move southward or disperse into neighboring areas. Arnold and Jirovec (1978) reported similar dates for fall arrivals and peak numbers of wintering snipe in east-central Texas, but they recorded first arrivals in the third week of September in 3 of 7 study years. They noted the first heavy fall flights were correlated with arrival of the first cold weather fronts. However, migrant birds may still be passing through in late November (Arnold and Jirovec 1978).

Common snipe have great fidelity to wintering sites (Arnold 1981). However, the ephemeral nature of much snipe habitat on the wintering grounds masks this fidelity. An area that does not represent good snipe habitat during one part of the winter season can become excellent habitat with the onset of rains that may deluge the area. Conversely, excellent habitat can become poor habitat for an extended period without significant rains. However, wintering areas with significant snipe populations usually have permanent wetlands.

Diet

Snipe probe moist soil or mud for earthworms, insect larvae, snails, and other animal foods (Fig. 1). On wintering grounds in Texas, Jirovec (1971) found that common snipe often foraged in drying cow manure. Along with earthworms and insect larvae, pond snails also constituted a significant part of the diet. White (1963) and Jirovec (1971) both reported high occurrence of plant materials in diets of wintering snipe. However, Booth (1968) disputed the importance of plant matter for common snipe. Although a variety of techniques have been tried, gizzard analyses remain the most reliable means of obtaining food habits data. However, differential digestion can give misleading results (Rundle 1982).

Whitehead (1965) in extreme southwestern Louisiana and Owens (1967) in pasture lands of central Louisiana reported early morning and late afternoon peaks of daily feeding by wintering snipe. However, Booth (1968) reported data from rice fields of southwestern Louisiana that indicated a feeding peak around mid-day. In Texas, Jirovec (1971) found that feeding activity peaked in early morning and late afternoon, but that birds would forage at any time of the day and during moonlit nights.

Non-hunting Mortality

Tuck (1972) documented loss of nests from inadvertent destruction by grazing livestock. However, Mason and McDonald (*in* Green 1985*a*) reported nest destruction by predators as well as from grazing livestock. Other reported mortality sources include poisoning from organophosphates (Flickinger et al. 1984), and striking a lighthouse in Denmark (Fog 1978).

HABITAT

Common snipe use a wide variety of shallow wetlands, including many that lack standing water or that are temporary. Shallow wetlands are the primary habitat during breeding, wintering, and migration.

Breeding Habitat

Tuck (1972) described the breeding habitat of common snipe in North America as restricted to organic soils, mostly peatlands, that lie within the northern forest region or boreal forest biome. In Newfoundland, Tuck (1972) found that nesting occurred mainly in sedge bogs, fens, and alder(*Alnus* spp.) or willow (*Salix* spp.) swamps.

McKibben and Hofmann (1985) described the breeding habitat in California, at the southwestern extreme of the breeding distribution. Although snipe used wetlands ranging from well-drained grass uplands to constantly wet bogs, they found that bogs and wet zones with 2 species of sedges (*Carex simulata* and *C. rostrata*) were of greatest importance. Late in the breeding season, only bogs and marshy areas within timber stands provided good nesting cover.

In Colorado, at the south-central edge of the breeding range, Johnson and Ryder (1977) stud-

ied breeding snipe at 12 sites. All study sites consisted of seasonal wetlands that received water from irrigation flow or were in proximity to permanent water sources such as ponds or streams. *Carex* spp. dominated at 7 of the 12 sites. Johnson and Ryder (1977) described suitable habitats as containing shallow, stable, discontinuous water levels, low and sparse vegetation, often grazed or mowed, with moist to saturated soils frequently characterized by hummocks.

In Europe, *G. g. gallinago* breeds in lowland wet grassland (Green 1985*a*), fens and marshes (Nilsson 1982), and bogs and marshy grassland (Green 1988). Tuck (1972) provided a good synopsis for snipe breeding habitat in all parts of the range.

Wintering Habitat

Common snipe use wintering habitat generally similar in structure to breeding habitat: moist soils and shallow waters. Wet pastures, plowed and fallow fields (e.g., rice fields), along with marshlands all receive use in California, Louisiana, and Texas (White 1963, Booth 1968, Arnold 1981). Common snipe will use almost any wet ground, including roadside ditches, cattle wallows, and even wet lawns if the ground remains moist for a sufficient length of time.

DISTRIBUTION AND ABUNDANCE

In North America, *G. g. delicata* breeds from northwestern Alaska through the northern Yukon and Northwest Territories to near Churchill, Manitoba on Hudson Bay; eastward from Fort Chimo, Quebec, north of James Bay, through central Labrador and Newfoundland (Fig. 2). To the south, common snipe formerly bred from Los Angeles, California northward through western Nevada and north-central Utah to south-central Colorado, eastward through central Iowa, northern Illinois and Ohio, northeastern West Virginia, northwestern Pennsylvania and southern New York to the east coast of the United States (Am. Ornithol. Union 1983). Studies by McKibben and Hofmann (1985) showed a much diminished breeding distribution in California, limited to the extreme northeastern part of the state. Isolated breeding has been reported from east-central Arizona and central New Mexico (Fogarty et al. 1977).

The winter distribution of this species extends from the panhandle of Alaska along the coast

Fig. 2.   Breeding and winter distribution of common snipe (after Fogarty et al. 1977).

of Canada, through western and southern Washington, southern Idaho, and much of Utah and Colorado; the range extends east through Kansas, the southern half of Missouri, extreme southern Illinois and Indiana, and most of Kentucky and North Carolina. The range extends south to southern California and west-central Arizona into central and eastern Mexico, and southward through Central America and Panama into South America; in the east, the range extends from Florida through the West Indies (Am. Ornithol. Union 1983).

No estimates of population numbers are available for common snipe. Also, the ability of the common snipe to use small patches of habitat on both breeding and wintering grounds makes it difficult to derive meaningful density estimates. However, Tuck (1972) recorded densities on the breeding grounds in Ontario, Manitoba, and Newfoundland as ranging from 3.6 to 17.2 pairs/100 ha; he recorded the lowest density in fen habitat and highest in swamp habitat. McKibben and Hofmann (1985) reported a density of 14.5 pairs/100 ha in California. In contrast, the Colorado study sites of Johnson and Ryder (1977) held densities of 25–85 pairs/100 ha.

Estimates of wintering populations are more difficult since snipe often move between patches of habitat in any given area (Arnold 1981). White (1963) reported large fluctuations in numbers of wintering snipe using his study areas near Humboldt Bay, California.

HARVEST

Tuck (1972) reported that at one time many hunters considered common snipe their prime target. He recorded individuals from the mid-1800's and the early 1900's that shot hundreds, sometimes thousands of snipe in a day, and tens of thousands in a single season. Current regulations preclude the taking of such large num-

Table 1.   Common snipe harvest data from states with hunter surveys.

State	Hunters (n)	Snipe harvested (n)	Year	Average
Alabama	700	2,400	1991	4,233[a]
Arizona	73	181	1992	293[a]
Florida	4,093	51,351	1992	59,503[a]
Illinois	878	1,492	1992	
Maryland	149	864	1992	885[a]
Minnesota	3,000	9,000	1992	13,000[a]
Nebraska	140	373	1992	500[a]
Ohio	1,006	1,341	1991	[b]
South Carolina	1,917	13,782	1991	
South Dakota	100	500	1989	715[a]
Texas	2,936	6,617	1992	8,459[a]
Utah	377	758	1992	1,437[a]
Virginia	212	637	1989	
Wyoming	67	112	1992	215[a]

[a] Based on latest 3 years of available data.
[b] Harvest for 1984–91 averaged 2,280.

Table 2.   Reporting states with no harvest data for common snipe; all have light hunting pressure.

Delaware	New Hampshire	Rhode Island
Iowa	North Dakota	Tennessee
Maine	Oklahoma	Vermont
Mississippi	Pennsylvania	Wisconsin

bers even in a season, and traditional snipe hunters are rare.

Hunting seasons and bag limits for common snipe are liberal. Season limits in Canada and the northern United States are within the fall migration time period. Within the wintering range, the season usually coincides with the waterfowl season. The season in Texas for 1992–93 was from 24 October through 7 February, with a daily bag limit of 8 and 16 in possession (Texas Parks and Wildl. Dep. 1992). The length of the season and the bag limits have remained essentially the same in Texas since 1967.

Lévesque et al. (1993) reported declining harvests for 1989 through 1991 in Canada: 49,585, 39,676, and 30,927, respectively. The largest harvests occurred in Quebec, Newfoundland, and Ontario, with averages for the 3 years of 17,201, 9,112, and 5,775, respectively.

A query to state wildlife agencies yielded harvest data for 14 states (Table 1), while another 12 states either reported no information or considered harvest pressure as "light" (Table 2). Martin (1993) reported an estimated harvest for the United States in 1991 of 184,900 and 137,100 in 1992. These numbers represent significant declines from the 422,000 snipe which he reported as the average for 1964–76 (Martin 1979). Louisiana, which had the highest annual statewide average harvest of 96,000 snipe for 1964–76 (Martin 1979), averaged 54,400 and 47,800 for 1991 and 1992. Florida averaged over 50,000 birds per year for the 1964-76 period, but de-

creased to 43,200 in 1991 and 16,000 in 1992 (Martin 1993). California also averaged over 50,000 birds harvested in the earlier period, but Martin (1993) reported 19,300 for 1991 and 6,900 in 1992. Almost every state which had significant harvests in the earlier period had much reduced numbers in the 1991 and 1992 surveys (Martin 1979, 1993), with many showing large decreases between the latter 2 years.

MANAGEMENT NEEDS
Habitat Management

Common snipe use seasonal wetland habitat, even in the breeding season (Johnson and Ryder 1977, McKibben and Hofmann 1985). The unstable nature of these habitats makes it difficult to assess the status of snipe habitat. Furthermore, local climatic conditions dictate which particular wetlands are suitable for snipe, especially on the wintering grounds (Arnold 1981). Geographic Information Surveys for snipe habitat on breeding and wintering grounds could be used to identify potential available habitat for this species. Since temporary wetlands often are the first to be drained for agricultural use, snipe populations using such habitats may be in jeopardy.

Population Management

Sufficient concern exists about the current Breeding Bird Survey programs conducted by the U.S. Fish and Wildlife Service and the Canadian Wildlife Service that special surveys are needed. Surveys are needed on both breeding and wintering grounds to estimate current population size and/or significant population trends. These surveys should be established at least in states and provinces that have the largest known harvests. The proposed National Migratory Bird Harvest Information Program will provide some of the needed data.

The display flights of common snipe have long been used for estimating numbers of breeding pairs. However, this survey technique has been challenged as inaccurate because even migrant birds will sometimes display while in route to breeding areas. Furthermore, the intensity of displays varies with weather, time of day, stage of the nesting cycle, and other factors (Tuck 1972). Smith (*in* Green 1985*a*) felt that early season surveys overestimated numbers of breeding pairs. In contrast, Green (1985*a*) found that 3 surveys conducted in April and early May underestimated numbers of breeding pairs. Nilsson (1982) found the highest efficiency (about 80%) for surveying snipe on fens and marshes in southern Sweden was 2 visits between 21 April and 31 May.

In the Netherlands, Nijland and Azn (1990) evaluated ways to survey migrating common snipe on 16 grassland areas, including moorlands and open water. They report that extrapolation of survey results by grassland type gave much more reliable estimates than a general extrapolation to the entire region. They suggest that social behavior and varying field conditions account for these differences, but that data can be extrapolated on a large scale if vegetation types are considered as strata.

Surveying winter populations of common snipe is complicated because of the variable nature of the winter habitat due to local weather conditions. Like habitat used by migrants, the wintering grounds consists of both permanent and temporary areas that birds use. More permanent areas can be surveyed on an annual basis if no other factors intervene. However, temporary areas should be surveyed due to their high use by wintering populations.

Busche and Staudte (1985) discussed a promising method of estimating total populations by using quantitative grid mapping. The exact area of usable habitat, bird counts in different grids, and calculation of confidence limits affected the usefulness of this technique. This approach was also time consuming; it took 88 minutes to examine 100 ha.

Harvest Management

Current information suggests that substantial harvest of this species is limited to a few states and provinces. In the United States, significant harvest occurs in Michigan, Minnesota and Wisconsin before fall migration, while the highest harvests occur in states within the winter range (California, Florida, Louisiana, and Texas). Reliable population estimates will be required to determine the effects of hunting on snipe populations. Precision and accuracy of harvest estimates should improve with implementation of the National Migratory Bird Harvest Information Program.

RESEARCH NEEDS

Lack of continent-wide data on common snipe populations preclude proper management of this species. Appropriate state and federal agencies need to establish programs that will lead to the needed data base. Research needs by priority follow.

1. Establish a data base on common snipe breeding populations.
2. Identify annual trends in common snipe breeding densities across their range.
3. Measure reproductive success using sampling across the breeding range for a minimum of 5 years to assess climatic effects on reproductive effort.
4. Identify relationships of permanent vs. temporary habitat on wintering grounds. This effort must extend for ≥5 years to assess shifts in populations due to changing habitat.
5. Estimate proportions of common snipe populations wintering in Latin America. The U.S. Fish and Wildlife Service should collaborate with appropriate agencies, especially in Mexico and Venezuela.
6. Estimate harvest at state and province levels.
7. Identify sex and age ratios of birds harvested.
8. Test use of discriminant function analyses for age and sex classification of harvested birds.

RECOMMENDATIONS

For each of the following recommendations, appropriate state or provincial agencies should conduct the indicated surveys or contract them to an appropriate university or private wildlife research entity. The Canadian Wildlife Service, U.S. Fish and Wildlife Service, and the appropriate federal agencies for Latin American countries should coordinate these surveys. For some Latin American countries, the federal agency may also be responsible for the surveys.

1. Conduct censuses on breeding grounds to identify populations trends.
2. Conduct hunter surveys in states and provinces of Canada, United States, and Latin America to estimate harvests during migration and on wintering grounds.
3. Survey wintering grounds for trends in habitat loss and condition.

4. Develop and enhance techniques to classify age and sex of harvested birds.

ACKNOWLEDGMENTS

N. J. Silvy and R. D. Slack graciously reviewed an early draft of this manuscript. Personnel of many state agencies responded to my query for harvest information, while K. M. Dickson of the Canadian Wildlife Service and E. M. Martin of the U.S. Fish and Wildlife Service supplied harvest information on a nationwide basis for Canada and the United States, respectively.

LITERATURE CITED

AMERICAN ORNITHOLOGISTS' UNION. 1983. Checklist of North American birds. 6th ed., Allen Press, Lawrence, Kans. 877pp.

ARNOLD, K. A. 1981. Fidelity of common snipe *Gallinago gallinago* to wintering grounds with comments on local movements. Southwest. Nat. 26:319–321.

———, AND D. J. JIROVEC. 1978. Arrivals and departures of wintering common snipe in central Brazos Valley of Texas. North Am. Bird Bander 3:45–47.

BENT, A. C. 1927. Life histories of North American shorebirds. U.S. Natl. Mus. Bull. 142. 420 pp.

BOOTH, T. W., JR. 1968. The availability and utilization of the foods of the common snipe (*Capella gallinago delicata*) in the rice growing region of southwestern Louisiana. M.S. Thesis, Louisiana State Univ., Baton Rouge. 160pp.

BRYANT, H. C. 1915. Two records of the nesting of the Wilson snipe in California. Calif. Fish and Game 1:76–77.

BUSCHE, G., AND A. STAUDTE. 1985. [An estimation of the total population of four bird species based on grid mapping.] Vogelwelt 106:142–149. (In German with English summary).

FLICKINGER, E. L., D. H. WHITE, C. A. MITCHELL, AND T. G. LAMONT. 1984. Monocrotophos and dicrotophos residues in birds as a result of misuse of organophosphates in Matagorda County, Texas. J. Assoc. Off. Anal. Chem. 67:827–828.

FOG, J. 1978. Studies in migration and mortality of common snipe (*Gallinago gallinago*) ringed in Denmark. Dan. Rev. Game Biol. 11:1–12.

FOGARTY, M. J. 1970. Capturing snipe with mist nets. Proc. Southeast. Assoc. Game and Fish Comm. 23:78–84.

———, K. A. ARNOLD, L. MCKIBBEN, L. B. POSPICHAL, AND R. J. TULLY. 1977. Common snipe. Pages 189–209 *in* G. C. Sanderson, ed. Management of migratory shore and upland game birds. Int. Assoc. Fish and Wildl. Agencies, Washington, D.C.

GREEN, R. E. 1984. Feeding and breeding of common snipe. Ibis 126:457.

———. 1985a. Estimating the abundance of breeding snipe. Bird Study 32:141–149.

———. 1985b. Growth of snipe chicks *Gallinago gallinago*. Ringing and Migration 6:1–6.

———. 1988. Effects of environmental factors on the timing and success of breeding of common snipe *Gallinago gallinago* (Aves: Scolopacidae). J. Appl. Ecol. 25:79–93.

———. 1991. Sex differences in the behaviour and measurements of common snipes *Gallinago gallinago* in Cambridgeshire England. Ringing and Migration 12:57–60.

———, G.J.M. HIRONS, AND B.H. CRESSWELL. 1990. Foraging habitats of female common snipe *Gallinago gallinago* during the incubation period. J. Appl. Ecol. 27:325–335.

HOFFPAUIR, J. W. 1969. The development of external aging and sexing techniques and trapping methods for common snipe (*Capella gallinago delicata*) in Louisiana. M.S. Thesis, Louisiana State Univ., Baton Rouge. 104pp.

JIROVEC, D. J. 1971. Food habits and migratory movements of the common snipe (*Capella gallinago*) in the central Brazos Valley of Texas. M.S. Thesis, Texas A&M Univ., College Station. 124pp.

JOHNSON, B. R., AND R. A RYDER. 1977. Breeding densities and migration periods of common snipe in Colorado. Wilson Bull. 89:116–121.

LÉVESQUE, H., B. COLLINS, AND A. M. LEGRIS. 1993. Migratory game birds harvested in Canada during the 1991 hunting season. Can. Wildl. Serv., Progress Notes 204. 42pp.

MARTIN, E. M. 1979. Hunting and harvest trends for migratory game birds other than waterfowl: 1964–76. U.S. Fish and Wildl. Serv., Spec. Sci. Rep. Wildl. 218. 37pp.

———. 1993. Trends in harvest and hunting activity for migratory game birds other than waterfowl and coots: 1992 season update. U.S. Fish and Wildl. Serv., Migratory Bird Manage. Off., Laurel, Md. Adm. Rep. 12 pp.

MCKIBBEN, L. A., AND P. HOFMANN. 1985. Breeding range and population studies of common snipe in California. Calif. Fish and Game 71:68–75.

NIJLAND, F., AND A. T. AZN. 1990. Counts of migrant common snipe *Gallinago gallinago* on wet grasslands in the province of Friesland, The Netherlands. Limosa 63:95–101.

NILSSON, S. G. 1982. Seasonal changes in census efficiency of birds at marshes and fen mires in southern Sweden. Holarct. Ecol. 5:55–60.

OWENS, J. 1967. Food habits of the common snipe (*Capella gallinago delicata*) in the pastures of south central Louisiana. M.S. Thesis, Louisiana State Univ. Baton Rouge. 107pp.

RUNDLE, W. D. 1982. A case for esophageal analysis in shorebird food studies. J. Field Ornithol. 53: 249–257.

SLOAN, N. L. 1967. An external sexual character of the common snipe. Michigan Tech. Univ., Houghton. Wharve-Graduate School Publ.:11–12.

SUTTON, G. M. 1923. Notes on the nesting of Wilson's Snipe in Crawford County. Pennsylvania. Wilson Bull. 35:191–202.

———. 1981. Aerial and ground displays of snipes throughout the world. Wilson Bull. 93:457–477.

TEXAS PARKS AND WILDLIFE DEPARTMENT. 1992. Texas late season migratory game bird 1992–1993 hunting regulations. PWD-BR-N7100-129-9/92.

TUCK, L. M. 1972. The snipes: a study of the genus *Capella*. Can. Wildl. Serv. Mongr. Ser. 5. 429pp.

WHITE, M. 1963. Occurrence, habitat ecology, food habits, and sex and age studies of the Wilson snipe in the Humboldt Bay region. M.S. Thesis, Humboldt State Univ., Arcata, Calif. 90 pp.

————, AND S. W. HARRIS. 1966. Winter occurrence, foods, and habitat use of snipe in northwest California. J. Wildl. Manage. 30:23–34.

WHITEHEAD, C. J., JR. 1965. Foods and feeding habits of the common snipe (*Capella gallinago delicata*) in Cameron Parish, Louisiana, with ecological notes and a discussion of methods of sexing and aging. M.S. Thesis, Louisiana State Univ. Baton Rouge. 199 pp.

Chapter 9

AMERICAN COOT

RAY T. ALISAUSKAS, Canadian Wildlife Service, 115 Perimeter Road, Saskatoon, SK S7N 0X4, Canada

TODD W. ARNOLD, Institute for Wetland and Waterfowl Research, Ducks Unlimited Canada, Stonewall P.O. Box 1160, Oak Hammock Marsh, MB R0C 2Z0, Canada

Abstract: American coots (*Fulica americana*) breed over much of North America, reaching maximum densities in the Northern Great Plains. Analysis of band recoveries suggests the North American coot population is panmictic. Coot populations have increased since breeding-ground surveys began in the 1950's, although the reliability of these estimates is unknown. Annual coot harvest over the last 3–4 decades has averaged approximately 8,000 in Canada and 800,000 in the United States, but has declined in recent years in both countries. Harvest is concentrated in the Mississippi Flyway (60% of U.S. harvest), California (13%), and Florida (5%). Major population management needs include evaluation of breeding- and wintering-ground surveys (and establishment of such surveys in Mexico), updated estimates of survival and recovery rates, and assessment of possible bias in harvest surveys (unretrieved kill and non-response). Wetland habitats traditionally have not been managed for coots, but coots nevertheless appear to benefit from many waterfowl management activities. Detailed studies of nutritional ecology, habitat preferences, and sources of mortality of wintering coots constitute important research needs.

American coots are an abundant and conspicuous component of North America's wetland avifauna (Kantrud and Stewart 1984). Three subspecies of American coots are commonly recognized (Howard and Moore 1984): *F. a. americana* from mainland North America, *F. a. alai* from Hawaii (hereafter "Hawaiian coots"), and *F. a. columbiana* from South America. In addition, the Caribbean coot (*F. caribaea*) from the Antilles is sometimes regarded as a morph of *F. americana* (Am. Ornithol. Union 1983). Unless stated otherwise, our review deals exclusively with *F. a. americana* (hereafter "American coots," or simply "coots").

DESCRIPTION

Adult coots superficially resemble ducks, but the bill and legs are chicken-like. Coots are sexually monochromatic; the plumage is slate gray, appearing black from a distance. White undertail coverts and white tips on the secondaries are conspicuous during certain displays (Gullion 1952). The tarsi and toes are greenish-yellow; the toes are lobed rather than webbed. The bill is white with a red callus on top of the frontal shield (Gullion 1951) and has a faint red stripe near the tip. Coots are sexually dimorphic; however, external measurements of sexes overlap considerably (Alisauskas 1987). Eddleman and Knopf (1985) obtained 93% correct gender clas-

sification using a discriminant function derived from 19 morphological variables. Boersma and Davies (1987) used cloacal vent measurements to correctly classify gender of 22/22 coots. There is some evidence of geographic size variation, with systematic increases in culmen length from California to Iowa to Manitoba (Alisauskas 1987). Spring body mass (including ingesta) averaged 530 g for females (SE = 5.7, n = 99) and 670 g for males (SE = 8.0, n = 98) (Arnold 1990); comparable weights for postbreeding coots were about 60 g heavier (C. D. Ankney and T. W. Arnold, unpubl. data). Both sexes develop brood patches. Voice differences are the most reliable way of classifying gender of coots in the field (Gullion 1950). Age class of adults can be determined from tarsal coloration, which progresses from green to yellow-green to yellow to orange/red as coots mature (Crawford 1978).

Coots build large floating nests that are anchored to surrounding emergent vegetation. Eggs are tan with extensive dark brown flecking and measure approximately 45 × 25 mm. Hatchlings are covered with grayish-black down, except in the head region, which is brightly colored with orange and blue. Chicks begin to acquire a light gray juvenal plumage when they are about 3 weeks old (Gullion 1954). Juveniles can be distinguished from adults with varying accuracy during the fall and winter using iris

Fig. 1. A typical coot nest. The two darker colored eggs on the outer edge of the clutch (top and lower left) were laid parasitically. Up to one third of coot clutches are parasitized by conspecifics (Photo by T. W. Arnold).

color, head plumage color, bill color, bill stripe characteristics, external morphological measurements, and size of the bursa of Fabricius (Eddelman and Knopf 1985).

LIFE HISTORY

Annual Cycle

American coots migrate at night, singly or in loose flocks (Hochbaum 1955, Yocum et al. 1978). Spring migration occurs from late February through mid-May (Gorenzel et al. 1981a, Alisauskas and Ankney 1985, Eddleman et al. 1985), with males and older coots migrating first (Ryan and Dinsmore 1979, Alisauskas and Ankney 1985, Eddleman et al. 1985). Coots are weakly philopatric to previous breeding areas (Crawford 1978, Bartelt and Rusch 1980). Pair formation is poorly understood, but apparently occurs on terminal staging areas and/or on breeding wetlands (Sooter 1941, Gullion 1953b, Ryan and Dinsmore 1979, Alisauskas and Ankney 1985). All-purpose territories are vigorously defended against conspecifics (Gullion 1953b), and sometimes against other species of wetland birds (Ryder 1959, Ryan and Dinsmore 1979). Coots are monogamous, and both parents assist in territorial defense, nest building, incubation, and brood rearing (Ryan and Dinsmore 1979). Breeding begins at age 1 (Crawford 1980), although many yearlings are non-breeders (Alisauskas 1987). Breeding performance increases with age, especially between 1- and 2-year-olds (Crawford 1980; Ryan and Dinsmore 1980; Alisauskas and Ankney 1985, 1987).

Adult coots undergo 1 complete annual molt at the end of the breeding season when they are flightless (late Jul–early Sep) (Gullion 1953a; C. D. Ankney and T. W. Arnold, unpubl. data); this may occur on the breeding territory, or on large molting wetlands where coots congregate after the breeding season (Ward 1953, Bergman 1973). Fall migration occurs from late August through December (Gorenzel et al. 1981a, Eddleman et al. 1985). Some coots exhibit fidelity to previous wintering locations (Yocum et al. 1978).

Reproduction

Coots usually begin nesting within 10–14 days of arrival on breeding grounds (Kiel 1955, Arnold 1990). Peak nest initiation occurs from late-April through May across most of the breeding range, with smaller numbers of clutches being initiated in June and July (Fredrickson 1970, Gorenzel et al. 1982, Alisauskas and Ankney 1985, Arnold 1990). Hawaiian coots nest throughout the year, although most nesting occurs from April through August (Schwartz and Schwartz 1952, Byrd et al. 1985). One egg is usually laid per day (Arnold 1990). Some individuals are intraspecific brood parasites, laying eggs in the nests of other coots before producing clutches of their own (Lyon 1991) (Fig. 1). Average clutch size ranges from 6 to 11 and declines seasonally in most populations (Arnold 1990). The mean clutch size of Hawaiian coots is 4.9 (Byrd et al. 1985). Both sexes incubate (Crawford 1977), but the relative contribution of each sex has not been adequately determined. The hatching pattern is asynchronous; incubation usually commences with the 3rd- to 6th-laid egg and eggs generally hatch 22–26 days after being laid ($\bar{x} = 23.4$) (T. W. Arnold, unpubl. data). Nest success generally exceeds 80% (Kiel 1955, Ryder 1957, Arnold 1992), but may be lower during drought years (Sutherland 1991; T. W. Arnold, unpubl. data). Coots are persistent renesters; individuals can renest up to 4 times following clutch or brood losses (Ryder 1957, Arnold 1992). Coots occasionally raise 2 sequential broods in southern portions of their breeding range (including Hawaii) (Gullion 1954, Ryder 1957, Byrd et al. 1985); elsewhere, a 2nd clutch may be laid while the 1st clutch is still being incubated (Bett 1983, Hill 1986).

Chicks can leave the nest within hours of hatching (Fig. 2), although they return to the nest or to special brood platforms for frequent

Fig. 2. Two newly hatched coot chicks wait in the nest. Coot clutches hatch asynchronously, with large clutches often requiring a week or more to hatch completely (Photo by T. W. Arnold).

Fig. 3. A young (ca. 1-week old) coot chick waits to be fed. Chicks are almost completely reliant on their parents for food for the first 2–3 weeks after hatch (Photo by T. W. Arnold).

brooding. Chicks obtain food almost exclusively from their parents for the first 2 weeks after hatching, but gradually become independent of their parents over the next 3–10 weeks (Ryan and Dinsmore 1979, Desroschers and Ankney 1986, Driver 1988). Fledging occurs at about 60–70 days of age (Gullion 1954). Total brood mortality is rare (<5%) (Lyon 1992; T. W. Arnold, unpubl. data), except during droughts (Sutherland 1991; T. W. Arnold, unpubl. data). However, partial brood losses are common; fledging success averaged just over 50% in 2 studies using marked chicks (Lyon 1992; T. W. Arnold, unpubl. data). Brood size data derived from visual counts of unmarked birds are not always reliable (Gullion 1956).

Survival and Non-hunting Mortality

Ryder (1963) estimated survival rates from 2,325 recoveries of coots banded west of Ontario and the Mississippi River using composite-dynamic life table analyses. Survival averaged 49% per year for adults (≥ 1 yr), 44% for juveniles, and 45% overall (Ryder 1963). Burton (1959) calculated an annual adult survival rate of 43% with a smaller sample of recoveries ($n = 139$) using a maximum-likelihood estimate.

Adult and juvenile coots are preyed upon by a wide variety of predators, including alligators (*Alligator mississippiensis*) (Delaney 1986), mink (*Mustela vison*) (Arnold and Fritzell 1989), great horned owls (*Bubo virginianus*) (Gilmer et al. 1983), northern harriers (*Circus cyaneus*) (Sowls 1955), bald eagles (*Haliaeetus leucocephalus*) (Griffin et al. 1982), and great black-

backed gulls (*Larus marinus*) (Sobkowiak and Titman 1989). Because they migrate at night, they often hit powerlines (R. T. Alisauskas and T. W. Arnold, pers. observ.). Coots rarely ingest lead shot (Jones 1939, Fredrickson 1969). Avian cholera (*Pasteurella multocida*) occurs commonly in coots (Vaught et al. 1967, Klukas and Locke 1970, Paullin 1987). In northern California, coots are more vulnerable to avian cholera than are waterfowl (Hazelwood et al. 1978, Oddo et al. 1978, Mensik and Botzler 1989). Extensive mortality sometimes occurs during periods of severe spring weather (Fredrickson 1969).

Diet and Nutrition

The 2 primary foraging methods used by coots are diving in shallow water and pecking at food items near the water's surface (Desroschers and Ankney 1986, Driver 1988) (Fig. 3). Some infrequently-used foraging methods include flycatching, tipping-up, scavenging, and terrestrial grazing (Fredrickson et al. 1977, Paullin 1987, Driver 1988).

Adult coots are primarily herbivorous throughout the annual cycle; prominent foods include pondweeds (*Potamogeton* spp.), duckweeds (*Lemna* spp.), water milfoils (*Myriophyllum* spp.), bulrushes (*Scirpus* spp.), and muskgrass algae (*Chara* spp.) (Jones 1940, Sooter 1941, Stollberg 1949, Fitzner et al. 1980, Swiderek et al. 1988). Consumption of animal foods, primarily aquatic insects and molluscs, increases during the summer breeding season (Jones 1940). In some studies, aquatic invertebrates have comprised a large (45–85%) proportion of the diet of young chicks (Jones 1940, Sooter 1941, Driver

Fig. 4. A typical breeding territory in southwestern Manitoba. Note the thick growth of cattail used for nesting and the open-water areas used for feeding (Photo by T. W. Arnold).

1988; but see Fitzner et al. 1980, Eichhorst 1986); important taxa include Trichoptera and Diptera larvae, Coleoptera, and Gastropoda (Driver 1988). Most early studies of food habits of coots were based on gizzard contents (e.g., Jones 1940, Sooter 1941, Stollberg 1949; but see Driver 1988), and probably underestimated the proportion of animal matter in the diet (Swanson and Barto-nek 1970).

Conflicting evidence exists as to the importance of nutrients during egg formation. Alisauskas and Ankney (1985) showed that female coots nesting at Delta Marsh, Manitoba, used endogenous lipid and protein reserves during egg laying. Nutrient reserves did not decline among laying females at Minnedosa, Manitoba, but coots that received food supplements during the nesting season nested earlier, laid larger clutches, and fledged more offspring (Arnold 1990). In contrast, Hill (1988) found that availability of natural and supplemental food had no effect on laying date and clutch size of coots in eastern Washington.

HABITAT

Coots attain maximum nesting densities on well-flooded, persistent emergent wetlands that have good interspersion of emergent vegetation and open water (Weller and Fredrickson 1973, Gorenzel et al. 1981b). Nest densities are usually highest on semipermanent wetlands (Kiel 1955, Stewart and Kantrud 1971, Sugden 1979, Kantrud 1985), except during severe droughts when coots may be restricted to permanent wetlands (Sutherland 1991). Seasonal wetlands are used when water levels are high (Kiel 1955, Sugden 1979, Kantrud 1985). Coots prefer fresh water

and avoid brackish or saline wetlands (Byrd et al. 1985, Kantrud 1985) (Fig. 4). A Habitat Suitability Index model has been prepared for breeding coots (Allen 1985). Nests are usually within stands of residual emergent vegetation, but some late season nests may be constructed in new-growth emergents (Kiel 1955, Sugden 1979, Gorenzel et al. 1982). Cattail (*Typha* spp.) and bulrush (*Scirpus* spp.) are preferred nesting cover, but whitetop rivergrass (*Scholochloa festucacea*), sedges (*Carex* spp.), and willows (*Salix* spp.) are also used, especially in wet years (Kiel 1955, Sugden 1979, Gorenzel et al. 1982, Sutherland and Maher 1987).

Although coots will molt on their breeding wetlands if water levels remain high throughout the summer (C. D. Ankney and T. W. Arnold, unpubl. data), many coots apparently migrate to larger northern wetlands for molting (Bergman 1973; T. W. Arnold, pers. observ.). However, no detailed information is available about postbreeding habitat requirements of coots.

Coots use a wide variety of wetland and deep-water habitats during migration (Fredrickson et al. 1977). In Oklahoma, where turnover of coots was high and most stayed for ≤3 days, habitat selection by fall migrants varied with time since arrival (Eddleman 1983); coots initially loafed in open water areas, but those that remained >6 days used feeding habitats that were distinguishable from random sites in having greater vegetative cover, shallower water, lower pH, higher alkalinity, and higher conductivity. During spring migration through Oklahoma, coots used smaller wetlands (Heitmeyer 1980).

White and James (1978) described winter habitat use of coots in coastal Texas. Coots were usually intermediate between dabbling and diving ducks in their use of specific microhabitats; on average, they fed in areas that were 90 cm deep with 20% cover of emergent vegetation and 40% cover of floating plus submerged vegetation. Coots use several types of man-made wetlands in winter including brackish impoundments (Swiderek et al. 1988), crayfish ponds (Nassar et al. 1988), catfish ponds (Dubovsky and Kaminsky 1987, Christopher et al. 1988), and coal mine sediment ponds (Reynolds 1989). Hydrilla (*Hydrilla verticillata*) was an important component of wintering habitat in Florida (Montalbano et al. 1979, Hardin et al. 1984), and coot abundance was positively correlated with hydrilla cover in Texas (Esler 1990).

Perceptions of coots as urban (e.g., golf cours-

Fig. 5.   Distribution and abundance of American coots by political boundary as determined by the Breeding Bird Survey in Canada and the United States but not Mexico (Robbins et al. 1986). Values shown are average number of coots per survey route in each state and province. Trace numbers are not shown.

es) and agricultural (e.g., rice production) pests during winter has motivated discussion and research about control methods (Van Way 1986, Woronecki et al. 1990). Nevertheless, there is little published information on winter ecology of coots. Studies about habitat selection and habitat-specific mortality rates would be useful for understanding coot population dynamics.

DISTRIBUTION AND ABUNDANCE

American coots breed throughout most of North America (given suitable wetland habitat), being absent only from arctic and boreal regions (Am. Ornithol. Union 1983, Lang 1991). Hawaiian coots are restricted to freshwater wetlands on major islands of the Hawaiian archipelago (Byrd et al. 1985). *F. a. columbiana* is found from central Colombia to northern Ecuador (Howard and Moore 1984).

Although range maps are useful for delimit-

ing distribution boundaries, they give little information on geographic variation in density during the breeding season. The Breeding Bird Survey (Robbins et al. 1986) is the only population survey that provides an index to geographic patterns of relative abundance of breeding coots throughout Canada and the United States. Average numbers of coots detected per route were highest in the Canadian Prairie Provinces (particularly Saskatchewan), North and South Dakota, and Oregon (Fig. 5). Lower densities of coots occurred in the western United States. Few coots are observed in eastern North America (Fig. 5), where coots were once abundant before extensive wetland drainage occurred (Lang 1991). The Breeding Bird Survey may be inadequate in areas where coots are patchily distributed in a few large breeding marshes; Cadman et al. (1987) estimated a population of 1,600 to 14,000 breeding coots in an

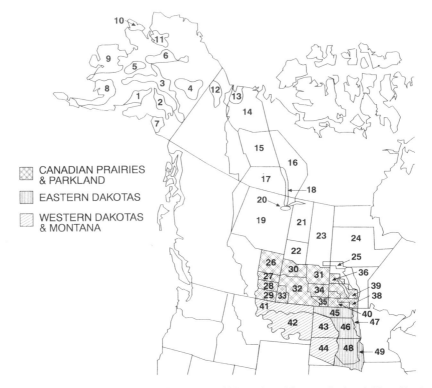

Fig. 6.   Strata for the Breeding Ground Survey (Smith et al. 1991) conducted for waterfowl each May.   Numbers are stratum codes. Strata most important to American coots are shaded: Canadian Prairies and Parklands 26–40; western Dakotas and Montana 41–44; eastern Dakotas 45–49.

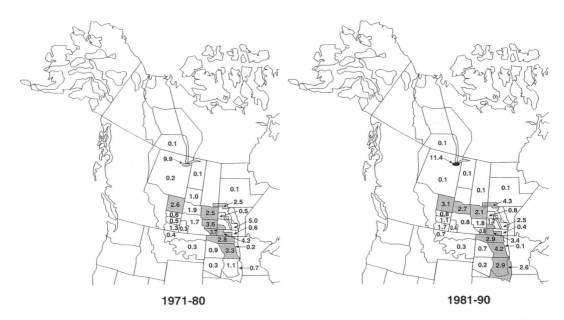

1971-80   **1981-90**

Fig. 7.   Long-term patterns of geographic distribution of American coots within areas censused by the Breeding Ground Survey (Smith et al. 1991). Within each stratum, the value shown (American coots/km²) is the estimated number of American coots divided by the stratum size (km²). High density areas (>2 American coots/km²) are shaded.

STRATA 26 TO 49 (1981-1991)

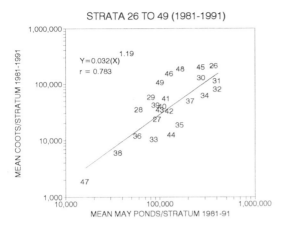

Fig. 8. Spatial relation of long-term averages of American coots with long-term averages in number of May ponds. Numbers indicate stratum codes.

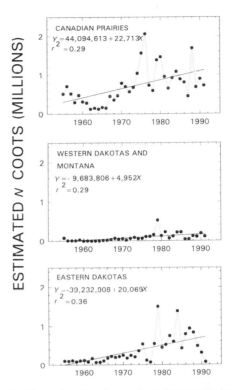

Fig. 9. Time series of American coot populations on the Northern Great Plains (Canadian Prairies, western Dakotas and Montana, eastern Dakotas) estimated from the Breeding Ground Survey (Smith et al. 1991). For all linear regression models, $P < 0.0006$.

area of Ontario where no coots were registered by the Breeding Bird Survey (Fig. 5). Comparable data are not available for areas outside Canada and the United States where coots are known to breed (e.g., Mexico and Central America) (Am. Ornithol. Union 1983).

Annual Breeding Ground Surveys for waterfowl are conducted each spring across much of the Northern Great Plains, western Canada, and Alaska (Smith et al. 1991); these surveys also record coot numbers. Breeding Ground Surveys provide only relative indices of coot abundance; aerial surveys detect fewer birds than ground surveys (Martin et al. 1979), and ground surveys detect only about half of known nesting populations of coots (Kiel 1955, Sugden 1979, Gorenzel et al. 1981b). Breeding Ground Surveys are geographically partitioned into 50 strata (Fig. 6), but most coots occur in the prairie-parkland region (strata 26–49), particularly in the Canadian parklands and eastern Dakotas (Fig. 7). Long-term spatial distributions of coots in the prairie-parkland region are positively correlated with long-term averages of wetland abundance (May pond index, Fig. 8).

Estimates of coot numbers in the prairie-parkland region have increased in the last 3 decades (Fig. 9). Unexpectedly, these increases were not correlated with annual estimates of May pond abundance in the Canadian Prairies (1961–91), in the western Dakotas and Montana (1974–91), in the eastern Dakotas (1963–91), or when compared to May ponds in all areas in the Northern Great Plains covered by the Breed-

ing Ground Survey (Smith et al. 1991). The ratio of coots to May ponds has increased in the Canadian Prairies and eastern Dakotas, but not in the western Dakotas and Montana or across the entire prairie-parkland region (Fig. 10; the latter 2 analyses were restricted to 1974–91). These analyses (Fig. 10) suggest that coot populations in the prairie-parkland region have not been limited by habitat availability, but 2 alternative explanations warrant consideration. First, the lack of correlation between coots and May ponds may result from variation in availability of specific wetland types (e.g., ephemeral and seasonal wetlands) that are most vulnerable to drought and drainage, but are not used by breeding coots. Second, early waterfowl surveyers may not have taken estimation of coot numbers as seriously as later surveyers. Aerial surveyors are responsible for counts that include May ponds, 18 species of waterfowl, and coots; coot estimation probably has had the lowest priority over the years, but with diminished duck populations, observers may be more apt to count more coots on

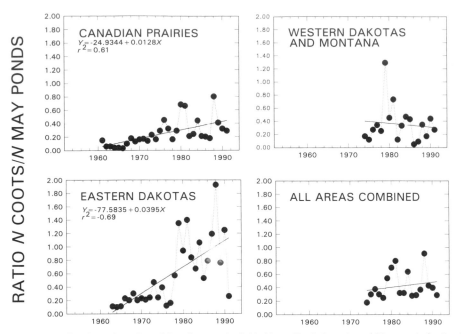

Fig. 10.   Time series of estimated number of American coots divided by estimated number of May ponds for the Canadian Prairies (1961–91), western Dakotas and Montana (1974–91), eastern Dakotas (1963–91), and for all areas on the Northern Great Plains censused by the Breeding Ground Survey (Smith et al. 1991). Only equations for models with $P < 0.05$ are shown. Both significant models have $P < 0.0003$.

survey lines. An evaluation of temporal changes in the ratio of coots observed from the ground to those observed from the air (i.e., visibility correction factor) may help explain the apparent long term increase of coots on the breeding grounds.

Most coots winter in the southern United States (California, Florida, Louisiana, Texas) and Mexico. Using Christmas Bird Counts, Root (1988) found that highest wintering concentrations in the United States were on Conchas Lake, New Mexico, and in the Imperial, San Joachin, and Sacramento valleys of California. In the eastern United States, wintering coots are widely associated with the Mississippi Alluvial Valley and the Louisiana and Texas coasts. Smaller numbers of coots are distributed continuously along the Atlantic Coast from Florida to New York. Since 1955, coot numbers have been estimated regularly in most of the continental United States during coordinated surveys of waterfowl during December of each year. Coots occur in appreciable numbers in all coastal states and in the northwest mainland of Mexico (Fig. 11). States that have averaged over 100,000 coots counted in years that surveys have been conducted include California, Florida, Louisiana, Texas, and

Sonora, Mexico. Unknown numbers of coots winter along other portions of the eastern and western coasts of Mexico, and through Central America to Panama and northern Colombia (Am. Ornithol. Union 1983). Since 1955, coot winter indices increased until the 1970's, then declined below 1950's levels in the 1980's (Fig. 12). Most of this reflects patterns of abundance in the Mississippi Flyway (Fig. 13). Long-term shifts in winter distribution have occurred during 1955–92, with more coots wintering consistently in the Mississippi Flyway, and a substantial decline in Pacific Flyway states. As most coots in the Pacific Flyway formerly wintered in California, the long-term decline may be the result of habitat deterioration either through wetland destruction or, more recently, drought in that state. Abundance of coots in the Atlantic and Central Flyway states has been rather stable (Figs. 13, 14).

American coots are apparently panmictic over most of their North American breeding range. Coots banded during the post-breeding season in the Northern Great Plains have been recovered in all 4 waterfowl flyways (Ryder 1963). Conversely, coots banded during the winter in Louisiana have been recovered from Yukon to

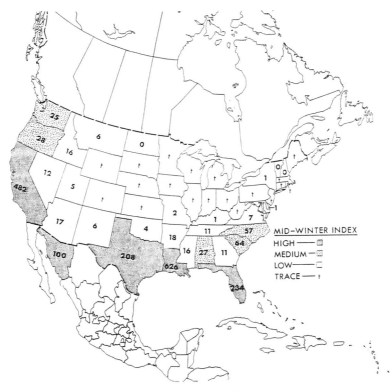

Fig. 11.   Midwinter indices of coots in the United States and northwest Mexico. Values shown are average numbers counted each year during coordinated waterfowl surveys. Averages of <1,000 were considered to be trace abundance. Counts were incomplete in California 1983–88, and the west coast of Mexico and Baja California were surveyed only in 1955–56, 1962–65, 1967–85, 1988, and 1991.

Virginia, and coots banded during winter in California have been recovered from Alaska to Manitoba (Ryder 1963). Many coots are probably sedentary in the southern portions of their range (southern U.S., Mexico, and Central America), where they are observed during both summer and winter (Gullion 1954).

HARVEST

About 8,000 coots were harvested in Canada each year between 1976 and 1991, with the greatest percentages being taken in Ontario (33%) and Quebec (28%) (Fig. 15). Most birds shot in these 2 provinces likely originated from the prairies (Lang 1991). Annual retrieved kill of coots in the United States during 1952–91 averaged 882,000 (Fig. 16). Large numbers of coots are consistently harvested in California, Florida, Louisiana, and the upper Midwest (Fig. 15). The greatest proportion of the harvest occurrs in the Mississippi Flyway (60%), with smaller proportions occurring in the Pacific (20%), Atlantic (13%), and Central (7%) flyways

(Fig. 17). Harvest data are not available for Mexico.

Geographic patterns of harvest likely result from a combination of abundance of coots dur-

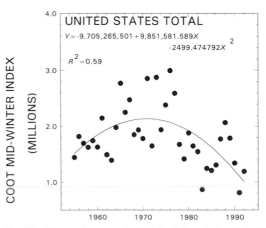

Fig. 12.   Time series of coot midwinter indices in the United States excluding Alaska and Hawaii. Smoothed curve is a second order polynomial determined with least squares regression, $P < 0.0006$; linear model was $P > 0.05$.

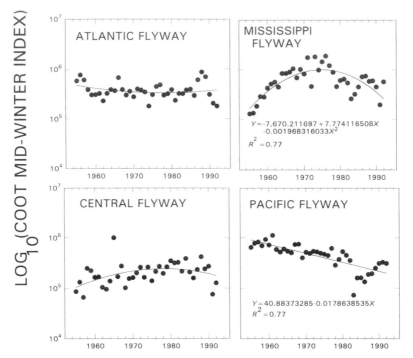

Fig. 13. Patterns of change in coot midwinter indices in the United States for each flyway. Only equations for models with $P < 0.05$ are shown. Both significant models have $P < 0.0001$. Either a linear or second order polynomial model was chosen depending on the highest coefficient of variation.

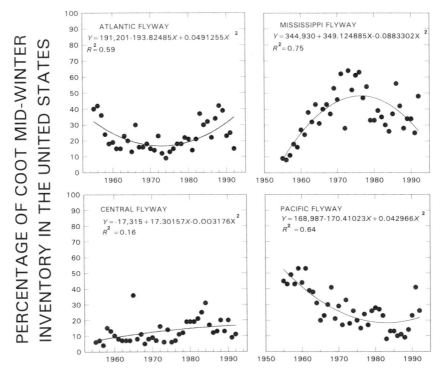

Fig. 14. Patterns of change in proportional midwinter distribution of coots by flyway. Shown are nonlinear trends in numbers from 1955 to 1992. Only equations for models with $P < 0.05$ are shown. All significant models have $P < 0.0001$. Either a linear or second order polynomial model was chosen depending on the highest coefficient of variation.

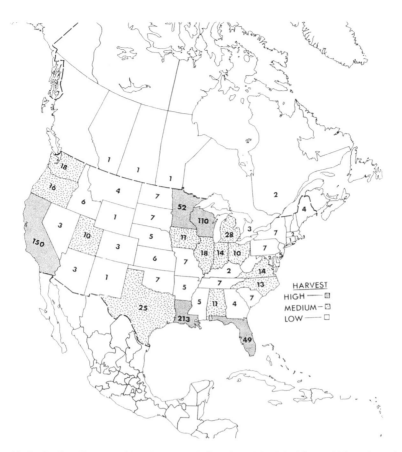

Fig. 15.   Geographic distribution of harvest of American coots in Canada and the United States. Values shown for each province (1976–91) and state (1952–91) are average number (in thousands) of American coots reported killed and retrieved annually. Areas of high (>40,000), medium (10,000–40,000), and low (<10,000) harvest are shaded. Harvest estimates are not available for Mexico or the Caribbean.

ing migration and winter, and variation in regional traditions for shooting coots (Kiel and Hawkins 1953). Also, those states with high annual coot harvests have waterfowl seasons that overlap peak coot migration, or have special seasons for coots (Fredrickson et al. 1977). Eddleman et al. (1985) suggested that low harvests in some states could be increased by adjusting seasons to correspond with peak of coot migration. They noted that special seasons on coots should not put added pressure on any non-target waterfowl, as the 2 groups are readily discernible in the field. Bartelt (1977) suggested that more restrictive waterfowl seasons could result in increased local harvest of coots.

Coot harvest in Canada has declined dramatically from about 18,000 in the late 1960's to under 3,000 in 1990 (Fig. 18). This systematic decline in harvest was correlated with a concurrent decline in hunter effort, and was independent of coot abundance in the prairie-park-

land region (Lang 1991). Total annual coot harvest in the U.S. has fluctuated in association with annual numbers of May ponds (Fig. 16). This was probably not caused by variation in size of the fall coot flight, because (unexpectedly) there was no correlation between number of breeding coots and number of May ponds ($P > 0.05$ for each population listed in Fig. 9). Coot harvest in each flyway (Fig. 19) was relatively high in the mid-1950's and late 1960's and early 1970's, moderate in the early 1960's and late 1970's, and comparatively low in the 1980's and into the 1990's. Higher coot harvest in years of abundant May ponds probably occurred incidentally as a result of greater hunter effort by waterfowl hunters that also shot coots. A local study in Wisconsin (a state with high harvest, Fig. 15) indicated that most coots were shot incidentally by duck hunters, with <1% of hunters responding that hunting effort was directly primarily at coots (Bartelt 1977).

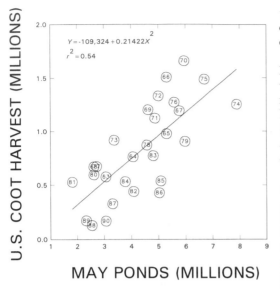

Fig. 16. Relation of American coot harvest in the United States and number of May ponds in the Canadian Prairies and Park-lands (strata 26–40) and the eastern Dakotas (strata 45–49). Numbers within symbols represent specific years.

There have been geographic shifts in proportional harvest of coots in the United States since 1952 (Fig. 17). Harvest in the Mississippi Flyway has increased from about 50% in the 1950's to 70% in recent years. Proportional har-vest in the Atlantic and Pacific flyways has concurrently declined. No significant change was evident in the Central Flyway.

Band recovery rate for coots was about 7% in Ryder's (1963) analysis; the direct recovery rate would have been about 4%. Band reporting rate is not known for coots, but we suspect that it is lower than for mallards (*Anas platyrhynchos*) (circa 30%; Nichols et al. 1991), in which case an annual harvest rate of ≥13% is suspected for coots before 1960.

Coots have a much lower incidence of imbedded body shot than do ducks (Elder 1955), suggesting much lower harvest pressure. However, because of their small size, coots are more likely to be downed by 1 shot pellet than are larger ducks. Locally, coots can be extremely vulnerable to heavy shooting; Bellrose (1944) reported an example where over 90% of coots using an Illinois marsh were harvested in 1 day. In Wisconsin, Bartelt (1977) found that unretrieved kill of coots comprised 25–45% of total coots shot by hunters.

MANAGEMENT NEEDS

Habitat Management

Coots prefer semipermanent wetlands for breeding and so have probably been less affected by wetland drainage on the breeding grounds

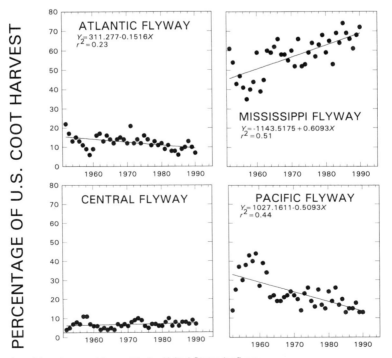

Fig. 17.   Time series of American coot harvest in the United States by flyway.

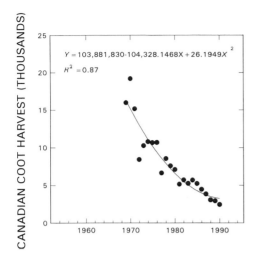

Fig. 18.   Patterns of change in American coot harvest in Canada from 1969 to 1990.

than have dabbling ducks that use more seasonal and temporary wetlands (Kantrud and Stewart 1977). Nevertheless, wetland loss has undoubtedly reduced the potential breeding population of coots, particularly in Iowa and Minnesota where almost all wetlands, regardless of per-

manence, have been drained (Kantrud et al. 1989). Coots are known for their ability to pioneer new habitats (Weller and Fredrickson 1973), and they would likely respond well to wetland restoration efforts in drained areas.

Coots attain their highest breeding densities when cover-water interspersion is maximal (Weller and Fredrickson 1973). On open marshes with water-control structures, drawdowns can be effective in establishing emergent vegetation, whereas deep flooding, mowing, or burning of closed marshes can help reduce vegetation and create open water areas (Kantrud et al. 1989).

The majority of the North American coot population winters in California, Mexico, Texas, Louisiana, Mississippi, and Florida. Maintenance and management of productive wetland habitats in these areas is undoubtedly important to overwinter survival. The effects of saltwater intrusion on freshwater habitats used by coots in important wintering states such as Florida, Louisiana, and Texas are unknown.

Population and Harvest Management

The annual Breeding Ground Survey for waterfowl has provided information on coot abun-

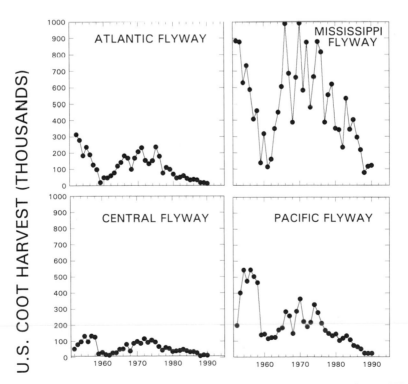

Fig. 19.   Temporal changes in harvest of American coots in each flyway in the United States from 1952 to 1990. Only equations for models with $P < 0.05$ are shown. All significant models have $P < 0.002$. Either a linear or second order polynomial model was chosen depending on the highest coefficient of variation.

dance in the most important breeding areas since 1955. Visual surveys can underestimate coot numbers by ≥50% (Kiel 1955; Sugden 1979; T. W. Arnold, unpubl. data), so such counts are not indicative of actual population size. Nevertheless, visual counts were highly correlated with nest density in southern Manitoba (Kiel 1955; T. W. Arnold, unpubl. data), and likely serve as valid indices of population fluctuations. However, the efficiency of the Breeding Ground Survey at estimating changes in coot abundance has not been adequately addressed. An index of coot brood abundance is also recorded during the July waterfowl production surveys (Martin et al. 1979), but the relationship between this index and actual breeding success is unknown.

Winter surveys for coots are conducted in conjunction with midwinter waterfowl surveys in the United States, but surveys are also needed for major wintering habitats in Mexico. Research into biases associated with the midwinter indices would be useful to gain insight into total midwinter numbers.

Recent harvest levels are probably not of concern because population indices of coots in the most important breeding areas show apparent long-term increases. The relationship between recent low harvest rates and apparent population increases on the breeding grounds is unclear. Historically, the harvest in the United States may have been a significant source of mortality and resulted in populations that were depressed, but adequate for sustained harvest. For harvest management to surpass its present level on a continental scale, more information is needed about the reliability of the Breeding Ground Survey and total harvest estimates. The National Migratory Bird Harvest Information Program should evaluate reliability of harvest estimates in the United States.

RESEARCH NEEDS

1. Evaluate bias and precision of the Breeding Ground Survey and Breeding Bird Survey in estimating breeding coot populations.
2. Conduct studies of marked coot populations to assess natal and breeding philopatry, and winter site fidelity (this may require development of better marking techniques).
3. Conduct an updated analysis of band recovery data to estimate survival and recovery rates, and migration routes.
4. Identify food habits throughout the annual cycle based on analysis of esophageal contents.
5. Obtain data on postbreeding, migratory, and wintering habitat requirements.
6. Evaluate potential sources of bias in harvest surveys including band reporting rates, failure to retrieve, crippling losses, and illegal kill.
7. Experiment with special seasons to increase hunter interest in coots.
8. Evaluate geographic variation in mitochondrial DNA and morphometry of coots dispersed throughout North America during the breeding and wintering seasons to learn if identifiable subpopulations occur.
9. Identify sources of variation in recruitment of young coots, especially brood and postfledging survival.
10. Examine dynamics of diseases, especially avian cholera, in limiting coot populations.
11. Study ecological relationships between coots and winter habitat, specifically habitat-dependent mortality rates.

RECOMMENDATIONS

1. In conjuction with Mexican federal wildlife agencies, the U.S. Fish and Wildlife Service (USFWS) should conduct research to assess harvest, abundance, and distribution of coots in Mexico.
2. The USFWS and Canadian Wildlife Service (CWS) should ensure that coots captured opportunistically during all regularly scheduled waterfowl banding efforts be banded.
3. The USFWS and CWS should ensure that regular annual population surveys of coots continue to be conducted in conjunction with breeding ground and wintering waterfowl surveys.
4. The USFWS should ensure that the National Migratory Bird Harvest Information Program is able to obtain reliable estimates of coot harvest in the United States.
5. The USFWS and CWS should promote funding of identified research needs.

ACKNOWLEDGMENTS

We thank J. P. Bladen and F. A. Johnson for supplying data on May pond numbers and American coot populations determined during Breeding Ground Surveys; E. L. Martin provided harvest survey data for the United States, and J. C. Bartonek, D. E. Sharp, K. E. Gamble, and J. R. Serie kindly compiled and supplied midwinter index data for coots. G. C. Gentle drafted distribution and abundance maps. L. H. Fredrickson reviewed an early draft of the manuscript.

LITERATURE CITED

ALISAUSKAS, R. T. 1987. Morphological correlates of age and breeding status in American coots. Auk 104:640–646.

———, AND C. D. ANKNEY. 1985. Nutrient reserves and the energetics of reproduction in American coots. Auk 102:133–144.

———, AND ———. 1987. Age-related variation in the nutrient reserves of breeding American coots (*Fulica americana*). Can. J. Zool. 65:2417–2420.

ALLEN, A. W. 1985. Habitat suitability index models: American coot. U.S. Fish and Wildl. Serv., Biol. Rep. 82(10.115). 17pp.

AMERICAN ORNITHOLOGISTS' UNION. 1983. Checklist of North American birds, 6th ed. Allen Press, Lawrence, Kans. 877pp.

ARNOLD, T. W. 1990. Food limitation and the adaptive significance of clutch size in American coots (*Fulica americana*). Ph.D. Thesis, Univ. Western Ontario, London. 219pp.

———. 1992. Continuous laying by American coots in response to partial clutch removal and total clutch loss. Auk 109:407–421.

———, AND E. K. FRITZELL. 1989. Spring and summer prey remains collected from male mink dens in southwestern Manitoba. Prairie Nat. 21:189–192.

BARTELT, G. A. 1977. Aspects of the population ecology of the American coot in Wisconsin. M.S. Thesis, Univ. Wisconsin, Madison. 38pp.

———, AND D. H. RUSCH. 1980. Comparison of neck bands and patagial tags for marking American coots. J. Wildl. Manage. 44:236–241.

BELLROSE, F. C. 1944. Waterfowl hunting in Illinois: its status and problems. Illinois Nat. Hist. Surv., Biol. Notes 17:3–35.

BERGMAN, R. D. 1973. Use of southern boreal lakes by postbreeding canvasbacks and redheads. J. Wildl. Manage. 37:160–170.

BETT, T. A. 1983. Influences of habitat composition on the breeding ecology of the American coot (*Fulica americana*). M.S. Thesis, Univ. Wisconsin, Oshkosh. 281pp.

BOERSMA, P. D., AND E. M. DAVIES. 1987. Sexing monomorphic birds by vent measurements. Auk 104:779–783.

BURTON, J. H., II. 1959. Some population mechanics of the American coot. J. Wildl. Manage. 23:203–210.

BYRD, G. V., R. A. COLEMAN, R. J. SHALLENBERGER, AND C. S. ARUME. 1985. Notes on the breeding biology of the Hawaiian race of the American coot. 'Elepaio 45:57–63.

CADMAN, M. C., P. F. J. EAGLES, AND F. M. HELLEINER. 1987. Atlas of the breeding birds of Ontario. Univ. Waterloo Press, Waterloo, Ont. 617pp.

CHRISTOPHER, M. W., E. P. HILL, AND D. E. STEFFEN. 1988. Use of catfish ponds by waterfowl wintering in Mississippi. Pages 413–418 in M. W. Weller, ed. Waterfowl in winter. Univ. Minnesota Press, Minneapolis.

CRAWFORD, R. D. 1977. Comparison of trapping methods for American coots. Bird-Banding 48:309–313.

———. 1978. Tarsal color of American coots in relation to age. Wilson Bull. 90:536–543.

———. 1980. Effects of age on reproduction in American coots. J. Wildl. Manage. 44:183–189.

DELANEY, M. F. 1986. Bird bands recovered from American alligator stomachs in Florida. North Am. Bird. Bander 11:92–94.

DESROSCHERS, B. A., AND C. D. ANKNEY. 1986. Effect of brood size and age on the feeding behavior of adult and juvenile American coots (*Fulica americana*). Can. J. Zool. 64:1400–1406.

DRIVER, E. A. 1988. Diet and behaviour of young American coots. Wildfowl 39:34–42.

DUBOVSKY, J. A., AND R. M. KAMINSKI. 1987. Estimates and chronology of waterfowl use of Mississippi catfish ponds. Proc. Southeast. Assoc. Fish and Wildl. Agencies 41:257–265.

EDDLEMAN, W. R. 1983. A study of migratory American coots, *Fulica americana*, in Oklahoma. Ph.D. Thesis, Oklahoma State Univ., Stillwater. 105pp.

———, AND F. L. KNOPF. 1985. Determining age and sex of American coots. J. Field Ornithol. 56:41–55.

———, ———, AND C. T. PATTERSON. 1985. Chronology of migration by American coots in Oklahoma. J. Wildl. Manage. 49:241–246.

EICHHORST, B. 1986. The food habits of juvenile American coots (*Fulica americana*) on Rush Lake, Winnebago County, Wisconsin. M.S. Thesis, Univ. Wisconsin, Oshkosh. 46pp.

ELDER, W. H. 1955. Flouroscopic measures of hunting pressure in Europe and North America. Trans. North. Am. Wildl. Conf. 20:298–332.

ESLER, D. 1990. Avian community responses to hydrilla invasion. Wilson Bull. 102:427–440.

FITZNER, R. E., E. T. SIPCO, AND R. G. SCHRECKHISE. 1980. American coot nesting and feeding habits in southeastern Washington. Northwest Sci. 54:244–252.

FREDRICKSON, L. H. 1969. Mortality of coots during severe spring weather. Wilson Bull. 81:450–453.

———. 1970. The breeding biology of American coots in Iowa. Wilson Bull. 82:445–457.

———, J. M. ANDERSON, F. M. KOZLIK, AND R. A. RYDER. 1977. American coot (*Fulica americana*). Pages 123–147 in G. C. Sanderson, ed. Management of migratory shore and upland game birds in North America. Int. Assoc. Fish and Wildl. Agencies, Washington, D.C.

GILMER, D. S., P. M. KONRAD, AND R. E. STEWART. 1983. Nesting ecology of red-tailed hawks and great horned owls in central North Dakota and their interactions with other large raptors. Prairie Nat. 5:133–143.

GORENZEL, W. P., R. A. RYDER, AND C. E. BRAUN. 1981a. American coot distribution and migration in Colorado. Wilson Bull. 93:115–118.

———, ———, AND ———. 1981b. American coot response to habitat change on a Colorado marsh. Southwest. Nat. 26:59–65.

———, ———, AND ———. 1982. Reproduction and nest site characteristics of American coots at different altitudes in Colorado. Condor 84:59–65.

GRIFFIN, C. R., T. S. BASKETT, AND R. D. SPARROWE. 1982. Ecology of bald eagles wintering near a waterfowl concentration. U.S. Fish and Wildl. Serv., Spec. Sci. Rep. 247. 12pp.

GULLION, G. W. 1950. Voice differences between sexes in the American coot. Condor 52:272–273.

———. 1951. The frontal shield of the American coot. Wilson Bull. 63:157–166.

———. 1952. The displays and calls of the American coot. Wilson Bull. 64:83–97.

———. 1953a. Observations on molting of the American coot. Condor 55:102–103.

———. 1953b. Territorial behavior in the American coot. Condor 55:169–186.

———. 1954. The reproductive cycle of American coots in California. Auk 71:366–412.

———. 1956. An observation concerning the validity of coot brood counts. J. Wildl. Manage. 20:465–466.

HARDIN, S., R. LAND, M. SPELMAN, AND G. MORSE. 1984. Food items of grass carp, American coots, and ring-necked ducks from a central Florida lake. Proc. Southeast. Assoc. Fish and Wildl. Agencies 38:313–318.

HAZELWOOD, R. M., A. F. ODDO, R. D. PAGAN, AND R. G. BOTZLER. 1978. The 1975–76 avian cholera outbreaks in Humboldt County, California. J. Wildl. Dis. 14:229–232.

HEITMEYER, M. E. 1980. Characteristics of wetland habitats and waterfowl populations in Oklahoma. M.S. Thesis, Oklahoma State Univ., Stillwater. 263pp.

HILL, W. L. 1986. Clutch overlap in American coots. Condor 88:96–97.

———. 1988. The effect of food abundance on the reproductive patterns of coots. Condor 90:324–331.

HOCHBAUM, H. A. 1955. Travels and traditions of waterfowl. Univ. Minnesota Press, Minneapolis. 301pp.

HOWARD, R., AND A. MOORE. 1984. A complete checklist of the birds of the world. Macmillan, London, U.K. 732pp.

JONES, J. C. 1939. On the occurrence of lead shot in stomachs of North American Gruiiformes. J. Wildl. Manage. 3:353–357.

———. 1940. Food habits of the American coot with notes on distribution. U.S. Dep. Inter., Wildl. Res. Bull. 2. 52pp.

KANTRUD, H. A. 1985. American coot habitat in North Dakota. Prairie Nat. 17:23–32.

———, AND R. E. STEWART. 1977. Use of natural basin wetlands by breeding waterfowl in North Dakota. J. Wildl. Manage. 41:243–253.

———, AND ———. 1984. Ecological distribution and crude density of breeding birds on prairie wetlands. J. Wildl. Manage. 48:426–437.

———, J. B. MILLAR, AND A. G. VAN DER VALK. 1989. Vegetation of wetlands in the Prairie Pothole Region. Pages 132–187 in A. G. van der Valk, ed. Northern prairie wetlands. Iowa State Univ. Press, Ames.

KIEL, W. H., JR. 1955. Nesting studies of the coot in southwestern Manitoba. J. Wildl. Manage. 19:189–198.

———, AND A. S. HAWKINS. 1953. Status of the coot in the Mississippi Flyway. Trans. North Am. Wildl. Conf. 18:311–322.

KLUKAS, R. W., AND L. N. LOCKE. 1970. An outbreak of fowl cholera in Everglades National Park. J. Wildl. Dis. 6:77.

LANG, A. L. 1991. Status of the American coot, Fulica americana, in Canada. Can. Field-Nat. 105:530–541.

LYON, B. E. 1991. Brood parasitism in American coots: avoiding the constraints of parental care. Proc. Int. Ornithol. Congr. 20:1023–1030.

———. 1992. The ecology and evolution of conspecific brood parasitism in American coots (Fulica americana). Ph.D. Thesis, Princeton Univ., Princeton, N.J. 159pp.

MARTIN, F. W., R. S. POSPAHALA, AND J. D. NICHOLS. 1979. Assessment and population management of North American migratory birds. Pages 187–239 in J. Cairns, Jr., G. P. Patil, and W. E. Waters, eds. Environmental biomonitoring, assessment, prediction, and management—certain case studies and related quantitative issues. Statistical ecology. Vol. 11. Int. Coop. Publ. House, Fairland, Md.

MENSIK, J. G., AND R. G. BOTZLER. 1989. Epizootiological features of avian cholera on the north coast of California. J. Wildl. Dis. 25:240–245.

MONTALBANO, F., III, S. HARDIN, AND W. M. HETRICK. 1979. Utilization of hydrilla by ducks and coots in central Florida. Proc. Southeast. Assoc. Fish and Wildl. Agencies 33:36–42.

NASSAR, J. R., R. H. CHABRECK, AND D. C. HAYDEN. 1988. Experimental plantings for management of crayfish and waterfowl. Pages 427–439 in M. W. Weller, ed., Waterfowl in winter, Univ. Minnesota Press, Minneapolis.

NICHOLS, J. D., R. J. BLOHM, R. E. REYNOLDS, R. E. TROST, J. E. HINES, AND J. P. BLADEN. 1991. Band reporting rates for mallards with reward bands of different dollar values. J. Wildl. Manage. 55:119–126.

ODDO, A. F., R. D. PAGAN, L. WORDEN, AND R. G. BOTZLER. 1978. The January 1977 avian cholera epornitic in northwest California. J. Wildl. Dis. 14:317–321.

PAULLIN, D. C. 1987. Cannibalism in American coots induced by severe spring weather and avian cholera. Condor 89:442–443.

REYNOLDS, L. A. 1989. Waterfowl use of sediment ponds on an east Texas coal mine. M.S. Thesis, Texas A&M Univ., College Station. 63pp.

ROBBINS, C. S., D. BYSTRACK, AND P. H. GEISSLER. 1986. The breeding bird survey: its first fifteen years, 1965–1979. U. S. Fish and Wildl. Serv., Resour. Publ. 157. 196 pp.

ROOT, T. L. 1988. Atlas of wintering North American birds: an analysis of Christmas Bird Count data. Univ. Chicago Press, Chicago, Ill. 312 pp.

RYAN, M. R., AND J. J. DINSMORE. 1979. A quantitative study of the behavior of breeding American coots. Auk 96:704–713.

———, AND ———. 1980. The behavioral ecology of breeding American coots in relation to age. Condor 82:320–327.

RYDER, R. A. 1957. Coot-waterfowl relations on some northern Utah marshes. Utah Acad. Arts, Letters, and Sci. Proc. 34:65–68.

———. 1959. Interspecific intolerance of the American coot in Utah. Auk 76:424–442.

———. 1963. Migration and population dynamics of American coots in western North America. Proc. Int. Ornithol. Congr. 13:441–453.

SCHWARTZ, C. W., AND E. R. SCHWARTZ. 1952. The Hawaiian coot. Auk 69:446–449.

SMITH, G. W., F. A. JOHNSON, J. B. BORTNER, J. P. BLADEN, AND P. D. KEYWOOD. 1991. Trends in duck breeding populations, 1955–91. U.S. Fish and Wildl. Serv., Adm. Rep., Off. Migratory Bird Manage., Laurel, Md. 25 pp.

SOBKOWIAK, S., AND R. D. TITMAN. 1989. Bald eagles killing American coots and stealing coot carcasses from greater black-backed gulls. Wilson Bull. 101:494–496.

SOOTER, C. A. 1941. Ecology and management of the American coot, *Fulica americana* Gmelin. Ph.D. Thesis, Iowa State Univ., Ames. 109pp.

SOWLS, L. K. 1955. Prairie ducks. Wildl. Manage. Inst., Washington, D.C. 193 pp.

STEWART, R. E., AND H. A. KANTRUD. 1971. Classification of natural ponds and lakes in the glaciated prairie region. U.S. Bur. Sport Fish. and Wildl., Res. Publ. 92. 67pp.

STOLLBERG, B. P. 1949. Competition of American coots and shoal-water ducks for food. J. Wildl. Manage. 13:423–424.

SUGDEN, L. G. 1979. Habitat use by nesting American coots in Saskatchewan parklands. Wilson Bull. 91:599–607.

SUTHERLAND, J. M. 1991. Effects of drought on American coot, *Fulica americana*, reproduction in Saskatchewan parklands. Can. Field-Nat. 105:267–273.

———, AND W. J. MAHER. 1987. Nest-site selection of the American coot in the aspen parklands of Saskatchewan. Condor 89:804–810.

SWANSON, G. A., AND J. C. BARTONEK. 1970. Bias associated with food analysis in gizzards of blue-winged teal. J. Wildl. Manage. 34:739–746.

SWIDEREK, P. K., A. S. JOHNSON, P. E. HALE, AND R. L. JOYNER. 1988. Production, management, and waterfowl use of sea purslane, Gulf Coast muskgrass, and widgeongrass in brackish impoundments. Pages 441–457 *in* M. W. Weller, ed., Waterfowl in winter. Univ. Minnesota Press, Minneapolis.

VAN WAY, V. 1986. Approaches to coot management in California. Proc. Vert. Pest Conf. 12:292–294.

VAUGHT, R. W., H. C. McDOUGLE, AND H. H. BURGESS. 1967. Fowl cholera in waterfowl at Squaw Creek National Wildlife Refuge, Missouri. J. Wildl. Manage. 31:248.

WARD, P. 1953. The American coot as a game bird. Trans. North. Am. Wildl. Conf. 18:322–329.

WELLER, M. W., AND L. H. FREDRICKSON. 1973. Avian ecology of a managed glacial marsh. Living Bird 12:269–291.

WHITE, D. H., AND D. JAMES. 1978. Differential use of fresh water environments by wintering waterfowl of coastal Texas. Wilson Bull. 90:99–111.

WORONECKI, P. P., R. A. DOLBEER, AND T. W. SEAMANS. 1990. Use of alpha-chloralose to remove waterfowl from nuisance and damage situations. Proc. Vert. Pest Conf. 14:343–349.

YOCUM, C. F., R. J. BOGIATTO, AND J. C. ESHELMAN. 1978. Migration of American coots wintering in California. Calif. Fish and Game 64:302–305.

Radovich. 94.

Chapter 10

COMMON MOORHEN

ELDON D. GREIJ, Hope College, Holland, MI and Birder's World, 44 East 8th Street, Suite 410, Holland, MI 49423

Abstract: Common moorhens (*Gallinula chloropus*) are marsh-dwelling rallids distributed throughout eastern and locally in the southwestern United States. Population estimates are unknown but moorhens are uncommon throughout most of their range. Moorhens are most abundant in the coastal region from south Texas to North Carolina and states bordering the Great Lakes in the eastern United States, and the Central Valley of California, the coast south of San Francisco, and isolated regions from the Salton Sea to western Texas in the western United States. They prefer deep, dynamic marsh systems that provide robust emergent vegetation interspersed about equally with open water. Moorhens receive little hunting pressure in most areas, but hunters in Louisiana take over 75% of the total harvest. Moorhen habitat needs to be conserved, especially deep fresh-water marshes. Population assessment and harvest estimates need improvement. The daily bag (15) and possession limit (30) should be examined in view of moorhen population estimates.

DESCRIPTION

Common moorhens are members of the Rallidae and are larger than purple gallinules (*Porphyrula martinica*) and smaller than American coots (*Fulica americana*) (Bell 1976). They are the most aquatic of the rails with the exception of coots (Miller 1946). Moorhens prefer deep water marshes and tend to stay close to emergent vegetation (Bent 1926, Miller 1946). They have long toes like purple gallinules that allow them to walk on large floating leaves or mats of vegetation (Bent 1926). Both moorhens and gallinules lack lobes that characterize the feet of coots. When alarmed, moorhens prefer to maneuver through vegetation rather than fly. When they do take flight, they fly in typical rail fashion—a running take-off from the water followed by rapid laborious wing beats, dangling legs, and a quick return to the marsh (Ripley 1977). Moorhens swim with a jerky motion of the head, walk slowly in shallow water and over floating vegetation by raising their feet with quick steps, and can dive both to obtain food and escape predators (Bent 1926). When they dive for escape, they often hide underwater with head or bill concealed in vegetation (Ripley 1977, Cramp et al. 1980), and can remain underwater by holding on to vegetation with their bills (Bent 1926, Witherby et al. 1941).

Adult moorhens are slate gray with a series of small oblique white stripes on the sides that sometimes appear as a continuous band, a crissum that is white laterally and black centrally,

green legs with a red garter near the distal tibia, and a red bill with the distal third yellow (Oberholser 1974, Ripley 1977). The frontal shield is also red, becoming more intensely red, smooth, and enlarged during the breeding season, and less colorful and wrinkled during the winter (Bent 1926, Oberholser 1974). Immatures in both juvenal and first-basic plumages are lighter and more brown with greenish-brown legs, bill, and frontal shields (Oberholser 1974). Plumages are sexually monomorphic, and have been described in detail by Grant (1914) and Ripley (1977).

Adult moorhens are sexually dimorphic in all body measurements, with males being larger (Mulholland 1983). Immatures are also dimorphic, but less so. In Mulholland's (1983) Florida sample, males were 18.6% larger than females, while at Slimbridge, England, males were 14.3% larger than females (Anderson 1975). The most accurate discriminant function (88%) for predicting gender from England was based on tarsus, middle toe, and culmen (Anderson 1975). Mulholland (1983) determined the most accurate discriminant function (87.3%) in Florida to be based on weight and middle toe including the claw. Body weight fluctuates during the year and decreases when wing feathers are growing following molt (Karhu 1973). Karhu (1973) lists a number of measurements, especially of chicks, and proposed a method of classifying age of chicks using wing growth. Chick development was described in detail by Fredrickson (1971), Krauth (1972), and Helm (1982).

LIFE HISTORY

Courtship and Pair Formation

Courtship behavior in Louisiana is reported to occur soon after the birds arrive on nesting grounds (Bell 1976); the earliest observation by Helm (1982) was during the first week of April. Krauth (1972) did not observe courtship in Wisconsin, and hypothesized that birds were paired when they arrived. In England, pair-formation occurs in winter before pairs leave to establish breeding territories (Petrie 1983). The size of the frontal shield correlates positively with gonad development (Krauth 1972) and body weight, and is important during pair formation, and establishing and maintaining territories (Petrie 1988). Detailed descriptions of courtship, pair formation, and copulation were given by Howard (1940), Fredrickson (1971), Krauth (1972), Wood (1974), Ripley (1977), Helm (1982), and Matthews (1983).

While moorhens breed in their first year, first-year birds are less likely to obtain a preferred mate (Petrie 1983), and are thought to arrive later in breeding areas resulting in exclusion from prime habitat (Helm 1982). First-year moorhens in Scotland nested about a month later and had smaller clutches than older birds (Anderson 1975). Young moorhens in Louisiana also nested later than older birds (Helm 1982).

Breeding

Common moorhens arrive in the northern part of their breeding grounds in the United States (Wis. to Pa.) during the 2nd and 3rd week of April (Miller 1910, Krauth 1972, Brackney and Bookhout 1982). Stragglers appear in the Philadelphia area through the middle of May (Miller 1946). In Michigan, a similar pattern occurs, with moorhens arriving from mid-April through mid-May, and stragglers continuing through early June (E. D. Greij, unpubl. data). Previously-banded birds returned with the earlier group and later arriving individuals were thought to be young birds.

Timing of emergence and height of emergent vegetation may be important to initiation of nests of marsh birds (Weller and Spatcher 1965). Nest initiation of moorhens in Ohio peaked when cattail (*Typha* spp.) growth rate was greatest, and when cattail height was between 45 and 100 cm above the water surface (Brackney 1979).

Nest initiation of moorhens began in early April along the Gulf Coast in both Texas (Cottam and Glazener 1959) and Louisiana (Helm 1982). Moorhens began using rice fields in Louisiana 6–7 weeks after they began nesting in nearby marshes, about 7 weeks after rice was planted, and when rice plants were 80–90 cm tall (Helm 1982). Nesting moorhens did not cause significant damage to rice crops, although harvesting of rice was harmful to both moorhen nests and young broods. Rice harvest had a greater impact with earlier maturing strains of rice (Helm 1982). Nest initiation peaked in late April and mid-June in Louisiana (Helm 1982). In the northern part of their range, moorhens initiated nests in early May and nest initiation peaked during the 3rd week of May and the 2nd to 3rd week of June (Brackney 1979). Nest initiation varied over a period of 122 and 131 days in marshes and 70 days in rice fields during a 2-year study in Louisiana (Helm 1982). The period for nest initiation by moorhens in Michigan was about 85 days (E. D. Greij, unpubl. data). Thus, the moorhen nesting season in the south is typically from 5.5–6.5 weeks longer than in the north. Occasionally the nesting season is extended; 5 records of downy moorhen chicks observed in December and February demonstrated late nesting in Florida (Bryan 1981).

Nesting

Moorhens build a variety of nest structures that can be classified into 4 basic types: sham or false nests, egg nests, brood nests, and platforms (Helm 1982). Sham or false nests appear to be the same as Howard's (1940) platforms and Wood's (1974) display nests. They are built early in the season and their function is not fully understood. Howard (1940) describes a "platform stage" that occurs in advance of nesting and involves the use of platforms. Helm (1982) believed sham nests were constructed to help strengthen the pair bond. Egg nests function to hold eggs. Brood nests are used for brooding young, which occurs for about the first 2 weeks after hatching (although chicks are sometimes brooded on egg nests). The term platform has been used to describe flat structures used for roosting (Miller 1946, Fredrickson 1971, Bell 1976) and brood rearing (Fredrickson 1971). Moorhens sometimes use platforms built by coots and muskrats (*Ondatra zibethicus*) (Fredrickson 1971). Moorhens build more platforms if natural sites such as muskrat houses, dead mats of cattail, and logs are not available (L. H. Fredrickson, pers. commun.).

Table 1. Reproductive parameters of common moorhens in the United States.

Clutch size			Nest		Hatching			
$\bar{x}$	Range	n	Success (%)	n	Success (%)	n	Location	Reference
7.1	5–10	13					IA	Fredrickson 1971
7.6[a]	3–10	100	63.3	158			LA	Helm et al. 1987
7.9	3–13	325	64.5	473	81.7	2,083	MI	E. D. Greij, unpubl. data
8.0	3–15	55	77[b]	61	83	456	OH	Brackney and Bookhout 1982
8.1	5–12	18	61	18	50.7	146	WI	Krauth 1972
8.1	5–15	11					LA	Bell 1976
8.3[c]	4–16	39					LA	Causey et al. 1968
9.1	4–17	142	52.8	197			TX	Cottam and Glazener 1959
10.0	6–14	26					PA	Harlow 1918
			75	61			HI	Byrd and Zeillemaker 1981

[a] Includes 6.7, $n = 59$ in marshes; 8.8, $n = 41$ in rice fields.
[b] 66% when corrected using Mayfield (1975) method.
[c] Adjusted by Fredrickson (1971).

Moorhen nests are oval platforms of emergent leaves and stems. They are larger in the north (Krauth 1972) than the south (Helm 1982) with the following size range (cm): outside diameter 24–30, depth 10–20, inside bowl diameter 12–17, and bowl depth 3–7 (Krauth 1972, Wood 1974, Byrd and Zeillemaker 1981, Helm 1982).

Both sexes are involved in nest construction (Bell 1976, Ripley 1977). Males bring most of the material to the nest site and females place it in position (Krauth 1972, Ripley 1977). Moorhens usually construct nests from dead vegetation obtained at the nest site, and the nest material is usually of the same plant species occurring where the nest is located (Fredrickson 1971, Reagan 1977). Occasionally, living material is used. Nests in cattail stands are usually constructed of cattail (Miller 1946, Fredrickson 1971, Krauth 1972). In the northeast, a nest in a *Spirea* thicket was constructed from cattail, with the closest cattail being 8 m away (Brewster 1891). Cattail was the most common substrate for nest construction in the northeast (Miller 1946), but other plants are used. Moorhen nests in Louisiana contained parts of 13 plant species (Helm 1982), but 78% of the nests were constructed from material within 1 m of the nest.

Ramps are common on moorhen nests, especially in the north and central states, and have been described by Fredrickson (1971), Krauth (1972), Brackney (1979), and Helm (1982). Ramps were not as common on the Gulf Coast (Bell 1976, Helm 1982). Most floating nests on water hyacinth (*Eichhornia crassipes*) or nests associated with maidencane (*Panicum hemitomon*) and common arrowhead (*Sagittaria latifolia*) in Louisiana didn't require ramps, but

nests in cattail did (Bell 1976). Plant nomenclature follows Scott and Wasser (1980). Both Bell (1976) and Helm (1982) suggested that ramps are constructed only when the growth form of the vegetation where the nest is located necessitates a walkway for access.

Most clutch sizes of moorhens in North America vary between 7 and 9 (Table 1). Helm et al. (1987) believed that differences in observed clutch sizes were related to differences in habitat—marsh vs. rice fields. Cottam and Glazener (1959) indicated their estimate of 9.1 included large clutches that appeared to represent contributions of 2 different hens. Clutch sizes larger than 13 (Huxley and Wood 1976, Cramp et al. 1980) or 14 (Witherby et al. 1941, Ripley 1977) are thought to result from laying by a second female. Mean clutch size, based on a comprehensive nest card survey in England and excluding large clutches thought to involve more than 1 female, was 6.6 ($n = 2,278$) (Huxley and Wood 1976). There are 2 types of intraspecific parasitism or "dumping" (Gibbons 1986). One occurs when a female with her own nest lays an egg in the nest of another; the second occurs when 2 females lay and incubate eggs in the same nest. Gibbons (1986) suggests that, in England, the 2 birds sharing a nest are mother and daughter.

Clutch sizes became smaller in England as the season progressed (Wood 1974), and clutches laid after mid-June (largely replacement and second clutches) in England were smaller than original clutches (Relton 1972, Hornbuckle 1981). Second and 3rd clutches in Pennsylvania also were smaller than the 1st (Miller 1946).

The incubation period is 20–22 days and both

sexes incubate (Bent 1926, Deusing 1941, Fredrickson 1971, Krauth 1972, Ripley 1977, Matthews 1983). Incubation usually begins before the clutch is complete (Allen 1931), resulting in a staggered hatch. Incubation typically began with the laying of the 5th egg in Wisconsin (Krauth 1972). Frequently, adult moorhens took recently hatched chicks away, leaving eggs in the nest. Few of these eggs were infertile, and most were either pipped or close to hatching. Many of the chicks in these pipped eggs died (Miller 1946, Krauth 1972). While some of the chicks left behind may hatch and join their parents and siblings, others are on their own with an uncertain fate (Cottam and Glazener 1959). While most studies show low levels of egg infertility, Hornbuckle (1981) in England noted an infertility rate of 14.4% that he attributed to a shortage of males.

Nest success for moorhens varies from about 50 to 75% (Table 1). In England, nest success varied from 65.3% ($n = 1,766$) (Huxley and Wood 1976) to 71.1% ($n = 135$) (Hornbuckle 1981). Nest success increased as the season progressed in England due to development of vegetation (Huxley and Wood 1976).

Predators and flooding are the primary causes of nest loss. The most common nest predators in Louisiana were raccoons (Procyon lotor), alligators (Alligator mississippiensis), boat-tailed grackles (Quiscalus major), and probably rice rats (Oryzomys palustris) (Helm 1982). In Texas, nest losses were associated with boat-tailed grackles, gray foxes (Urocyon cinereoargenteus), raccoons, water moccasins (Ancistrodon piscivorus), and cattle (trampling) (Cottam and Glazener 1959). Long-tailed weasels (Mustela frenata) were possible nest predators in Wisconsin (Krauth 1972). Raccoons were the most common nest predators in Ohio (Brackney 1979) and were especially destructive during periods of low water. Snakes were reported as predators by Bent (1926) and Brackney (1979).

Hatching success varies from about 50 to 80% (Table 1). Hatching success was 53.4% ($n = 470$) in England (Hornbuckle 1981). Following hatching, adult moorhens either dropped egg shells in the water (Krauth 1972), or ate the shells (Fredrickson 1971). Chicks stayed in the nest 1–4 days following hatching (Pitt 1918, Helm 1982).

At hatching, moorhen chicks have an enlarged spur on the alula which permits grasping like the thumb of a mitten. This spur is used to assist in climbing on vegetation, to enter egg and brood nests (Bent 1926, Bell 1976, Helm 1982), and to grasp vegetation while swimming underwater (Miller 1946).

Broods

Young moorhens are brooded either on special brood nests or the egg nest for about 14 days (Wood 1974). Survivorship of moorhen chicks is difficult to ascertain because of their secretive nature. In Louisiana, broods 1–10 days old averaged 4.7 chicks, while broods 3.5–5.5 weeks old had decreased to 2.6 chicks (Bell 1976). These brood sizes were similar to brood sizes at about 2 and 6.5 weeks observed in Louisiana (Helm 1982, Matthews 1983). In Lake Erie marshes, 28 broods (6 weeks old) averaged 3.6 young each (Brackney and Bookhout 1982); in Pennsylvania, the number of young seen with parents was usually 3 or 4 (Miller 1946). Brood size at fledging in Hawaii was 2.3 ($n = 55$) (Byrd and Zeillemaker 1981). Mortality of chicks in their first 10 days must exceed 40% (Miller 1946, Bell 1976). Largemouth bass (Micropterus salmoides) were the most important predator on chicks in Louisiana; floating mats served as important foraging substrates for moorhens and their broods (Bell 1976, Helm 1982). Snapping turtles (Chelydra serpentina) were likely predators of moorhen chicks in Ohio (Brackney 1979).

Multiple broods are common and important to moorhen production. Two broods are common in England (Relton 1972, Hornbuckle 1981), Germany (Muthorst 1971), Norway (Norderhaug 1962), Finland (Karhu 1973), Hawaii (Byrd and Zeillemaker 1981), and in the United States (Miller 1946; E. D. Greij, unpubl. data). Three broods have been produced in England (Brown 1943) and Germany (Muthorst 1971), and 4 broods in England (Bentham 1931). In England, 36% of pairs had 2 broods (Relton 1972, Hornbuckle 1981). Moorhen nesting occurred continuously throughout the year in South Africa, although supplemental food was made available (Siegfried and Frost 1975).

The significance of the interval length between broods (20 days) (Hornbuckle 1981), (25–30 days) (Huxley and Wood 1976) is likely related to the 3-week period young moorhens are dependent on parents for food. As parents spend less time feeding young, there is more time to begin a second nest.

The interval between loss of a nest and renesting is much shorter than the interval between broods. Typical averages are 8 (3–18, $n = 15$) (Hornbuckle 1981), 8.5 (1–18, $n = 16$)

(Wood 1974), and 7–10 days (Miller 1946). The large variation is likely related to condition of the female when the nest is interrupted. Laying females or those in early incubation can quickly start another nest. If nest interruption occurs well into incubation, the interval between nesting attempts is greater because there is a lag time for females to reach the physiological condition necessary to lay again. For double-brooded species, the renesting interval is usually shorter if the nest is destroyed late in incubation (Sowls 1955, Wood 1974).

Juvenile moorhens from the 1st brood sometimes join chicks and adults of the 2nd brood (Miller 1946, Helm 1982), presumably as "helpers." The presence of juvenile helpers occurs regularly in England (Gibbons 1986, Eden 1987), although not all juveniles help, and the amount of help given by individuals varies. Juveniles not only help with feeding younger chicks, but also in predator and territorial defense (Leonard et al. 1989). Parents with helpers reared more chicks to independence (Gibbons 1986), but questions remained as to the effect of other variables such as age and experience of parents and habitat quality.

Nesting Densities

Marshes on the southwest shore of Lake Erie had an overall density of 1.5 pairs/ha (Brackney 1979). Densities were higher in areas of better marsh condition (4.6 pairs/ha) and lower in recently flooded wetlands (0.2 pairs/ha). In Pennsylvania, densities of 3 pairs/ha and 10 nests/ha were documented (Miller 1946). In marshes near southern Lake Michigan, 5.2 nests/ha were observed (Beecher 1942).

The home range (minimum polygon method) of nesting moorhens estimated for birds marked with radio transmitters was 1.22 ha (0.21–3.20, $n = 12$) based on an average of 41.9 (11–89) locations for each pair; non-nesting moorhens occupied 5.61 ha (5.2–6.01, $n = 2$) based on an average of 75 (42–108) locations each (Matthews 1983). Juvenile moorhens used 6.76 ha (0.61–17.75, $n = 6$) based on an average of 35.5 (20–46) locations each. Nesting adults maintained home ranges that were adjacent and approximately parallel to roads and adjacent canals, apparently making territorial defense easier.

Diet

The common moorhen diet is primarily plant material, although a variety of animals also are eaten (Bent 1926, Simpson 1939, Ripley 1977, Mulholland 1983). Plant/animal percentages were 93/7 in north-central Florida (Mulholland 1983); 80/20 in Florida lakes, and 88/12 in Florida phosphate mine settling ponds (O'Meara et al. 1982); 97/3 in Puerto Rico (Wetmore 1916); and 75/25 (Ripley 1977). Plant material includes leaves and stems of submerged plants such as hydrilla (*Hydrilla* spp.), hornwort (*Ceratophyllum* spp.), and water pondweeds (*Potamogeton* spp.); floating plants such as *Wolffia* and duckweed (*Lemna* spp.); and seeds from aquatic plants such as waterlily (*Nymphea* spp.), giant southern-wildrice (*Zizaniopsis miliacea*), smartweed (*Polygonum* spp.), and bulrush (*Scirpus* spp.) (Bent 1926, Simpson 1939, Haag et al. 1987, O'Meara et al. 1982, Mulholland 1983). Moorhens fed on the flowers of water hyacinth and insects associated with them (Matthews 1983). Animal foods included a variety of insects such as beetles (Coleoptera), giant water bugs (Hemiptera: Belostomatidae), water scorpions (Hemiptera: Nepidae), water striders (Hemiptera: Gerridae), dragonfly larvae (Odonata), caddisfly larvae (Trichoptera), midge larvae (Diptera: Chironomidae), and grasshoppers (Orthoptera), as well as earthworms (Oligochaeta), snails (especially *Planorbella* spp.), other molluscs, several spiders, and small fish (Bent 1926, Howell 1932, Simpson 1939, Miller 1946, Fredrickson 1971, Reagan 1977, Mulholland and Percival 1982). Moorhens forage by grasping submerged plants while swimming, tilting, or diving; picking food from the surface of floating mats while walking on them; and picking food items from emergents (Bent 1926).

In Florida, moorhens were opportunistic feeders and fed largely on the leaves and stems of hydrilla that was abundant (Mulholland 1983). Smartweed seeds were consumed in the fall. A significant increase of animal matter (largely leaf beetles [Chrysomelidae]) appeared in the diet of moorhens in April (Mulholland 1983). This increase in invertebrate consumption coincided with emergence of these beetles and may reflect opportunism. Nevertheless, nutritional requirements for egg laying may require greater consumption of protein (Krapu and Swanson 1975) and represents selection of animal foods to meet these laying requirements. In other cases, moorhens demonstrated no apparent selectivity for foods (Reagan 1977).

Adult moorhens fed chicks on the nest as early as 1 hour after hatching (Fredrickson 1971, Bell 1976). Moorhen chicks are totally dependent on parents for 7–10 days and are partially

Fig. 1.   Common moorhen (Photo by Millard Sharp).

dependent for 45 days (Helm 1982). Most stud-ies indicate that chicks feed independently at about 3 weeks (Karhu 1973, Byrd and Zeille-maker 1981). Moorhen chicks were observed begging for as long as 4 weeks in Wisconsin (Krauth 1972). Witherby et al. (1941) reported that moorhen chicks can forage for themselves at 3 weeks of age, but depend on parents for about 5 weeks. Chicks are capable of flight at 6–7 weeks of age (Witherby et al. 1941, Helm 1982).

Longevity

Longevity was examined from 201 recoveries of 5,470 moorhens banded in the United States from 1921 to 1992. Seventy-eight (38.8%) were recaptured or recovered within a year of band-ing, and 71 (35.3%) 1 year after banding. Twen-ty-four (11.9%) birds were recaptured or recov-ered 2 years after banding and 9 (4.5%) birds 3 years after banding. Ten (5%) birds were re-captured or recovered 5 or more years after banding. Of the oldest birds, 2 were recaptured or recovered after 8 years and 1 was recaptured 9 years after banding.

HABITAT

Moorhens depend on fresh-water marshes for both breeding and wintering (Bent 1926, Ripley 1977), and deep-water marshes are preferred when available (Miller 1946, Brackney 1979) (Fig. 1). The key to good moorhen habitat is availability of a permanent water supply. The species of plants used by moorhens may not be as important as having robust growth of emer-gents (Karr and Roth 1971, Weller and Fred-rickson 1974). The most common emergents used by moorhens in the eastern range are cattail, burreed (*Sparganium* spp.), bulrush, and to a lesser extent, pickerelweed (*Pontederia* spp.), smartweed, and cowlily (*Nuphar* spp.) (Braislin 1906, Miller 1946, Fredrickson 1971, Krauth 1972, Brackney and Bookhout 1982). In Ohio, moorhens prefer habitats where old cattail stalks from the previous year persist the following spring (Brackney and Bookhout 1982). In south-eastern coastal marshes, moorhens use marshes characterized by bulrush, southern-wildrice, common arrowhead, marshhay cordgrass (*Spar-tina patens*), maidencane, and cowlily (Bell 1976, Matthews 1983, Mulholland 1983, Helm et al. 1987). Moorhens nest in rice fields as well (Helm 1982). In Texas, moorhens also nest in panicum (*Panicum* spp.) and paspalum (*Pas-palum* spp.) (Reagan 1977). In southern marsh-es, moorhens regularly use extensive floating vegetation, primarily water hyacinth, alligator-weed (*Alternanthera philoxeroides*), penny-wort (*Hydrocotyl* spp.) (Helm et al. 1987) and watershield (*Brasenia* spp.) (Bell 1976).

In the Central Valley of California, moorhens occupy marshes characterized by cattail and bulrush (G. R. Zahm, pers. commun.) and in the Salton Sea area, cattail and common reed (*Phragmites communis*) (W. R. Radke, pers. commun.). In Arizona, New Mexico, Utah, and Nevada, moorhens occur in cattail marshes as-sociated with rivers at low elevation (R. L. Todd, C. G. Schmitt, O. A. Knorr, and F. P. Howe, pers. commun.). In Arizona, moorhens use woody vegetation around the edges of small tributaries of rivers (R. L. Todd, pers. commun.). The most common shrub is introduced tamarisk (*Tamarix gallica*). While stream habitats with shrubs are not commonly used by moorhens in North America, they are in England (Witherby et al. 1941, Cramp et al. 1980, Hornbuckle 1981).

Water depth determines the kind and abun-dance of emergents that will be present and, along with turbidity, the presence and accessibility of submerged plants for feeding. Vegetation also determines the abundance and kind of invertebrate food present (Krull 1970). In northern and central portions of their eastern breeding range, moorhens prefer overwater nest sites with water depths up to 1 m (Fredrickson 1971, Krauth 1972, Brackney 1979, Helm 1982) and >1 m (Miller 1946). Moorhens will nest over deeper water in northern areas if they use plants such as cowlily and pickerelweed (E. D. Greij, unpubl. data), or pennywort and water hyacinth in southern areas (Helm 1982). Moorhens will nest in shallow to dry marshes, but success is greatly reduced. Brackney (1979) and Helm (1982) reported that moorhens abandoned marshes left dry by a sudden drawdown in early spring. Moorhens nesting in dry marshes in Ohio (Brackney 1979) received significantly higher predation by raccoons.

Nest Sites

While moorhens use a variety of marsh vegetation for nest sites, they apparently prefer cattail, at least when Gulf Coast marshes are excluded. Most state and regional references of birds and birding atlases list cattail as one of the emergents characteristic of moorhen habitat. Cattail and muskrats were part of moorhen habitat in the northeast (Miller 1946). Cattail was selected for 75% of 267 nests constructed in the Philadelphia area (Miller 1946), and 93% of 67 nests in the southwest Lake Erie marshes (Brackney and Bookhout 1982).

Most moorhen nests are built in 2 distinctly different plant life forms, a mat of floating vegetation (Cottam and Glazener 1959, Bell 1976, Helm 1982) or within a clump of emergent vegetation (Fredrickson 1971, Krauth 1972, Brackney 1979, Helm 1982). Floating nests may be positioned away from emergent vegetation (Helm 1982), or they may be attached to a stand of emergent vegetation (Oberholser 1974, Mulholland 1983). Floating nests are usually restricted to coastal marshes, generally from Texas to Florida, where floating mats of vegetation accumulate. Common mat species are water hyacinth, alligatorweed, pennywort, and watershield (Bell 1976, Helm 1982, Mulholland 1983). Although uncommon, floating nests in Michigan (E. D. Greij, unpubl. data) and Iowa (M. W. Weller, pers. commun.) were built on mats of dead floating cattail stalks that accumulated large concentrations of duckweed later in the season. Nests within clumps of emergent veg-

etation are found throughout the range (Bent 1926, Krauth 1972, Bell 1976). Elevation of the nest varies from just above to 1 m above the water (Miller 1946, Krauth 1972, Helm 1982). Height of the nest above water is limited by the vegetation type. When moorhens nest in plants lacking a robust upright structure such as common arrowhead in southern areas (Helm 1982), or cowlily and pickerelweed in northern areas (Brackney 1979), nests are attached in the base of the stems near the water surface. These nests are subject to flooding because birds cannot add significantly to the height of the nests. Apparently, vertical stems and leaves are needed as anchors for increasing the height of nests. In emergents with vertical life forms, such as southern-wildrice in southern areas (Bell 1976, Helm 1982) or cattail in northern areas (Miller 1946), nests are placed from near the water surface to a height >1 m. Elevated nests offer protection from flooding but are more vulnerable to wind damage. Nests built near the water surface in taller vegetation can easily be increased in height to avoid destruction by flooding if water levels rise gradually. In Wisconsin, only 1 of 18 nests was lost over 2 years to flooding (Krauth 1972). A nest that was raised at least 25 cm by a pair of moorhens to stay ahead of rising water (Burtch 1917) demonstrates the importance of nest location.

Breeding Habitat

Moorhen production depends on the quality of marshes. Marshes are dynamic habitats that change dramatically and predictably with fluctuating water levels (Weller and Spatcher 1965, Weller and Fredrickson 1974). Moorhens prefer the stage of the marsh cycle characterized by dense stands of emergents with openings approximating a nearly equal interspersion of cover and open water.

Moorhens are opportunistic and respond to habitat changes quickly. In California, high water in the Central Valley in winter 1982–83 resulted in an increase in moorhens both that winter and the following spring and summer (G. R. Zahm, pers. commun.). Tule Lake, near Sinton, Texas, was nearly dry for several years, but had enough water to produce submergent and emergent plants (Cottam and Glazener 1959). Heavy rains in spring 1957 created favorable nesting habitat and water birds used the area in June. Similar events occurred in adjacent Pollito Lake, except conditions were even dryer during previous years, and vegetation took longer to respond. Moorhens and other waterbirds nested in these lakes throughout August (later than expected), presumably because of the unusual timing of vegetation development.

The relationship of moorhen production to habitat quality was pronounced in Michigan. During an 11-year (1973–83) study, moorhen production was documented for different habitat conditions caused by rising and falling water levels in semi-permanent marshes at the junction of a river and small lake that opens into Lake Michigan (E. D. Greij, unpubl. data). During 6 of 11 years, habitat quality was considered good, having fairly dense stands of emergents with good interspersion and up to 1 m of standing water. During 5 years, habitat was considered poor because little or no standing water was present in the vegetation, or water was so high that vegetation deteriorated. Production factors associated with good habitat were increased number of pairs, increased number of renests following 1st nesting attempts, increased number of 2nd nests, decreased predation, and more chicks produced per pair. Predation was highest during dry years.

The highest densities of nesting moorhens in Ohio occurred in semi-permanently flooded wetlands with persistent emergent vegetation (Brackney 1979). Brackney (1979) sampled 5,188 ha of wetlands composed of 54% open water, 8% deep marsh, 17% shallow marsh, 16% drawdown marsh, and 5% wet meadow. Highest densities of moorhens occurred in deep marshes with robust growth of emergents and a nearly equal interspersion of cover to open water. Medium nesting densities were associated with seasonally flooded and undiked, intermittently-exposed wetlands with persistent emergent vegetation. Lowest nesting densities were in wetlands with nonpersistent emergent vegetation; mixtures of scrub-shrub and persistent emergent vegetation; and seasonally flooded or undiked, intermittently-exposed wetlands with a high ratio of open water to persistent emergent vegetation.

DISTRIBUTION AND ABUNDANCE

Common moorhens are present on all continents except Australia (Ripley 1977). Ripley (1977) described 12 subspecies, but omitted *G. c. barbadensis* from Barbados (Ripley and Beehler 1985) for a total of 13. *G. c. cachinnans* occurs in North and Central America. It differs from its closest neighbor *G. c. cerceris*, of the

Greater and Lesser Antilles, by having more brown on the back, rump, wing coverts, and secondaries (Ripley 1977). *G. c. sandvicensis* is a permanent resident on Hawaii and differs from *G. c. cachinnans* by having a larger frontal shield and more red on the legs (Ripley 1977). *G. c. quami* occurs on the Mariana Archipelago in the western Pacific and differs from other subspecies described here by having a frontal shield rounded on top (Ripley 1977).

Common moorhens have a widespread distribution in North America south of Canada, but are not particularly abundant throughout most of their range. Because of the disjunct distribution of suitable wetlands in most regions, moorhen populations are generally described as local, although density in these marshes can vary. Sizeable populations of moorhens are associated with extensive areas of emergent vegetation with good interspersion that are regularly flooded.

Moorhens are concentrated in eastern and southwestern United States, Mexico, Central America, Bermuda, the West Indies, and the Galapagos (Ripley 1977) (Fig. 2). For ease of discussion, moorhens in the United States are treated as eastern and western populations, even though they may not be distinct. These populations are generally separated by a region from North Dakota, where their status is accidental (Konrad 1983), to west-central Texas where they are uncommon to rare (Oberholser 1974). The breeding range of the eastern population includes the southern tip of Canada from Ontario east to Nova Scotia, and the eastern portion of the United States generally from southeastern Minnesota to the eastern half of Texas. Within this range, moorhens are most abundant in coastal areas from south Texas (Oberholser 1974) to North Carolina (Potter et al. 1980). In the northeast from Maryland (Stewart and Robbins 1958) to Maine (Adamus 1987), moorhens are locally abundant. In the Great Lakes states, moorhens are common in southeastern Wisconsin (Robbins 1991), northeastern Illinois (Bohlen 1989), northern Indiana (Mumford and Keller 1984), and northern Ohio (Peterjohn and Rice 1991). In Pennsylvania, moorhens are most abundant in the northwest and along the Delaware River (Poole 1964). In New York, moorhens are common throughout the state, especially the northwest region (Anderle and Carroll 1988). In centrally located eastern states, moorhens are generally rare to uncommon, but can be locally abundant in isolated pockets.

The western population occurs primarily in

Fig. 2.   Distribution of moorhens in the United States and Canada.

the Central Valley of California, coastal areas south of San Francisco, emergent marsh habitats around the Salton Sea, and east through Arizona and New Mexico, including parts of Nevada and Utah, to the western tip of Texas.

Most of the eastern population is migratory and winters along coastal areas from North Carolina to Texas (Ripley 1977, Root 1988), and south through eastern Mexico to Panama (Ripley 1977). Some individuals remain throughout parts of the northern breeding range during winter. Moorhens also winter in the West Indies (Ripley 1977). Two bands have been recovered from south of the United States mainland—one each from Cuba and Haiti. The extent to which moorhens migrate to northern South America is not clear, although it is mentioned by Allen (1931).

The western population is much less migratory, with many birds being permanent resi-

dents (Grinnell and Miller 1944, Hubbard 1978, Rosenberg et al. 1991). Moorhens are present year-round in both the Sacramento Valley (northern) and San Joaquin Valley (southern) of the Central Valley of California (Root 1988; G. R. Zahm, pers. commun.), although Zahm believes some of these birds migrate in the fall. Moorhens are generally thought to be absent from the coast north of San Francisco (Unitt 1984), although there is 1 record from near Arcata (Wheeler 1967). Moorhens are permanent residents in coastal areas from San Francisco south to San Diego (Unitt 1984), and in the Salton Sea area (W. R. Radke, pers. commun.). Moorhens are locally common in parts of Arizona, particularly along the Colorado and Gila rivers in the southwestern portion of the state (Monson and Phillips 1981; R. L. Todd, pers. commun.), and have been recorded during Christmas Bird Counts near Phoenix (Root 1988).

Table 2. Gallinule hunting activity and success in the United States.[a]

Year	Hunters[b] (n)	Birds/hunter	Totals
1976–77	5,800	11.0	63,500
1977–78	5,800	6.1	35,400
1978–79	5,700	6.3	35,800
1979–80	5,400	7.9	42,600
1980–81	5,500	8.9	48,500
1981–82	6,300	10.0	63,600
1982–83	4,900	7.3	35,900
1983–84	6,600	10.5	69,000
1984–85	5,300	9.1	48,000
1985–86	5,700	12.4	70,700
1986–87	4,500	10.0	44,500
1987–88	3,700	9.2	33,800
1988–89	2,138	8.6	18,300
1989–90	3,200	11.9	38,700
1990–91	3,542	11.5	40,700
1991–92	3,400	13.1	43,800

[a] Martin (1979) and unpublished data from the Office of Migratory Bird Management, U.S. Fish and Wildlife Service, Laurel, Maryland.
[b] Based on percent of waterfowl stamp buyers who indicate they hunt gallinules.

Moorhens in Arizona are thought to be permanent residents. In New Mexico, moorhens are rare to locally common in marshlands at lower elevations (Hubbard 1978). These include the Gila, Rio Grande, and Pecos River valleys in the southern portion of the state, and the San Juan River Valley in the northwest. There is some seasonal altitudinal movement in both Arizona and New Mexico, with birds wintering at elevations below 1,000 m (R. L. Todd, pers. commun.) Moorhens are rare in Nevada, with the exception of Stillwater marsh east of Reno, and Las Vegas Wash leading to Lake Mead (O. A. Knorr, pers. commun.). Moorhens are generally rare in Utah, although they are considered permanent residents in 5 isolated pockets in the northern, eastern, and southern portions of the state and summer residents at Bear River National Wildlife Refuge (Behle et al. 1985). Moorhens are considered rare to uncommon in west and central Texas (Oberholser 1974), although a breeding record occurs in the El Paso region, and there are several breeding records in the panhandle (Seyffert 1989). Additional breeding records exist for the El Paso area, and in the panhandle (Texas Breeding Bird Atlas Project). Moorhens in Texas are thought to be permanent residents. Although moorhens are considered permanent residents in most regions of the west, they are reported to winter in Baja California and western Mexico (Ripley 1977). The extent of this migration is not known.

Historically, moorhens were present on all 5 major islands of Hawaii but are currently restricted to Oahu and Kauai (Byrd and Zeillemaker 1981). The last moorhen sighting on Molokai was in 1973. Six moorhens were released on Molokai in 1983, but the status of these birds is not known (Griffin et al. 1989). The lack of appropriate habitat on Molokai precludes a significant population from developing (C. R. Griffin, pers. commun.). Mariana common moorhens were originally distributed on the islands of Guam, Saipan, Tinian, Pagan, and Rota (Stinson et al. 1991). These moorhens are classified as endangered, with estimates of from 75 to 125 moorhens each on Tinian, Saipan, and Guam, with no birds currently found on Rota and Pagan.

HARVEST

The U.S. Fish and Wildlife Service (USFWS) includes both the purple gallinule and the common moorhen as "gallinules," in their tabulation of data on hunter and harvest trends (Martin 1979). However, most gallinule data in USFWS publications refers to common moorhens.

Estimated gallinule harvest during the past 15 years (1977–92) averaged 44,597 per year (18,300–70,700) (Table 2). Louisiana accounted for 60% of participating hunters and 77.5% of the harvest. During these years, 90.6% of the harvest was from Louisiana (77.5%), Florida (9.0%), and Texas (4.1%). In the most recent 5-year period, Louisiana averaged 85.3% of the gallinule harvest.

MANAGEMENT NEEDS
Habitat Management

Habitat loss and degradation significantly impact moorhens. Because of the relatively small harvest, managing moorhens is best implemented by managing habitat, including marsh protection, development, and manipulation. The following are habitat management priorities.

1. Identify the characteristic types of marsh habitats favored by breeding and wintering moorhens and prepare a priority list of key habitats for conservation. It is vital to maintain large, dynamic wetland complexes because these seem to be most important to long-term moorhen use. These complexes should include large areas for refugia and smaller satellite marshes into which moorhens can disperse for breeding.
2. Smaller marshes are also important, especial-

ly with the continued loss of wetland habitat. Regional marsh management should be conducted to have some marshes with good interspersion of emergents and open water. This could require coordination between government and private agencies, as well as individuals.

Population Management

Management of moorhen populations and harvest requires an understanding of population levels and dynamics, the capacity of habitats to sustain these populations, and the number and origin of birds harvested. The following points need to be addressed.

1. Data on moorhen population sizes and trends are lacking, which limits management of this species.
2. The present U.S. Fish and Wildlife Service (USFWS) method of estimating harvest of moorhens is inadequate. The sampling system centers around duck stamps and not all moorhen hunters buy duck stamps. The new National Migratory Bird Harvest Information Program is currently being developed by USFWS. This program is expected to provide a sampling base allowing a more accurate harvest estimate for moorhens.
3. Origins and distribution of harvest of eastern and western populations are needed. Given the lack of information about moorhen populations and the origin of hunted birds, bag limits of 15 daily, with 30 in possession may be too high, especially if the populations are resident, as they could receive continual intense pressure.

RESEARCH NEEDS

An understanding of common moorhen biology is limited by a lack of information on population dynamics, migration patterns, and distribution. The following research needs are necessary to properly manage this species.

1. Techniques are needed to provide better population indices. Population estimates based on banded birds have not been successful because of the limited number of birds banded and recovered. A vocal survey technique (Brackney 1979) was effective in estimating size of moorhen populations of a large marsh in Ohio, and may be useful in obtaining estimates elsewhere. While this technique will work with breeding popula-

tions, it is worth investigating to test its effectiveness on winter and resident populations.
2. Examine the integrity of eastern and western populations. A color-marking system should be devised to more readily recognize birds from particular sources.
3. Delineate migration patterns of eastern and western moorhen populations, and identify permanent resident populations.
4. Estimate numbers and trends of moorhen populations. In the eastern United States, these populations should minimally include the Great Lakes region and coastal freshwater marshes of both the Atlantic and Gulf coasts. In the West, sampled populations should include the Sacramento and San Joaquin valleys of central California, the southern Colorado River, and selected wetlands in Utah, Arizona, and New Mexico.
5. Examine age and sex ratios, survival rates, and estimate effects of hunting regulations on moorhen populations.

RECOMMENDATIONS

The following recommendations are suggested to facilitate moorhen management and research.

1. The U.S. Fish and Wildlife Service (USFWS) should encourage, coordinate, and fund moorhen research working cooperatively with state agencies.
2. Specific wetlands to be conserved and managed for moorhens, and other wetland species, should be identified by the USFWS and appropriate state and federal agencies. The North American Waterfowl Management Plan has been expanded to include all wetland wildlife and can be important in wetland conservation. Private organizations such as The Nature Conservancy, National Audubon Society, and Ducks Unlimited have influence over significant wetlands and should be included in conservation/management of moorhens.
3. Because moorhens require quality wetland habitat, they should be promoted through public education as good indicators of wetlands.

ACKNOWLEDGMENTS

I thank M. W. Weller and L. H. Fredrickson for reviewing an early draft of this manuscript and D. D. Beamish for help in preparing it.

LITERATURE CITED

ADAMUS, P. R. 1987. Atlas of breeding birds in Maine, 1978–1983. Dep. Inland Fish. and Wildl., Augusta. 366pp.

ALLEN, A. A. 1931. Florida gallinule—the water chicken. Bird-Lore 33:284–293.

ANDERLE, R. F., AND J. R. CARROLL. 1988. The atlas of breeding birds in New York state. Cornell Univ. Press, Ithaca, N.Y. 548pp.

ANDERSON, A. 1975. A method of sexing moorhens. Wildfowl 26:77–82.

BEECHER, W. J. 1942. Nesting birds and the vegetative substrate. Chicago Ornithol. Soc., Chicago, Ill. 69pp.

BEHLE, W. H., E. D. SORENSON, AND C. M. WHITE. 1985. Utah birds. Utah Mus. Nat. Hist., Occas. Publ. 4, Salt Lake City. 108pp.

BELL, G. R. 1976. Ecological observations of common and purple gallinules on Lacassine National Wildlife Refuge. M.S. Thesis, Univ. Southwestern Louisiana, Lafayette. 59pp.

BENT, A. C. 1926. Life histories of North American marsh birds. U.S. Natl. Mus. Bull. 135. 490pp.

BENTHAM, H. 1931. Moorhens rearing four broods. Brit. Birds 25:106.

BOHLEN, H. D. 1989. The birds of Illinois. Indiana Univ. Press, Bloomington. 221pp.

BRACKNEY, A. W. 1979. Population ecology of common gallinules in southwestern Lake Erie marshes. M.S. Thesis, Ohio State Univ., Columbus. 69pp.

———, AND T. A. BOOKHOUT. 1982. Population ecology of common gallinules in southwestern Lake Erie marshes. Ohio J. Sci. 82:229–237.

BRAISLIN, W. C. 1906. The Florida gallinule nesting on Long Island, New York. Auk 23:189–193.

BREWSTER, W. 1891. Florida gallinule notes. Auk 8:1–7.

BROWN, R. H. 1943. Notes on a pair of moorhens. Brit. Birds 37:202–204.

BRYAN, D. C. 1981. Winter breeding of the common gallinule in the Florida panhandle. Florida Field Nat. 9:8–9.

BURTCH, V. 1917. Nesting of the Florida gallinule. Auk 34:319–321.

BYRD, G. V., AND C. F. ZEILLEMAKER. 1981. Ecology of nesting Hawaiian common gallinules Gallinula chloropus sandvicensis at Hanalei, Hawaii, USA. West. Birds 12:105–116.

CAUSEY, M. K., F. L. BONNER, AND J. B. GRAVES. 1968. Dieldrin residues in the gallinules Porphyrula martinica and Gallinula chloropus and its effect on clutch size and hatchability. Bull. Environ. Contam. Toxicol. 3:274–283.

COTTAM, C., AND W. C. GLAZENER. 1959. Late nesting of water birds in south Texas. Trans. North Am. Wildl. Conf. 24:382–395.

CRAMP S., K. E. L. SIMMONS, R. GILLMOR, P. A. D. HOLLOM, R. HUDSON, E. M. NICHOLSON, M. A. OGILVIE, P. J. OLNEY, C. S. ROSELAAR, K. H. VOOUS, D. I. M. WALLACE, AND J. WATTEL. 1980. Handbook of the birds of Europe, the Middle East, and North Africa. The birds of the western Palearctic, Vol. II. Oxford Univ. Press, Oxford, U.K. 695pp.

DEUSING, M. 1941. Notes on the nesting of the Florida gallinule. Passenger Pigeon 3:79–81.

EDEN, S. F. 1987. When do helpers help? Food availability and helping in the moorhen, Gallinula chloropus. Behav. Ecol. Sociobiol. 21:191–196.

FREDERICKSON, L. H. 1971. Common gallinule breeding biology and development. Auk 88:914–917.

GIBBONS, D. W. 1986. Brood parasitism and cooperative nesting in the moorhen Gallinula chlorpus. Behav. Ecol. Sociobiol. 19:221–232.

GRANT, C. 1914. The molts and plumages of the common moorhen. Ibis 56:298–304.

GRIFFIN, C. R., R. J. SHALLENBERGER, AND S. I. FEFER. 1989. Hawaii's endangered waterbirds: a resource management challenge. Hawaiian waterbird management. Pages 1165–1175 in Freshwater wetlands and wildlife. U.S. Dep. Energy Symp. Ser. 61. Oak Ridge, Tenn.

GRINNELL, J., AND A. H. MILLER. 1944. The distribution of the birds of California. Cooper Ornithol. Club Publ. 27. Berkeley, Calif. 615pp.

HAAG, K. H., J. C. JOYCE, W. M. HETRICK, AND J. C. JORDAN. 1987. Predation on water hyacinth weevils and other aquatic insects by three wetland birds in Florida, USA. Florida Entomol. 70:457–471.

HARLOW, R. C. 1918. Notes on the breeding birds of Pennsylvania and New Jersey. Auk 35:18–22.

HELM, R. N. 1982. Chronological nesting study of common and purple gallinules in the marshlands and rice fields of southwest Louisiana. M.S. Thesis, Louisiana State Univ., Baton Rouge, 114pp.

———, D. N. PASHLEY, AND P. J. ZWANK. 1987. Notes on the nesting of the common moorhen and purple gallinule in southwestern Louisiana USA. J. Field Ornithol. 58:55–61.

HORNBUCKLE, J. 1981. Some aspects of the breeding biology of the moorhen. Magpie 2:45–56.

HOWARD H. E. 1940. A waterhen's world. Cambridge Univ. Press, Cambridge, U.K. 84pp.

HOWELL, A. H. 1932. Florida bird life. Florida Dep. Game and Fresh Water Fish, Tallahassee. 579pp.

HUBBARD, J. P. 1978. Revised checklist of the birds of New Mexico. New Mexico Ornithol. Soc. Publ. 6. 110pp.

HUXLEY, C. R., AND N. A. WOOD. 1976. Aspects of the breeding of the moorhen in Britain. Bird Study 23:1–10.

KARHU, S. 1973. On the development stages of chicks and adult moorhens Gallinula chloropus at the end of a breeding season. Ornis Fenn. 50:1–17.

KARR, J. R., AND R. R. ROTH. 1971. Vegetation structure and avian diversity in several new world areas. Am. Nat. 105:423–435.

KONRAD, P. M. 1983. Third record of a common moorhen in North Dakota. Prairie Nat. 15:144.

KRAPU, G. L., AND G. A. SWANSON. 1975. Some nutritional aspects of reproduction in prairie nesting pintails. J. Wildl. Manage. 39:156–162.

KRAUTH S. 1972. The breeding biology of the common gallinule. M.S. Thesis, Univ. Wisconsin, Oshkosh. 74pp.

KRULL, J. N. 1970. Aquatic plant-macroinvertebrate associations and waterfowl. J. Wildl. Manage. 34:707–718.

LEONARD, M. L., A. G. HORN, AND S. F. EDEN. 1989.

Does juvenile helping enhance breeder reproductive success? A removal experiment on moorhens. Behav. Ecol. Sociobiol. 25:357–362.

MARTIN, E. M. 1979. Hunting and harvest trends for migratory game birds other than waterfowl 1964–1976. U.S. Fish and Wildl. Serv., Spec. Sci. Rep. Wildl. 218. 37pp.

MATTHEWS, W. C., JR. 1983. Home range, movements and habitat selection of nesting gallinules in a Louisiana freshwater marsh. M.S. Thesis, Louisiana State Univ., Baton Rouge. 134pp.

MAYFIELD, H. F. 1975. Suggestions for calculating nest success. Wilson Bull. 87:456–466.

MILLER, R. F. 1910. Notes on the Florida gallinule (*Gallinula galeata*) in Philadelphia County, Pa. Auk 27:181–184.

———. 1946. The Florida gallinule: breeding birds of the Philadelphia region. Cassinia 36:1–15.

MONSON, G., AND A. PHILLIPS. 1981. Annotated checklist of the birds of Arizona. Univ. Arizona Press, Tucson. 240pp.

MULHOLLAND, R. 1983. Feeding ecology of the common moorhen (*Gallinula chloropus*) and purple gallinule (*Porphyrula martinica*) on Orange Lake, Florida. M.S. Thesis, Univ. Florida, Gainesville. 79pp.

———, AND H. F. PERCIVAL. 1982. Food habits of the common moorhen and purple gallinule in north-central Florida. Proc. Southeast. Assoc. Fish and Wildl. Agencies 36:527–536.

MUMFORD, R. E., AND C. E. KELLER. 1984. The birds of Indiana. Indiana Univ. Press, Bloomington. 376pp.

MUTHORST, B. H. 1971. Zur biologie des teichhuhns (*Gallinula c. chloropus*) und des blesshuhns (*Fulica a. atra*) (Aves). Abh. Verh. Naturwiss. Ver. Hamburg NF 15:107–126.

NORDERHAUG, M. 1962. Fra sivhonas (*Gallinula chloropus*) forekomst og levevis ved Tonsberg. Sterna 5:53–61.

OBERHOLSER, H. C. 1974. The bird life of Texas. Univ. Texas Press, Austin. 530pp.

O'MEARA, T. E., W. R. MARION, O. B. MYERS, AND W. M. HETRICK. 1982. Food habits of three bird species on phosphate-mine settling ponds and natural wetlands. Proc. Southeast. Assoc. Fish and Wildl. Agencies 36: 515–526.

PETERJOHN, B. G., AND D. L. RICE. 1991. The Ohio breeding bird atlas. Ohio Dep. Nat. Resour., Columbus. 416pp.

PETRIE, M. 1983. Female moorhens compete for small fat males. Science 220:413–415.

———. 1988. Intraspecific variation in structures that display competitive ability: large animals invest relatively more. Anim. Behav. 36:1174–1179.

PITT, F. 1918. Notes and observations on the moorhen. Brit. Birds 11:170–176.

POOLE, E. L. 1964. Pennsylvania birds. An annotated list. Delaware Valley Ornithol. Club., Livingston Publ. Co., Naberth, Pa. 94 pp.

POTTER, E. F., J. F. PARNELL, AND R. P. TEULINGS. 1980. Birds of the Carolinas. Univ. North Carolina Press, Chapel Hill. 408pp.

REAGAN, W. W. 1977. Resource partitioning in the North American gallinules in southern Texas. M.S. Thesis, Utah State Univ., Logan. 72pp.

RELTON, J. 1972. Breeding biology of moorhens on Huntingdonshire farm ponds. Brit. Birds 65:248–256.

RIPLEY, S. D. 1977. Rails of the world. M. F. Fehelel Publ. Ltd., Toronto, Ont. 406pp.

———, AND B. M. BEEHLER. 1985. Rails of the world: a compilation of new information, 1975–1983, Aves: Rallidae. Smithson. Contrib. Zool. 417. 28pp.

ROBBINS, S. D., JR. 1991. Wisconsin bird life: population and distribution, past and present. Univ. Wisconsin Press, Madison. 702pp.

ROOT, T. 1988. Atlas of wintering North American birds, an analysis of Christmas Bird Count data. Univ. Chicago Press, Chicago, Ill. 312pp.

ROSENBERG, K. V., R. D. OHMART, W. C. HUNTER, AND B. W. ANDERSON. 1991. Birds of the Lower Colorado River Valley. Univ. Arizona Press, Tucson. 416pp.

SCOTT, T. G., AND C. H. WASSER. 1980. Checklist of North American plants for wildlife biologists. The Wildl. Soc., Washington, D. C. 58pp.

SEYFFERT, K. 1989. Common moorhens nesting in the Texas panhandle. Bull. Oklahoma Ornithol. Soc. 22(3):23.

SIEGFRIED, R. W., AND G. H. FROST. 1975. Continuous breeding and associated behavior in the moorhen (*Gallinula chloropus*). Ibis 117:102–109.

SIMPSON, T. W. 1939. The feeding habits of the coot, Florida gallinule, and least bittern on Reelfoot Lake. J. Tenn. Acad. Sci. 14:110–115.

SOWLS, L. K. 1955. Prairie ducks: a study of their behavior, ecology, and management. Stackpole, Harrisburg, Pa. 193pp.

STEWART, R. E., AND C. S. ROBBINS. 1958. Birds of Maryland and the District of Columbia. Bur. Sport Fish. and Wildl., Washington D.C. 401pp.

STINSON, D. W., M. W. RITTER, AND J. D. REICHEL. 1991. The Mariana common moorhen: decline of an island endemic. Condor 93:38–43.

UNITT, P. 1984. The birds of San Diego County. San Diego Soc. Nat. Hist., San Diego, Calif. 276pp.

WELLER, M. W., AND L. H. FREDERICKSON. 1974. Avian ecology of a managed glacial marsh. Living Bird 12:269–291.

———, AND C. S. SPATCHER. 1965. Role of habitat in the distribution and abundance of marsh birds. Iowa State Univ. Agric. and Home Econ. Exp. Stn., Spec. Rep. 43. 31pp.

WETMORE, A. 1916. Birds of Puerto Rico. U.S. Dep. Agric., Bull. 326. 140pp.

WHEELER, R. 1967. Common gallinule in Humboldt County, California. Condor 69:219.

WITHERBY, H. F., F. C. R. JOURDAIN, N. F. TICEHURST, AND B. W. TUCKER. 1941. The Handbook of British birds. Vol. 5. H. F. & G. Witherby Ltd., London, U.K. 381pp.

WOOD, N. A. 1974. The breeding behavior and biology of the moorhen. Brit. Birds 67:104–115, 137–158.

Chapter 11

PURPLE GALLINULE

ROBERT N. HELM, Louisiana Department of Wildlife & Fisheries, Post Office Box 98000, Baton Rouge, LA 70898

Abstract: Purple gallinules (*Porphyrula martinica*) are migratory Rallidae that nest in the southern United States and winter primarily in the tropics. They are highly dependent on freshwater wetlands with a wide range of plant diversity, particularly robust emergent and floating vegetation communities. There is little quantitative information on population status and trends, and no reliable methods to estimate purple gallinule harvest or hunter numbers. Management and research efforts should focus on methods of developing estimates of baseline population parameters at representative sites. Wetland habitat preservation and management are keys to maintaining populations of purple gallinules.

DESCRIPTION

Purple gallinules are among the larger and most brightly colored members of the Rallidae in North America. The attractive plumage may be the most notable attribute of this species. The head, neck, and underparts are purplish-blue, back and wings are olive-green, and the white undertail coverts are often flashed when walking. The legs and feet are bright yellow and dangled during short flights; the bill is red, tipped in yellow with a blue frontal shield. The bright blue plumage and yellow legs and feet readily distinguish this bird from the darker-plumaged common moorhen (*Gallinula chloropus*), a sympatric species with which it is most often confused. Plumage characteristics are similar between sexes; however, differences have been noted in body weight and lengths of the middle toe and tarsus (Mulholland 1983). Juveniles at fledging are 75% adult size and have a dark brown head and neck, olive-green back and wings, light brown breast and flanks, legs and feet that are light yellow, and a dark bill and culmen shield (Helm 1982). Chicks are covered with black down with some silver-tipped down encircling the neck and dispersed over the back; the culmen shield area is flesh-colored, bills are black anteriorly grading to red on the posterior with a white egg tooth. Mean weight of 1 day-old chicks was 13.4 g. Ripley (1977:295) and Krekorian (1978) provide further descriptions of adult and juvenile purple gallinules.

LIFE HISTORY

Several sets of missing information about basic life history of purple gallinules as noted by Holliman (1977:106) have been addressed during the past 17 years. Many of these research efforts are in unpublished M.S. theses (Bell 1976, Reagan 1977, Helm 1982, Matthews 1983, Mulholland 1983).

Social Organization

Social structure of purple gallinules in North America is limited to a breeding pair and their young of the year. These family units are maintained through the breeding season and probably until fall migration. There is no information on social structure during winter from South and Central America where purple gallinules that nest in the United States winter. However, in Costa Rica, a non-migratory group of cooperatively-breeding purple gallinules have a more elaborate social structure where adult helpers and old and young juvenile helpers aid the mated pair with feeding and defending chicks and territories (Krekorian 1978, Hunter 1987*b*).

Purple gallinules are trans-Gulf migrants that arrive in their breeding areas in Georgia (Meanley 1963), Texas (Reagan 1977), and Louisiana (Helm 1982) in mid-April. Gallinules either arrive paired or pair immediately after arrival. Krekorian (1978) suggested purple gallinules were monogamous in the tropics. However, there is little information on the mating system in North America. Age of initial breeding is unknown, although purple gallinules probably begin to breed when they are 1 year old. Pairing activities and courtship displays include billing, bowing and nibbling, swaying, and the squat arch (Meanley 1963, Helm 1982). Territories are established prior to the nesting season and maintained through the brood-rearing period. Charging, chasing, and bowing are intraspecific territorial displays. The average home range for 4 nesting purple gallinules as established by ra-

Fig. 1.   Purple gallinule nest in rice field near Jennings, Jefferson Davis Parish, Louisiana (Photo by Guy LaBranche (LDWF)).

diotelemetry was 1.03 ha in a Louisiana freshwater marsh (Matthews 1983).

Nesting Ecology

Both sexes share responsibilities associated with the entire reproductive cycle, from nest construction and incubation through brood rearing. Nests are constructed from readily available plant materials (Fig. 1). Twenty-six of 28 (92.9%) purple gallinule nests were built from plants within 1 m of the nest site in a Louisiana marsh (Helm et al. 1987). Extensive ramps or walkways for access into nests are constructed in emergent vegetation.

Purple gallinules begin nesting in May and cease egg laying in early August. Nest initiation periods ranged from 72 to 95 days in Louisiana (Helm 1982). Nesting in some habitats, such as rice fields, is delayed until plant density is adequate for nesting purposes. Purple gallinules lay 1 egg per day and have an incubation period of 18–20 days (Matthews 1983). Incubation begins before the clutch is complete. There is a wide range of average clutch size reported: 4.5

($n = 12$) in Louisiana (Bell 1976), 6.5 ($n = 87$) in Texas (Cottam and Glazener 1959), 5.8 ($n = 32$) and 8.6 ($n = 60$) in Louisiana (Helm et al. 1987). Nest success rates also vary widely but are normally high: 91% ($n = 87$) and 49% ($n = 87$) in a 2-year Texas study (Cottam and Glazener 1959), and 85% ($n = 39$) and 50% ($n = 28$) in a 2-year Louisiana study (Helm 1982). Purple gallinules will sometimes renest following an unsuccessful first attempt (Matthews 1983), but there is no definitive information on double brooding in North America. However, sedentary purple gallinules in Costa Rica produce a clutch of eggs every 2–4 months throughout the year (Hunter 1987b).

Brood Rearing Ecology

Precocial gallinule chicks are fed in the nest for 2–4 days after hatch. Mollusks, crayfish, insects, and insect larvae are common foods provided to hatchlings. Chicks begin to feed themselves at 7–10 days of age and are primarily self feeding by 21 days of age (Helm 1982). The juvenile plumage is complete and young are capable of short flights by 7 weeks. Average brood size at fledging ranged from 1.5 (Matthews 1983) to 3.1 (Helm 1982). Purple gallinule surveys conducted from airboats each August on Lacassine National Wildlife Refuge (NWR) in southwest Louisiana indicated an average production rate of 1.6 (range 0.6–2.8) immatures/adult during 1979–92 (Lacassine NWR, unpubl. data).

Molt

Adult purple gallinules undergo a complete molt in late summer prior to southern migration (Helm 1982). Flight feathers are lost simultaneously and birds are flightless for 3–4 weeks. The entire plumage becomes drab and faded during the molt that requires 6 weeks to complete. The brightly-colored bill and culmen shield become dark brown during molt, making it difficult to distinguish molting adults from fully-developed juveniles in fall.

Foods

Purple gallinule diets in a Florida study consisted of 71% plant material (mostly seeds) and 29% animal matter (Mulholland and Percival 1982). These proportions of plant and animal foods are almost identical to the food habits of purple gallinules nesting in Colombian rice fields (McKay 1981) but in contrast to the 58% plant

Fig. 2. Purple gallinule nesting habitat. Good interspersion of floating leaved plants in foreground bordering emergents. Lacassine NWR, Cameron Parish, Louisiana (Photo by Guy LaBranche (LDWF)).

and 42% animal matter reported in Florida by Sprunt (1954). Gallinules are opportunistic in their feeding habits and will take advantage of locally abundant foods. Common food items include seeds of annual grasses and sedges, seeds of floating and submergent vegetation, flowers of water hyacinth (*Eichhornia crassipes*) (plant nomenclature follows Radford et al. 1968), domestic rice grains, aquatic insects and larvae, and dragonflies (Anisoptera).

HABITAT

Purple gallinules breed primarily in fresh to intermediate salinity (<5 ppt. salt content) marshes. Deep water marshes (0.25–1 m depth), lakes, and impoundments (primarily coastal, but also inland), with stable water levels and dense stands of floating, emergent and submergent vegetation provide excellent habitat for nesting gallinules (Fig. 2).

Nests are built on floating vegetative mats of species such as water hyacinth and alligator-weed (*Alternanthera philoxeroides*), or in emergent vegetation such as cattail (*Typha* spp.) and Southern wild rice (*Zizaniopsis miliacea*). Nests in emergent vegetation are normally near the edge of dense stands of emergents, where they interface with open water ponds that contain submergents such as common hornwort (*Ceratophyllum demersum*) and pondweeds (*Potamogeton* spp.) or floating vegetation.

The structure provided by floating vegetation appears particularly important because purple gallinules seldom use open water areas void of vegetation (Fig. 3). Mulholland (1983) found floating-leaved aquatics, especially cow-lily (*Nuphar luteum*), were necessary to insure the presence of purple gallinules in a Florida study site, and that loss of this plant type would adversely impact purple gallinules. Helm (1982) also observed that floating aquatics and submergents were essential constituents of brood rearing habitat, providing food, cover, and protection from aquatic predators. This dependence on floating vegetation may explain why purple gallinules do not use some seemingly good

Fig. 3. Adult purple gallinule on water lily. Lacassine NWR, Cameron Parish, Louisiana (Photo by Guy LaBranche (LDWF)).

nesting habitats that are occupied by common moorhens. Purple gallinules have not been observed nesting in an area that did not also contain nesting common moorhens (R. N. Helm, unpubl. data). Additionally, purple gallinules consistently appear to be present in smaller numbers than common moorhens when nesting sympatrically in natural wetlands. This may be related to selection of wetlands by purple gallinules that contain floating vegetation, and suggests that purple gallinules have more specific habitat requirements than common moorhens.

Preferred breeding habitats also include a large amount of edge created by the interspersion of robust emergents with open water ponds. Mulholland (1983) found purple gallinules used closed habitat (<25% open water) significantly more than open habitat (50–75% open water) during the June nesting season, but this difference was not detected in September.

Rice fields are also important nesting sites for purple gallinules. Relatively high nesting densities have been reported in rice fields of the southern United States (Meanley 1963, Causey 1968, Meanley 1969, Fowler 1970, Helm 1982) and in Colombia, South America (McKay 1981). Rice fields provide a dependable source of food, cover, and water that appears to meet the ecological requirements of nesting gallinules. Following rice harvest and before migration, gallinules use either adjacent unharvested fields or the numerous canals associated with rice cultivation.

Little is known on habitat use during migration, and on wintering areas south of the United States.

DISTRIBUTION AND ABUNDANCE

The recorded breeding range of purple gallinules in North America includes many states, but highest breeding densities occur near the Gulf and lower Atlantic coasts of Florida, Georgia, Louisiana, South Carolina, and Texas (Fig. 4). The breeding range extends throughout Mexico and Central and South America southward to Chile and Argentina (Ripley 1977:295, Am. Ornithol. Union 1983:158). Gallinules migrate to wintering areas south of the United

Fig. 4.   Breeding and winter range of purple gallinules.

States in October and November, with a few lingering in coastal states into December. Specific wintering areas of purple gallinules that nest in North America are unknown within the general wintering region of Mexico to Argentina. Purple gallinules are uncommon in the United States from December through March with the exception of southern Florida.

The vagrant characteristics of Rallidae during migration are well recognized (Silbernagl 1982). The champion vagrant of this family may be the purple gallinule (Parkes et al. 1978, Remsen and Parker 1990) because of numerous extralimital locations in South Africa, Europe, and several islands in the Atlantic and Pacific oceans. In North America, purple gallinules have been recorded in many of the lower 48 states, as far west as California, and into Canada northward to Labrador (Am. Ornithol. Union 1983:158). The vagrant tendency of purple gallinules will require regular updating of their range.

Holliman (1977:106) noted the lack of information on population status and trends of purple gallinules. Seventeen years later there is still no useable information. States within the primary breeding range were contacted in 1992 and all indicated there was no population monitoring of gallinules. Population estimates in rice fields based on flush counts (McKay 1981) and nest counts (Meanley 1969, Helm 1982) have pro-

vided only limited bird density information on specific sites, but have not been repeated in those areas for comparisons over time. The results of the 1966–91 U.S. Fish and Wildlife Service (USFWS) Breeding Bird Surveys were reviewed, but provided no useful population trends due to low reporting of purple gallinules. Wetland habitat quantity and quality are keys to population stability for purple gallinules. The population trend is, therefore, probably decreasing as related to fresh water wetlands loss in southern and southeastern United States and throughout South and Central America.

HARVEST

There is no reliable method to estimate purple gallinule harvest or hunter numbers in the United States or for any individual state. The only quantitative data on harvest in the United States are from USFWS reports (Martin 1979) and from Louisiana Small Game Harvest Surveys. Because the number of gallinule hunters is relatively small compared to the total number of small game and migratory bird hunters, obtaining reliable estimates of their numbers and harvest is currently impractical. The inability of hunters to distinguish between common moorhens and purple gallinules further complicates efforts to estimate harvest of these species. Another basic problem that prohibits use of information from the above 2 harvest surveys is that no distinction is made in surveys between purple gallinules and common moorhens; the 2 are grouped as "gallinules."

Thirty-one of the contiguous 48 states selected a common moorhen/purple gallinule (no distinction made between species) hunting season in 1992. This consisted of 11 states in each of the Atlantic and Mississippi flyways, 2 in the Central Flyway, and 7 in the Pacific Flyway. Hunting was permitted in all southern and southeastern states, excluding Florida, where purple gallinules are a relatively common nesting species. Despite liberal hunting regulations (70 days, 15 birds/day), harvest of purple gallinules is likely small due to low hunter interest and secretive nature of the species. Even if interest in purple gallinules among hunters was enhanced, harvest would remain low because purple gallinules migrate south of the United States prior to late fall hunting seasons in many states.

MANAGEMENT NEEDS

Habitat Management

Conservation and management of freshwater wetlands along the lower Atlantic and Gulf Coast states are critical for purple gallinules in the United States. Because purple gallinules reside outside of the United States for about 50% of the year, similar habitat conservation efforts are needed for sites south of the United States. Cooperative efforts with conservation organizations such as Ducks Unlimited in Mexico, and the Organization for Tropical Studies in Costa Rica, could expedite this process.

Population Management

Purple gallinules have continued to receive minimal management. Currently, there is little effort to monitor population status/trends or harvest. During 1970–91 only 210 purple gallinules were banded in the United States and Mexico, with no recoveries reported (U.S. Fish and Wildl. Serv., Migratory Bird Manage. Off., unpubl. reps.).

The most pressing management need is for surveys that will provide baseline information on population status, (including annual productivity), hunting and non-hunting mortality, and survival rates. Attempts to monitor purple gallinule harvests in selected states where potential for harvests are greatest should be implemented. The National Migratory Bird Harvest Infor-

mation Program may assist in estimating harvests, but separation of common moorhen and purple gallinule harvests will be required. Estimates of recreational/subsistence harvest south of the United States are also needed.

RESEARCH NEEDS

The following research is needed to support management.

1. Population survey techniques that have proven successful for other Rallidae should be tested for purple gallinules. Because gallinules are so secretive and highly vociferous, auditory survey techniques should be evaluated. These techniques have been used for surveying rails (Griese 1977), common moorhens (Brackney 1979), and other waterbirds (Gibbs and Melvin 1993). Nest counts, roadside counts, and air boat surveys using transect lines should also be evaluated. Should a survey technique prove effective, standardized surveys conducted on consistent sites or routes on an annual basis could yield information on population status and trends, and habitat preferences.

2. Studies to estimate productivity and annual recruitment necessary to maintain population levels are needed. Studies should be conducted on intensive study sites for at least 5 consecutive years.

3. An operational banding program on intensive study sites could yield information relative to nesting area fidelity and, possibly, migration patterns and survival. Such a program may be dependent on recapturing marked birds because of low probability of band recoveries away from banding sites.

4. Information on available habitat, habitat use and preferences, and habitat management practices is essential for basic management planning. Management practices should be developed to enhance habitat conditions for breeding populations. Methods have been applied in the tropics (Hunter 1987a), and habitat manipulations such as those suggested by Eddleman et al. (1988) should be tested in wetlands and rice fields of the southern United States.

RECOMMENDATIONS

The following recommendations should be implemented to address management and research needs.

1. The USFWS should coordinate testing of survey techniques and banding procedures at representative sites on national wildlife refuges and/or rice fields in the southern United States.
2. Once reliable survey techniques are established, the USFWS and appropriate states should conduct cooperative standardized population surveys on national wildlife refuges, state management areas, and private rice lands with substantial numbers of purple gallinules.
3. Purple gallinules should be distinguished from common moorhens when sampling hunters via the National Migratory Bird Harvest Information Program.
4. States within the primary range of purple gallinules should designate a coordinator to facilitate research and management, and to stimulate interest for the species within resource agencies and consumptive and nonconsumptive public users.

LITERATURE CITED

AMERICAN ORNITHOLOGISTS' UNION. 1983. Checklist of North American birds. 6th ed., Allen Press, Lawrence, Kans. 877pp.

BELL, G. 1976. Ecological observations of common and purple gallinules on Lacassine National Wildlife Refuge. M.S. Thesis, Univ. Southwestern Louisiana, Lafayette. 59pp.

BRACKNEY, A. W. 1979. Population ecology of common gallinules in southwestern Lake Erie marshes. M.S. Thesis, Ohio State Univ., Columbus. 69pp.

CAUSEY, M. K. 1968. Dieldrin residues in gallinules and its effect on clutch size and hatchability. Ph.D. Thesis, Louisiana State Univ., Baton Rouge. 48pp.

COTTAM, C., AND W. C. GLAZENER. 1959. Late nesting of water birds in south Texas. Trans. North Am. Wildl. Conf. 24:383–395.

EDDLEMAN, W.R., F.L. KNOPF, B. MEANLEY, F.A. REID, AND R. ZEMBAL. 1988. Conservation of North American Rallidae. Wilson Bull. 100:458–475.

FOWLER, J. F. 1970. Effect of dieldrin on egg hatchability and chick survival in purple and common gallinules. Ph.D. Thesis, Louisiana State Univ., Baton Rouge. 65pp.

GIBBS, J. P., AND S. W. MELVIN. 1993. Call-response surveys for monitoring breeding waterbirds. J. Wildl. Manage. 57:27-34.

GRIESE, H. J. 1977. Status and habitat utilization of rails in Colorado. M.S. Thesis, Colorado State Univ., Fort Collins. 65pp.

HELM, R. N. 1982. Chronological nesting study of common and purple gallinules in the marshlands and rice fields of southwest Louisiana. M.S. Thesis, Louisiana State Univ., Baton Rouge. 114pp.

————, D. N. PASHLEY, AND P. J. ZWANK. 1987. Notes on the nesting of the common moorhen and purple gallinule in southwestern Louisiana. J. Field Ornithol. 58:55–61.

HOLLIMAN, D. C. 1977. Purple gallinule. Pages 105–109 *in* G. C. Sanderson, ed. Management of migratory shore and upland game birds in North America. Int. Assoc. Fish and Wildl. Agencies, Washington, D.C.

HUNTER, L. A. 1987*a*. Acquisition of territories by floaters in cooperatively breeding purple gallinules. Anim. Behav. 35:402–410.

————. 1987*b*. Cooperative breeding in purple gallinules: the role of helpers in feeding chicks. Behav. Ecol. Sociobiol. 20:171–177.

KREKORIAN, C. O. 1978. Alloparental care in the purple gallinule. Condor 80:382–390.

MARTIN, E. M. 1979. Hunting and harvest trends for migratory game birds other than waterfowl, 1964–76. U.S. Fish and Wildl. Serv., Spec. Sci. Rep., Wildl. 218. 30pp.

MATTHEWS, W. C. 1983. Home range, movements and habitat selection of nesting gallinules in a Louisiana freshwater marsh. M.S. Thesis, Louisiana State Univ., Baton Rouge. 134pp.

MCKAY, W. D. 1981. Notes on purple gallinules in Colombian ricefields. Wilson Bull. 93:267–271.

MEANLEY, B. 1963. Pre-nesting activity of the purple gallinule near Savannah, Georgia. Auk 80:545–547.

————. 1969. Natural history of the king rail. U.S. Fish and Wildl. Serv., North Am. Fauna 67. 108pp.

MULHOLLAND, R. 1983. Feeding ecology of the common moorhen and purple gallinule on Orange Lake, Florida. M.S. Thesis, Univ. Florida, Gainesville. 79pp.

————, AND H. F. PERCIVAL. 1982. Food habits of the common moorhen and purple gallinule in north-central Florida. Proc. Southeast. Assoc. Fish and Wildl. Agencies 36:527–536.

PARKES, K. C., D. P. KIBBE, AND E. L. ROTH. 1978. First records of the spotted rail for the United States, Chile, Bolivia, and western Mexico. Am. Birds 32:295–299.

RADFORD, A.E., H.E. AHLES, AND C.R. BELL. 1968. Manual of the vascular flora of the Carolinas. Univ. North Carolina Press, Chapel Hill. 1,183pp.

REAGAN, W. W. 1977. Resource partitioning in the North American gallinules in southern Texas. M.S. Thesis, Utah State Univ., Logan. 62pp.

REMSEN, J. V., AND T. A. PARKER. 1990. Seasonal distribution of the Azure gallinule with comments on vagrancy in rails and gallinules. Wilson Bull. 102:380–399.

RIPLEY, S. D. 1977. Rails of the world. David R. Godine Publ., Boston, Mass. 406pp.

SILBERNAGL, H. P. 1982. Seasonal and spatial distribution of the American purple gallinule in South Africa. Ostrich 53:236–240.

SPRUNT, A. 1954. Florida bird life. Coward-McCann, New York, N.Y. 527pp.

Radovich '94

Chapter 12

CLAPPER RAIL

WILLIAM R. EDDLEMAN, Department of Natural Resources Science, 210B Woodward Hall, University of Rhode Island, Kingston, RI 02881

COURTNEY J. CONWAY, Montana Cooperative Wildlife Research Unit, University of Montana, Missoula, MT 59812

Abstract: The 8 North American subspecies of clapper rail (*Rallus longirostris*) occur in coastal habitats from southern New England to south Texas, and in the Florida Keys, lower Colorado River ecosystem, and West Coast salt marshes from San Francisco Bay to Mexico. All but the northernmost races are non-migratory. Clapper rails have high nesting success in good quality habitat, and often repeatedly renest and produce second broods. The size of hunted populations is controlled mainly by severe climatic events; hunting mortality is probably low. Call-count or tape-playback surveys conducted in a standardized format are probably the most efficient techniques for estimating population trends. Harvest trends of clapper rails are unknown because reliable methodology for assessing harvest is lacking. State and provincial migratory bird biologists believe hunting pressure is low and not likely to increase because hunter interest in clapper rails is static or decreasing. Population management needs include development and application of breeding population surveys, continuation and expansion of banding programs, and implementation of a harvest survey. Habitat management of clapper rails in the East should involve continued protection of coastal marshes, restoration of degraded marshes, inventory of habitats, and evaluation of existing management practices that affect coastal marshes. Research needs for clapper rails include refining breeding population survey techniques, conducting basic life history studies of the (particularly southern) subspecies, identifying migration pathways and behavior, assessing effects of habitat management on both breeding and wintering birds, and improving techniques for external sex and age classification.

The following account includes information from all subspecies of clapper rail. Endangered taxa are relatively well-studied because of recent emphasis on identifying aspects of their life history; this information is discussed under the appropriate sections. Insofar as information is available, we emphasize hunted populations. Plant names follow Scott and Wasser (1980).

DESCRIPTION

Clapper rails are crow-sized birds with a laterally flattened body. The bill is thin, decurved, longer than the head, and is orange to orange-red in breeding adults and pinkish to pale orange in juveniles and non-breeding adults (Meanley 1985:103). The tail is short and inconspicuous unless the bird is agitated. One row of undertail coverts is white, the remainder are barred black and white. Legs and toes are long relative to body length and are flesh-colored to dark gray-brown.

Adult clapper rails are uniformly gray or brown ventrally from the neck to the abdomen, white on the abdomen, and have black and white barring on the flanks. The back is darker, with black centers on feathers of the neck, back, and scapulars. A faint superciliary line is present on adults. The cheeks and auricular area are paler than the top of the head and neck. The throat is white or off-white. The remiges are uniformly dark brown or gray, and a richer shade often characterizes the upper wing coverts. The sexes are identical in coloration.

Eight subspecies of clapper rail have been recognized in North America north of Mexico (Am. Ornithol. Union 1957, Ripley 1977, Meanley 1985), including northern (*R. l. crepitans*), Wayne's (*R. l. waynei*), Florida (*R. l. scotti*), mangrove (*R. l. insularum*), Louisiana (*R. l. saturatus*), California (*R. l. obsoletus*), light-footed (*R. l. levipes*), and Yuma (*R. l. yumanensis*) (Fig. 1). All except the Yuma clapper rail occur in tidal wetlands, mainly salt marshes and mangroves, but also brackish marshes (Meanley 1985).

The northernmost and westernmost subspecies generally have longer wing chord, tail, and tarsus; but the western subspecies have a shorter culmen (Ridgway and Friedmann 1941, Ripley 1977). The smallest race overall is the mangrove clapper rail of the Florida Keys and the largest is the California clapper rail of San Francisco

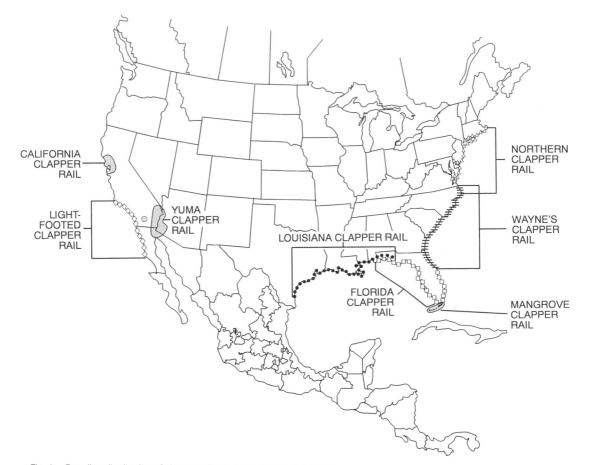

Fig. 1.   Breeding distribution of clapper rail subspecies in North America.

Bay. Weights of adult clapper rails of the Yuma, northern, Wayne's, and Louisiana races range from 160 g for a small female *yumanensis* (W. R. Eddleman, unpubl. data) to 401 g for a large male *saturatus* (Bateman 1965). Males average 20% larger than females (Meanley 1985).

LIFE HISTORY

Ripley (1977) and Meanley (1985) summarized much of what is known about the life history of eastern clapper rail subspecies. We review information on reproduction, survival, and diet relative to their importance to habitat and population management of clapper rails.

Social Organization

Clapper rail pair bonds are formed on breeding areas (Meanley 1985:43). Males begin giving their mate attraction call (*kik* or *kek* repeated in a monotonous series) in late January or early February in western and southern areas and

March in northern areas (Sharpe 1976, Meanley 1985:42, Massey and Zembal 1987, Eddleman 1989). Paired birds give a duet *clapper* or *clatter* call, which may be heard within 2 days of the initiation of male advertising calls. The age of first breeding is unknown, but presumably yearlings are capable of nesting. Sex ratios are poorly documented; studies suggest either even or male-dominated ratios (Adams and Quay 1958, Sharpe 1976:63). Surplus males are suspected in Yuma clapper rails because solitary males occur during the breeding season, and trapped samples consist of 2.2 males/female (Bennett and Ohmart 1978, Eddleman 1989). The latter documentation is suspect, however, because trapping techniques may have been biased toward males.

Clapper rails are probably annually monogamous, and both sexes share in incubation duties (Meanley 1985:43). Individuals may or may not pair with the same mate in subsequent years, although mated pairs in non-migratory subspecies will continue to maintain adjacent home ranges after the breeding season (Eddleman 1989, Zembal et al. 1989).

Juveniles stay in loosely-organized family groups until about 5–6 weeks of age, when they become independent (Adams and Quay 1958). Individual clapper rails are solitary after the breeding season, although there may be considerable overlap among home ranges (Eddleman 1989). After pairs and family groups break up in June–September, individuals begin local wandering and migration. No differential migration by birds of different age and sex has been noted.

Reproduction and Recruitment

The southernmost races (Yuma and Louisiana clapper rails) begin nesting in mid to late March (Sharpe 1976:20, Eddleman 1989). Nest initiation at mid-latitudes in North America is about 1 month later, ranging from early to mid-April in northern clapper rails (Stewart 1951a, MacNamara and Udell 1970, Mangold 1974, Meanley 1985:47), 1 April for Wayne's clapper rails (Adams and Quay 1958), and 10–25 April for California clapper rails (DeGroot 1927, Harvey 1988). The peak of nesting shows little geographic pattern, and may sometimes occur later in Yuma clapper rails (mid-May) (Eddleman 1989) than in Wayne's clapper rails (late Apr) (Adams and Quay 1958). Peak nesting of northern clapper rails varies from the second week of May in New York to late May–mid-June in Virginia (Stewart 1951a, MacNamara and Udell 1970, Meanley 1985: 47). Late nesting dates that probably represent renesting attempts or second nests show no evident geographic variation, and range from 2 June (Adams and Quay 1958) to mid-August (Stewart 1951b, Sharpe 1976:18).

Clutch size in first nests ranges from 4 to 12, although dump nests with up to 20 eggs have been found (Meanley 1985:55). Mean clutch size varies from 8.2 to 10.0 in the range of northern clapper rails (Schmidt and McLain 1951, Mangold 1974), from 8.2 to 10.5 for Wayne's clapper rails (Oney 1954, Adams and Quay 1958), and average 8.2 for Louisiana clapper rails (Sharpe 1976:23), 7.3 for California clapper rails (Harvey 1988), 6.4 for light-footed clapper rails (Massey et al. 1984), and 7.8 for Yuma clapper rails (Bennett and Ohmart 1978). Similar data are lacking for Florida and mangrove clapper rails. Second nests have smaller clutches, averaging 1 fewer egg in Georgia (Oney 1954), 2.2

fewer in Louisiana (Sharpe 1976:28), and 3.4 fewer in Virginia (Stewart and Meanley 1960).

Incubation commences before the last egg is laid (Meanley 1985:58). Both sexes incubate, the male typically during the night and sporadically during the day, and the female during most of the day (Eddleman 1989). The incubation period is 21–29 days; the range is explained by the variation in hatching sequence because incubation starts before the last egg is laid (Johnston 1956, Harvey 1988, Eddleman 1989).

Nesting success varies widely, but is generally high in good habitat and given good tidal and weather conditions. Nest success of 10–100% has been observed, but most observations exceed 80% (Stewart 1951a, Blandin 1965, Mangold 1974, Sharpe 1976:29, Bennett and Ohmart 1978, Ferrigno 1990). Most nest failures result from flooding by extreme high tides (Adams and Quay 1958, Mangold 1974), but predation may be the primary source of nest loss on the Gulf Coast (Sharpe 1976:29). The only consistently low nesting success observed in clapper rails was in the California subspecies that experience only 38% nesting success because of Norway rat (*Rattus norvegicus*) predation (Harvey 1988). Egg success is also high, often exceeding 90% (Mangold 1974). Renesting has been observed in nearly all subspecies of clapper rail, and most subspecies will average successful completion of >1 nests (Blandin 1963, Mangold 1974, Massey et al. 1984, Meanley 1985).

One parent will usually take the first chicks while the second incubates the remainder of the clutch (Adams and Quay 1958). Chicks are semiprecocial and are brooded on a number of brood nests during the first few days of life (Meanley 1985:63). Brood nests are platforms constructed by muskrats (*Ondatra zibethicus*), old nest sites of water birds, or platforms constructed by adult rails. The family forages in a loosely-organized group over an area that may exceed 50 m in diameter (Adams and Quay 1958). Survival of young between hatching and fledging is generally <80%, and may be <50% (Blandin 1965, Bennett and Ohmart 1978). Broods of 2–7 chicks ($\bar{x}$ = 3.2) are observed after hatching (Meanley 1985:62).

Fall populations are mainly hatch-year birds, depending on productivity. Age ratios as high as 13.6 young/adult have been observed in New Jersey (Mangold 1977). During fall, age ratios in the harvest range from 2.0 to 5.8 young/adult (Adams and Quay 1958, Sharpe 1976:64, Meanley 1985:62).

Fig. 2.   Clapper rail habitat in low salt marsh at high tide, dominated by smooth cordgrass and needle rush, Big Bend Wildlife Management Area, Dixie County, Florida (Photo by W. R. Eddleman).

Survival and Non-hunting Mortality

Banding programs for clapper rails have been limited in size and geographic extent, and recovery rates have been low (0.63–2.3%) (Stewart 1954, Mangold 1974, Ferrigno 1990). Consequently, no estimates of survival using band recovery data are available. Annual adult survival of Yuma clapper rails ranged from 49 to 67% using patterns of mortality of radio-marked birds (Eddleman 1989). These estimates may be biased by the effects of transmitter harnesses on bird survival. Most natural mortality of *R. l. yumanensis* has been attributed to predation during postbreeding and winter.

A variety of predators prey on nests, eggs, and adults of eastern clapper rails (Meanley 1985: 92–95). Introduced predators, especially red fox (*Vulpes vulpes*) and Norway rats, are the principal factors implicated in the recent decline of California clapper rails (Harvey 1988, Anon. 1991*b*).

Natural catastrophes may cause local or regional mortality of clapper rails, but populations usually recover (Meanley 1985:87). For exam-

ple, New Jersey had record low breeding populations of clapper rails in 1990 (Ferrigno 1990). An examination of banding data showed 80% of birds banded in New Jersey during 1948–88 and recovered in the southern U.S. were wintering in the South Carolina–Georgia coastal area where Hurricane Hugo struck in October 1989. The decline in New Jersey breeding populations was therefore attributed to mortality of wintering birds during the hurricane.

Coastal estuaries often act as settling basins for environmental contaminants that may enter clapper rails through the detrital food chain. For example, mercury levels in the Brunswick and Savannah estuaries in Georgia exceeded the Food and Drug Administration limit of 0.5 ppm in clapper rails, prompting a warning to hunters (Odom 1975). DDE levels in light-footed clapper rail eggs were also elevated (Eddleman et al. 1988), but clapper rails appeared to be less susceptible to eggshell thinning caused by chlorinated hydrocarbons than other birds (Klaas et al. 1980). Selenium levels in Yuma clapper rail tissues were within the range that causes hatching defects in many other birds, but the implications for population biology were unknown (Rusk 1991).

Diet and Nutrition

Clapper rails feed on a variety of invertebrates in tidal marshes (Heard 1983). They feed opportunistically on the most common and available foods in a given marsh type or geographic location. Clapper rails forage visually, using mainly surface gleaning and shallow probing into the substrate (Meanley 1985:37–38, Zembal and Fancher 1988). The highest intensity of foraging occurs in late evening.

Subspecies on the Atlantic and Gulf coasts most often eat fiddler crabs (*Uca* spp., *Sesarma* spp.), grasshoppers, crayfish (especially *Procambarus* spp.), periwinkle snails (*Littorina inornata*), and clam worms (*Nereis* spp.) in summer and fall (Oney 1954, Bateman 1965, Roth et al. 1972, Meanley 1985:33–36). Fiddler crabs are dormant in winter when temperatures drop below 13.5 C, but clapper rails nonetheless are capable of locating them (Meanley 1985:36). Diets of eastern clapper rails change slightly in winter, when some individuals eat more seeds (Roth et al. 1972).

West Coast clapper rails have diets similar to those of eastern subspecies, consisting of crabs (*Pachygrapsus crassipes, Hemigrapsus oregonensis*), snails, clams, insects, and a variety of other invertebrates (Moffitt 1941, Zembal and Fancher 1988). Yuma clapper rails eat mostly crayfish (*Procambarus clarki, Orconectes virilis*), isopods, freshwater shrimp (*Palaeomonetes paludosis*), freshwater clams (*Corbicula* spp.), water beetles, and fish (Ohmart and Tomlinson 1977, Eddleman 1989). Prey items become less abundant in winter, resulting in increased foraging movements and larger home range size of rails in autumn and winter (Conway et al. 1993).

Nothing is known about seasonal changes in body lipid levels in clapper rails, or whether there is variation between migratory and sedentary subspecies. Yuma clapper rails that are mostly sedentary [although possibly a partial migrant (Tomlinson and Todd 1973, Bennett and Ohmart 1978)], show wide variation in body weights (Eddleman 1989). Adult males weigh the least in late summer ($\bar{x} = 241$ g), and reach peak weight in November–February ($\bar{x} = 314$ g). Females show similar annual patterns. The significance of this weight change is unknown, although the combined stresses of nesting, brooding, and prebasic molt coincide with low summer weights.

HABITAT

Optimal habitat of clapper rails is low tidal salt marsh (low being defined as sites flooded at least once daily during high tide) dominated by cordgrass of moderate height and salinity levels exceeding 7,100 ppm at low tide and 5,600 ppm at high tide (Meanley 1985:31) (Fig. 2). This requirement is met by low salt marsh dominated by smooth cordgrass (*Spartina alterniflora*) in eastern areas and Pacific cordgrass (*S. foliosa*)-pickleweed (*Salicornia virginica*) on the West Coast (Hon et al. 1977, Holliman 1981, Massey et al. 1984, Foin and Benchley-Jackson 1991). Sharpe (1976:33) found Louisiana clapper rails were most abundant in dense smooth cordgrass, but comparisons with other studies were not made because of small sample sizes.

Nesting habitat of California clapper rails has 4 important characteristics: low marsh vegetation, tidal sloughs, tall high marsh (high being defined as sites flooded irregularly by the highest high tides), and abundant prey (Harvey 1988). High marsh is not often mentioned in nesting habitat needs on the East Coast, but uninterrupted tidal flow is essential to maintain vegetational communities preferred by clapper rails (Ferrigno et al. 1987). Nests of clapper rails are typically in smooth cordgrass of medium height, and grass height is the major cue used in selecting nest sites on the East Coast (Adams and Quay 1958, Storey et al. 1988). Early nests may be placed in needle rush (*Juncus roemerianus*), perhaps because of the greater cover provided by this plant in early spring (Adams and Quay 1958). Most nests are also within 15 m of tidal creeks or pool edges (Lewis and Garrison 1983); nests averaged 1.7 m from open water in Virginia (Meanley 1985:51) and 7.8 m in California (Harvey 1988). Nest placement shows no apparent pattern relative to creeks for Louisiana clapper rails (Sharpe 1976). Yuma clapper rails nest in riverine wetlands that were historically exposed to periodic flooding (Todd 1986). Consequently, nest sites selected by this subspecies are near uplands in shallow sites dominated by mature marsh vegetation, often in the base of a shrub (Conway et al. 1993).

Foraging habitat of clapper rails is mostly along tidal creeks and mud flats adjacent to dense emergent or mangrove (*Rhizophora* spp.) cover (Clark and Lewis 1983, Lewis and Garrison 1983,

Conway et al. 1993). Sites with at least 50% of the shoreline adjacent to emergent marsh are optimal (Lewis and Garrison 1983). These sites are selected because of prey abundance, ease of movement by foraging rails, and presence of nearby escape cover that is especially important for chicks that are unable to fly (Harvey 1988, Conway et al. 1993).

Habitat needs of clapper rails after nesting are poorly known, and rail density may vary during post-breeding as a result of tides, winds, ice coverage, and cold rather than vegetation structure or prey abundance (Meanley 1985:82). Habitat use by migrating birds is unknown. Clapper rails in North Carolina move from low marsh into mixed cordgrass and needle rush or high marsh during November to early April (Adams and Quay 1958). Yuma clapper rails also move into different cover types in winter, showing preference for denser cover than in summer (Anderson and Ohmart 1985, Eddleman 1989).

DISTRIBUTION AND ABUNDANCE

Clapper rails are distributed throughout North America (Fig. 1) in tidal salt and brackish marshes that are dominated by cordgrass. Three subspecies (Yuma clapper rail, light-footed clapper rail, and California clapper rail) are listed as federally endangered (U.S. Fish and Wildl. Serv. 1989a). Yuma clapper rails nest in freshwater wetlands along the lower Colorado River from Needles, California, to the mouth of the river, on the lower Gila River, in marshes associated with the Salton Sea, and at isolated sites in Arizona (Todd 1986). Light-footed and California clapper rails are restricted to tidal marshes in coastal southern California and San Francisco Bay, respectively.

The 5 eastern subspecies of clapper rail occur from coastal southern New England to southeastern Texas (Am. Ornithol. Union 1957, 1983; Ripley 1977; Meanley 1985) (Fig. 1). Northern clapper rails breed from Rhode Island to coastal North Carolina, where they intergrade with Wayne's clapper rail. Wayne's clapper rail ranges southward to the central east coast of Florida (Crawford et al. 1983), where it is replaced by the Florida clapper rail. Florida clapper rails nest in southern and western Florida and the Florida panhandle. Mangrove clapper rails are resident in the Florida Keys, while Louisiana clapper rails range from extreme western Florida to southern Texas.

All subspecies except the northern clapper rail are thought to be non-migratory (Am. Ornithol. Union 1957). Northern clapper rails winter as far north as the southern part of their breeding range (Stewart 1954) (Fig. 1), but principally winter in South Carolina, Georgia, and northeastern Florida; a few go as far south as the central east coast of Florida (Crawford et al. 1983). Stragglers may also remain in the northern portions of the breeding range (Meanley 1985:81).

Movements observed for other subspecies of clapper rail might not be true migration (Hon et al. 1977, Crawford et al. 1983, Eddleman 1989). Five types of dispersal movements are recognized in Yuma clapper rails: juvenile dispersal, breeding season movements by unmated males, postbreeding dispersal by adults, movements in late winter associated with acquisition of breeding territories, and home range shifts associated with high water or drying of habitat (Smith 1975, Bennett and Ohmart 1978, Eddleman 1989). Similar movements have been documented or suggested for other subspecies (Orr 1939, Crawford et al. 1983, Am. Ornithol. Union 1983, Zembal et al. 1985), but the scale of these movements does not suggest long-distance migration.

Home range size of clapper rails varies widely in different marsh habitat types, among years at a given site, and among seasons. Radio-telemetry is the most accurate technique for identifying spatial use by clapper rails and other rallids, because mapping locations of vocalizing birds usually underestimates home range size (Eddleman 1989). Yuma clapper rails have the largest home ranges, averaging 7.6 ha for males and 10.0 ha for females (Conway et al. 1993). The relatively low production of preferred foods in their habitat and their need for different marsh types for foraging and nesting explain their large spatial needs. In coastal salt marshes, home ranges of clapper rails are substantially smaller, ranging from 0.04 ha (Roth et al. 1972) to 1.66 ha (Zembal et al. 1989) during the nesting season, and 0.10 to 2.00 ha in winter (Roth et al. 1972). Home range size and movements increase after the nesting season and in winter, ranging up to 43 ha for Yuma clapper rails (Eddleman 1989). Winter home range size in coastal marshes is ≤2.00 ha (Roth et al. 1972).

Density of breeding clapper rails also varies among marsh types, ranging from a low of 0.15/ ha for *yumanensis* (Smith 1975) to 10.0/ha for *crepitans* in Virginia (Meanley 1985:49). In coastal cordgrass marshes, densities usually exceed 1 bird/ha (Oney 1954:32; Mangold 1974, 1977; Sharpe 1976:32; Harvey 1988; Zembal et al. 1989). Densities of calling clapper rails are recorded annually in 8 different marsh habitats in New Jersey (Mangold 1974, Ferrigno 1990). Salt hay (diked and farmed) and common reed (*Phragmites communis*) typically supported no clapper rails. Low numbers (<0.5 calls/station) occurred in marshhay cordgrass (*Spartina patens*) and mixed vegetation types. Smooth cordgrass had the highest number of calling rails (0.5 to 8 birds/station), and birds preferred sites dominated by the short growth-form of smooth cordgrass (Mangold 1974).

Densities of wintering clapper rails have not been estimated because their secretive nature and low rate of calling in winter makes detection difficult (Adams and Quay 1958). Winter abundance is highest from Camp Lejeune, North Carolina, to Titusville, Florida, based on Audubon Christmas Bird Count data (Root 1989: 73).

Current Survey Techniques

Few surveys are currently conducted to monitor population trends of clapper rails except for endangered subspecies (W. R. Eddleman, unpubl. data). An annual tape-playback survey is conducted to census Yuma clapper rails throughout the U.S. portions of their range (Tomlinson and Todd 1973, Powell 1990). An inter-agency team of cooperating federal and state biologists from Arizona and California conduct this survey by playing tapes of the primary advertising and territorial vocalizations of clapper rails throughout suitable habitat. However, results should be interpreted with caution. Problems include observers changing between years, variation in time of survey relative to breeding stage, and many areas of suitable habitat that are surveyed sporadically between years (Eddleman 1989). Additional problems include inconsistent response rates of clapper rails known to be present (Conway et al. 1993), unfamiliarity of many biologists with all vocalizations of clapper rails (Eddleman 1989), the dynamic nature of some habitat areas, and failure to survey suitable habitat where rails occur in Mexico.

Light-footed clapper rails and California clapper rails are also surveyed regularly using a combination of evening vocalization counts, tape-playback, nest searches, flushing counts, and counts of birds seen at high tide (Gill 1979, Zembal and Massey 1985, Harvey 1988).

A variety of techniques has been suggested for surveying clapper rails in the eastern United States including counting calling birds, tape-playback, nest counts, track counts, and sightings (Stewart 1951*a*, Mangold 1974, Meanley 1985:108). Call-counts are used in New Jersey to census clapper rails along standardized routes (Mangold 1974). These routes are patterned after those used for mourning doves (*Zenaida macroura*), with periodic stops to listen for calling rails during 2-minute periods. A tape recorder is used to record responses for later analysis to avoid differences in observers' ability to detect calls. Call-counts are conducted in the evening to avoid confusion with singing passerines (Mangold 1974). These data are stratified into 8 habitat types and the area of each habitat type is estimated by aerial surveys. The number of calls heard/minute is averaged for each cover type and multiplied by the percentage of mapped wetlands in each cover type to obtain an index. The indices are totaled for all 8 cover types to derive an annual statewide index of clapper rail abundance, and allows rough comparison of relative abundance among years. This method has documented a recent upward trend in clapper rail numbers in New Jersey, but populations fluctuate in relation to weather, territorial behavior, and tidal destruction of nests (Ferrigno 1990).

Surveys of clapper rails using tape-playback may increase the probability of locating clapper rails (Tomlinson and Todd 1973, Mangold 1974), but an inconsistent proportion of birds respond depending on population size, stage of the nesting cycle, time of day, and weather (Meanley 1985:109, Eddleman 1989, Conway et al. 1993). Nest counts have been used on a local basis to estimate breeding density (Stewart 1951*a*), but are labor-intensive, not applicable on a regional scale (Stewart 1951*a*), and impractical in dense habitats (Eddleman 1989). Track counts and sightings have been used to provide an index to relative abundance on a local scale, but are useful only where rails occur in relatively low density, such as in winter (Meanley 1985:108).

Population Status and Trends

No estimate of the total size of clapper rail populations in the eastern U.S. is available because of sporadic and inconsistent application of population estimation techniques. A total of

46 Breeding Bird Survey (BBS) routes include coastal marsh habitats, so this technique may also be used to monitor numbers of clapper rails in the East (U.S. Fish and Wildl. Serv., unpubl. data). Analyses of BBS data for clapper rails during 1966–91 indicate a mean annual increase ($P < 0.01$) of 4.3% in populations in the northeastern United States, and no change for southeastern and the entire United States. Similar analyses for the last 10 years show a mean annual increase ($P < 0.05$) of 6.8% in the southeastern United States and no change for the entire United States.

Information on population trends of clapper rails in eastern states in the last 15 years was obtained in response to a questionnaire sent in 1992 to state migratory bird biologists (W. R. Eddleman, unpubl. data). Biologists in Connecticut, Georgia, New Jersey, New York, Rhode Island, and Virginia were confident enough to estimate trends in clapper rail populations in their states. Clapper rail populations are believed to be increasing in New Jersey, decreasing in New York (especially on Long Island), and stable in the other states. No eastern state lists clapper rails as warranting special management status, although Florida indicates the species may be deserving of closer monitoring (Millsap et al. 1990).

The gross trend for Yuma clapper rails based on the annual tape-playback survey was stable to slightly increasing between the late 1970's and 1983 (Powell 1990). Extensive flooding on the lower Colorado River in 1983 degraded much of the available habitat (Powell 1990). At least 700 birds have responded during counts in the late 1980's to 1991.

Call-count surveys in the United States indicate a decline from 500–700 light-footed clapper rails in the early 1970's (Wilbur 1974) to 470 birds in 1991 (Anon. 1991a). An additional 500–700 birds occur in salt marshes in Baja California. California clapper rails have declined rapidly from an estimated 4,200–6,000 birds in the early 1970's to 1,500 birds in the early 1980's (Harvey 1988), to only 400 birds in 1991 (Anon. 1991a).

HARVEST

Clapper rail hunting is most effective when exceptionally high tides force clapper rails into the open and allow hunters to pole boats through the marsh and flush birds (Meanley 1985:77). The unpredictable nature and annual occurrence of these "marsh hen tides" results in extreme fluctuations in annual harvest. Additionally, a long-term, steady decline in interest in hunting rails may contribute to variation in the harvest (W. R. Eddleman, unpubl. data). The combination of unpredictability of conditions for good hunts, poor harvest monitoring, and declining hunter interest make assessment of trends in clapper rail harvest difficult.

Thirteen states on the East and Gulf coasts from Rhode Island to Texas allow harvest of clapper rails, and New York is the only coastal state in this region with no clapper rail season (W. R. Eddleman, unpubl. data). However, few reliable estimates of clapper rail annual harvest are available (Mangold 1977; W. R. Eddleman, unpubl. data). Current and past U.S. Fish and Wildlife Service estimates are based on samples of waterfowl hunters who also hunt rails, and may represent only 60% of the total harvest (Banks 1979, Martin 1979, U.S. Fish and Wildl. Serv. 1989b). Estimates also group clapper rail harvest with king rails (*Rallus elegans*) and Virginia rails (*R. limicola*), although clapper rails comprise most of the harvest in coastal states (U.S. Fish and Wildl. Serv. 1988, Conway and Eddleman 1994). Estimated mean annual harvest for 1964–86 using these data was 100,983 (95% C.I. = 74,100–127,400) in the coastal states that allow hunting of clapper rails, ranging from a low of 24,100 in the 1965–66 season to a high of 175,200 in 1970–71 (Conway and Eddleman 1994). An average of 1.6% of waterfowl hunters hunted rails other than soras (*Porzana carolina*) in the Atlantic Flyway during 1964–76, with an average annual bag of 9.7/hunter. Similar data for the Mississippi Flyway were 0.9% of waterfowl hunters that bagged an average of 3.58 clapper rails/hunter/year. The percentage of waterfowl hunters who hunted rails showed significant annual increases of 0.06 and 0.08% in the Atlantic and Mississippi flyways, respectively, during the same period. Recent estimates of clapper rail, king rail, and Virginia rail harvest in the coastal states of the Atlantic Flyway were 18,500 during the 1987–88 hunting season and 33,900 during 1988–89 (U.S. Fish and Wildl. Serv. 1989b).

A few states within the range of clapper rails (Louisiana, Maryland, New Jersey, Texas, and Virginia) have conducted harvest surveys for rails (W. R. Eddleman, unpubl. data). Louisiana averages a higher total rail harvest than the other 4 states, but discontinued its survey of rail harvest in 1988 because of the imprecision of the estimates. These state surveys have the advantage of including all rail hunters in the sampling scheme and not just waterfowl hunters. The most recent (1987–88 for Louisiana, 1991–92 for other states) estimates of rail harvest for these states are 20,000 for Louisiana; 9,549 in Virginia; 1,200 in Texas; 800 in New Jersey; and 200 in Maryland. New Jersey's harvest estimate in the late 1970's was 15,000–25,000 annually, suggesting a substantial decrease in that state's clapper rail harvest over a period of only 10–15 years (Mangold 1977). Reasons for this decline are unknown, but could be due to unfavorable weather during the hunting season or decline in hunter interest.

Most state regulations for harvest of clapper rails have not changed in the last 15 years (W. R. Eddleman, unpubl. data). Bag limits range from 10 to 15 daily (in aggregate with king rails in Texas, Delaware, and Georgia), and possession limits are double the daily bag limit. Season opening dates range from 19 August in Virginia to 19 September in Louisiana. The season continues for about 2.0 to 2.5 months in most states. Louisiana had a split season in 1992, with a short rail season during the September teal season (19–27 Sep) and a longer second season (21 Nov–20 Jan).

MANAGEMENT NEEDS

Habitat Management

Habitat management for clapper rails consists mostly of maintaining the structure and function of tidal salt marshes (Meanley 1985). Despite losses of salt marshes to coastal development, and degradation of these habitats by adjacent development and pollution, large areas of suitable habitat still remain on the East Coast (Meanley 1985:17). The stable to increasing trends noted for eastern clapper rails on BBS routes (U.S. Fish and Wildl. Serv., unpubl. data) imply that clapper rails have benefitted from coastal wetland protection laws (Eddleman et al. 1988).

Most habitat management of clapper rails involves either prevention of tidal flow alteration or restoration of altered tidal flows (Shisler and Schulze 1976, Ferrigno et al. 1987). Interference with tidal flow has a number of effects on salt marshes, including drying of habitats so that high marsh plants become dominant in former low salt marshes (Ferrigno et al. 1987); lowering

of salt content, allowing invasion by common reed; or permanent flooding of impoundments for waterfowl management, which can result in change to brackish or freshwater wetlands dominated by submerged or floating-leaved plants (Chabreck 1988:82). One method for restoration of diked areas used for salt hay production is the tidal restoration of salt hay impoundments (TRSHI) that has been initiated on several altered salt marshes in New Jersey. In New Jersey, clapper rails were absent on salt hay impoundments that were dominated by high marsh vegetation, but occurred on restored salt marshes (Ferrigno et al. 1987).

Open marsh water management (OMWM) is another practice that might affect clapper rail habitat (Shisler and Schulze 1976). This technique is used to control salt marsh mosquitos, and includes connecting existing pools in salt marshes and allowing fish to move between pools to eat mosquito larvae. The effects of OMWM on clapper rails are poorly known, but spoil from ditches may provide nest sites for clapper rails. Additional evaluation of the effects of TRSHI, OMWM, restorations of degraded marshes, and impoundments on clapper rails are needed for proper habitat management.

Western clapper rails have many of the same habitat management problems as the eastern races, although degradation of tidal marshes is much more severe in coastal California (Massey et al. 1984, Eddleman et al. 1988, Anon. 1991*b*). Yuma clapper rails are affected by water flow management on the lower Colorado River, but respond positively to water level manipulations on diked freshwater management units. Marshes of all ages should be maintained in managed wetland complexes to increase suitability for clapper rails (Eddleman et al. 1988, Conway et al. 1993).

Population Management

Subspecies.—Management of eastern subspecies should be as an Atlantic Coast Unit consisting of northern and Wayne's clapper rails, and a Gulf Coast Unit consisting of Florida and Louisiana clapper rails. Separate management of mangrove clapper rails is justified because they are little-known and probably insignificant as a game bird. The rationale for these management units is that the biology of the eastern races is relatively well-known, they seem to have similar habitat needs and occur together over a wide area in winter (Stewart 1954, Crawford et al. 1983, Ferrigno 1990), probably have higher harvest pressure, and share similar reproductive biology. Florida and Louisiana clapper rails are less well-known in almost all aspects of their biology, do not seem to have significant distributional overlap with the 2 Atlantic coast races, have relatively low harvest pressure, and may have somewhat different habitat and reproductive needs. Additional research on the Gulf Coast subspecies should clarify the validity of this management scheme. Season opening dates might also be different between these 2 regions, because existing frameworks sometimes result in rail seasons opening after many local birds have migrated south on the Atlantic Coast (W. R. Eddleman, unpubl. data). Seasons could be opened earlier on the Atlantic Coast to allow hunting opportunity prior to autumn migration, and split or opened later on the Gulf Coast where clapper rails are resident and birds may still be breeding in early autumn. The specific needs of the 3 endangered western subspecies are being addressed (Powell 1990, Anon. 1991a).

Surveys.—Surveys for clapper rails need refinement to obtain results that are comparable among years over the species' range. Call-count surveys using broadcasts of taped vocalizations show the most promise of standardization and require the least effort. However, calling behavior of clapper rails needs to be assessed to determine optimal timing and methodology for conducting surveys.

Current surveys for clapper rails are conducted regularly only in New Jersey, but general trends can be obtained from the BBS. The BBS is not designed to provide good trend data for birds of specialized habitats such as marshes, and surveys specifically designed for marsh birds may be needed (Gibbs and Melvin 1993). Such surveys could be designed to include all marsh birds, and would be more justifiable given the level of interest in clapper rails as game birds and the relative difficulty of access to their habitats.

Harvest Management

Implementation of the National Migratory Bird Harvest Information Program should provide accurate information on harvest of clapper rails. Analysis of data obtained under this program should help clarify if separate management of Atlantic and Gulf Coast subspecies is appropriate.

Obtaining estimates of population parameters should be a priority to insure effective harvest management of clapper rails. Additional banding studies are needed to identify migration routes, survival, and hunting mortality for northern, Wayne's, Florida, and Louisiana clapper rails. Techniques to assign age and sex of clapper rails must be developed before age and sex composition of the harvest can be estimated (Mangold 1974, Eddleman 1989).

RESEARCH NEEDS

Research needs for clapper rails have changed little in the last 15 years (Mangold 1977), and are listed in priority order.

1. Identify relative abundance, distribution, and population trends. This will involve assessment of the relative efficacy of call-count, tape playback, or other techniques for large-scale monitoring of clapper rail relative abundance and population trends, perhaps in concert with similar studies of other rails or marsh birds.
2. Develop additional banding programs at several sites throughout the eastern range to estimate survival rates of local breeding populations using mark-recapture techniques (Pollock et al. 1990). These programs might also result in additional clarification of dispersal patterns in sedentary subspecies, and wintering patterns in migratory races.
3. Identify habitat use and effects of existing habitat management techniques. Existing information on habitat requirements of eastern subspecies is largely qualitative and has been examined only on a local scale during the nesting season. Additionally, well-designed manipulative studies on effects of tidal marsh management techniques will clarify their effects on clapper rails. Application of radio-telemetry to study of western subspecies has revealed considerable detail on the range and characteristics of habitats used by clapper rails during all seasons of the year. Similar studies should be conducted on eastern and southern subspecies.
4. Develop and refine harvest surveys in conjunction with the National Migratory Bird Harvest Information Program. The U.S. Fish and Wildlife Service should cooperate with states that currently conduct such surveys to develop standardized methodologies.
5. Investigate aspects of basic biology that are currently unknown or poorly known. Such

studies should emphasize basic life history (especially annual variation in productivity and survival of the different subspecies, calling behavior, and habitat preferences), external age and sex criteria, post-breeding biology (including movements, migration, and habitat preferences), and wintering biology (including movements, survival, and habitat preferences).

RECOMMENDATIONS

The following is a summary of specific recommendations presented in descending order of priority.

1. The U.S. Fish and Wildlife Service (USFWS) and the Atlantic and Mississippi Flyway councils should implement programs to monitor population and harvest trends for clapper rails based on Atlantic Coast and Gulf Coast management units.
2. The USFWS and Atlantic and Mississippi flyway councils should conduct, assist, fund, and/or promote funding of identified applied research needs.

ACKNOWLEDGMENTS

We thank the state and provincial migratory bird biologists who provided information on population and habitat management and information needs for their states. M. E. Salerno assisted with preparation of the range map. This is Contribution #2870 of the College of Resource Development, University of Rhode Island, with support from the Rhode Island Agricultural Experiment Station.

LITERATURE CITED

ADAMS, D. A., AND T. L. QUAY. 1958. Ecology of the clapper rail in southeastern North Carolina. J. Wildl. Manage. 22:149–156.

AMERICAN ORNITHOLOGISTS' UNION. 1957. Checklist of North American birds. 5th ed. Port City Press, Baltimore, Md. 691pp.

———. 1983. Check-list of North American birds. 6th ed. Allen Press, Lawrence, Kans. 877pp.

ANDERSON, B. W., AND R. D. OHMART. 1985. Habitat use by clapper rails in the lower Colorado River Valley. Condor 87:116–126.

ANONYMOUS. 1991a. Regional News. Endangered Spp. Techn. Bull. 6(9–12):3.

———. 1991b. The California clapper rail: a beleaguered bird faces new threats. Endangered Spp. Techn. Bull. 6(2):2,5–6.

BANKS, R. C. 1979. Human related mortality of birds in the United States. U.S. Fish and Wildl. Serv., Spec. Sci. Rep. Wildl. 215. 16pp.

BATEMAN, H. A., JR. 1965. Clapper rail (*Rallus longirostris*) studies on Grand Terre Island, Jefferson Parish, Louisiana. M.S. Thesis, Louisiana State Univ., Baton Rouge. 144pp.

BENNETT, W. W., AND R. D. OHMART. 1978. Habitat requirements and population characteristics of the clapper rail (*Rallus longirostris yumanensis*) in the Imperial Valley of California. Unpubl. Rep., Univ. California, Lawrence Livermore Lab., Livermore. 55pp.

BLANDIN, W. W. 1963. Renesting and multiple brooding studies of marked clapper rails. Proc. Southeast. Assoc. Game and Fish Comm. 17:60–68.

———. 1965. Clapper rail studies in South Carolina: a preliminary report with particular emphasis on productivity. Progr. Rep., Proj. W–31-R. South Carolina Wildl. Resour. Dep., Charleston. 19pp.

CHABRECK, R. H. 1988. Coastal marshes—ecology and wildlife management. Univ. Minnesota Press, Minneapolis. 138pp.

CLARK, J. D., AND J. C. LEWIS. 1983. A validity test of a habitat suitability index model for clapper rail. Proc. Southeast. Assoc. Fish and Wildl. Agencies 37:95–102.

CONWAY, C. J., AND W. R. EDDLEMAN. 1994. Virginia rail. Pages 192–206 in T. C. Tacha and C. E. Braun, eds. Migratory shore and upland game bird management in North America. Int. Assoc. Fish and Wildl. Agencies, Washington, D.C.

———, ———, S. H. ANDERSON, AND L. R. HANEBURY. 1993. Seasonal changes in Yuma clapper rail vocalization rate and habitat use. J. Wildl. Manage. 56:282–290.

CRAWFORD, R. L., S. L. OLSON, AND W. K. TAYLOR. 1983. Winter distribution of subspecies of clapper rails (*Rallus longirostris*) in Florida with evidence for long-distance and overland movements. Auk 100:198–200.

DEGROOT, D. S. 1927. The California clapper rail: its nesting habits, enemies, and habitat. Condor 29:259–270.

EDDLEMAN, W. R. 1989. Biology of the Yuma clapper rail in the southwestern United States and northwestern Mexico. Final Rep., Intra-agency Agreement 4-AA–30–02060. U.S. Bur. Reclam., Yuma Proj. Off. Yuma, Ariz. 127pp.

———, F. L. KNOPF, B. MEANLEY, F. A. REID, AND R. ZEMBAL. 1988. Conservation of North American rallids. Wilson Bull. 100:458–475.

FERRIGNO, F. 1990. Wetlands ecology—Clapper rail nesting survey. Performance Rep., Proj. W–58-R–14. New Jersey Div. Fish, Game, and Shellfisheries, Trenton. 21pp.

———, J. K. SHISLER, J. HANSEN, AND P. SLAVIN. 1987. Tidal restoration of salt hay impoundments. Pages 284–296 in W. R. Whitman and W. H. Meredith, eds. Waterfowl and wetlands symposium. Delaware Dep. Nat. Resour. and Environ. Control, Dover.

FOIN, T. C., AND J. L. BENCHLEY-JACKSON. 1991. Simulation model evaluation of potential recovery of endangered light-footed clapper rail populations. Biol. Conserv. 58:123–148.

GIBBS, J. P., AND S. M. MELVIN. 1993. Call-response

surveys for monitoring breeding waterbirds. J. Wildl. Manage. 57:27–34.

GILL, R., JR. 1979. Status and distribution of the California clapper rail (*Rallus longirostris obsoletus*). Calif. Fish and Game 65:36–49.

HARVEY, T. E. 1988. Breeding biology of the California clapper rail in south San Francisco Bay. Trans. West. Sect., The Wildl. Soc. 24:98–104.

HEARD, R. W. 1983. Observations on the food and food habits of clapper rails (*Rallus longirostris* Boddaert) from tidal marshes along the East and Gulf Coast of the United States. Gulf Res. Rep. 7:125–135.

HOLLIMAN, D. C. 1981. A survey of the September 1979 hurricane damage to Alabama clapper rail habitat. Northwest Gulf Sci. 5:95–98.

HON, T., R. R. ODOM, AND D. P. BELCHER. 1977. Results of Georgia's clapper rail banding program. Proc. Southeast. Assoc. Fish and Wildl. Agencies 31:72–76.

JOHNSTON, R. F. 1956. The incubation period of the clapper rail. Condor 58:166.

KLAAS, E. E., H. M. OHLENDORF, AND E. CROMARTIE. 1980. Organochlorine residues and shell thicknesses in eggs of the clapper rail, common gallinule, purple gallinule, and limpkin (Class Aves), eastern and southern United States, 1972–74. Pestic. Monitor. J. 14:90–94.

LEWIS, J. C., AND R. L. GARRISON. 1983. Habitat suitability index models: clapper rail. U.S. Fish and Wildl. Serv. FWS/OBS–83/10. 15pp.

MACNAMARA, E. E., AND H. F. UDELL. 1970. Clapper rail investigations on the south shore of Long Island. Proc. Linnean Soc. N.Y. 71:120–131.

MANGOLD, R. E. 1974. Research on shore and upland game migratory birds in New Jersey: clapper rail studies. Final Rep., New Jersey Div. Fish, Game, and Shellfisheries, Trenton. 17pp.

———. 1977. Clapper rail (*Rallus longirostris*). Pages 84–92 *in* G. C. Sanderson, ed. Management of migratory shore and upland game birds in North America. Int. Assoc. Fish and Wildl. Agencies, Washington, D.C.

MARTIN, E. M. 1979. Hunting and harvest trends for migratory game birds other than waterfowl: 1964–76. U.S. Fish and Wildl. Serv., Spec. Sci. Rep. Wildl. 218. 37pp.

MASSEY, B. W., AND R. ZEMBAL. 1987. Vocalizations of the light-footed clapper rail. J. Field Ornithol. 58:32–40.

———, ———, AND P. D. JORGENSEN. 1984. Nesting habitat of the light-footed clapper rail in southern California. J. Field Ornithol. 55:67–80.

MEANLEY, B. 1985. The marsh hen: a natural history of the clapper rail of the Atlantic coast salt marsh. Tidewater Publ., Centreville, Md. 123pp.

MILLSAP, B. A., J. A. GORE, D. E. RUNDE, AND S. I. CERULEAN. 1990. Setting priorities for the conservation of fish and wildlife species in Florida. Wildl. Monogr. 111. 57pp.

MOFFITT, J. 1941. Notes on the food of the California clapper rail. Condor 43:270–273.

ODOM, R. R. 1975. Mercury contamination in Georgia rails. Proc. Southeast. Assoc. Game and Fish Comm. 28:649–658.

OHMART, R. D., AND R. E. TOMLINSON. 1977. Foods of western clapper rails. Wilson Bull. 89:332–336.

ONEY, J. 1954. Clapper rail survey and investigation study. Final Rep., Proj. W-9-R. Georgia Game and Fish Comm., Atlanta. 50pp.

ORR, R. T. 1939. Fall wanderings of clapper rails. Condor 41:151–152.

POLLOCK, K. H., J. D. NICHOLS, C. BROWNIE, AND J. E. HINES. 1990. Statistical inference for capture-recapture experiments. Wildl. Monogr. 107. 87pp.

POWELL, R. 1990. 1990 Yuma clapper rail census. Yuma Clapper Rail Recov. Team, Blythe, Calif. 4pp.

RIDGWAY, R., AND H. FRIEDMANN. 1941. The birds of North and Middle America. U.S. Natl. Mus. Bull. 50. 254pp.

RIPLEY, S. D. 1977. Rails of the world: a monograph of the family Rallidae. David R. Godine, Boston, Mass. 406pp.

ROOT, T. 1989. Atlas of wintering North American birds. Univ. Chicago Press, Chicago, Ill. 336pp.

ROTH, R. R., J. D. NEWSOM, T. JOANEN, AND L. L. MCNEASE. 1972. The daily and seasonal behavior patterns of the clapper rail (*Rallus longirostris*) in the Louisiana coastal marshes. Proc. Southeast. Assoc. Game and Fish Comm. 26:136–159.

RUSK, M. K. 1991. Selenium risk to Yuma clapper rails and other marsh birds of the lower Colorado River. M.S. Thesis, Univ. Arizona, Tucson. 75pp.

SCHMIDT, F. V., AND P. A. MCLAIN. 1951. The clapper rail in New Jersey. Proc. Northeast. Fish and Wildl. Conf. 7:164–172.

SCOTT, T. G., AND C. H. WASSER. 1980. Checklist of North America plants for wildlife biologists. The Wildl. Soc., Washington, D.C. 58pp.

SHARPE, T. L. 1976. Productivity and distribution of the clapper rail in a Louisiana salt marsh. M.S. Thesis, Louisiana State Univ., Baton Rouge. 91pp.

SHISLER, J. K., AND T. L. SCHULZE. 1976. Some aspects of open marsh water management procedures on clapper rail production. Trans. Northeast. Sect., The Wildl. Soc. 32:101–104.

SMITH, P. M. 1975. Habitat requirements and observations on the clapper rail, *Rallus longirostris yumanensis*. M.S. Thesis, Arizona State Univ., Tempe. 35pp.

STEWART, R. E. 1951a. Clapper rail populations of the Middle Atlantic states. Trans. North Am. Wildl. Conf. 16:421–430.

———. 1951b. Clapper rail studies. Pages 56–58 *in* Investigations of woodcock, snipe, and rails in 1951. U.S. Fish and Wildl. Serv., Spec. Sci. Rep. Wildl. 14.

———. 1954. Migratory movements of the northern clapper rail. Bird-Banding 25:1–5.

———, AND B. MEANLEY. 1960. Clutch size of the clapper rail. Auk 77: 221–222.

STOREY, A. E., W. A. MONTEVECCHI, H. F. ANDREWS, AND N. SIMS. 1988. Constraints on nest site selection: a comparison of predator and flood avoidance in four species of marsh-nesting birds (Genera: *Catoptrophorus*, *Larus*, *Rallus*, and *Sterna*). J. Comp. Psychol. 102:14–20.

TODD, R. L. 1986. A saltwater marsh hen in Arizona: a history of the Yuma clapper rail (*Rallus longirostris yumanensis*). Final Rep., Fed. Aid Proj. W-95-R, Arizona Game and Fish Dep., Phoenix. 290pp.

TOMLINSON, R. E., AND R. L. TODD. 1973. Distribution of two western clapper rail races as determined by responses to taped calls. Condor 75: 177-183.

U.S. FISH AND WILDLIFE SERVICE. 1988. Final supplemental environmental impact statement: issuance of annual regulations permitting the sport hunting of migratory birds. SEIS 88. U.S. Gov. Print. Off., Washington, D.C. 340pp.

———. 1989a. Endangered and threatened wildlife and plants. 50 CFR 17.11 and 17.12. U.S. Gov. Print. Off., Washington, D.C. 34pp.

———. 1989b. Trends in harvest and hunting activity for migratory game birds other than waterfowl. U.S. Fish and Wildl. Serv. Admin. Rep., Laurel, Md. 11pp.

WILBUR, S. R. 1974. The status of the light-footed clapper rail. Am. Birds 28:868–870.

ZEMBAL, R., AND J. M. FANCHER. 1988. Foraging behavior and foods of the light-footed clapper rail. Condor 90:959–962.

———, AND B. W. MASSEY. 1985. Distribution of the light-footed clapper rail in California, 1980–1984. Am. Birds 39:135–137.

———, ———, AND J. M. FANCHER. 1989. Movements and activity patterns of the light-footed clapper rail. J. Wildl. Manage. 53:39–42.

———, ———, C. S. NORDBY, AND R. J. BRANSFIELD. 1985. Intermarsh movements by light-footed clapper rails indicated in part through regular censusing. Calif. Fish and Game 71:164–171.

Chapter 13

KING RAIL

FREDERIC A. REID, Ducks Unlimited, 9823 Old Winery Place, Sacramento, CA 95827
BROOKE MEANLEY, P.O. Box 87, Fishersville, VA 22939
LEIGH H. FREDRICKSON, Gaylord Memorial Laboratory, School of Natural Resources, University of Missouri–Columbia, Puxico, MO 63960

Abstract: King rails (*Rallus elegans*) are large North American rallids with a strong decurved bill and rusty-brown plumage. Wetland habitats inhabited by king rails have been lost or degraded over the last 40 years. In 1992, 13 states or provinces recognized a special status for king rails, including 6 states which classify them as endangered. Thirteen Atlantic or Gulf Coast states list the king rail as a game bird. Basic population trends are unknown. Conservation efforts for king rails should protect or restore complexes of marsh and slough wetland habitats. Habitat management should protect hummocky topography and natural swales for nesting and foraging. Research is needed on basic ecology, including energetics and habitat use. Information on hunter activity, harvest, and population dynamics is needed to evaluate harvest impacts.

Life history information for king rails has been well summarized (Meanley 1969, 1992). Biologists or students interested in this species are urged to consult these references.

DESCRIPTION

King rails are the largest of the true North American rails (although it is smaller and lighter than the more aquatic American coot [*Fulica americana*]). King rails have a laterally compressed body with a long, decurved bill, and rusty-buff plumage. Wing spans reach up to 40 cm and body mass ranges from 300 to 490 g in males and 250 to 360 g in females (Meanley 1969, Ripley 1977). King rails are slightly larger and heavier than northern clapper rails (*R. longirostris crepitans*). Sexes are monochromatic, but differ from some subspecies of clapper rails by being rusty-brown instead of gray. King rails have rich chestnut wing coverts and distinct barring on the flanks (Meanley 1969, 1992). The juvenal plumage shows whiter underparts and less distinct markings above the face. Chicks are solid black in plumage. All plumages are described in detail elsewhere (Meanley and Meanley 1958; Meanley 1969, 1992).

Two subspecies are generally recognized (Am. Ornithol. Union 1957, 1983) and consist of *R. e. elegans* of North America and *R. e. remsdeni* of Cuba (Meanley 1992). A third less recognized subspecies, *R. e. tenuirostris*, has been described from the highlands of central Mexico (Warner and Dickerman 1959), but is considered by some to be a race of clapper rail. Most recent taxonomic considerations place *R. elegans* and *R. longirostris* as a superspecies (Am. Ornithol. Union 1983), while others consider them conspecific (Ripley 1977). Mixed pairings and hybrids have been seen on both Atlantic and Gulf coasts (Meanley and Wetherbee 1962, Meanley 1992). Systematic investigations using mitochondrial DNA of the 2 species were inconclusive (Avise and Zink 1988).

LIFE HISTORY

Detailed life history descriptions of king rail have been reviewed by Meanley (1969, 1992). We present information on social organization, reproduction, and diet because they are important to habitat and population management.

Social Organization

Mated adult pairs and families with broods are the primary social units of king rails. King rails are semi-precocial; thus adults not only feed young, but must lead the young to areas of sufficient food. Young stay grouped within a brood for 6–10 weeks and then separate from adults and siblings. Social structure of these secretive birds during migration and wintering is unknown. It is unclear if courtship, displays, or pairing occur outside of the breeding grounds. However, displays and vocalization by males occur on the breeding grounds. The primary advertising call is given by adults year-round, but the greatest array and complexity of calls occurs between courtship and nesting (Meanley 1992). Present evidence indicates annual monogamy as a mating system (Meanley 1957, 1992; Reid 1989). Age at first breeding, life span, and

Fig. 1.   King rail incubating in nest constructed in common cattails (*Typha latifolia*) in roadside ditch on the Grand Prairie, Arkansas, April 1952 (Photo by Brooke Meanley).

survivorship are unknown, but a nesting female with what appeared to be first-year plumage was collected in the Delaware Bay marshes (Meanley 1969).

Reproduction

Phenology of nesting varies with latitude, beginning as early as February in St. Johns County, Florida, and occurring as late as August in Louisiana (Meanley 1992) (Fig. 1). Nest initiation begins in mid-May to June in more northern breeding areas such as Iowa and Ohio (Trautman 1940, Tanner and Hendrickson 1956).

Spring arrival dates in the Upper Mississippi Valley vary little, where the first king rails arrived on 2 May in glacial marshes of northwestern Iowa (43°N, 95°W), and peak of migration occurred during the first week of May in 1951 (Tanner and Hendrickson 1956). The mean date (±SE) of first nest initiation during a 5-year study in Missouri was 9 May ± 5.7 days. Peak nest initiation occurred between the second week of May and the second week of June. The mean hatch date of all nests was 30 June ± 15.3 days (Reid 1989). In contrast to conditions in the Upper Mississippi Valley where king rails arrive in late-April or early-May and initiate nesting in mid-May to late-May, the lower Mississippi Alluvial Valley may provide a longer period for breeding. An adult king rail was seen in late February 1984 in the vicinity of Mingo National Wildlife Refuge (NWR), Missouri (37°N, 90°W), and broods have been seen on the refuge as early as 5 April 1987 and

27 April 1988. By back-dating the early April brood, it appears that nest initiation began by late February or the first week of March. At the southern extreme of the U.S. breeding range, in Florida and Louisiana, the breeding season may last as long as 7 months (Meanley 1992).

Little variation in clutch size has been found among populations; means ranged from 10.5 to 11.2 eggs/clutch in 4 different populations (Reid 1989). No trends in clutch size are apparent in relation to either latitude or longitude. However, differences exist among populations of king rails ($\bar{x} \pm SE = 10.8 \pm 1.3$, $n = 122$ clutches) and clapper rails ($\bar{x} \pm SE = 9.1 \pm 1.5$, $n = 162$ clutches) (Reid 1989). These differences in clutch size may reflect the relative unpredictability of foods and nest predators in freshwater habitats used by king rails, as compared to more predictable coastal habitats used by clapper rails.

Both sexes incubate (Meanley 1969), beginning with the laying of the last egg and lasting 21–23 days. Nest success was relatively high at the Ted Shanks Wildlife Area (WA), Missouri, where 54 (81%) of 67 nests were successful and 39 (58%) nests hatched complete clutches (Reid 1989). All 13 unsuccessful nests were apparently destroyed by mammalian predators. Analyses of nest success for the egg-laying and incubation periods (after Mayfield 1975) revealed daily survival rates ranging from 0.97 to 1.0 and interval survival rates ranging from 0.74 to 1.0. Span survival rate (±SE) from first egg laid to hatch was 0.695 ± 0.071 (Reid 1989). These trends were similar to the 75% apparent success rate observed in Arkansas (Meanley 1969). The cryptic plumage of both sexes and the secretive behavior of adults certainly aid success.

Nest predation may occur from raccoons (*Procyon lotor*), mink (*Mustela vison*), red fox (*Vulpes vulpes*), and striped skunks (*Mephitis mephitis*). Predators of adults include northern harriers (*Circus cyaneus*), great-horned owls (*Bubo virginianus*), and alligators (*Alligator mississipiensis*) (Meanley 1992). With expanded human development around wetlands, mortality because of domestic cats and dogs may also occur among these slow-flushing birds. No disease or parasite data are available.

Diet and Foraging

King rails are omnivores, but specialize on crustaceans and insects. Crayfish are a critical food item in freshwater marshes, whereas fiddler crabs are important in brackish tidal systems (Meanley 1992). Birds cast pellets consisting of exoskeleton fragments of crustaceans and insects. Aquatic insects, fish, frogs, grasshoppers, crickets, and moist-soil plants seeds are frequently consumed (Meanley 1969, 1992). In the only quantitative study with viable sample size (118 individuals), Meanley (1956) found that animal material constituted 95% by volume of foods in spring, 90% in summer, 74% in fall, and 58% in winter.

A crepuscular pattern of activity was suggested for diurnal-foraging king rail broods in Missouri (Reid 1989), whereas chicks were fed throughout the day in Arkansas (Meanley 1992). King rails display dramatic shifts in foraging habitat between migration and breeding periods (Reid 1989). Sites used during spring migration and nesting/incubation are in dense vegetation where water is relatively deep (2.5–20 cm), but broods tend to forage in open mud flats with shallow water (saturated soil to 7.5-cm water depth) (Reid 1989). Brood foraging sites are closely associated with drier sites that have dense, tall vegetation where broods hide during midday. Sites used during fall migration have relatively deep water (1.0–24.5 cm) and include mosaics of drying swales and not large expanses of exposed mud flats. The lack of dense vegetation associated with larger mud flats may explain in part the lack of brood use. Use of drying freshwater sites by foraging king rails may be similar to use of tidal exposed mud flats by clapper rails (Meanley 1985), except that foraging pattern related to time of day for the latter species would be more regulated by tidal action. Prey densities at foraging sites used by king rail adults and broods have more predictable prey base than foraging sites used by adults during nesting and migration periods that contain patchy food resources (Reid 1989). The protein-rich diets that invertebrates provide are important for rapid growth rates of young waterbirds (Krapu and Reinecke 1992).

HABITAT

Breeding habitat includes freshwater (tidal and non-tidal) marshes, brackish marshes, shrub swamps, and, occasionally, ricefields. Nesting occurs in association with perennial vegetation, especially grasses (Poaceae), sedges (Cyperaceae) and rushes (Juncaceae) where water depths are <1 to 25 cm (Meanley 1992) (Fig. 2). Selection of nest sites in shallow water is characteristic of this species. Six king rail nests at Dew-

Fig. 2.   King rail nest in roadside ditch near Stuttgart, Arkansas, 30 May 1952. Nest constructed in common rush (*Juncus effusus*) (Photo by Brooke Meanley).

ey's Pasture, Iowa, were in slightly deeper water than most areas, ranging from 10 to 46 cm, with a mean depth of 27 cm (Tanner and Hendrickson 1956). Nesting in the Lake Erie marshes occurred at water depths of about 60 cm (Trautman 1940), but this value seems high for a species with a short tarsus (approximately 6 cm) that relies so heavily on walking. The description of king rails as essentially a damp habitat species (Meanley 1953) seems most appropriate. Water depth at nest sites ranged from 15 to 20 cm in the Grand Prairie, Arkansas (Meanley 1953), and moist to 22 cm in northeastern Missouri (Reid 1989).

The Atlantic Coastal Plain and Mississippi Valley are the principal migration corridors for king rails (Meanley 1969). Migrating rails associate with damp or shallow water conditions in marsh, or seasonally flooded freshwater wetlands and tidal guts in coastal areas. Winter concentrations occur in floodplain wetlands of riverine systems along the Atlantic and Gulf coasts. Coastal Louisiana probably has the largest remaining wintering concentration of king rails.

DISTRIBUTION AND ABUNDANCE

The North American subspecies (*R. e. elegans*) has a broad geographic range across much of the eastern United States (Fig. 3). Breeding habitats range from the Gulf Coast to southern Ontario and from the Atlantic Coast to about the 100th meridian in the Great Plains (Am. Ornithol. Union 1983, Meanley 1992). The winter range coincides with the highest breeding densities and includes the Atlantic seaboard from Delaware to the Everglades, westward through

Fig. 3.   Breeding and year-round distributions of king rail (after Meanley 1992).

BREEDING
WINTER

the Gulf Coast, and north into seasonally flooded wetlands and the rice belt of the Mississippi Delta.

Visual surveys are difficult because of the secretive nature of king rails. No accurate estimate is available for total population size or even density estimates across most of the range. Estimates in the early 1960's ranged from 74–267 birds/100 ha using strip censuses to 4–24 birds/1.2 km route using a roadside count (Meanley 1992). More recent estimates of king rail density range from 7 to 22 adults/100 ha in semi-permanent wetlands on the Ted Shanks WA in northeastern Missouri (Reid 1989).

Alarming declines in king rail populations have occurred in the last 30 years, despite the broad geographic and habitat distribution (Meanley 1992). These declines mimic the decline of other small rail species in North America (Eddleman et al. 1988), Europe (Reichholf 1982), and Pacific islands (Ripley 1977). Specific locations of recent king rail declines include the southwestern shore of Lake Erie, glacial marshes of northwestern Iowa, western shore of Maryland, Smyrna River marshes of Delaware, and

Arkansas rice belt (Meanley 1969, Weller 1979, Eddleman et al. 1988). Much of this decline can be directly related to wetland habitat losses and degradations across North America. Approximately 54% of the original wetlands in the conterminous United States has been lost (Tiner 1984); agriculture specifically has accounted for 87% of wetland losses from the mid–1950's to mid–1970's (Frayer et al. 1983). Palustrine emergent wetlands are probably the most important habitat type for king rails (Meanley 1969), and have declined by 1.9 million ha during that 20-year period (Frayer et al. 1983). These losses represented approximately 17% of all existing palustrine wetlands in the conterminous United States.

Several states have recently recognized the king rail as a species of special status (Table 1) because of wetland conversion and declining observations of rails. Most of these states are in the Upper Midwest where densities of king rails may not have approached those on the Gulf or Atlantic coasts. However, ornithological reports from the turn of the century (Widmann 1907, Meanley 1969) list king rails as a common breed-

Table 1. States and provinces that recognize special status for king rails.

State/province	Status	Trend[a]
Pennsylvania	Endangered	Stable
Ohio	Endangered	Decreasing
Michigan	Endangered	Decreasing
Iowa	Endangered	NI[b]
Missouri	Endangered	Decreasing
Kentucky	Endangered	NI
Massachusetts	Threatened	NI
Connecticut	Threatened[c]	Stable
New Jersey	Special Concern	NI
Wisconsin	Special Concern	NI
Minnesota	Special Concern	NI
Arkansas	Special Concern	NI
Ontario	Rare species	NI

[a] Trends of population based on 1992 reports (W. R. Eddleman, unpubl. data) from state and provincial fish and wildlife biologists.
[b] No information.
[c] Breeding population.

er along major river floodplains. Six states now list king rails as endangered, and 3 of these states suggest recent decreasing populations. Missouri has identified only 8 counties where king rails have nested in the last 15 years. Massachusetts and Connecticut list the species as threatened. Four states consider king rails to have a status of special concern, while Ontario lists the species as rare. Arkansas had high densities of rails in both seasonally flooded wetlands and ricelands just 30 years ago (Meanley 1969), but now lists the species in special status. Of the 12 states that list king rails in special status, all consider wetland habitat reduction as the major factor responsible. New York and Kansas also list habitat loss as the reason for declining populations. Populations at Cheyenne Bottoms, Kansas, may have been drastically reduced during recent extended drought in the region.

HARVEST

Thirteen Gulf and Atlantic coastal states list king rails as a game bird (Table 2). A recent survey of state game bird biologists was used to identify hunting seasons, limits, and population trends (W. R. Eddleman, unpubl. data). Nine of the states allow an aggregate take of 15 king or clapper rails per day; 3 states allow an aggregate take of 10 king or clapper rails; while Connecticut allows a single king rail in a daily bag. The daily bag and possession limits in Connecticut were changed in 1992 because of concern over a breeding king rail population of threatened status.

The federal hunting season framework allows for hunting to begin 1 September and end 20 January. The federal limit on season length extends for 70 days in each state (U.S. Fish and Wildl. Serv. 1987). Currently, 5 states open their season on 1 September, and Louisiana closes its season on 20 January. South Carolina, Florida, and Louisiana have opted for a split season to

Table 2. Season dates, daily bag and possession limits, and population trends for states that allow hunting of king rails—1993.

State	Season	Bag/possession[a]	Trend[b]
Rhode Island	14 Sep–22 Nov	10/20	NI[c]
Connecticut	01 Sep–09 Nov	1/1[d]	Stable
Delaware	01 Sep–09 Nov	10/20	NI
Maryland	01 Sep–09 Nov	10/20	NI
Virginia	19 Sep–27 Nov	15/30	NI
North Carolina	05 Sep–13 Nov	15/30	NI
South Carolina	23 Sep–30 Sep[e]	15/30	NI
	12 Oct–12 Dec		
Georgia	26 Sep–04 Dec	15/30	Stable
Florida	01 Sep–30 Sep[e]	15/30	NI
	25 Nov–03 Jan		
Alabama	12 Nov–20 Jan	15/15	Stable
Mississippi	12 Oct–20 Dec	15/30	NI
Louisiana	19 Sep–27 Sep[e]	15/30	NI
	21 Nov–20 Jan		
Texas	01 Sep–09 Nov	15/30	Declining

[a] In aggregate with clapper rails.
[b] Trends in population based on 1992 reports from state fish and wildlife biologists (W. R. Eddleman, unpubl. data).
[c] No information.
[d] Connecticut changed its daily bag and possession limits in the 1992 season because of concern over a threatened breeding king rail population. Prior limits had been 10/20 and remained the same for clapper rails, but was modified for king rails.
[e] South Carolina, Florida, and Louisiana had a split season in 1993 to accommodate both rail and teal hunting during the early split season.

Fig. 4.　Method of hunting rails in Patuxent River wildrice (*Zizania* spp.) marshes in Maryland. Boat is poled through marshes at flood tide (September 1958) (Photo by Brooke Meanley).

accommodate both rail and teal hunting during the early split, and rail and duck hunting during the later split.

Historically, king rails were prized game birds (Bent 1926), but the difficulty of finding concentrated numbers, and the inability to maneuver in slough habitats, has resulted in the species seldom being hunted (Meanley 1969) (Fig. 4). Only in local areas are they even considered an important game species. Meanley (1969) reported that Gulf Coast domestic rice producing areas of Louisiana and Texas probably experienced the greatest hunting effort, but even there <1% of the local population was harvested. Most of the king rails harvested throughout its range are incidentally taken by hunters shooting sora (*Porzana carolina*) or clapper rails.

The 2 most common means of hunting king rails are to "push" or "pole" shallow-draft boats in coastal areas at high tide, or to wade through freshwater marshes or harvested rice fields (Meanley 1969). An example occurs in Connecticut, where currently <20 active rail hunt-

ers are estimated. There, most hunting occurs in tidal marshes near the mouths of the Housatonic and Connecticut rivers. Access is only available by boat to the best hunting areas on the highest tides in September. The rail harvest in Connecticut is estimated at 95% sora, 4% Virginia rail (*Rallus limicola*), 1% clapper rail, and incidental take of king rail. The Delaware Valley of New Jersey, Patuxent River marshes in Maryland, lower James River of Virginia tidewater, and ricefields at Eagle Lake, Texas, and Grand Prairie, Arkansas, are historic hunting areas for king rails (Meanley 1969). Meanley (1969:93) writes "In the days of the market gunner, rails were shot in much greater numbers than at present, and were sold in the markets of most of the large cities along the eastern seaboard. To the epicures, the king rail of the freshwater marsh was far superior to the clapper rail of the salt marsh." Meanley (1969: 93) further quotes Charles Westcott writing in "Forest and Stream" magazine in the 1880's saying, "Many of the latter [clapper rails], however, carefully plucked were palmed off for king rails on those less expert in identifying them."

MANAGEMENT NEEDS

Habitat Management

King rails, like most North American water-birds, have adapted life history strategies that allow them to exploit the seasonal resources in wetlands. Most palustrine wetlands in temperate portions of North America have been converted to agricultural developments or degraded in quality (Tiner 1984). Although certain large tracts of wetland habitats have been protected (usually by public ownership), most lack dynamic water regimes that promote good habitat quality (Fredrickson and Reid 1990, Wentz and Reid 1992). As an example, the Mississippi River corridor historically provided important habitat for breeding and migrating king rails. Major degradations to this ecosystem have occurred and include constriction of banks that modify flow and flood capacity, dike constriction that impacts channel direction, and addition of toxicants through point and non-point pollution (Reid et al. 1989). Today, most quality wetland habitats remain on public refuges.

Loss of wetlands and habitat degradation continues across the range of king rails. All state biologists surveyed suggested that habitat decreases should be the primary concern for king rail management (W. R. Eddleman, unpubl. data). Human influences such as drainage, dredging, pollution, filling, mosquito drainage projects, and agricultural or urban expansion modify the hydrologic integrity of systems along the Atlantic and Gulf coasts (Smith et al. 1989).

Florida's interior palustrine wetlands have been subjected to extensive drainage, flood-control, and navigation projects. Artificial regulation of water levels continues to pose the greatest continuing threat to the quality of rail habitat. The levels of most Florida lakes have been stabilized to prevent flooding and to insure adequate water supplies during dry periods. Stabilization of water levels reduces the extent of emergent plants and increases the inundation frequency in much of the littoral zone (Johnson and Montalbano 1989), as well as decreases the availability of invertebrate prey.

The marshes of the deltaic and Chenier plains of the Gulf Coast are the most important coastal wetlands for king rails (Meanley 1969). With a national trend toward increasing human activity

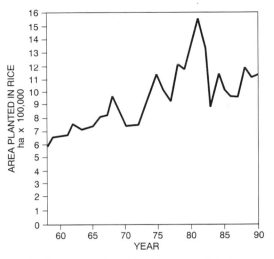

Fig. 5.   Area of rice planted 1958–90 for the United States (after U.S. Dep. Agric. 1992).

along coastal zones, problems of wetland loss (Tiner 1984), and subsidence and salinity modification (Gosselink 1984), the impact of humans on waterbird habitats will continue to increase.

The Mississippi Alluvial Valley has been severely impaired by human activity. Publically managed habitats important for waterbirds in this region equal less than 100,000 ha (Reinecke et al. 1989). Agricultural subsidies, flood insurance, technological advances in farming equipment (allowing tillage of wet and large, unbroken tracts), and high grain yields during drought periods may continue to encourage conversion of existing wetlands and intensified drainage of wet agricultural lands (Reid et al. 1989).

Agricultural conversion of wetlands has been expedited through the production of crops such as cotton, corn, soybeans, pasture for cattle, and rice. Row crops, other than rice (Meanley 1969), have little value for any rallid species. Much of the rice ground in the Mississippi Alluvial Valley and Gulf Coast was formally wet prairie and marsh habitat. These areas include the Beaumont, Katy, Lissie, and Garwood prairies of Texas and Grand Prairie of Arkansas. In much of the Mississippi Delta, total area and field size has increased dramatically over the last 30 years, while total area in the United States converted to rice has more than doubled in that period (U.S. Dep. Agric. 1992) (Fig. 5). Today, greater than 45% of all rice area in the United States is in Arkansas, and greater than 85% of the total rice area is in Arkansas, Mississippi, Louisiana, and Texas. Since the early 1960's, after Meanley (1953) documented king rail use of rice fields, several cultural practices have changed. Second cropping has become much more common, and fall or winter land preparation leaves minimal residual plant cover. Herbicide use has reduced moist-soil "weed" plants in the fields. Intensive cattle grazing may occur in idle growing years. Increased herbicide and pesticide use from the late 1950's to mid-1970's resulted in acute poisoning of some waterbirds, and probably a dramatic decline in the aquatic invertebrate prey base.

King rails nest in floodplain habitats. As such, hummocky topography and natural swales should be maintained for nesting and foraging. Allowing small depressions to dry naturally during the brood period may more closely mimic floodplain conditions to which king rails have adapted. Artificial land leveling should be discouraged. Beds of perennial vegetation, especially sedges, grasses, and water smartweed (*Polygonum* spp.), should be encouraged where water depths are moist to 25 cm. In a continuum of preferred water depths at nest sites for inland-breeding rallids, king rails and black rails (*Laterallus jamaicensis*) nest in the most shallow water areas (Fredrickson and Reid 1986). These shallow, seasonally-flooded sites are most easily drained and impacted by agriculture.

Nest success is significantly related to water depth and distance to open water (Reid 1989). Location of a nest within a management unit appears most important in predicting nest success. King rail nests constructed in borrow ditches, wetlands during drawdowns, or within 3 m of any managed unit edge were far more likely to be destroyed than nests constructed in the interior of a managed unit that was not drawn down during the nesting period (Reid 1989). Fragmentation of habitats can adversely affect nest predation for avian species (Diamond 1975). Borrow areas along the edges of units may serve as travel lanes for mammalian predators (Brown and Dinsmore 1986). Ditches also may be susceptible to rapid and higher flooding spates that can flood nests (Meanley 1969). Borrow areas may, however, be the only remaining habitat available in intensively farmed regions (Meanley 1969), and roadside mowing of borrow areas should be discouraged during the nesting and brood period. On intensively managed refuges, a complex of wetland units should include marsh habitats that naturally dry during the summer

and may include extensive perennial vegetation (Reid 1993).

Population and Harvest Management

There is no evidence identifying subpopulations of king rails in the United States. Only Virginia currently conducts standardized surveys for king rails, and these are locally restricted to the eastern shore. Because the species is so secretive, state-wide surveys may not yield precise estimates or trends. Local surveys may reveal trends at critical breeding or wintering sites. Breeding surveys may be most productive during the brood period, when young may be seen and counted in more open habitat. Coastal surveys may record the most flushes during winter high tides. Repeatable methods to estimate or index populations across the range need to be developed and implemented.

Of the 13 states that list the king rail as a game bird, harvest surveys are only currently conducted by Maryland, Virginia, and Texas. Biologists in Maryland have suggested that current harvest opportunity exceeds participation by hunters. A 1991 Maryland survey identified 117 total hunters for all rail species (excluding coots), and 2,136 ± 18.2 total rails harvested. No specific estimate of harvest for king rails was made. The king rail season in Virginia was shifted to later in September in 1992 to allow late-hatched clapper and king rails time to mature. A 1989 Virginia harvest survey estimated 978 clapper rail hunters taking 9,549 birds. This estimate probably includes any king rails harvested. An annual average during 1989–91 in Texas suggested 960 days of hunting and a harvest of 1,200 rails of all 4 hunted species.

Louisiana discontinued rail harvest surveys following the 1987–88 season because of large confidence intervals resulting from small numbers of hunter responses. Clapper and king rails constituted the majority of rails harvested in that state. The 1987–88 Louisiana harvest survey indicated 6,100 ± 2,000 hunters taking 49,000 ± 29,300 total rails. Rhode Island, Connecticut, and Delaware biologists suggest there is minimal king rail harvest in those states.

The National Migratory Bird Harvest Information Program should provide a more precise estimate of recreational harvest of king rails in the United States. If populations continue to decline, reduced bag limits, season lengths, or eliminating hunting seasons must be considered by state and federal authorities. If concern exists over not restricting clapper rail hunting opportunities, hunting of king rails could be restricted to coastal counties within a state, thus protecting inland, freshwater populations (e.g., the Catahoula Lake, Louisiana population).

RESEARCH NEEDS

Little research to improve management for king rails has occurred over the last 30 years. Studies of basic ecological processes that have important management applications should include the following, in order of priority.

1. A study of general habitat use at primary wintering, migration, and breeding areas.
2. An understanding of how size, isolation, and configuration of management units on natural swales impacts nesting success and juvenile survival needs further elucidation for king rails and other waterbirds (Brown and Dinsmore 1986, Reid 1989).
3. An evaluation of population assessment techniques is needed.
4. The basic foraging ecology of king rails and relationships to energetic patterns are relatively unknown. The development of learned foraging could be compared among siblings and among broods, and then compared to chick survival.
5. A basic understanding of king rail nutrition and energetics is needed. American coots, the largest of North American rallids, store most lipid reserves required for egg production as reserves prior to arrival on breeding grounds (Alisauskas and Ankney 1985). This suggests that condition of wintering or migration habitats directly influences whether a coot will nest and the size of her clutch (Alisauskas and Ankney 1985). The pattern of nutrient acquisition among rallids probably varies among species in relation to niche and reproductive strategies, as seen in waterfowl (Krapu and Reinecke 1992), but specific nutritional and physiological strategies that king rails use are unknown.
6. Controlled drawdowns in managed wetlands offer the advantage in experimental design of (relatively) predictable timing and drawdown of declining water levels (Fredrickson and Taylor 1982, Fredrickson and Reid 1986). How closely these controlled drawdowns mimic natural drying pattern in floodplains or long-term water regimes of prairie marsh-

es (Weller and Fredrickson 1974) needs further investigation.
7. Managers need to examine relationships of bag limits, season lengths, and season dates to magnitude of harvest and annual survival.

RECOMMENDATIONS

1. Public agencies and private organizations should protect areas where viable populations of king rails still exist. Enhancement of water delivery systems or management should be developed on public refuges to emulate natural hydrologic cycles of the region. Restoration of tidal and freshwater marshes should be a habitat management priority in the historic range of king rails. Atlantic and Gulf Coast states should set priorities and fund protection and management of key coastal and riverine wetlands where king rails exist. Major wintering areas in Louisiana, Florida, and Texas should be priorities for aquisition and management.
2. The U.S. Fish and Wildlife Service (USFWS) in association with the Mississippi and Atlantic Flyway councils (MAFC) should develop and implement population and harvest assessments of king rails. Population and harvest surveys should be conducted on public refuges where viable populations exist.
3. The USFWS and MAFC should conduct and/or facilitate funding of identified applied research.
4. Enhancement of rice or associated wetlands should be encouraged with the rice industry. Incentives should be made available for modification to cultural practices that allow conjunctive use of rice production areas and enhance king rail survival and recruitment.
5. Wetland restoration programs should encourage natural swales for king rail foraging areas.

ACKNOWLEDGMENTS

We thank N. A. Bicknese, P. R. Covington, W. R. Eddleman, M. E. Heitmeyer, and W. A. Wentz for reviewing an early draft of this manuscript.

LITERATURE CITED

ALISAUSKAS, R. T., AND C. D. ANKNEY. 1985. Nutrient reserves and the energetics of reproduction in American coot. Auk 102:133–144.

AMERICAN ORNITHOLOGISTS' UNION. 1957. Checklist of North American birds, 5th ed., Lord Baltimore Press, Baltimore, Md. 691pp.

———. 1983. Checklist of North American birds, 6th ed., Allen Press, Lawrence, Kans. 877pp.

AVISE, J. C., AND R. M. ZINK. 1988. Molecular genetic divergence between avian sibling species: king and clapper rails, long-billed and short-billed dowitchers, boat-tailed and great-tailed grackles, and tufted and black-crested titmice. Auk 105: 516–528.

BENT, A. C. 1926. Life histories of North American marsh birds. U.S. Natl. Mus. Bull. 135, 490pp.

BROWN, M., AND J. J. DINSMORE. 1986. Implications of marsh size and isolation for marsh bird management. J. Wildl. Manage. 50:392–397.

DIAMOND, J. M. 1975. The island dilemma: lessons of modern biogeographic studies for the design of natural reserves. Biol. Conserv. 7:129–146.

EDDLEMAN, W. R., F. L. KNOPF, B. MEANLEY, F. A. REID, AND R. ZEMBAL. 1988. Conservation of North American rallids. Wilson Bull. 100:458–475.

FRAYER, W. E., T. J. MONAHAN, D. C. BOWDEN, AND F. A. GRAYBILL. 1983. Status and trends of wetlands and deepwater habitats in the conterminous United States, 1950's to 1970's. Dep. Forest and Wood Sci., Colorado State Univ., Fort Collins. 32pp.

FREDRICKSON, L. H., AND F. A. REID. 1986. Wetland and riparian habitats: a nongame management overview. Pages 59–96 in J. B. Hale, L. B. Best, and R. L. Clawson, eds., Management of nongame wildlife in the Midwest: a developing art. North Central Sect., The Wildl. Soc., Chelsea, Mich.

———, AND ———. 1990. Impacts of hydrologic alteration on management of freshwater wetlands. Pages 71-90 in J. M. Sweeney, ed. Management of dynamic ecosystems, North Central Sect., The Wildl. Soc., West Lafayette, Ind.

———, AND T. S. TAYLOR. 1982. Management of seasonally flooded impoundments for wildlife. U.S. Fish and Wildl. Serv., Resour. Publ. 148. 29pp.

GOSSELINK, J. G. 1984. The ecology of delta marshes of coastal Louisiana: a community profile. U.S. Fish and Wildl. Serv., FWS/OBS–84/09. 134pp.

JOHNSON, F. A., AND F. MONTALBANO, III. 1989. Southern reservoirs and lakes. Pages 93–116 in L. M. Smith, R. L. Pederson, and R. M. Kaminski, eds., Habitat management for migrating and wintering waterfowl in North America. Texas Tech Univ. Press, Lubbock.

KRAPU, G. L., AND K. J. REINECKE. 1992. Foraging ecology and nutrition. Pages 1–29 in B. D. J. Batt, A. D. Afton, M. G. Anderson, C. D. Ankney, D. H. Johnson, J. A. Kadlec, and G. L. Krapu, eds. Ecology and management of breeding waterfowl. Univ. Minnesota Press, Minneapolis.

MAYFIELD, H. F. 1975. Suggestions for calculating nest success. Wilson Bull. 87:456–466.

MEANLEY, B. 1953. Nesting of the king rail in the Arkansas ricefields. Auk 70:262–269.

———. 1956. Food habits of the king rail in the Arkansas ricefields. Auk 73:252–258.

———. 1957. Notes on the courtship behavior of the king rail. Auk 74:433–440.

———. 1969. Natural history of the King Rail. North Am. Fauna 67. 108pp.

———. 1985. The marsh hen: a natural history of the clapper rail of the Atlantic Coast salt marsh. Tidewater Publ., Centreville, Md. 123pp.

———. 1992. King rail (Rallus elegans). In A. Poole, P. Stettenheim, and F. Gill, eds. The birds of North America, No. 3. Philadelphia Acad. Nat. Sci., and Am. Ornithol. Union, Washington, D.C. 12pp.

———, AND A. G. MEANLEY. 1958. Growth and development of the king rail. Auk 75:381–386.

———, AND D. K. WETHERBEE. 1962. Ecological notes on mixed populations of king rails and clapper rails in Delaware Bay marshes. Auk 79:453–457.

REICHHOLF, J. 1982. Der Niedergang der kleinen Rallen. Anz. orn. Ges. Bayern 21:165–174.

REID, F. A. 1989. Differential habitat use by waterbirds in a managed wetland complex. Ph.D. Thesis, Univ. Missouri, Columbia. 243pp.

———. 1993. Managing wetlands for waterbirds. Trans. North Am. Wildl. and Nat. Resour. Conf. 58:345–350.

———, J. R. KELLEY, T. S. TAYLOR, AND L. H. FREDRICKSON. 1989. Upper Mississippi Valley wetlands—Refuges and moist-soil impoundments. Pages 181–202 in L. M. Smith, R. L. Pederson, and R. M. Kaminski, eds. Habitat management for migrating and wintering waterfowl in North America. Texas Tech Univ. Press, Lubbock.

REINECKE, K. J., R. M. KAMINSKI, D. J. MOORHEAD, J. D. HODGES, AND J. R. NASSER. 1989. Mississippi Alluvial Valley. Pages 203–247 in L. M. Smith, R. L. Pederson, and R. M. Kaminski, eds. Habitat management for migrating and wintering waterfowl in North America. Texas Tech Univ. Press, Lubbock.

RIPLEY, S. D. 1977. Rails of the world: a monograph of the family Rallidae. David R. Godine, Publ., Boston, Mass. 406pp.

SMITH, L. M., R. L. PEDERSON, AND R. M. KAMINSKI, EDITORS. 1989. Habitat management for migrating and wintering waterfowl in North America. Texas Tech Univ. Press, Lubbock. 560pp.

TANNER, W. D., JR., AND G. O. HENDRICKSON. 1956. Ecology of the king rail in Clay County, Iowa. Iowa Bird Life 26:54–56.

TINER, R. W., JR. 1984. Wetlands of the United States: current status and recent trends. National Wetlands Inventory. U.S. Fish and Wildl. Serv., Washington, D.C. 59pp.

TRAUTMAN, M. B. 1940. The birds of Buckeye Lake, Ohio. Univ. Michigan, Mus. Zool. Misc. Publ. 44, 466pp.

U.S. DEPARTMENT OF AGRICULTURE. 1992. Rice situation and outlook. Commodity Econ. Div., U.S. Dep. Agric., Washington, D.C. 43pp.

U.S. FISH AND WILDLIFE SERVICE. 1987. Supplemental environmental impact statement: issuance of annual regulations permitting the sport of hunting migratory birds. Washington, D.C. 250pp.

WARNER, D. W., AND R. W. DICKERMAN. 1959. The status of Rallus elegans tenuirostris in Mexico. Condor 61:49–51.

WELLER, M. W. 1979. Birds of some Iowa wetlands in relation to concepts of faunal preservation. Proc. Iowa Acad. Sci. 86:81–88.

————, AND L. H. FREDRICKSON. 1974. Avian ecology of a managed glacial marsh. Living Bird 12: 269–291.

WENTZ, W. A., AND F. A. REID. 1992. Managing refuges for waterfowl purposes and biological diversity: can both be achieved? Trans. North Am. Wildl. and Nat. Resour. Conf. 57:581–585.

WIDMANN, O. 1907. A preliminary catalog of the birds of Missouri. Trans. Mo. Acad. Sci. 17:1–288.

Chapter 14

VIRGINIA RAIL

COURTNEY J. CONWAY,[1] Department of Natural Resources Science, 210B Woodward Hall, University of Rhode Island, Kingston, RI 02881

WILLIAM R. EDDLEMAN, Department of Natural Resources Science, 210B Woodward Hall, University of Rhode Island, Kingston, RI 02881

Abstract: One subspecies of Virginia rail (*Rallus limicola limicola*) is recognized in North America. Populations have declined over the past 10 years and declines are most evident in the central United States, where wetland loss and degradation have been severe. Virginia rails prefer warm, freshwater marshes with dense emergent vegetation interspersed with open water or mud flats. Natural wetlands with heterogeneous topography, 0–15 cm water depths, and high invertebrate abundances are selectively used by Virginia rails. Migration routes, migration chronology, and important staging areas are unknown. Adequate population and harvest surveys are lacking, but vocalization surveys could be used to effectively monitor rail population trends throughout their range. Thirty-seven states and Ontario consider Virginia rails a game species, but few hunters take rails. Hunting pressure is highest in Atlantic and Gulf Coast states. Major management needs include better knowledge of seasonal distributions and population trends, increased wetland acquisition and restoration, active manipulation of man-made wetlands to increase productivity, and establishment of national population and harvest surveys. Research priorities include better estimates of survival, nesting success, and chick mortality; identification of environmental features affecting these population parameters; and effects of existing wetland management programs on rail populations.

DESCRIPTION

Virginia rails are small (23–27 cm) reddish-colored birds with gray cheeks and a long, slightly decurved bill (Peterson 1980). Wings are rich chestnut with a 1-mm long claw on the outer digit (Bent 1926, Mousley 1940). Legs and bill are reddish, and flanks are banded black and white. Sexes are similar in plumage, but females are smaller than males (C. J. Conway, unpubl. data). There is no adequate technique for ascertaining gender of Virginia rails in the field. Adults weigh 55–124 g. Wing chords range from 95 to 117 mm.

Newly-hatched Virginia rail chicks are covered in black natal down (Gillette 1897, Billard 1948) (Fig. 1) that is replaced by juvenal plumage by mid- to late-summer when young are fully grown (Bent 1926). Juvenile Virginia rails are blackish-brown above and mottled black/gray below. Wing coverts acquire the reddish-brown adult color by 4 weeks of age and full adult plumage is attained at 14 weeks (Billard 1948). Pairs of Virginia rails make antiphonal, duetting calls known as "grunts" (Brewster 1902, Walkinshaw 1937, Irish 1974, Ripley 1977).

Only 1 subspecies of Virginia rail (*R. l. limicola*) is recognized in North America (Am. Ornithol. Union 1957; but see Dickey 1928, Dickerman 1966). Lacking better information on seasonal distributions, this species should be managed as 1 continental race.

LIFE HISTORY

Breeding Virginia rails are monogamous and territorial. As pair bonds are formed, pairs engage in allo- and autopreening, precopulatory chases, courtship displays, copulations, exchanges of calls, and vigorous defense of their territory (Audubon 1842; Ehrlich et al. 1988; Kaufmann 1988, 1989). Males perform the majority of territorial defense (Kaufmann 1989). Mated pairs perform courtship feeding (Ehrlich et al. 1988) and may defend their territory for up to 9 weeks before nesting (Kaufmann 1989). The actual courtship period is brief and can be identified by the short duration of the "tick-it" or "kid-ick" calls in spring (Bent 1926, Glahn 1974, Irish 1974). However, territory defense may be rare within several weeks after territory establishment (Johnson and Dinsmore 1985). Copula-

[1] Present address: Montana Cooperative Wildlife Research Unit, University of Montana, Missoula, MT 59812.

Fig. 1. Virginia rail chicks are covered in black natal down (Photo by C. J. Conway).

tions have been observed as long as 20 days prior to laying of the first egg.

Females select the nest site and nest-building begins with laying of the first egg (Short 1890, Kaufmann 1989), or shortly prior to egg laying (Shaw 1887), or more than a week prior to egg laying (Mousley 1940). Both sexes construct the nest and nests are completed within a week (Pospichal and Marshall 1954, Kaufmann 1989). In the northeastern United States, nest construction normally begins in early May (Wood 1937, Billard 1948). Both sexes can breed in their first year, and pairs probably have 2 broods (Pospichal and Marshall 1954, Ehrlich et al. 1988).

The peak of egg laying occurs in mid-May in Iowa (Johnson and Dinsmore 1986). Nesting females lay 1 egg/day (Mousley 1940, Pospichal and Marshall 1954), usually early in the day, and clutch size averages 8.5 eggs (range 4–13, $n = 115$) (Walkinshaw 1937, Ripley 1977, Kaufmann 1989). Egg laying has been recorded as early as 17 April in New York (Orman and Swift 1987). Peak incubation is late-May through mid-June (Bent 1926). Incubation usually begins 1 day (range 0–5 days) before laying of the last egg (Bent 1926, Walkinshaw 1937, Mousley 1940) and is shared by both sexes, with changeovers occurring every 1.5–2 hours.

Incubation length for Virginia rails is normally 19 days (range 18–20 days) (Walkinshaw 1937, Wood 1937, Mousley 1940, Billard 1948,

Pospichal and Marshall 1954, Ripley 1977). Eggs are pipped about 48 hours before they hatch, and newly hatched young average 6.7 g (Walkinshaw 1937). Both sexes engage in nest defense and continue to defend their young after they leave the nest, but the female is usually more aggressive (Weber 1909, McLean 1916, Burtch 1917, Mousley 1940, Pospichal and Marshall 1954, Wiens 1966, Ripley 1977). Hatching has been described as synchronous, or nearly so (within 48 hr) (McLean 1916; Burtch 1917; Bent 1926; Walkinshaw 1937; Mousley 1940; but see Pospichal and Marshall 1954; Ehrlich et al. 1988). Precocial rail chicks leave the nest within 3 days after hatching (Gillette 1897; McLean 1916; Bent 1926; Kaufmann 1987, 1989), and can feed on their own by day 7 (Kaufmann 1987, 1989). Both male and female parents feed and brood the chicks, often dividing up large broods (Kaufmann 1987, 1989). Young rails grow rapidly during their first 5 weeks: metatarsi and toes reach adult size by their third week (Kaufmann 1987).

Chicks are brooded by their parents as a family group within the breeding territory for 3–4 weeks (Kaufmann 1989), after which adults shift their home range out of their territory as young become independent (Johnson and Dinsmore 1985, Kaufmann 1987). Chicks are preened frequently by brooding parents and are fed for >23 days. The pair bond breaks down before dispersal, shortly after young fledge (Johnson and Dinsmore 1985). Adults may return to a nest site the following year if habitat conditions are stable (Mousley 1931, Pospichal and Marshall 1954).

Estimates of nest success are few: 50% (4/8 nests) in Minnesota (Pospichal and Marshall 1954), 75% (18/24 nests) in Connecticut (Billard 1948), 78% (21/27 nests) in Iowa (Tanner and Hendrickson 1954), and 53% ($n = 81$ nests) throughout North America (Conway et al. 1994). Documented nest predators include snakes, weasels (*Mustela erminea* and *M. frenata*), raccoon (*Procyon lotor*), hawks, blackbirds, and wrens (Gillette 1897, Allen 1934, Walkinshaw 1937, Tanner and Hendrickson 1954). Likely nest predators include muskrat (*Ondatra zibethica*), skunk (*Mephitis* spp.), crows, terns, and yellow-billed cuckoo (*Coccyzus americanus*) (Randall 1946, Billard 1948, Pospichal and Marshall 1954, Tanner and Hendrickson 1954, Andrews 1973, Tacha 1975). Pike (*Esox* spp.), bass (*Micropterus* spp.), sandhill cranes (*Grus canadensis*), and frogs prey on young chicks (Forbush 1925, Cramer 1932, Ehrlich et al. 1988), and mink (*Mustela vison*) (Audubon 1842, Billard 1948, Baird 1974, Tacha 1975), coyote (*Canis latrans*), feral house cats (Pospichal and Marshall 1954, Robbins 1967), great egret (*Egretta alba*) (Campbell and Wolf 1977), northern harrier (*Circus cyaneus*) (Audubon 1842), and owls (C. J. Conway, unpubl. data) prey on adult and juvenile rails.

Many nests are lost to flooding in some areas (Walkinshaw 1937, Tanner and Hendrickson 1954, Post and Enders 1970). Changing water levels adversely affect rails by increasing nest loss, disrupting breeding activities, increasing chick mortality, restructuring location of optimal foraging sites, and increasing rail movements (Baird 1974, Tacha 1975, Griese et al. 1980).

Chick mortality is probably high prior to fledging; most broods are small (range 2–5) relative to published estimates of clutch size (Hunt 1908, Lowther 1961, Wiens 1966, Irish 1974). The daily survival rate of 36 radio-marked birds was 0.998 ± 0.001 and the annual survival rate was 0.526 ± 0.195 in Arizona for all age/sex classes and seasons combined (Conway et al. 1994). Mortality was highest in winter.

Virginia rails primarily forage at dawn and dusk (Gillette 1897) by probing the mud and shallow water with their long bill (Bent 1926). Diet includes slugs, snails, small fish, insect larvae, aquatic invertebrates, caterpillars, beetles, flies, earthworms, amphipods (*Gammarus* spp.), crayfish, frogs, and small snakes (Audubon 1842, Shaw 1887, Cahn 1915, Bent 1926, Richter 1948, Pospichal and Marshall 1954, Brocke 1958). Virginia rails also eat a variety of aquatic plants and seeds of emergent plants (Fassett 1940, Pospichal and Marshall 1954, Irish 1974), but insects comprise nearly 62% of their diet (Horak 1970). Plant material is more commonly consumed in fall and winter compared to spring and summer (Martin et al. 1951). Virginia rails undergo simultaneous wing and tail molt prior to fall migration, usually during July–August (Andrews 1973).

HABITAT

Virginia rails inhabit stands of robust emergent vegetation within freshwater and brackish marshes and wetlands, and occasionally coastal salt marshes (Horak 1964, Weller and Spatcher 1965, Post and Enders 1970, Johnson 1984, Sayre

and Rundle 1984, Eddleman et al. 1988, Manci and Rusch 1988, Gibbs et al. 1991). Virginia rails prefer freshwater marshes (Ripley 1977) and are most common in moist-soil emergent wetlands and along seasonal or semipermanent ponds and lakes (Fredrickson and Reid 1986) (Fig. 2). Virginia rails may feed in adjacent upland habitats in some areas (Horak 1970).

Shallow water, emergent cover, and substrate with high invertebrate abundance are the most important features of Virginia rail habitat (Berger 1951, Andrews 1973, Baird 1974, Glahn 1974, Tacha 1975, Griese et al. 1980, Rundle and Fredrickson 1981, Sayre and Rundle 1984, Fredrickson and Reid 1986, Gibbs et al. 1991). In Maine, wetlands used by Virginia rails have greater abundance of emergent vegetation compared to unused wetlands (Gibbs et al. 1991). In Iowa and Arizona, Virginia rails use relatively homogeneous stands of emergent vegetation compared to other rails (Johnson 1984, Conway 1990). In other areas, Virginia rails seem to prefer heterogeneous stands with more vegetative edge (Allen 1934, Pospichal and Marshall 1954, Glahn 1974, Sayre and Rundle 1984).

Virginia rails need standing water, moist-soil, or mud flats for foraging and avoid dry stands of emergents (Johnson 1984, Fredrickson and Reid 1986, Manci and Rusch 1988, Gibbs et al. 1991). Virginia rails will use deep-water habitats, but prefer shallow and intermediate water depths (0–15 cm) with muddy, unstable substrates for foraging (Billard 1948, Pospichal and Marshall 1954, Irish 1974, Tacha 1975, Griese et al. 1980, Rundle and Fredrickson 1981, Sayre and Rundle 1984, Johnson and Dinsmore 1986). Virginia rails in Kansas were most frequently observed in areas with 5–15 cm of standing water (Baird 1974), and were most frequently heard calling from areas with 0–5 cm of water (Tacha 1975). If adequate upright emergent cover exists, Virginia rails will occupy deeper water habitats where there is substantial collapsed or floating vegetation that give the birds a substrate upon which to walk and forage (Sayre and Rundle 1984, Johnson and Dinsmore 1985).

A moderate cover : water ratio within wetlands is important for Virginia rails; they are often absent from wetlands lacking adequate shallow water pools or mud flats. An equal mixture of emergent vegetation and flooded openings increases macroinvertebrate production (Voigts 1976, Kaminski 1979, Nelson and Kadlec 1984), and some species may use intersper-

Fig. 2.   Virginia rails prefer shallow, freshwater marshes with muddy substrates and 40–70% emergent vegetation interspersed with open water or mudflats (Photo by C. J. Conway).

sion as a proximate cue in selecting habitats rich in macroinvertebrates (Kaminski and Prince 1981, Reid 1985). Management for rails should target 40–70% (optimally 60%) upright emergent vegetation interspersed with open water, mud flats, and/or matted vegetation (Fredrickson and Reid 1986). Nests of Virginia rails were repeatedly found in semipermanent wetlands with 45–65% emergent cover in North Dakota, but were absent from an otherwise similar wetland with 95% emergent cover (Krapu and Green 1978). Additionally, Virginia rails were abundant in a marsh with 25% open water in Iowa (Horak 1970). Management of wetlands for migrating rails should provide a diversity of plant species with annuals predominating (Fredrickson and Reid 1986).

Virginia rails avoid emergent stands with high stem densities or large amounts of residual vegetation (Johnson 1984, Conway 1990). These features are common in older marshes and impede rail movement. Vegetation height is not considered important for optimal Virginia rail habitat as long as there is adequate overhead cover. Virginia rails will move into regrowing marshes as soon as there is adequate cover.

Wetland size may be an important component of optimal Virginia rail habitat (Gibbs et al. 1991; but see Brown and Dinsmore 1986). Virginia rails in Maine used large wetlands more commonly and wetland use correlated with shoreline length, but area of emergent vegetation within a wetland was more important (Gibbs et al. 1991). Within a wetland complex, Virginia rails prefer littoral sites (Weller and Spatcher 1965, Zimmerman 1977, Johnson and Dinsmore 1986, Swift 1989) and areas of relatively high pH and conductivity (Gibbs et al. 1991).

In Maine, Virginia rails are uncommon in glacial wetlands (Gibbs et al. 1991), preferring beaver- or human-created wetlands with fertile soil, heterogeneous topography, and more understory herbs. Moist-soil management in manmade impoundments can be effective in attracting Virginia rails when it results in diverse habitat conditions with shallow water and a mix of open water and mud flats interspersed within dense vegetation. These conditions support great

Fig. 3. The highest density of wintering Virginia rails is in the lower Colorado River Valley where extensive backwaters and oxbows provide optimal habitat (Photo by J. C. Rorabaugh).

diversity and abundance of invertebrates available for potential prey and provide adequate cover (Rundle and Fredrickson 1981, Fredrickson and Reid 1986).

During migration, Virginia rails use flooded annual grasses or forbs with shallow water (<10 cm) for optimal foraging (Sayre and Rundle 1984, Fredrickson and Reid 1986). Migrating rails require a variety of water depths, robust vegetative cover, and short-stemmed seed-producing plants (Andrews 1973, Rundle and Fredrickson 1981). Winter habitat includes both freshwater and salt marshes (Zimmerman 1977) (Fig. 3).

Nest Site Selection

Virginia rails nest in robust emergent vegetation (e.g., *Typha*, *Scirpus*). Rails will nest within a wide variety of emergents (reviewed by Walkinshaw 1937 and Horak 1964), so the dominant plant species in a marsh is not considered a good indication of habitat suitability for rails. Virginia rails use the most abundant emergent plants at the nest site for nest construction (Walkinshaw 1937, Billard 1948, Horak 1964). Nests are well-concealed and are built touching, slightly submerged, or a short distance (<15 cm) above the water surface.

Virginia rails nest at sites with a wide variety of water depths ranging from 0 to 71 cm (Walkinshaw 1937, Billard 1948, Tanner 1953, Pospichal and Marshall 1954, Andrews 1973, Baird 1974, Griese et al. 1980, Johnson 1984). Nests are most often placed near a border between vegetative types (Allen 1934), but not near open water (Andrews 1973; but see Pospichal and Marshall 1954). Virginia rails build "dummy" or brood nests near the active nest (Billard 1948, Pospichal and Marshall 1954, Kaufmann 1989). These dummy nests may number as many as 5/active nest and are probably used for feeding, brooding, resting, or as alternates in case of destruction or predation (Billard 1948, Pospichal and Marshall 1954, Kaufmann 1989).

Wetland Management

There have been few, if any, management activities implemented specifically for rails, but rails have responded well to some waterfowl management programs (Rundle and Fredrickson 1981). Management activities that promote growth of diverse emergent vegetation will benefit Virginia rails and other waterbirds (Johnson 1984, Gibbs et al. 1991). Activities that increase wetland cover of emergent perennial vegetation, while retaining 30–60% of the wetland in open water or mud flats, will provide both optimal nesting and foraging habitat for Virginia rails.

Manipulation of water levels in man-made wetlands can increase invertebrate productivity for rails and other wildlife. Shallow flooding of areas with heterogeneous topography, or partial drawdowns of more homogeneous man-made wetlands, concentrates invertebrate prey (Fredrickson and Reid 1986, Eddleman et al. 1988), resulting in ideal foraging conditions for breeding rails. Wetland productivity is determined in part by daily, seasonal, and annual hydrologic fluxes (Batema et al. 1985, Reid 1985, Fredrickson and Reid 1986), and manipulations are often essential where hydrology has been modified or habitats degraded (Fredrickson and Reid 1986).

Shallow flooding (<15 cm) of grasses and forbs in spring and again in late summer will provide optimal rail habitat during spring and fall migration (Griese 1977, Rundle and Fredrickson 1981, Johnson 1984, Eddleman et al. 1988). Also, spring flooding in emergent marshes allows increased colonization by macroinvertebrate communities (Nelson and Kadlec 1984). Additionally, shallow flooding of wetland complexes in early fall has been suggested for managing migrant rails in Missouri (Fredrickson and Reid 1986). Fall flooding will stimulate growth and productivity of many invertebrate species (Reid 1985). However, flooding areas too deeply will reduce habitat quality for Virginia rails, as well as other rallids (Fredrickson and Reid 1986, Eddleman et al. 1988).

Drawdowns promote high productivity, diversity, and germination rates in man-made wetlands, but subsequent control of water depth is essential in maintaining plant species diversity (Weller and Fredrickson 1974, Weller 1981, Fredrickson and Reid 1986). Shallow flooding following drawdowns encourages growth of dense emergents and submergents. Partial drawdown of impoundments in early spring will benefit nesting and migrating rails by stimulating emergent growth, while still restricting weed succession (Andrews 1973, Johnson 1984, Fredrickson and Reid 1986). Late summer draw-downs produce seeds and other foods attractive to migrant rails (Rundle and Fredrickson 1981, Weller 1981). Both summer and winter drawdowns can be used to reduce high muskrat populations where excessive damage to marshes has occurred (Weller 1981). Fall or winter drawdowns maintained through August can also provide attractive fall habitat for migrating rails (Johnson 1984). However, overly aggressive drawdown/flooding strategies can increase turbidity and reduce seed stocks, thereby preventing establishment of persistent emergents and increasing open water areas (Weller et al. 1991) which reduce benefits to rails. Whatever the timing of a drawdown, reflooding should be gradual to avoid scouring, turbidity, and plant mortality (Weller 1981).

Achieving stable water levels and reduced turbidity are essential steps in gaining a diversity of emergent plants (Weller et al. 1991) and attracting a variety of rail species. Managers should encourage a diversity of emergent vegetation and seed-producing annuals well interspersed with aquatic bed vegetation (Cowardin et al. 1979) and open water. Management activities that eliminate ground topographic diversity (e.g., grading) reduce vegetation/water interfaces preferred by foraging rails (Sayre and Rundle 1984, Eddleman et al. 1988).

DISTRIBUTION AND ABUNDANCE

The breeding range of Virginia rails extends from southern British Columbia, northern Alberta (Lowther 1961), northern Saskatchewan, central Manitoba, southern Ontario, southern Quebec, Nova Scotia, and New Brunswick south through California, southern Arizona, northern New Mexico, Oklahoma, northern Texas, northern Missouri, Illinois, Indiana, and Ohio, across to southern Virginia, extending south along the coast to North Carolina (Fig. 4), and rather widespread throughout Mexico (Goldman 1908, Bent 1926, Billard 1948, Robbins 1949, Am. Ornithol. Union 1957, Dickerman 1966, Binford 1972, Natl. Geogr. Soc. 1987). Virginia rails have been reported at elevations up to 2,730 m (Goldman 1908, Griese et al. 1980), but generally breed in marshlands where spring air temperatures are warmer when compared to sora (*Porzana carolina*) breeding marshes (Griese et al. 1980).

The winter range extends from southern British Columbia south through California, across southern Nevada, northern Arizona, New Mex-

Fig. 4. Breeding and wintering ranges of Virginia rails in North America.

ico, Colorado (Griese et al. 1980), Wyoming, Nebraska, Oklahoma, and northern and southern Texas, and the lower Mississippi Valley states (Fig. 4). The Great Lakes harbor a limited wintering population. On the East Coast, Virginia rails winter from Massachusetts to southern Florida (Billard 1948, Natl. Geogr. Soc. 1987, Root 1988). Most wintering rails occur along the East, West, and Gulf coasts, but the highest density is in the lower Colorado River Valley (Root 1988). The winter range also extends south through Mexico to central Guatemala (Bent 1926, Am. Ornithol. Union 1957, Natl. Geogr. Soc. 1987).

Within their breeding (and probably winter) range, Virginia rails have restricted distributions, but are relatively abundant at sites where habitat conditions are acceptable (Gibbs et al. 1991). Wintering distributions follow major

drainage systems, water storage impoundments, irrigation districts, wet meadows, and irrigated hayfields. Environmental factors affecting winter distribution include freshwater marshes and warm (> -7 C) temperatures (Root 1988).

Home range size varies seasonally (Conway 1990) and varies with habitat quality. Estimates of average home range size are limited: 0.18 ha during the breeding season in Iowa (Johnson and Dinsmore 1985), 1.64 ± 1.48 ha during the breeding season in Arizona (Conway 1990), and 2.41 ± 1.84 ha during winter in Arizona (Conway 1990).

Information on migration routes and chronology, and important staging areas is lacking. Birds return to their breeding grounds during early April in Colorado (Glahn 1974, Griese et al. 1980), during the 3rd week of April in Kansas (Baird 1974), and during the 3rd week of April through the 1st week of May in Connecticut, Iowa, Michigan, Minnesota, Ohio, and Wisconsin (Walkinshaw 1937, Billard 1948, Andrews 1973, Ripley 1977, Manci and Rusch 1988, Kaufmann 1989). Virginia rails have returned to breeding grounds in Kansas, New York, and Ohio as early as 10–17 March (Crandall 1920, Bent 1926, Tacha 1975). Migrating birds fly low during the night and males usually arrive 7–10 days before females (Audubon 1842).

Returning migrants seldom vocalize during the first 1–3 weeks after arrival (Walkinshaw 1937, Pospichal and Marshall 1954, Tanner and Hendrickson 1954, Andrews 1973, Baird 1974, Glahn 1974, Kaufmann 1989; but see Griese et al. 1980). Peaks in vocalization frequency occur during the last week in April through the 2nd week in May in Colorado and Kansas (Glahn 1974, Griese et al. 1980, Zimmerman 1984), the 3rd week of May in Wisconsin and Maine (Manci and Rusch 1988, Gibbs and Melvin 1993), throughout May in Ohio and Iowa (Andrews 1973, Johnson and Dinsmore 1986), late-April to mid-June in Kansas (Tacha 1975), and mid-April in Arizona (C. J. Conway, unpubl. data). A second peak in vocalization frequency has been reported in several studies and may coincide with hatching (Kaufmann 1971, Glahn 1974, Gibbs and Melvin 1993). Vocalization frequency is low after July (Brewster 1902, Glahn 1974, Irish 1974). Peaks in Virginia rail vocalizations vary among years (Tacha 1975).

Density of breeding rails depends on habitat quality, but Virginia rails tend to occur at lower densities compared to soras (Pospichal and Marshall 1954). Densities vary from 0.1–8.9 pairs/ha (Tanner and Hendrickson 1954, Post and Enders 1970, Glahn 1974, Tacha 1975, Griese et al. 1980, Johnson 1984, Manci and Rusch 1988), but the highest density of Virginia rails documented was 25 breeding pairs/ha in Michigan (Berger 1951). Distance between Virginia rail nests averaged 46 m in Minnesota (Pospichal and Marshall 1954). Availability of adequate food and nesting cover probably determines territory size and breeding density.

Fall migration is not obvious and extremely variable (Pospichal and Marshall 1954, Griese et al. 1980), and departure dates vary with latitude and altitude. Birds concentrate on larger marshes prior to fall migration (Pospichal and Marshall 1954). In Kansas, rails are present through October, although vocalizations end in late September (Baird 1974). Virginia rails in Ohio depart by the first week in October, but have been recorded as late as 18 October (Andrews 1973). Birds in Michigan leave in late September or early October and have been recorded as late as 18 October (Walkinshaw 1937). Peak migration in Colorado occurs between the 2nd week in August and the 3rd week in September (Griese et al. 1980). Vocalizations are rare and difficult to evoke in August and September, and cannot be used to assess migration chronology.

Current Survey Techniques

Visual surveys are inadequate because Virginia rails are difficult to flush (Walkinshaw 1937) and visible only in open habitats. Because rails are so secretive, surveys have primarily used broadcast recordings of vocalizations to elicit detections (Johnson et al. 1981) and provide indices of abundance (Baird 1974, Glahn 1974, Tacha 1975, Griese et al. 1980, Marion et al. 1981, Tyser 1982, Zimmerman 1984, Johnson and Dinsmore 1986, Manci and Rusch 1988). Playback recordings increase response rates of Virginia rails (Baird 1974, Glahn 1974, Johnson and Dinsmore 1986, Manci and Rusch 1988, Gibbs and Melvin 1993), but response rate may still vary (22–72%) (Glahn 1974). Response rate is influenced by breeding density (Kaufmann 1971, Glahn 1974), season, and time of day (Gibbs and Melvin 1993), but weekly counts appear adequate to provide crude estimates of rail densities (Baird 1974, Manci and Rusch 1988). Surveys should be conducted between 1 hour before and 3 hours after sunrise and between 3 hours before and 1 hour after sunset (Glahn 1974, Tacha 1975). Evening surveys are equally or more effective than morning surveys (Tacha 1975, Johnson and Dinsmore 1986). Most importantly, surveys should be conducted during the period of peak vocalizations (prior to egg-laying) that varies annually and latitudinally. The peak calling season is usually the 2nd to 4th week of April in southern parts of the breeding range, and the 2nd to 4th week of May near the northern extent of the breeding range. However, several surveys should be conducted throughout the spring and early summer to avoid missing the peak season. Calling activity also is affected by weather (Tacha 1975, Gibbs and Melvin 1993), and surveys should not be conducted with wind >8 km/hour or with temperature/overcast extremes. Useful descriptions of Virginia rail calls have been provided by

Allen (1934), Walkinshaw (1937), and Callin (1968).

A 1992 mail survey of all states and Canadian provinces (W. R. Eddleman, unpubl. data) found that only 4 states (Virginia, New Jersey, Ohio, and California), and no provinces have standardized rail population surveys.

Population Status and Trends

Virginia rail populations have declined 22% ($P < 0.05$, $n = 93$) throughout North America over the past 10 years based on Breeding Bird Surveys (Conway et al. 1994). Trend data are not adequate to address specific states or provinces, but declines were greatest in the central United States. Only 18 states/provinces were able to comment on 15-year Virginia rail population trends within their boundaries (W. R. Eddleman, unpubl. data). Of these, Pennsylvania, Kansas, Connecticut, Kentucky, Alabama, New York, Rhode Island, Georgia, West Virginia, and New Brunswick reported that population size had stayed the same, while Alberta, Ohio, Indiana, Michigan, Washington, Wyoming, and Oregon reported that populations were decreasing, and Iowa reported populations were increasing. Virginia, Indiana, and Ohio classify Virginia rails as a "species of special interest" because of lack of adequate information.

HARVEST

There are no national surveys to estimate numbers of hunters or harvested Virginia rails in North America. Hunting pressure on Virginia rails has probably decreased since the early part of this century (Billard 1948), but surveys of waterfowl hunters buying duck stamps indicate that numbers of hunters and harvest of rails other than soras increased from 1964 through 1975 (Martin 1979, U.S. Fish and Wildl. Serv. 1988) and then decreased from 1975 through 1986 (Table 1). Annual rail harvest varied greatly during 1964–86 (Table 1), averaging 13,374 hunters and 100,983 rails other than soras taken annually (U.S. Fish and Wildl. Serv. 1988). However, most harvested rails were probably clapper rails (*Rallus longirostris*) in coastal states. Because the U.S. Fish and Wildlife Service survey included only waterfowl hunters, it is incomplete, but the only survey available. Both soras and clapper rails are more popular with hunters than are Virginia rails. Only 0.9% of waterfowl hunters from 3 eastern flyways har-

Table 1. Hunting activity and harvest of rails other than soras by waterfowl hunters in the United States, 1964–86.[a]

Year	Hunters (*n*)	Harvest
1964	8,000	41,300
1965	5,800	24,100
1966	6,700	50,600
1967	10,800	94,300
1968	10,400	67,400
1969	19,900	130,000
1970	21,400	175,200
1971	14,900	118,300
1972	19,900	147,100
1973	18,000	148,100
1974	16,400	108,300
1975	18,900	160,300
1976	19,800	165,600
1977	15,400	95,400
1978	15,800	97,400
1979	13,300	98,800
1980	12,500	99,000
1981	12,200	130,400
1982	10,000	69,600
1983	9,400	63,300
1984	10,900	85,900
1985	9,100	73,100
1986	8,100	79,100
Mean 1964–88	13,374	100,983

[a] From U.S. Fish and Wildlife Service (1988:Table 26).

vested rails other than soras during 1964–75. The total number of rails harvested increased significantly in the Atlantic Flyway, and the number of waterfowl hunters harvesting rails also increased significantly in the Atlantic and Mississippi flyways during 1964–75 (Martin 1979).

Thirty-seven states and Ontario consider the Virginia rail a game species (W. R. Eddleman, unpubl. data). Vermont, New Hampshire, South Dakota, North Dakota, Utah, Nevada, Montana, Arizona, California, Idaho, Washington, Oregon, Alaska, Saskatchewan, Alberta, Manitoba, Nova Scotia, Quebec, and New Brunswick do not consider the Virginia rail a game species. Virginia rails are hunted by a limited number of sportsmen. Hunting pressure is highest on their wintering grounds along the south Atlantic and Gulf coasts (Horak 1964, Andrews 1973). Virginia rails are also hunted more intensively in Connecticut, New Jersey, Delaware, and Maryland. Virginia rail hunting in midwestern states is minimal and by only a few individuals (Andrews 1973). Of the 38 states/provinces that allow hunting of rails, only 11 (Virginia, Nebraska, Kentucky, Missouri, Colorado, Minnesota, Ohio, Maryland, Wyoming, New Mexico, and Texas) have harvest surveys.

In all but 1 state, the rail hunting season is in the fall, and in most states (22/35), seasons are from 1 or 2 September through 4–9 November. Daily bag and possession limits are set at 25 birds in most (30/35) states. Nebraska and Ontario have a daily bag limit of 10 and a possession limit of 20 birds. New Mexico has bag and possession limits of 10 birds, Alabama has bag and possession limits of 15 birds, and Iowa has a bag limit of 12 and a possession limit of 24 birds. Bag limits have stayed the same for the past 15 years in 36/39 state/provinces. Bag limits in New Mexico have decreased, and Vermont and Alberta have closed their rail hunting seasons. Additional harvest opportunities exist in 14 states and provinces, while no additional opportunities are thought to exist in 17 other states and provinces (W. R. Eddleman, unpubl. data).

Effects of harvest on Virginia rail populations are not known, but annual harvest is probably within sustainable levels, at least on a national scale (Eddleman et al. 1988, U.S. Fish and Wildl. Serv. 1988). Of 1,688 Virginia rails banded prior to 1950, none was reported harvested by hunters (U.S. Fish and Wildl. Serv. 1988). Despite liberal bag limits, seasonal hunter success averaged only 7.5 rails (other than soras) per active hunter during 1964–84 (U.S. Fish and Wildl. Serv. 1988). None of 37 agencies responding to a United States and Canadian rail harvest survey was able to estimate the number of rail hunters in their state/province, and only Kentucky was able to provide a minimum number of birds (1,000) harvested annually. Five states and provinces indicated a need for decreased season lengths or bag limits, while 25 states/provinces reported no need for such changes (W. R. Eddleman, unpubl. data).

MANAGEMENT NEEDS

State and provincial managers were asked to rank their needs based on information necessary for more effective management of rails (W. R. Eddleman, unpubl. data). Needs identified were:

1. better data on abundance, distribution, population trends, and other population parameters,
2. better data on habitat needs,
3. data on effects of existing habitat management programs,
4. improved harvest surveys,

5. evaluation of census techniques,
6. basic life history information,
7. public education, and
8. improved sex/age criteria.

Habitat Management

Habitat loss, primarily draining of inland freshwater wetlands for agricultural purposes, is the greatest threat to Virginia rail populations. Habitat management programs should favor acquisition and restoration of natural wetland areas that have been degraded. Management of man-made or severely degraded natural wetlands should strive to maintain or emulate natural water fluctuations of the region.

Marshes should be managed where build-up of residual vegetation is evident. Such marshes should be burned, disked and flooded, mowed, or plowed to remove residual vegetation that impedes rail movement (Rundle and Fredrickson 1981, Johnson 1984, Fredrickson and Reid 1986, Conway et al. 1993). Rail use can be encouraged by maintaining marshes in early successional stages and promoting moderate cover : water interspersions of wetland types 3–4 (Stewart and Kantrud 1971). Moderate cover : water ratios are also preferred by dabbling ducks (Kaminski and Prince 1981, Murkin et al. 1982). In general, avian productivity and species diversity are highest when cover-to-water ratios are 50–70% (Weller and Spatcher 1965, Weller and Fredrickson 1974). Disking followed by shallow flooding in man-made wetlands reduces woody vegetation and stimulates growth of robust annuals used by migrating rails (Rundle and Fredrickson 1981, Fredrickson and Reid 1986). Because rails use a variety of water depths and depth is affected by soils, hydrology, rainfall, and evaporation, there is no single optimal initial flooding depth. Rather, the management goal should be water interspersion and habitat heterogeneity, incorporating a large range (0–40 cm) of water depths (Rundle and Fredrickson 1981).

It is important to maintain or create diverse wetland complexes. Rails have different habitat requirements during different seasons and life stages (Conway 1990, Conway et al. 1993), and effective management must satisfy all habitat needs of a species (Fredrickson and Reid 1986, Conway et al. 1993). Therefore, a mosaic of wetland types, conditions, and compositions is encouraged for management and conservation of a wide-array of species, including rails.

Although 37 states and provinces consider Virginia rails a game species, few ($n = 10$) have habitat management programs for rails (W. R. Eddleman, unpubl. data). Many states/provinces ($n = 31$) address rail management in existing management plans for other species, but knowledge of the effects of existing management activities on rails is limited. Managers need to consider rails in wetland management plans, and to examine the effects of existing programs on rail productivity and survival.

Population Management

Survey techniques for all rails need to be standardized, so that relative densities can be compared among studies and annual trends can be discerned. All states should participate in statewide rail surveys of major wetland habitats. These surveys would require relatively little time and results would provide more accurate information on rail distribution, abundance, densities, and annual trends in North America. Surveys should:

1. include samples of all available marsh habitats and estimate total area of marsh including classification of vegetative cover when possible,
2. playback recordings of paired duets should be broadcast for 5 minutes,
3. count stations should be placed 60 m apart, using tapes broadcast at ≥ 80 db amplitude, (Virginia rails will respond up to 200 m away, but 90% of responding rails were within 60–75 m of the speaker [Glahn 1974, Gibbs and Melvin 1993]), and
4. surveys of important wetlands should be repeated 3 times to ensure detection of rails (Glahn 1974, Gibbs and Melvin 1993).

Pollution and pesticide accumulation in wetlands is a great hazard to Virginia rails (Odom 1975, Eddleman et al. 1988). Rails are especially susceptible to bioaccumulation because they feed upon invertebrates within the substrate. Pesticides can also reduce the invertebrate prey base available to rails (Eddleman et al. 1988).

Hunting of migratory game birds is a socioeconomically important activity in the United States (Tautin et al. 1989) and accurate surveys are needed to regulate harvest of sensitive populations. The lack of nationwide data on hunters and harvest pressure on non-waterfowl species places significant limitations on management of rails. The National Migratory Bird Harvest In-

formation Program should provide more accurate estimates of Virginia rail harvest in the United States.

Better information is needed on seasonal distributions of Virginia rails (Odom 1977, Zimmerman 1977, Johnson and Dinsmore 1986). Without adequate knowledge of identifiable Virginia rail populations, effective management will remain limited.

RESEARCH NEEDS

Basic information on biology and habitat needs is limited for Virginia rails, and severely restricts ability to properly manage rail populations (Tacha 1975, Johnson and Dinsmore 1986). Virginia rails have been studied infrequently because of their limited economic importance and the difficulty in observing individuals within the dense vegetation they inhabit (Billard 1948, Horak 1964).

Priorities for research are:

1. estimate adult and brood survival, nesting success, site fidelity, and recruitment,
2. examine environmental factors affecting survival, nest success, site fidelity, and recruitment,
3. examine effects of common wetland management programs on Virginia rails,
4. evaluate effectiveness of vocalization surveys for estimating population density or indexing population trends, and
5. develop effective techniques for ascertaining gender of Virginia rails in the field.

RECOMMENDATIONS

1. Relevant private, state, provincial, and federal agencies should collaborate to acquire and protect important natural wetlands, especially in the central United States. Although large wetland complexes should be given priority, even small wetlands are valuable to Virginia rails.
2. The U.S. Fish and Wildlife Service (USFWS) should establish a national population survey of rails in cooperation with state wildlife agencies. This could be accomplished by an annual spring vocalization survey for rails within major wetland areas.
3. The USFWS should insure the National Migratory Bird Harvest Information Program provides estimates of harvest of Virginia rails, so that managers and research biologists can

make informed decisions when setting harvest policy.

4. The USFWS, Canadian Wildlife Service, and state wildlife agencies should promote funding of, or conduct, the research identified.

5. The National Wildlife Refuge System should incorporate rail management into their wetland management plans, and identify refuges that will make rail management a stated priority. One of the refuges on the lower Colorado River should be managed for rails because of the importance of this wetland complex to Virginia rails, Yuma clapper rails (*Rallus longirostris yumanensis*), soras, and black rails (*Laterallus jamaicensis*).

ACKNOWLEDGMENTS

We thank M. E. Salerno for help with figure preparation. S. M. Melvin and J. P. Gibbs commented on early drafts of the manuscript. This is contribution #2871 of the College of Resource Development, University of Rhode Island with support from the Rhode Island Agricultural Experiment Station.

LITERATURE CITED

ALLEN, A. A. 1934. The Virginia rail and the sora. Bird-Lore 36:196–204.

AMERICAN ORNITHOLOGISTS' UNION. 1957. Checklist of North American birds. Lord Baltimore Press, Baltimore, Md. 691pp.

ANDREWS, D. A. 1973. Habitat utilization by soras, Virginia rails and king rails near southwestern Lake Erie. M.S. Thesis, Ohio State Univ., Columbus. 112pp.

AUDUBON, J. J. 1842. The birds of America, Vol. 5. J. J. Audubon, New York, N.Y. 346pp.

BAIRD, K. E. 1974. Field study of the king, sora and Virginia rails at Cheyenne Bottoms in west-central Kansas. M.S. Thesis, Fort Hays Kansas State Univ., Fort Hays. 38pp.

BATEMA, D. L., G. S. HENDERSON, AND L. H. FREDRICKSON. 1985. Wetland invertebrate distribution in bottomland hardwoods as influenced by forest type and flooding regimes. Pages 196–202 *in* J. O. Dawson and K. A. Majerus, eds. Proc. 5th Central Hardwood Forest Conf., Dep. Forestry, Univ. Illinois, Champaign-Urbana.

BENT, A. C. 1926. Life histories of North American marsh birds. U.S. Natl. Mus. Bull. 135. 392pp.

BERGER, A. J. 1951. Nesting density of Virginia and sora rails in Michigan. Condor 53:202.

BILLARD, R. S. 1948. An ecological study of the Virginia rail and the sora in some Connecticut swamps, 1947. M.S. Thesis, Iowa State Univ., Ames. 84pp.

BINFORD, L. C. 1972. Virginia rail and Cape May warbler in Chiapas, Mexico. Condor 75:350–351.

BREWSTER, W. 1902. Voices of a New England marsh. Bird-Lore 4:43–56.

BROCKE, R. H. 1958. A Virginia rail defies a record winter. Jack-Pine Warbler 36:100.

BROWN, M., AND J. J. DINSMORE. 1986. Implications of marsh size and isolation for marsh bird management. J. Wildl. Manage. 50:392–397.

BURTCH, V. 1917. The summer life of the Virginia rail. Bird-Lore 19:243–248.

CAHN, A. R. 1915. Notes on a captive Virginia rail. Auk 32:91-95.

CALLIN, E. M. 1968. Vocalization of the Virginia rail: a mystery solved. Blue Jay 26:75–77.

CAMPBELL, E. G., AND G. A. WOLF. 1977. Great egret depredation on a Virginia rail. Western Birds 8:64.

CONWAY, C. J. 1990. Seasonal changes in movements and habitat use by three sympatric species of rails. M.S. Thesis, Univ. Wyoming, Laramie. 58pp.

———, W. R. EDDLEMAN, AND S. H. ANDERSON. 1994. Nesting success and survival of Virginia rails and soras. Wilson Bull. 106:466–473.

———, ———, ———, AND L. R. HANEBURY. 1993. Seasonal changes in Yuma clapper rail vocalization rate and habitat use. J. Wildl. Manage. 57:282–290.

COWARDIN, L. M., V. CARTER, F. C. GOLET, AND E. T. LaROE. 1979. Classification of wetlands and deepwater habitats of the United States. U.S. Fish and Wildl. Serv., Off. Biol. Serv. FWS/OBS–79/31. 103pp.

CRAMER, W. S. 1932. Virginia rail in the stomach of a green frog. Auk 49:80.

CRANDALL, L. S. 1920. Early Virginia rail in New York. Auk 37:452.

DICKERMAN, R. W. 1966. A new subspecies of the Virginia rail from Mexico. Condor 68:215–216.

DICKEY, D. R. 1928. A race of Virginia rail from the Pacific Coast. Condor 30:322.

EDDLEMAN, W. R., F. L. KNOPF, B. MEANLEY, F. A. REID, AND R. ZEMBAL. 1988. Conservation of North American rallids. Wilson Bull. 100:458–475.

EHRLICH, P. R., D. S. DOBKIN, AND D. WHEYE. 1988. The birder's handbook: a field guide to the natural history of North American birds. Simon and Schuster, New York, N.Y. 785pp.

FASSETT, N. C. 1940. A manual of aquatic plants. McGraw-Hill Book Co., New York, N.Y. 405pp.

FORBUSH, E. H. 1925. Birds of Massachusetts and other New England states. Part I: Water birds, marsh birds and shore birds. J. S. Cushing Co.-Berwick and Smith Co., Norwood, Mass. 481pp.

FREDRICKSON, L. H., AND F. A. REID. 1986. Wetland and riparian habitats: a nongame management overview. Pages 59–96 *in* J. B. Hale, L. B. Best, and R. L. Clawson, eds. Management of nongame wildlife in the midwest: a developing art. North Central Sect., The Wildl. Soc., Chelsea, Mich.

GIBBS, J. P., AND S. M. MELVIN. 1993. Call-response surveys for monitoring breeding waterbirds. J. Wildl. Manage. 57:27–34.

———, J. R. LONGCORE, D. G. McAULEY, AND J. K. RINGELMAN. 1991. Use of wetland habitats by selected nongame water birds in Maine. U.S. Fish and Wildl. Serv., Fish and Wildl. Res. Rep. 9. 57pp.

GILLETTE, D. C. 1897. Notes on the Virginia and sora rails. Oologist 14:21–23.

GLAHN, J. F. 1974. Study of breeding rails with recorded calls in north-central Colorado. Wilson Bull. 86:206–214.

GOLDMAN, E. A. 1908. The Virginia rail breeding in Mexico. Condor 10:181.

GRIESE, H. J. 1977. Status and habitat utilization of rails in Colorado. M.S. Thesis, Colorado State Univ., Fort Collins. 67pp.

———, R. A. RYDER, AND C. E. BRAUN. 1980. Spatial and temporal distribution of rails in Colorado. Wilson Bull. 92:96–102.

HORAK, G. J. 1964. A comparative study of Virginia and sora rails with emphasis on foods. M.S. Thesis, Iowa State Univ., Ames. 73pp.

———. 1970. A comparative study of the foods of the sora and Virginia rail. Wilson Bull. 82:207–213.

HUNT, C. J. 1908. *Rallus virginianus* a Delaware Valley breeder. Auk 25:81.

IRISH, J. 1974. Postbreeding territorial behavior of soras and Virginia rails in several Michigan marshes. Jack-Pine Warbler 52:115–124.

JOHNSON, R. R. 1984. Breeding habitat use and postbreeding movements by soras and Virginia rails. M.S. Thesis, Iowa State Univ., Ames. 52pp.

———, AND J. J. DINSMORE. 1985. Brood-rearing and postbreeding habitat use by Virginia rails and soras. Wilson Bull. 97:551–554.

———, AND ———. 1986. The use of tape-recorded calls to count Virginia rails and soras. Wilson Bull. 98:303–306.

———, B. T. BROWN, L. T. HAIGHT, AND J. M. SIMPSON. 1981. Playback recordings as a special avian censusing technique. Pages 68–75 *in* C. J. Ralph and J. M. Scott, eds. Estimating the numbers of terrestrial birds. Stud. Avian Biol. 6.

KAMINSKI, R. M. 1979. Dabbling duck and aquatic invertebrate responses to manipulated wetland habitat. Ph.D. Thesis, Michigan State Univ., Lansing. 62pp.

———, AND H. H. PRINCE. 1981. Dabbling duck and aquatic macroinvertebrate responses to manipulated wetland habitat. J. Wildl. Manage. 44:1–15.

KAUFMANN, G. W. 1971. Behavior and ecology of the sora, *Porzana carolina*, and Virginia rail, *Rallus limicola*. Ph.D. Thesis, Univ. Minnesota, Minneapolis. 114pp.

———. 1987. Growth and development of sora and Virginia rail chicks. Wilson Bull. 99:432–440.

———. 1988. Social preening in soras and in Virginia rails. Loon 60:59–63.

———. 1989. Breeding ecology of the sora, *Porzana carolina*, and the Virginia rail, *Rallus limicola*. Can. Field-Nat. 103:270–282.

KRAPU, G. L., AND R. K. GREEN. 1978. Breeding bird populations of selected semipermanent wetlands in south-central North Dakota—1977. Am. Birds 32:110–112.

LOWTHER, J. K. 1961. Virginia rail (*Rallus limicola limicola* Vieillot) breeding at Vermilion, Alberta. Auk 78:271.

MANCI, K. M., AND D. H. RUSCH. 1988. Indices to distribution and abundance of some inconspic-

uous waterbirds on Horicon marsh. J. Field Ornithol. 59:67–75.

MARION, W. R., T. E. O'MEARA, AND D. S. MAEHR. 1981. Use of playback recordings in sampling elusive or secretive birds. Pages 81–85 *in* C. J. Ralph and J. M. Scott, eds. Estimating the numbers of terrestrial birds. Stud. Avian Biol. 6.

MARTIN, A. C., H. S. ZIM, AND A. L. NELSON. 1951. American wildlife and plants. McGraw-Hill Book Co., New York, N.Y. 500pp.

MARTIN, E. M. 1979. Hunting and harvest trends for migratory game birds other than waterfowl: 1964–76. U.S. Fish and Wildl. Serv., Spec. Sci. Rep. Wildl. 218. 37pp.

MCLEAN, D. D. 1916. Nesting habits of the Virginia rail in Mariposa County, California. Condor 18:229.

MOUSLEY, H. 1931. Notes on the home life of the Virginia rail. Can. Field-Nat. 45:65–66.

———. 1940. Further notes on the nesting habits of the Virginia rail. Wilson Bull. 52:87–90.

MURKIN, H. R., R. M. KAMINSKI, AND R. D. TITMAN. 1982. Responses by dabbling ducks and aquatic invertebrates to an experimentally manipulated cattail marsh. Can. J. Zool. 60:2324–2332.

NATIONAL GEOGRAPHIC SOCIETY. 1987. Field guide to the birds of North America. 2nd ed. W. A. Krueger Company, New Berlin, Wis. 464pp.

NELSON, J. W., AND J. A. KADLEC. 1984. A conceptual approach to relating habitat structure and macroinvertebrate production in freshwater wetlands. Trans. North Am. Wildl. and Nat. Resour. Conf. 49:262–270.

ODOM, R. R. 1975. Mercury contamination in Georgia rails. Proc. Southeast. Assoc. Game and Fish Comm. 28:649–658.

ORMAN, S., AND B. SWIFT. 1987. Early nesting of a Virginia rail in New York. Kingbird 37:211.

PETERSON, R. T. 1980. A field guide to the birds. Houghton-Mifflin Co., Boston, Mass. 384pp.

POSPICHAL, L. B., AND W. H. MARSHALL. 1954. A field study of sora rail and Virginia rail in central Minnesota. Flicker 26:2–32.

POST, W., AND F. ENDERS. 1970. Notes on a salt-marsh Virginia rail population. Kingbird 20:61–67.

RANDALL, T. E. 1946. Virginia rail, *Rallus limicola limicola*, Vieillot, nesting in Alberta. Can. Field-Nat. 60:135.

REID, F. A. 1985. Wetland invertebrates in relation to hydrology and water chemistry. Pages 72–79 *in* M. D. Knighton, ed. Water impoundments for wildlife: a habitat management workshop. U.S. Dep. Agric., For. Serv. Gen. Tech. Rep. NC-100.

RICHTER, C. 1948. Virginia rail catches frog. Passenger Pigeon 10:32.

RIPLEY, S. D. 1977. Rails of the world. David Godine Publ., Boston, Mass. 406pp.

ROBBINS, C. S. 1949. Distribution of North American birds. Audubon Field Notes 3:238–239.

ROBBINS, C., JR. 1967. Virginia rail on Christmas count. Maine Field Nat. 23:13.

ROOT, T. 1988. Atlas of wintering North American birds: an analysis of Christmas bird count data. Univ. Chicago Press, Chicago, Ill. 312pp.

RUNDLE, W. D., AND L. H. FREDRICKSON. 1981. Managing seasonally flooded impoundments for migrant rails and shorebirds. Wildl. Soc. Bull. 9:80–87.

SAYRE, M. W., AND W. D. RUNDLE. 1984. Comparison of habitat use by migrant soras and Virginia rails. J. Wildl. Manage. 48:599–605.

SHAW, S. A. 1887. Nesting of the Virginia rail in New Hampshire. Ornithol. and Oologist 12:131–132.

SHORT, E. H. 1890. Breeding of the Virginia rail. Oologist 7:229–230.

STEWART, R. E., AND H. A. KANTRUD. 1971. Classification of natural ponds and lakes in the glaciated prairie region. U.S. Fish and Wildl. Serv., Resour. Publ. 92. 57pp.

SWIFT, B. L. 1989. Avian breeding habitats in Hudson River tidal marshes. Final Rep., New York Dep. Environ. Conserv., Delmar. 79pp.

TACHA, R. W. 1975. A survey of rail populations in Kansas, with emphasis on Cheyenne Bottoms. M.S. Thesis, Fort Hays Kansas State Univ., Fort Hays. 54pp.

TANNER, W. D. 1953. Ecology of the Virginia and king rails and the sora in Clay County, Iowa. Ph.D. Thesis, Iowa State Univ., Ames. 154pp.

———, AND G. O. HENDRICKSON. 1954. Ecology of the Virginia rail in Clay County, Iowa. Iowa Bird-Life 24:65–70.

TAUTIN, J., S. M. CARNEY, AND J. B. BORTNER. 1989. A national migratory gamebird harvest survey: a continuing need. Trans. North Am. Wildl. and Nat. Resour. Conf. 54:545–551.

TYSER, R. W. 1982. Species composition and diversity of bird communities in four wetland habitats of the Upper Mississippi River Floodplain. Passenger Pigeon 44:16–19.

U.S. FISH AND WILDLIFE SERVICE. 1988. Final supplemental environmental impact statement: issuance of annual regulations permitting the sport hunting of migratory birds. SEIS 88. U.S. Gov. Print. Off., Washington, D.C. 340pp.

VOIGTS, D. K. 1976. Aquatic invertebrate abundance in relation to changing marsh vegetation. Am. Midl. Nat. 93:313–322.

WALKINSHAW, L. H. 1937. The Virginia rail in Michigan. Auk 54:464–475.

WEBER, J. A. 1909. The Virginia and sora rails nesting in New York City. Auk 26:19–22.

WELLER, M. W. 1981. Freshwater marshes: ecology and wildlife management. Univ. Minnesota Press, Minneapolis. 150pp.

———, AND L. H. FREDRICKSON. 1974. Avian ecology of a managed glacial marsh. Living Bird 12: 269–291.

———, AND C. E. SPATCHER. 1965. Role of habitat in the distribution and abundance of marsh birds. Iowa Agric. and Home Econ. Exp. Stn., Spec. Rep. 43. 31pp.

———, G. W. KAUFMANN, AND P. A. VOHS, JR. 1991. Evaluation of wetland development and waterbird response at Elk Creek Wildlife Management Area, Lake Mills, Iowa, 1961 to 1990. Wetlands 11:245–262.

WIENS, J. A. 1966. Notes on the distraction display of the Virginia rail. Wilson Bull. 78:229–231.

WOOD, H. B. 1937. Incubation period of Virginia rail. Auk 54:535–536.

ZIMMERMAN, J. L. 1977. Virginia rail (Rallus limicola). Pages 46–56 in G. C. Sanderson, ed. Management of migratory shore and upland game birds in North America. Int. Assoc. Fish and Wildl. Agencies, Washington, D.C.

———. 1984. Distribution, habitat, and status of the sora and Virginia rail in eastern Kansas. J. Field Ornithol. 55:38–47.

Redovich- 94

Chapter 15

SORA

SCOTT M. MELVIN, Massachusetts Division of Fisheries and Wildlife, Field Headquarters, Westborough, MA 01581
JAMES P. GIBBS, School of Forestry and Environmental Studies, 206 Prospect Street, Yale University, New Haven, CT 06511

Abstract: Soras (*Porzana carolina*) are the most abundant and widely distributed of North American rails. Soras breed primarily in freshwater emergent wetlands and occur in fresh, brackish, and salt marshes during migration and in winter. Shallow marshes with high interspersion of fine-leaved and robust emergents, flooded annuals, and patches of open water constitute optimal habitat. Habitat continues to decline through much of the range. Population trends are uncertain. Soras are hunted in 31 states and 2 Canadian provinces. In most states and provinces, interest and participation in hunting soras are low, and surveys to monitor harvest and population trends are lacking. Bag limits range from 10 to 25 birds/day. The new National Migratory Bird Harvest Information Program should allow improved estimates of harvest in the United States. The most urgent management need for soras is identification, protection, and management of emergent wetlands used for breeding, migration, and wintering. We suggest a federal stamp be required for hunting rails (and other migratory shore and upland game birds) to provide funds for habitat acquisition and management. Standardized playback surveys using tape-recorded calls should be implemented to monitor population trends of soras.

DESCRIPTION

Soras are small, plump, grayish-brown rails with a stubby yellow bill, black mask on the face and throat, and greenish legs. Total length ranges from 20 to 25 cm; weight ranges from 60 to 110 g and averages 85 g (Ripley 1977). Subspecies or discrete populations have not been described. Adults of both sexes are generally similar, although females are slightly smaller and have darker bills. Sora chicks are covered with glossy black down. Buff-brown juvenile plumage begins to emerge at 2–3 weeks and is complete at about 4 weeks of age. Postjuvenal molt to first winter plumage begins around 12–14 weeks (Pospichal and Marshall 1954, Ripley 1977, Kaufmann 1987). Sora vocalizations include a high-pitched, descending "whinny," a whistled "kerwee," and a variety of short, sharp, "keek" calls when startled (Peterson 1980, Kaufmann 1983). The "whinny" call is given by both sexes and appears to function in territorial defense and as a contact call between members of a pair (Kaufmann 1983). It is given during spring migration and throughout the breeding season. The "kerwee" call often precedes the "whinny," and is given most commonly during spring migration. Soras move about mostly on foot, through or over marsh vegetation. They can also swim and dive. When flushed, they appear to be weak, awkward flyers, yet they migrate hundreds of kilometers each spring and fall and

have been encountered on ships hundreds of kilometers at sea (Ripley 1977).

LIFE HISTORY

Soras establish well-defined nesting and brood-rearing territories that are defended, primarily by males, against both conspecifics and other rail species. Kaufmann (1983) described displays and behaviors used by adult soras in territory defense, courtship, pair bonding, and copulation. Nests are loosely woven baskets of available vegetation, constructed over standing water, and usually in sedges (*Carex* spp.) or cattails (*Typha* spp.) (Fig. 1). Nests may be supported by stems of vegetation or built in a solid mass within clumps of vegetation, and often have a ramp constructed to the lip of the nest. Nests may be built up several centimeters to avoid rising water levels. Dummy nests are often constructed nearby and serve as resting platforms (Billard 1948, Pospichal and Marshall 1954, Ripley 1977). Eggs are usually laid at a rate of 1/day, and clutch size ranges from 5 to 15 eggs, with an average near 10 (Pospichal and Marshall 1954, Tanner and Hendrickson 1956, Kaufmann 1989). Incubation begins when the clutch is partially complete, and lasts 16–19 days (Walkinshaw 1940, Pospichal and Marshall 1954, Kaufmann 1989). Hatching is asynchronous, spanning 2–17 days, and is longer with increasing clutch size (Kaufmann 1989). During the

Fig. 1. Sora at nest (Photo by A. Cruickshank/VIREO).

hatching period, 1 adult continues to incubate unhatched eggs while the other stays nearby with the incomplete brood (Walkinshaw 1940, Greenlaw and Miller 1982). It is uncertain whether soras renest following an unsuccessful attempt. Both sexes incubate, brood, and feed young. Females contribute more to incubation and brooding, while males bring more food to young (Kaufmann 1989).

Sora chicks are precocial in ground and aquatic locomotion and semi-precocial in feeding themselves (Kaufmann 1987). Chicks appear dependent on adults for warmth and dryness for extended periods and are brooded by adults for about 1 month. Chicks are able to fly after about 4 weeks. Soras rear their broods to independence as family groups within nesting territories. Home ranges of radio-marked soras in Iowa averaged 0.19 ha during the brood-rearing period (Johnson and Dinsmore 1986). Family groups remained within home ranges until chicks were 16–32 days old. Dispersal from home ranges,

often out of the nesting wetland, occurred between 19 July and 1 August.

Ecology and behavior of soras during migration is poorly understood. Soras are cold-sensitive, and chronology of migration, especially in fall, may be determined in part by timing of frosts (Bent 1926, Walkinshaw 1940). Winter ecology, behavior, and social organization are poorly understood.

Soras eat a variety of plant material and invertebrates. Plant material constitutes a large proportion of the diet in summer and fall (Martin et al. 1951, Pospichal and Marshall 1954, Horak 1970, Rundle and Sayre 1983). Common plant foods include duckweed (*Lemna* spp.) and seeds of wild or cultivated rice (*Zizania* spp.), smartweeds (*Polygonum* spp.), sedges, and grasses (Fig. 2). Migrating soras also feed in cultivated rice fields (Meanley 1960). Fall migrants in salt marshes may feed more heavily on invertebrates, including grasshoppers, crickets, and larval cases of moths (Webster 1964).

Invertebrates and seeds of *Carex* constituted the majority of the diet of spring migrant soras in Missouri (Rundle and Sayre 1983).

Soras often occur sympatrically with Virginia rails (*Rallus limicola*). The 2 species appear not to segregate by wetland habitat type, but rather partition food resources (Horak 1970, Johnson and Dinsmore 1986). Soras eat more seeds and other vegetable matter than do Virginia rails. Kaufmann (1989) suggested interspecific competition between soras and Virginia rails occurs during the breeding season due to the sora's inefficiency in gathering food for its young. Because of their short, stubby bills, soras may be less efficient at procuring invertebrate foods for chicks than longer-billed Virginia rails. Soras search for food by raking mats of duckweed with their feet or pulling aside floating vegetation with their bills and visually searching for food. Soras appear to have evolved other morphological and behavioral mechanisms to ensure adequate food for their young. These include defense of nesting and brood-rearing territories against conspecifics and other rail species, evolution of conspicuous facial coloration to reinforce threat displays, larger repertoire of threat displays than Virginia rails, larger clutch size than Virginia rails, and asynchronous hatching that distributes the high energetic cost of feeding young over a longer period (Kaufmann 1983). Defense of a well-defined territory plays a greater role in the breeding biology of soras than Virginia rails (Kaufmann 1983).

Factors limiting sora populations are poorly understood. Estimates of chick and adult survival rates are lacking. Habitat loss and degradation most likely limit sora populations. Effects of annual harvest and incidental take by waterfowl and other bird hunters are unknown. Trapping of furbearers results in mortality to soras and other rails (Meanley 1969, Linscomb 1976, Eddleman et al. 1988). Relative impacts of predation on productivity or annual survival are poorly understood. Cold temperatures and heavy rainfall in late spring and early summer may reduce reproductive success by flooding nests or increasing chick mortality from drowning or exposure. Effects of pesticides and other environmental contaminants on soras are poorly understood. Pesticides may be a threat in southern commercial rice fields and in wetlands in California and Arizona (Eddleman et al. 1988). Soras are also potentially susceptible to mortality from lead shot; ingested lead shot was present

Fig. 2.   Typical foraging habitat for sora in Wisconsin (Photo by S. J. Lang/VIREO).

in gizzards of 7.4–12.3% of soras collected in Maryland, and 1.8% of birds from Missouri (Artmann and Martin 1975, Stendell et al. 1980).

HABITAT

Soras inhabit wetlands dominated by emergent vegetation. Preferred breeding, migration, and wintering habitats are freshwater marshes (Walkinshaw 1940, Odum 1977) (Fig. 3). Soras occasionally nest in salt marshes (Greenlaw and Miller 1982), and often occur in brackish and salt marshes during migration.

Soras breed in freshwater emergent wetlands with shallow and intermediate water depths (Pospichal and Marshall 1954, Griese et al. 1980, Johnson and Dinsmore 1986, Gibbs and Melvin 1990, Gibbs et al. 1991, Crowley 1994). Dominant plants at sora nest sites include cattail, sedges, and, less commonly, bulrush (*Scirpus* spp.). Preferred nest sites seem to be in sedges or cattails near borders of vegetation types or patches of open water (Walkinshaw 1940, Pospichal and Marshall 1954). Soras breeding in prairie pothole wetlands in North Dakota and Iowa (Kantrud and Stewart 1984, Johnson and Dinsmore 1986) occurred almost exclusively in wetlands classified (following Stewart and Kantrud 1971) as seasonal or semi-permanent. Wetlands used by breeding soras in Maine had more fine-leaved and robust emergents and aquatic-bed vegetation, and less ericaceous shrubs, compared to wetlands where soras were not present (Gibbs and Melvin 1990). In Massachusetts, breeding soras were present in wetlands with larger areas of cattail and greater interspersion of vegetation and water compared to wetlands where they were absent (Crowley 1994). Along the Atlantic Coast, soras may occasionally nest

Fig. 3.   Sora breeding habitat, Penjajawoc Marsh, Bangor Maine (Photo by S. M. Melvin).

in smooth cordgrass (*Spartina alterniflora*) or common reed (*Phragmites communis*) within brackish or salt marshes (Greenlaw and Miller 1982).

Breeding soras in Iowa were most abundant in relatively shallow, shoreward portions of wetlands, where water level instability produced a mosaic of fine and robust emergent vegetation (Johnson and Dinsmore 1986). Stands of emergents with abundant floating and submergent vegetation may be attractive to soras because they provide good substrates for invertebrate prey near the water's surface. Soras may be attracted to shallower portions of wetlands during brood-rearing and pre-migration periods, where seed-producing plants such as sedges, smartweeds, and beggarticks (*Bidens* spp.) are important foods (Johnson and Dinsmore 1986, Manci and Rusch 1988). In late summer in Iowa and Minnesota, soras left wetlands for short periods to feed in upland fields and row crops (Johnson and Dinsmore 1986).

Breeding soras appear to be relatively area-independent in their selection of wetlands. In Iowa and Maine, soras were present on 14–17% of wetlands <1 ha that were surveyed (Brown and Dinsmore 1986, Gibbs et al. 1991).

Rapid water level fluctuations can disrupt sora breeding activities. In Colorado, 13 of 15 nesting territories were deserted when water levels rose >20 cm (Griese et al. 1980). Decreasing water levels in other wetlands prevented renesting and apparently caused chick mortality in 1 instance.

Migrant soras in Missouri used water impoundments 0–46 cm deep, but were most common at sites <15 cm deep (Sayre and Rundle 1984). They preferred sites with tall, dense emergent vegetation. When available, stands of wild rice or portions of wetlands with flooded annual grasses or forbs are preferred feeding habitats (Walkinshaw 1940, Odom 1977, Fannucchi et al. 1986). Soras also occur in large numbers in brackish or salt marshes during migration (Odom 1977).

Wintering habitats are poorly known (Eddleman et al. 1988), but include both freshwater and salt marshes. Wintering soras use wetlands with high interspersion of shallow water and emergent vegetation (Gochfeld 1972, Conway 1990).

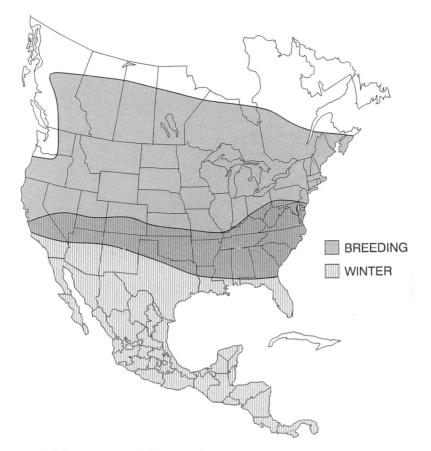

Fig. 4.   Breeding and winter ranges of sora in North America.

DISTRIBUTION AND ABUNDANCE

Soras are the most abundant and widely distributed of North American rails. Soras nest locally in suitable wetland habitats from Nova Scotia, New Brunswick, and Prince Edward Island west through the St. Lawrence Valley and Ontario to northern Saskatchewan and Alberta, southern Mackenzie, and central British Columbia, south to central California, and east to central Colorado and Kansas, northern Missouri, Ohio, and Maryland (Fig. 4) (Ripley 1977, Peterson 1980, Godfrey 1986). Density estimates of breeding soras were 0.1 birds/ha in 1,321 wetlands in central North Dakota (Kantrud and Stewart 1984), 1.3 birds/ha at Horicon Marsh in southern Wisconsin (Manci and Rusch 1988), 1.6 birds/ha in 28 wetlands in northwestern Iowa (Tanner and Hendrickson 1956) and 30 birds/ha at Fossil Creek Reservoir in northern Colorado (Odom 1977).

Winter distribution is dictated by the sora's apparent intolerance of freezing temperatures (Bent 1926, Root 1988). Soras winter from the southern United States, Mexico, and Central America south to Peru, Guyana, and the West Indies (Ripley 1977, Am. Ornithol. Union 1983). Most wintering soras are restricted to regions where minimum winter temperatures exceed −1 C. In the United States, they winter from Chesapeake Bay south through Florida, and west to Louisiana, Texas, southern Arizona, and central California (Fig. 4). Wintering populations extend into much colder regions along the Rio Grande into Colorado and up the Colorado River into Arizona. Power plants along these rivers may be discharging warm water, preventing adjacent wetlands from freezing (Root 1988).

Population trends of soras are unclear. From 1966 to 1987, sora numbers on Breeding Bird Survey routes declined at a non-significant rate of −2.2% annually (Droege and Sauer 1989). If

Table 1. Estimated numbers of hunters and annual harvest of soras in states and Canadian provinces, 1989–90 (nd = no data available).

State/ province	Hunters (n)	Soras harvested (n)
United States		
Colorado	100[a]	500[a]
Connecticut	<20	nd
Delaware	"negligible"	nd
Illinois	200–300[a]	1,000–2,000[a]
Kentucky	nd	<1,000
Louisiana	6,100 ± 2,000	49,000 ± 29,300
Maine	nd	300–500[b]
Maryland	117[b]	2,136 ± 18[b]
Minnesota	1,000	2,500
Missouri	159[b]	264[b]
Nebraska	40[b]	40[b]
New Jersey	300	2,300
New York	"small"	"small"
Ohio	335[b]	6,863[b]
Texas	960[a]	1,200[a]
Virginia	401	<100
Wyoming	21[b]	0[b]
Canada		
Ontario	nd	"very low"

[a] Sora and Virginia rails combined.
[b] All rails combined.

populations are declining, this would be consistent with continuing declines in quantity and quality of wetland habitats throughout much of the United States (Tiner 1984, Eddleman et al. 1988). State and provincial biologists we surveyed in 1992 were of the opinion that populations of breeding or migrant soras were increasing in Iowa, increasing or stable in Massachusetts, stable in Alabama, Connecticut, Kansas, Rhode Island, Wyoming, and New Brunswick, and decreasing in Michigan, New York, Pennsylvania, and Alberta. However, none of these trend estimates was supported by quantitative data from population surveys. Rather, they were based on general impressions, incidental observations made during late summer waterfowl surveys or banding programs, or deductions based on habitat trends. The remaining states and provinces offered no opinions on population trends.

HARVEST

Hunting of soras is currently allowed in 31 of the 48 contiguous states, but not in Arizona, California, Idaho, Montana, Nevada, New Hampshire, North Dakota, South Dakota, Utah, or Vermont. In Canada, soras are hunted only in Manitoba and Ontario. Vermont closed its rail season in 1990 due to the lack of information on population status and low hunter interest. Manitoba is considering closing its season for similar reasons.

An estimated 13,400 to 47,200 soras were harvested annually by waterfowl hunters between 1964 and 1976 (Martin 1979). These estimates probably represent only 50% of the total annual harvest of soras during this period; the rest were believed shot by non-waterfowl hunters. Five states each harvested >2,000 soras: Florida, Iowa, Louisiana, New Jersey, and Virginia. Nationwide, numbers of hunters taking soras and average number of soras bagged showed no change in 1964–76, although number of hunters declined in the Atlantic Flyway.

Only 14 of 31 states reported current estimates of sora hunters or harvest, based on state or federal surveys in 1990 or 1991 (Table 1). Only Illinois, Louisiana, Maryland, Minnesota, Ohio, and Texas estimated harvests of >1,000 birds; estimates were for soras and Virginia rails combined in Illinois and Texas, and for all rails combined in Ohio and Maryland. Estimated numbers of rail hunters were >500 only in Louisiana, Minnesota, and Texas, and were between 100 and 500 in Colorado, Illinois, Maryland, Missouri, New Jersey, Ohio, and Virginia. None of the Canadian provinces reported conducting either population or harvest surveys.

Seasons in 1991–92 extended from the 1st or 2nd week of September into the 2nd or 3rd week of November in 24 of 31 states and Manitoba. Seasons in Alabama, Lousiana, Tennessee, and Ontario extended into December and January. Bag limits were 25 birds/day and 25 in possession, either for soras alone or in aggregate with Virginia rails, in 27 of 31 states. Bag/possession limits in the remaining states were 12/24, 15/15, or 10/20, and were 10/20 in Manitoba and Ontario. State biologists in Maryland, Massachusetts, Michigan, Texas, and Wisconsin expressed concerns that reduced bag limits should be considered, not necessarily because overharvest is occurring, but because of lack of information on harvest or population trends, low hunter interest, and public perceptions.

Effects of annual harvest on populations are unknown. Although low hunter interest and the difficulty of hunting rails probably keeps the annual kill within sustainable levels (Eddleman et al. 1988), effects of incidental take by waterfowl and other bird hunters on local or regional populations are unknown. Biologists from 13 states and 3 Canadian provinces thought that additional harvest opportunities exist for soras. At present, however, there is little interest in rail hunting among sportsmen, and most soras are harvested incidental to other game species (Odom 1977). Much larger numbers were harvested earlier in this century. Bent (1926) reported that it was not uncommon for a skilled hunter to kill 100–150 rails/day along the Connecticut River in Connecticut, and estimated that 1,000 rails were killed at Longmeadow, Massachusetts, in 1908. Sora hunting is an old tradition in coastal marshes in Connecticut, Maryland, New Jersey, and Virginia, but substantial declines in both birds and rail hunters have occurred (Ripley 1977).

MANAGEMENT NEEDS

Habitat Management

The most urgent management need for soras is preservation of emergent wetlands that provide breeding, migration, and wintering habitats. An estimated 1.9 million ha of palustrine emergent wetlands were lost in the conterminous United States between the mid-1950's and mid-1970's (Tiner 1984). Many of the wetland types most important to soras remain among the most threatened in the United States. These include estuarine and coastal marshes in California, Florida, Louisiana, New Jersey, and Texas, palustrine emergent wetlands in south Florida and the Prairie Pothole Region, and western riparian wetlands. Soras will benefit from policies and management practices that eliminate or minimize impacts of wetland draining and filling, siltation, eutrophication and other forms of pollution, and invasion by exotic plants.

Habitat needs of soras and other rails should be considered when developing and implementing management plans on impoundments and other managed wetlands. Rail habitat managers should encourage growth of diverse stands of both fine-leaved and robust emergents, including sedges, bulrushes, and especially cattails, as well as moist-soil annuals around the edges of wetlands (Rundle and Sayre 1983, Johnson and Dinsmore 1986). Periodic gradual drawdowns that encourage horizontal zonation of wetland vegetation may maximize habitat quality for soras. Several authors have reported that soras were most abundant near edges of vegetation types or patches of open water (Walkinshaw 1940, Pospichal and Marshall 1954, Johnson and Dinsmore 1986). Management should maximize interspersion of emergent vegetation and open water areas (Weller and Spatcher 1965, Crowley 1994). Modifying or constructing wetland impoundments with sloping or irregular bottoms will provide greater diversity of water levels and topography and will increase vegetation/water edge (Eddleman et al. 1988). Complete drawdowns are not compatible with breeding rails. If early drawdowns are desired, they should be undertaken before April to avoid disrupting territory establishment and courtship. Effects of slow, incomplete drawdowns after nest initiation on nest success, renesting, or brood survival are poorly understood. In late summer and fall, manipulation of water levels to allow shallow (<15 cm) flooding of seed heads of annual grasses and smartweeds along wetland margins will maximize habitat quality for rails (Rundle and Frederickson 1981, Sayre and Rundle 1984). To improve habitat for rails during spring migration, impoundments vegetated with annual grasses and smartweed should be de-watered over winter to protect vegetation from ice and waterfowl, or allowed to advance successionally to a community of perennial emergents.

Population And Harvest Management

Although soras are hunted in 31 states, at present no standardized survey programs exist to provide indices of state, regional, or continental population trends. Standardized surveys of breeding populations using playback recordings should be implemented on a state-by-state basis, in conjunction with surveys of other wetland birds (Gibbs and Melvin 1993). Soras are quite responsive to broadcasts of taped vocalizations during the early part of the breeding season, from late April to early June in most states (Griese et al. 1980, Zimmerman 1984, Johnson and Dinsmore 1986, Gibbs and Melvin 1993, Crowley 1994). Soras respond less frequently to taped calls in summer and fall (Griese et al. 1980), and may respond better to loud noises such as sharply rapping the side of a canoe (Fannuchi et al. 1986). Surveys using loud noise, or flushing counts, could be used to develop indices of relative abundance of migrant and wintering soras (Gochfeld 1972, Sayre and Rundle 1984, Fannuchi et al. 1986). However, flushing counts may be biased by habitat type in that rails are less likely to flush from dense or tall vegetation

(Walkinshaw 1940, Kaufmann 1983, Conway 1990).

In most states, participation and interest in hunting soras is low, and standardized surveys to monitor harvest and hunter effort are lacking. Nevertheless, bag limits are high compared to other migratory game birds. Where survey data are collected, estimates are often inaccurate and imprecise due to small sample sizes. The National Migratory Bird Harvest Information Program should provide a sampling framework for sora hunters, allowing more precise estimates of statewide and U.S. harvests.

RESEARCH NEEDS

The following are priority research needs for soras.

1. Develop reliable techniques for monitoring population trends. Indices of population trends using playback recording surveys will require better distributional information on breeding soras within states and provinces, and identifying periods of peak response to tape-recorded calls.
2. Develop reliable harvest surveys in the United States using the National Migratory Bird Harvest Information Program.
3. Determine effects of habitat quality, predation, weather, and water level fluctuations on reproductive success of soras.
4. Describe habitat use and distribution patterns of wintering soras. Determine management actions necessary to maximize carrying capacity of winter habitats.
5. Describe migration chronology and habitat use of sora populations. Priority should be given to unstudied populations outside the midwestern United States.

RECOMMENDATIONS

The following is a summary of priority management recommendations for soras.

1. Federal, state, and provincial resource management agencies should use all means at their disposal to halt further loss and degradation of freshwater and coastal emergent wetlands.
2. Habitat needs of soras and other rails should be considered in habitat acquisition and management programs of state and federal agencies, and private conservation organizations.
3. The U.S. Fish and Wildlife Service should

institute a hunting stamp requirement for hunting rails and other migratory shore and upland game birds. Such a program would provide funds for wetland acquisition and management.
4. The U.S. Congress should resume funding of the Accelerated Research Program for Migratory Shore and Upland Game Birds (or an equivalent program) to support research on habitat and population management for rails.
5. The U.S. Fish and Wildlife Service, Canadian Wildlife Service, and individual states and provinces should cooperate to develop and implement standardized surveys to monitor trends in sora populations and habitats.

ACKNOWLEDGMENTS

We thank the state and provincial biologists who responded to our questionnaire on the status and harvest of soras. We thank C. J. Conway and W. R. Eddleman for their efforts in preparing and distributing the questionnaire. We thank C. J. Conway, T. C. Tacha, and C. E. Braun for helpful comments on previous drafts of this chapter.

LITERATURE CITED

AMERICAN ORNITHOLOGISTS' UNION. 1983. Checklist of North American birds. 6th ed. Allen Press, Lawrence, Kans. 877pp.

ARTMANN, J. W., AND E. M. MARTIN. 1975. Incidence of ingested lead shot in sora rails. J. Wildl. Manage. 39:514–519.

BENT, A. C. 1926. Life histories of North American marsh birds. U.S. Natl. Mus. Bull. 135. 490pp.

BILLARD, R. S. 1948. An ecological study of the Virginia rail (Rallus limicola) and the sora (Porzana carolina) in some Connecticut swamps. M.S. Thesis, Iowa State Coll., Ames. 84 pp.

BROWN, M., AND J. J. DINSMORE. 1986. Implications of marsh size and isolation for marsh bird management. J. Wildl. Manage. 50:392–397.

CONWAY, C. J. 1990. Seasonal changes in movements and habitat use by three sympatric species of rails. M.S. Thesis, Univ. Wyoming, Laramie. 58pp.

CROWLEY, S.K. 1994. Habitat use and population monitoring of secretive waterbirds in Massachusetts. M.S. Thesis, Univ. Massachusetts, Amherst. 108 pp.

DROEGE, S., AND J. R. SAUER. 1989. North American breeding bird survey annual summary 1988. U.S. Fish and Wildl. Serv., Biol. Rep. 89(13). 16pp.

EDDLEMAN, W. R., F. L. KNOPF, B. MEANLEY, F. A. REID, AND R. ZEMBAL. 1988. Conservation of North American rallids. Wilson Bull. 100:458–475.

FANNUCCHI, W. A., G. T. FANNUCCHI, AND L. E. NAUMAN. 1986. Effects of harvesting wild rice, *Zizania aquatica*, on soras, *Porzana carolina*. Can. Field-Nat. 100:533–536.

GIBBS, J.P., AND S. M. MELVIN. 1990. An assessment of wading birds and other avifauna and their habitats in Maine. Final Rep., Maine Dep. Inland Fish. and Wildl., Bangor. 73pp.

———, AND ———. 1993. Call-response surveys for monitoring breeding populations of grebes, bitterns, and rails. J. Wildl. Manage. 57:27–34.

———, J. R. LONGCORE, D. G. McAULEY, AND J. K. RINGELMAN. 1991. Use of wetland habitats by selected nongame waterbirds in Maine. U.S. Fish and Wildl. Serv., Resour. Publ. 9. 57pp.

GOCHFELD, M. 1972. Observations on the status, ecology, and behavior of soras wintering in Trinidad, West Indies. Wilson Bull. 84:200–201.

GODFREY, W. E. 1986. The birds of Canada. Natl. Mus. Nat. Sci., Ottawa, Ont. 596pp.

GREENLAW, J. S., AND R. F. MILLER. 1982. Breeding soras on a Long Island salt marsh. Kingbird 32:78–84.

GRIESE, H. J., R. A. RYDER, AND C. E. BRAUN. 1980. Spatial and temporal distribution of rails in Colorado. Wilson Bull. 92:96–102.

HORAK, G. J. 1970. A comparative study of the foods of the sora and Virginia rail. Wilson Bull. 82:207–213.

JOHNSON, R. R., AND J. J. DINSMORE. 1986. Habitat use by breeding Virginia rails and soras. J. Wildl. Manage. 50:387–392.

KANTRUD, H. A., AND R. E. STEWART. 1984. Ecological distribution and crude density of breeding birds on prairie wetlands. J. Wildl. Manage. 48:426–437.

KAUFMANN, G. W. 1983. Displays and vocalizations of the sora and the Virginia rail. Wilson Bull. 95:42–59.

———. 1987. Growth and development of sora and Virginia rail chicks. Wilson Bull. 99:432–440.

———. 1989. Breeding ecology of the sora *Porzana carolina*, and the Virginia rail *Rallus limicola*. Can. Field-Nat. 103:270–282.

LINSCOMB, G. 1976. An evaluation of the No. 2 Victor and 220 conibear traps in coastal Louisiana. Proc. Southeast. Assoc. Fish and Wildl. Agencies. 30:560–568.

MANCI, K. M., AND D. H. RUSCH. 1988. Indices to distribution and abundance of some inconspicuous waterbirds on Horicon Marsh. J. Field Ornithol. 59:67–75.

MARTIN, A. C., H. S. ZIM, AND A. L. NELSON. 1951. American wildlife and plants. McGraw-Hill Book Co., New York, N.Y. 500pp.

MARTIN, E. M. 1979. Hunting and harvest trends for migratory game birds other than waterfowl: 1964–76. U.S. Fish and Wildl. Serv., Spec. Sci. Rep. Wildl. 218. 37pp.

MEANLEY, B. 1960. Fall food of the sora rail in the Arkansas rice fields. J. Wildl. Manage. 24:339.

———. 1969. Natural history of the king rail. North. Am. Fauna 67. 108pp.

ODOM, R. R. 1977. Sora. Pages 57–65 *in* G.C. Sanderson, ed. Management of migratory shore and upland game birds in North America. Int. Assoc. Fish and Wildl. Agencies, Washington, D.C.

PETERSON, R. T. 1980. A field guide to the birds. Houghton Mifflin Co., Boston, Mass. 384pp.

POSPICHAL, L. B., AND W. H. MARSHALL. 1954. A field study of sora rail and Virginia rail in central Minnesota. Flicker 26:2–32.

RIPLEY, S. D. 1977. Rails of the world. David R. Godine, Publ. Boston, Mass. 406pp.

ROOT, T. 1988. Atlas of wintering North American birds. Univ. Chicago Press, Chicago, Ill. 312pp.

RUNDLE, W. D., AND L. H. FREDERICKSON. 1981. Managing seasonally flooded impoundments for migrant rails and shorebirds. Wildl. Soc. Bull. 9:80–87.

———, AND M. W. SAYRE. 1983. Feeding ecology of migrant soras in southeastern Missouri. J. Wildl. Manage. 47:1153–1159.

SAYRE, M. W., AND W. D. RUNDLE. 1984. Comparisons of habitat use by migrant soras and Virginia rails. J. Wildl. Manage. 48:599–605.

STENDELL, R. C., J. W. ARTMANN, AND E. MARTIN. 1980. Lead residues in sora rails from Maryland. J. Wildl. Manage. 44:525–527.

STEWART, R. E., AND H. A. KANTRUD. 1971. Classification of natural ponds and lakes in the glaciated prairie region. U.S. Fish and Wildl. Serv., Resour. Publ. 92. 57pp.

TANNER, W. D., AND G. O. HENDRICKSON. 1956. Ecology of the sora in Clay County, Iowa. Iowa Bird Life 26:78–81.

TINER, R. W., JR. 1984. Wetlands of the United States: current status and recent trends. National wetlands inventory. U.S. Gov. Print. Off., Washington, D.C. 59pp.

WALKINSHAW, L. H. 1940. Summer life of the sora rail. Auk 57:153–168.

WEBSTER, C. G. 1964. Fall foods of soras from two habitats in Connecticut. J. Wildl. Manage. 28:163–165.

WELLER, M. W., AND C. E. SPATCHER. 1965. Role of habitat in the distribution and abundance of marsh birds. Iowa Agric. Home Econ. Exp. Stn. Spec. Rep. 43. 31pp.

ZIMMERMAN, J. L. 1984. Distribution, habitat, and status of the sora and Virginia rail in interior Kansas. J. Field Ornithol. 55:38–47.

Migratory shore and upland game birds frequently occur in groups during migration and winter (Photo by G. L. Mills).

Chapter 16

MIGRATORY SHORE AND UPLAND GAME BIRD RESOURCES— STATUS AND NEEDS

THOMAS C. TACHA, Caesar Kleberg Wildlife Research Institute, Campus Box 218, Texas A&M University–Kingsville, Kingsville, TX 78363

CLAIT E. BRAUN, Colorado Division of Wildlife, Wildlife Research Center, 317 West Prospect Road, Fort Collins, CO 80526

ROY E. TOMLINSON, U.S. Fish and Wildlife Service, P.O. Box 1306, Albuquerque, NM 87103-1306

Migratory shore and upland game birds (MSUGBs) are valuable avian resources in North America. The mourning dove is the most widely distributed and, perhaps, the most important game bird in the United States. In 1991, mourning doves provided recreation for 1.9 million hunters that took 8.8 million hunting trips and spent about $418 million (U.S. Dep. Inter. and U.S. Dep. Commerce 1993). White-winged doves, band-tailed pigeons, American coots, American woodcock, and sandhill cranes also annually provide substantial hunting recreation and revenue in local areas. Perhaps even more value exists in the non-consumptive recreation provided by these species, such as the major tourist attraction of watching sandhill cranes in the North Platte River Valley of Nebraska in spring, the backyard feeding and watering stations for doves and pigeons, and the many photographic opportunities afforded by most species. Birders make special trips to view these birds and are particularly pleased to glimpse the secretive rails in marsh habitats.

In 1967, the International Association of Fish and Wildlife Agencies (IAFWA) recognized the importance of MSUGBs by establishing the Accelerated Research Program (ARP) that provided Congressional funding of $250,000 each year to the U.S. Fish and Wildlife Service (USFWS) for research on those species. Of that total, $175,000 were annually contracted to states and $75,000 were used for USFWS research and program administration. During the 15 years of its existence (1968–82), ARP funded 122 research projects, including 38 on woodcock and 34 on mourning doves, but also included projects on rails, snipe, band-tailed pigeons, sandhill cranes, white-winged doves, coots, and shorebirds. A considerable amount of supplementary work using state and Federal Aid funding also was generated by the existence of ARP projects.

Approximately 340 publications resulted directly from these ARP-funded projects, a substantial addition to the knowledge of these species.

During the 13 years since ARP was discontinued, populations of some MSUGB species (e.g., Western Management Unit mourning doves and Coastal band-tailed pigeons) have been discovered to exhibit alarming long-term declines. In addition, information gaps on species such as rails, moorhens, gallinules, and snipe have become apparent, making management decisions difficult. The Migratory Shore and Upland Game Bird Committee and the IAFWA have urged the USFWS to adopt a Webless Migratory Bird Research Program (WMBR), similar to ARP, but with an annual budget of $750,000. We recommend immediate implementation of this new program to help identify the reasons for population declines of doves and pigeons and to obtain base-line information on other species.

HABITAT

Maintenance of nesting, roosting, watering, and feeding habitats is the key to stabilizing or increasing population numbers of all wildlife. However this task can be difficult because most upland and many wetland habitats are privately owned. In many areas, MSUGB populations are dependent on agricultural and other land uses dictated by economic demand. If cotton propagation generates more income than grains, cotton will be the choice. If windbreaks and woodlots (that provide dove nesting habitat) are not economically productive, they will be destroyed. Biologists are faced either with working with individual landowners to enhance the habitats on their lands or buying or leasing lands for intensive management. However, state and federal managers cannot possibly acquire enough land to support the many species of wildlife entrusted to their care. Studies are needed to identify habitat requirements for species before sound habitat management recommendations can be made. While habitat requirements are being ascertained (and thereafter), a widespread extension program should be developed to work with landowners to implement habitat enhancement procedures. To be effective, such a program must be extensive and coordinated by a federal organization such as the USFWS, with designated state-organization and private co-operators.

MSUGB species and populations clearly have been adversely affected by habitat deterioration, but our knowledge and ability to monitor the extent of those changes have been limited. With the advent of aerial photography, satellite imagery, and computer technology, the ability to assess past, present, and future habitat changes has increased greatly. Wherever possible, managers should implement studies using Geographic Inventory Systems (GIS) to aid in monitoring habitat changes, so that ongoing habitat management activities are current.

Habitat requirements for MSUGBs are highly variable. Although doves, pigeons, and American woodcock principally select upland areas, 10 of the 14 MSUGB species are dependent upon wetland habitats. Sandhill cranes require shallow open water for roosting, especially saline, lacustrine, or estuarine areas during winter, and riverine areas during migration. The Platte and North Platte rivers in Nebraska provide spring roosting for about 80% of Mid-continent sandhill cranes. Less than 24 large saline lakes are used by more than 75% of mid-continent sandhill cranes during some winters. Both the Platte River systems and the salt lakes are vulnerable to present or planned human activities and must be conserved.

The 4 species of rails require shallow palustrine emergent wetlands with interspersion of open water, emergent vegetation, and mud flats. Some clapper rail populations also require estuarine emergent areas (coastal marsh) during winter. American coots, common moorhens, and purple gallinules depend on palustrine and lacustrine (deep marsh) areas with emergent and/ or floating-leaf vegetation. Common snipe require wetlands with soils that have high organic content and estuarine areas. Most wetland conservation activities by state and federal conservation agencies focus on shallow marshes preferred by ducks. Special provisions for wetland

habitats of MSUGBs, particularly deep marsh with floating-leaved plants, should be integrated into priorities of private, state, and federal conservation efforts.

DISTRIBUTION AND ABUNDANCE

In the first MSUGB book (Sanderson 1977), Ruckel and Sadler (1977) observed that MSUGBs, such as mourning doves and snipe were common and widely distributed, whereas others were locally distributed and apparently uncommon. During the 1970's, little indication was evident that populations were declining; indeed they were probably relatively stable then. Mourning dove populations had been estimated in the millions throughout the United States (Dunks et al. 1982), and Tomlinson et al. (1988) later estimated an average fall flight of about 475 million birds during 1967–75. Since then, some mourning dove population indices show significant long-term downward trends, particularly in the Western Management Unit. Populations of white-winged doves in the Lower Rio Grande Valley of Texas and northeastern Mexico decreased and became redistributed during the mid-1980's. White-winged doves in Arizona declined precipitously from the late 1960's to the late 1980's. Coastal band-tailed pigeons also experienced substantial declines since 1970, to the point that hunting seasons for this population have been substantially restricted. There are some indications that Interior band-tailed pigeons also may be declining. Both the Eastern and Central populations of woodcock have declined over the past 15–20 years. Sandhill cranes appear to have remained stable over the past several years, but habitat deterioration along the Platte and North Platte rivers does not bode well for this species. Population surveys specifically for snipe, rails, coots, moorhens, and gallinules are either nonexistent or rudimentary and the true status of these species is relatively unknown.

For the species affected, reasons for the population declines are either unknown or not fully understood. In the case of Western Management Unit mourning doves, a combination of factors (including habitat loss, changing agricultural practices, pesticides, and hunting) may be responsible (Reeves et al. 1993). Nesting habitat and foraging areas of Coastal band-tailed pigeons have undergone extensive alteration; these factors plus a susceptibility to pesticides and trichomoniasis are thought to have caused pigeon declines (West. Migratory Upland Game Bird Tech. Comm. 1994). White-winged dove nesting habitat has been cleared in south Texas and northeastern Mexico, where perhaps only 5–10% of the original potential nesting areas remain. In addition, severe winter freezes and an extended drought during the mid- to late-1980's markedly damaged the citrus nesting areas and caused deterioration of the remaining native brush areas. However, with favorable weather conditions during 1990–94, it appears that Eastern white-winged populations slowly are increasing.

American woodcock habitat has changed considerably because the early stages of alder and other important nesting habitats have deteriorated through successional maturation. Although this loss of nesting habitat may be the principal causative factor, biocides and other contaminants may have decreased the earthworm populations that woodcock depend on for food. Continued deterioration of the Platte and North Platte rivers may eventually eliminate spring staging areas upon which sandhill cranes depend.

Whatever the reasons, it is evident that populations and habitats for some migratory shore and upland game birds presently are substantially smaller than they were in the 1970's. Managers have a clear mandate to identify the causes and implement procedures to reverse the declines.

Population assessment continues to be a problem for most species. No standardized or coordinated population surveys are conducted for common snipe, common moorhens, purple gallinules, or any of the 4 species of rails. Varying methods currently are used for evaluating band-tailed pigeon populations, but little or no standardization is used. Call-playback surveys have been developed for use with some populations of rails, but their use is local and not standardized. The most important priority for management of MSUGBs is to develop and implement reliable population assessment procedures that provide unbiased annual estimates of or indices to population size with acceptable accuracy and precision.

HARVEST

As Harper and Sadler (1977) reported, management of MSUGBs is directed mainly toward annual appraisals of populations, together with an evaluation of proposed hunting regulations, to permit harvest of selected species by sport hunting. The objective is to permit optimal recreational opportunity that is consistent with the continuing well-being and abundance of the resource. Population evaluations are made by the USFWS, Canadian Wildlife Service (CWS), and cooperating state and provincial agencies. Regulatory decisions are reached through statutory authority by the Secretary of the Interior after careful consideration and in consultation with representatives from state conservation agencies, private organizations, other groups, and the general public. Sport hunting provides a means of harvesting a fraction of specific populations without lasting detriment to the resource. Although protection from hunting will not insure the maintenance of a population indefinitely, excessive harvest will surely cause a decline. Effective management includes regulating the harvest wisely.

Management problems arise when the means to estimate population status and size of harvest are inaccurate and/or imprecise. All species chapters reported the need to improve techniques for obtaining harvest estimates for MSUGB species. Although there has been a standardized and nationwide method used to estimate the waterfowl harvest and number of hunters for many years, a similar survey has not been conducted for MSUGBs. Harvest estimates for some species (e.g., mourning doves, white-winged doves, band-tailed pigeons, and American woodcock) routinely have been collected by state wildlife agencies, but surveys generally were not standardized, not conducted by all states, not run annually, and the data were usually obtained too late for annual regulations decision-making. No coordinated and standardized harvest surveys are conducted for rails, purple gallinules, or snipe. The only species considered in this book with a presently adequate harvest survey is the sandhill crane. Nevertheless, most states that hunt MSUGB species retain relatively long seasons and large bag/possession limits. We submit that this lack of adequate harvest knowledge is inconsistent with the wise use of these resources.

In response to the need for better MSUGB harvest information, the National Migratory Bird Harvest Information Program (HIP) has been established by the USFWS, in cooperation with state agencies, to provide harvest and hunter estimates for all migratory game birds, including those species treated in this book. Chapter authors in this book consistently cite development and full implementation of the HIP as the best alternative for improved harvest surveys for MSUGBs. HIP is scheduled to be operational for all states in 1998, but many obstacles remain. The primary problem at present is ensuring that all state wildlife agencies enter the program, and within the 5-year phase-in period. In addition, the program will need adequate USFWS staffing and funding to conduct surveys with sufficient sample size and detail to provide separate harvest estimates for each species, population, and subpopulation with acceptable accuracy and precision. For example, both parts (i.e., wings) and mail surveys may be required to ascertain species composition of rail harvest and to accurately separate harvests of purple gallinules and common moorhens. We see implementation of HIP as the only available alternative for providing sufficient harvest information to make knowledgeable decisions for hunting regulations as part of the overall management of MSUGB species.

RECOMMENDATIONS

1. The IAFWA (and its individual state agencies), the USFWS, and CWS should develop comprehensive planning and funding mechanisms for management of MSUGBs. These actions should include:
   a. maintain adequate USFWS and CWS staff dedicated to MSUGB issues;
   b. permanent adequate funding for annual population surveys for each species, population, and/or subpopulation;
   c. permanent adequate funding for HIP; and
   d. permanent adequate funding for the Webless Migratory Bird Research Program.
2. Comprehensive management plans should be developed for each MSUGB species, population, or subpopulation. Provision should be made for periodic review, amendment, and adherence to schedule.
3. Population monitoring techniques should be developed for species presently lacking them. Trend information should be gathered and analyzed annually for promulgation of hunting regulations and for making other management decisions.
4. All reasonable means should be used to ensure that HIP is implemented by all states during the scheduled phase-in period. Steps

should be taken to ensure that harvest estimates reflect all species, populations, and subpopulations accurately and with precision. Harvest estimates must be obtained annually and in time for the federal June regulations meetings.
5. Studies should be initiated to identify year-round habitat needs of all MSUGBs and recommendations developed for enhancing preferred habitats. MSUGB habitat management priorities should be actively integrated into existing waterfowl programs where practicable, including the North American Waterfowl Management Plan.
6. A nationwide extension network should be established and implemented by the USFWS, in cooperation with other federal and state conservation organizations, for MSUGB habitat improvement projects on private lands.
7. Information/education on MSUGB management needs should be integrated into existing undergraduate and graduate natural resources education programs, and in extension and private lands networks.

LITERATURE CITED

DUNKS, J. H., R. E. TOMLINSON, H. M. REEVES, D. D. DOLTON, C. E. BRAUN, AND T. P. ZAPATKA. 1982. Migration, harvest, and population dynamics of mourning doves banded in the Central Management Unit, 1967–77. U.S. Fish and Wildl. Serv., Spec. Sci. Rep.—Wildl. 249. 128pp.

HARPER, H. T., AND K. C. SADLER. Management approaches and benefits. Pages 327–332 in G. C. Sanderson, ed. Management of migratory shore and upland game birds in North America. Int. Assoc. Fish and Wildl. Agencies, Washington, D.C.

REEVES, H. M., R. E. TOMLINSON, AND J. C. BARTONEK. 1993. Population characteristics and trends in the Western Management Unit. Pages 341–376 in T. S. Baskett, M. W. Sayre, R. E. Tomlinson, and R. E. Mirarchi, eds., Ecology and management of the mourning dove. Stackpole Books, Harrisburg, Pa.

RUCKEL, J. M., AND K. C. SADLER. 1977. Distribution and abundance. Pages 323–327 in G. C. Sanderson, ed. Management of migratory shore and upland game birds in North America. Int. Assoc. Fish and Wildl. Agencies, Washington, D.C.

SANDERSON, G. C., EDITOR. 1977. Management of migratory shore and upland game birds in North America. Int. Assoc. Fish and Wildl. Agencies, Washington, D.C. 358pp.

TOMLINSON, R. E., D. D. DOLTON, H. M. REEVES, J. D. NICHOLS, AND L. A. McKIBBEN. 1988. Migration, harvest, and population characteristics of mourning doves in the Western Management

Unit, 1964–1977. U.S. Fish and Wildl. Serv., Fish and Wildl. Tech. Rep. 13. 101pp.

U.S. DEPARTMENT OF THE INTERIOR, FISH AND WILDLIFE SERVICE AND U.S. DEPARTMENT OF COMMERCE, BUREAU OF CENSUS. 1993. 1991 national survey of fishing, hunting, and wildlife-associated recreation. U.S. Gov. Print. Off., Washington, D.C. 124pp + 4 appendices.

WESTERN MIGRATORY UPLAND BIRD TECHNICAL COMMITTEE. 1994. Pacific Flyway management plan for the Pacific Coast population of band-tailed pigeons. Pacific Flyway Counc., Portland, Oreg. 39pp.